WHO'S NEXT
An Unofficial Guide to *Doctor Who*

WHO'S NEXT
An Unofficial Guide to *Doctor Who*

Mark Clapham, Eddie Robson
and Jim Smith

First published in Great Britain in 2005 by
Virgin Books Ltd
Thames Wharf Studios
Rainville Road
London
W6 9HA

A catalogue record for this book is available from the British Library.

ISBN 0 7535 0948 2

Typeset by TW Typesetting, Plymouth, Devon
Printed and bound in Great Britain by
Mackays of Chatham PLC

Acknowledgements

Kirstie Addis, Scott Andrews, Jon de Burgh Miller, James Ewart, Simon Guerrier, Craig Hinton, Barry Letts, Adrian Middleton, Lawrence Miles, Lance Parkin, Andrew Pixley, Andrew Plummer-Rodriguez, Dr Henry Potts, Jim Sangster, Dr Catherine Spooner, Ed Stradling, Christian Slater, Alan Stevens, Matt Symonds, Peter Ware, Tat Wood, Outpost Gallifrey, the Right Reverend Revolution e-zine and all the other writers of www.shinyshelf.com.

Paul Cornell, Martin Day, Keith Topping – may you never be DisContinued.

The authors would like especially to thank the management and staff of two businesses located on Great Russell Street, London, without whom the writing of this book would have been far more painful: Gosh! Comics, for all our important weekly supplies; and the Forum cafe, where much of this book was written and discussed. With special thanks to WHSmith for abruptly selling off most of its DVD and VHS stock for a pittance.

Featuring Special Guest Star Stephen Lavington as 'The Talons of Weng-Chiang'.

Introduction

'We are not of this race, we are not of this Earth. We are wanderers in the fourth dimension of space and time, cut off from our own planet and our own people by aeons and universes far beyond the reach of your most advanced sciences.'

From the *Doctor Who* pilot episode

Between 1963 and 2004 around seven hundred episodes of *Doctor Who* were made and broadcast by the BBC. The majority of these were shown on television, but more than a few have been transmitted on the radio and, more recently, made available for viewing over the Internet. The programme's return to primetime BBC1 in early 2005 (the first full series of television adventures for over fifteen years) is what's prompted this book, which is partially designed as a beginners'/viewers'/buyers' guide to the series' vast number of instalments. If you can't remember which order the Doctors come in, but know that you'd quite like to see 'that one with the Daleks in London/the giant maggots/that red-eyed creature in the basement that bellows "HUNGRY!!!"' again, then this is the place to start. If you're intimately familiar with the minutiae of the series and can instinctively list the titles of all *Doctor Who* stories backwards without breaking into a sweat, then this book is still going to contain some surprising opinions, fresh perspectives and new angles on that much-discussed body of material.

Doctor Who was originally devised as a semi-educational adventure series for children, and specifically tailored to fit into a pre-existing time slot between the Saturday football results and *Juke Box Jury*. *Doctor Who* has evolved more than any other long-running series; this is a testament to both the series' innate flexibility and the vast evolution of both television and the society it portrays over more than forty years. *Doctor Who*'s format is, if not actually unique, then certainly unusual (indeed most programmes that use a similar system can be successfully argued to have copied it). Most television programmes are 'series' (individual episodes with self-contained plots but recurring characters) or 'serials' (one ongoing plot split across a number of instalments).

An example of the former would be *Star Trek*; an example of the latter *The Singing Detective*. *Doctor Who* is, unusually, a series of serials. Each 'season' of *Doctor Who* comprised a number of serials, each broken down into episodes. For example the 26th season (1989) has fourteen episodes but consists of four serials 'Battlefield' (Parts One to Four), 'Ghost Light' (Parts One to Three), 'The Curse of Fenric' (Parts One to Four) and 'Survival' (Parts One to Three). The word 'season' (an Americanism in this context) is used sparingly in this book, because we prefer to see the programme in terms of serials and years.

During the first three years of the show's run, these serials did not have overarching on-screen story titles: every episode had its own individual title – hence the story usually referred to as 'The Rescue' comprises two episodes, individually entitled on screen 'The Powerful Enemy' and 'Desperate Measures'. What the overarching story titles for this period of the series are is open to debate and there is strong evidence to suggest that the people who were actually making the series didn't nail down any particular title for some serials. We use the story titles as used by the BBC on their official video, CD and DVD releases: as this book is intended as a viewers'/buyers' guide to the series, it's the only way to make sure everyone is thinking about the same set of episodes. In the interests of clarity, titles not used on screen are given in quotation marks at the top of the entry for them (again, for example, 'The Rescue').

This is a guide to all of broadcast *Doctor Who*. *Doctor Who* books, stage plays, comic strips, records and single- or multiple-voice talking books are not included. This is partially because including them would make any book an unwieldy length, but is mostly because of what *Doctor Who* is. It's a mass-market family entertainment created by the British Broadcasting Corporation, and made available, initially anyway, free at the point of use. *Doctor Who* is part of mainstream British culture, the stuff of a thousand references, stand-up jokes and playground chants. Even the biggest-selling original *Doctor Who* product has been experienced by approximately one per cent of the millions who watched even the least enthusiastically viewed episode of the television series.

BBC-produced *Doctor Who* stories that were shown as part of some charity telethons (**129**, 'The Five Doctors', **158**, 'Dimensions in Time', **161**, 'The Curse of Fatal Death') have been included, as have the radio serials, the animated and semi-animated Internet broadcasts and the 1996 TV movie co-produced with Universal

Television. The two theatrical motion pictures, *Dr. Who & the Daleks* (Gordon Flemyng, 1965) and *Daleks – Invasion Earth 2150 A.D.* (Gordon Flemyng, 1966) are briefly discussed within the sections for the television serials from which they were adapted – **2**, 'The Daleks' and **10**, 'The Dalek Invasion of Earth' respectively. We maintain there is a clear difference between such potential apocrypha as **158**, 'Dimensions in Time', **160**, 'The Movie' and **161**, 'The Curse of Fatal Death' (all of which were treated by the *Radio Times* on transmission as 'the return of *Doctor Who*') and sketches that used *Doctor Who* as a basis (examples include those made by Lenny Henry or for *Jim'll Fix It*). Equally, the radio serials are clearly marked in *Radio Times* as being part of an ongoing series called *Doctor Who* – and that's good enough for us. All transmission dates are the first UK broadcast and on BBC1 unless otherwise stated. All episodes are listed in original transmission order. We have not listed repeats, either terrestrially or on cable, digital or satellite television, or first broadcasts of the episodes in other territories – except when an episode's very first broadcast was somewhere other than the UK, as is the case with, for example, **129**, 'The Five Doctors'.

Continuity?

You could choose to look at *Doctor Who* as a series of interconnected one-offs; you could choose to see it as one story of seven-hundred-plus episodes. *Doctor Who* continuity – in this sense – has never been exact, and at times it has barely been sensible. The series has no fewer than three explanations for the destruction of Atlantis, two entirely incompatible origins for the Daleks and a lead character whose own beginnings and reasons for becoming a wanderer in space and time are presented so inconsistently, and with such frequent shifts of emphasis, that any attempt to create a coherent, comprehensive framework for his past is doomed to failure. It isn't even clear what the lead's name is, whether he's a medical doctor or even how old he is.

Doctor Who's attitude to its own past can be summed up by one fact: that **130**, 'Warriors of the Deep', is a sequel to **52**, 'Doctor Who and the Silurians', written by someone who had never *seen* it. Terrance Dicks, one of *Doctor Who*'s most durable writers, once claimed that his attitude to continuity was limited to what he could remember about his predecessors' shows. We'd go further and say that the only continuity that matters is what you like about what you can remember. Anything else would be inhibiting, and most of *Doctor Who*'s grossest continuity 'errors' have arisen out of the desire to correct or 'protect' the series' past, rather than the simple exercise of wilful creativity.

There are many things assumed to be universally true about *Doctor Who* that are actually mere transitory plot points that would have been discarded had a writer or producer felt the need to do so. (There are many equally solid 'facts' that were discarded in this manner when the need arose.) Most fans would concur that the Doctor is a Time Lord, from the planet Gallifrey, who can change his physical appearance twelve times (giving him thirteen lives) and that the character had, when played by William Hartnell, never yet changed his appearance. Yet these 'facts' are established in *Doctor Who*'s sixth, eleventh, fourteenth and twentieth years on air respectively, and as much of the series goes against them as with them. *Doctor Who* doesn't fit together and there's no reason why it should. No programme that has run for this long, and had so many writers, could possibly do so.

This is more a book that occasionally looks at the *way* that it doesn't, rather than trying to get a square peg to fit a round hole. It's both more honest and, seriously, much more fun this way. To deny multiple interpretations is indicative of a desire to force conformity out of something that shouldn't conform. There is no definitive timeline, lifeline or continuity of Hercules, King Arthur, Robin Hood or Superman – nor should there be. To attempt to create one would be pointless – it would be to deny the plurality of myth.

How to use this book

Each *Doctor Who* serial is laid out as below, with the commentary/ analysis laid out in handy categories. These categories are not always consistently in the same order, but rather in the best order for each serial.

Story No.
Story Title

Episode Title: (first transmission date)
Second Episode Title: (first transmission date)

Written by (name or names)
Directed by (name or names)

Note: All *Doctor Who* episodes are about 25 minutes in length unless stated otherwise. Individual episode titles are given on screen for episodes which have them; for instalments labelled as 'Part 1', 'Part One', 'Episode 1' or 'Episode One' the attribution is as given on screen on the episode.

Notable Cast: Where you've seen the more noticeable guest actors before, who they are and what they've done both before and since. Handy if you're wondering who that chap with the mutton chops is in **139**, 'The Mark of the Rani'. Actors who appear in multiple, distinct, significant roles across *Doctor Who* (for example Michael Sheard, *Grange Hill*'s Mr Bronson) are often cross referenced between stories they appear in but actors who play numerous minor parts usually aren't. What information there is on actors herein is a trade-off between their fame elsewhere and their importance to the serial under discussion. Numerous actors who appeared many times in *Doctor Who* but who aren't particularly recognisable outside it are often omitted. Actors considered stars at the time of their *Doctor Who* appearance but who have faded since are often mentioned to give context. This category is also where you'll find information on the various Doctors and actors who play other recurring characters, usually included on the entry related to their first appearance in the series. For film credits, director and year are noted. Dates given for TV credits have been given where available and/or pertinent.

Writer: Career summaries and judgements on *Doctor Who*'s many scriptwriters – again usually included on their first script for the series. If you can't find a particular author's biographical details, please refer to the index.

Director: As above, but for the directors.

Producer; Script Editor: These are the titles of the two people who, at any given time, are regarded as being responsible for the creative direction of a BBC series under the old-style BBC production system. Most of *Doctor Who*'s producers and script editors also worked on the series in other capacities: we tend to examine them upon their earliest credit. The script editor job was, until early 1968, termed story editor. In a *Doctor Who* context, the jobs are the same and the terms are used interchangeably.

Doctor Who?: The category for our main character. What do we learn about him in this serial? How is he played? To what extent is he involved in the storyline?

Other Worlds; Scary Monsters; Villains: Three self-explanatory categories looking at the elements of the adventure under discussion.

The Plan: Like most adventure fiction, *Doctor Who* works through conflict and resolution. This usually means someone has a plan and someone else tries to stop it.

Science/Magic: They might as well be the same thing in this series, despite some serials' earnest protestations of scientific accuracy. This is the category for all the bafflegab, technical nonsense, scientific name-dropping and occasional moments of actual educational value.

Things Fall Apart: All those things that go wrong, and then get the programme laughed at by Paul Merton on *Room 101*. Plot problems will only get a look-in here when they're so vast that they detract from the serial's other merits (if any). Again, as an adventure series, *Doctor Who* presents stories that rely on coincidence, momentum and conflict. It would be criticising an orange for not being a chair to go on endlessly about the plot problems of **82**, 'Pyramids of Mars', when the serial has so much more to offer an audience; **83**, 'The Android Invasion', however, deserves every criticism it gets.

Availability: Currently around a hundred black-and-white episodes of *Doctor Who* are known not to exist. This is because the BBC was not required to keep a comprehensive archive of its output. Some episodes appear to have been lost, but most were actually destroyed either as part of a deliberate process of space-clearing (and video tape reuse) or because one part of the organisation was unaware of what another part did and didn't have copies of. In the early 1980s the number of 'missing' episodes was much higher, and copies of episodes presumed gone for ever in 1980 have made their way to the BBC, from a variety of sources, over the last 25 years. It should not be assumed, however, that all 'missing' *Doctor Who* episodes are 'out there' somewhere and it is unfortunately probably more correct to think of them as 'destroyed' rather than 'absent'. These episodes are, however, represented in part by superb audio-only versions as recorded on to cassette during transmission by contemporary viewers. In addition a large number of off-screen photographs (known as 'telesnaps') exist for many episodes. These can all be seen at the BBC's official *Doctor Who* website – www.bbc.co.uk/cult/doctorwho.

There are, additionally, eight episodes of *Doctor Who* (**68**, 'Planet of the Daleks' – Episode Three; **71**, 'Invasion – Part One'; and all six episodes of **56**, 'The Mind of Evil'), which were originally made in colour but now exist only in black and white. This is because the BBC destroyed the colour originals but retained, or in some cases reacquired, black-and-white copies made for sale to foreign television services that had not yet gone over to colour transmissions. Additionally, **53**, 'The Ambassadors of Death', exists in a combination of colour and black-and-white scenes, making the VHS release not unlike watching Lindsay Anderson's *If . . .* (although with fewer tiger impressions).

Between 1983 and 2003 every single extant *Doctor Who* episode, both in colour and in black and white, was released on video at least once by the BBC. Since 2003 the BBC has, in line with its general policy of moving from VHS to DVD releases, made the majority of them technically unavailable. Many can be found in shops or from reputable online retailers for their original prices. Other sources may charge inflated sums because of 'rarity' (we recommend www.amazon.co.uk or www.sendit.com to avoid being fleeced). We include BBCV numbers in order to help you track down particular stories where there is no DVD issue. Out of print VHS and re-issues on VHS are mentioned only when there is something such as edits, which makes the item of special interest.

Most *Doctor Who* serials remain available on VHS in the USA, where the series was released by Warner Home Video/BBC America. In many cases it is cheaper for UK fans to order these from a reputable international dealer such as www.amazon.com. Ironically, the *Doctor Who* episodes that do not exist as video recordings or film prints, but only as audio tracks of destroyed visual originals, are now far more accessible than the 'existing' episodes. Virtually all have been released as audio CDs by the BBC Radio Collection and are on sale on high streets in larger book and record shops. The small remainder are due to be released during 2005. With these, and the radio episodes (all of which are also available), we include ISBN numbers. A number of these are also available as MP3 CDs for playing on computers. Again, we include ISBNs.

Verdict: This is our opinion, usually bargained out collectively between the three of us, all fans of the show, and prefaced by a quote from the serial that seems to sum it up. *Doctor Who* has been many things in its long existence, and people who love certain periods of the programme's run dislike others with equal intensity. This is usually connected with which episodes, or which *kinds* of episode, were the first *Doctor Who* an individual saw. While the opinions are subjective and might not always be wholly or even remotely positive, they are also entirely honest and, let's face it, no more subjective than anyone else's. Just because we'd like to think of this as a beginner's guide to *Doctor Who*, it doesn't mean we won't be delighted if you develop tastes in this series that are radically different from our own. Well, as long as you don't decide you love **44**, 'The Dominators', or **96**, 'Underworld' – that would just be bad and wrong.

1
'An Unearthly Child'

An Unearthly Child: 23 November 1963
The Cave of Skulls: 30 November 1963
The Forest of Fear: 6 December 1963
The Firemaker: 13 December 1963

Written by Anthony Coburn
Directed by Waris Hussein

Notable Cast: William Hartnell (1908–75) was a star of British films either side of World War Two, although he started his working life in Sir Frank Benson's touring Shakespeare company in the 1920s. He was versatile enough to play the 'wronged man' in *Murder in Reverse* (Montgomery Tully, 1945), the romantic lead in *Strawberry Roan* (Maurice Elvey, 1944) and a murderous antihero in *Appointment with Crime* (John Harlow, 1946). He had also been successful in comic pictures like *I'm An Explosive!* (Adrian Brunel, 1933). Despite this, he became typecast as tough guys and sergeants, thanks to his TV series *The Army Game* (1957–58, 1960–61) and films such as *The Way Ahead* (Carol Reed, 1944), *Private's Progress* (John Boulting, 1956) and *Carry On Sergeant* (Gerald Thomas, 1958). His best screen performances came in *The Yangtse Incident* (Michael Anderson, 1957), *Hell Drivers* (Cy Endfield, 1957), *Brighton Rock* (John Boulting, 1947) and *This Sporting Life* (Lindsay Anderson, 1963). The last of these led to his being offered the title role in *Doctor Who*.

William Russell (Ian Chesterton) was born in 1924 and had been the lead in *The Adventures of Sir Lancelot* for ATV (1956–57). He has a small but memorable role in *The Key* (Carol Reed, 1958) and has latterly been a leading member of the Royal Shakespeare Company, playing senior roles such as the Ghost of King Hamlet. He made memorable appearances in *The Black Adder* ('The Archbishop') and *Robin of Sherwood* ('The Pretender'), and played Ted Sullivan in *Coronation Street* (1992).

Jacqueline Hill (1929–93) plays Barbara. She was married to the noted theatrical director Alvin Rakoff. She can be seen as Lady Capulet in the BBC's *Romeo and Juliet* (1979).

Carole Ann Ford (Susan) played a small role in *Day of the Triffids* (Steve Sekely, 1963) and a larger one in an episode of *Dixon of Dock Green* (1961). Among her limited amount of post-*Doctor Who* work is an appearance in *Whatever Happened to the Likely Lads?* (1974).

Writer: The Australian author Anthony Coburn is the only writer credited on these episodes. However, BBC staff members, including Donald Baverstock, Rex Tucker and CE 'Bunny' Webber, all contributed material from character suggestions to actual lines of dialogue. The basic idea for *Doctor Who* as a series was worked out by Sydney Newman and Donald Wilson. Canadian Newman (1917–97) was the BBC's head of drama and had previously created *Armchair Theatre* and *The Avengers* (for ATV), while Wilson (1910–2002) was head of serials. Wilson was a well-regarded writer/producer whose greatest achievement remains his scripts for *The Forsyte Saga* (1967) – he resigned his position at the BBC in order to be allowed to write it. Anthony Coburn also wrote for *King of the River* (1966), wrote/produced *The Borderers* (1968) and was the producer of *Poldark* (1976) and Terry Nation's *The Incredible Robert Baldick* (1972), starring Robert Hardy. He wrote six more episodes of *Doctor Who* about a sentient computer. They were never produced, although the scripts have since been published under the title 'The Masters of Luxor'. He never worked on the series subsequently, and died in 1987.

Director: This story was the directorial debut of a 24-year-old Indian émigré, Waris Hussein. His later work encompasses the films *Henry VIII and his Six Wives* (1973) and *The Sixth Happiness* (1997), as well as the prestige TV serials *Edward and Mrs Simpson* (1980) and *The Glittering Prizes* (1976).

Producer: *Doctor Who*'s first producer was Verity Lambert. Previously a typist, and latterly a production assistant, working for Sydney Newman at ATV, she became British television's first ever female producer upon being put in charge of *Doctor Who*. It was a controversial appointment. Lambert's gender, relative youth and, inevitably, the fact that she was rather attractive were explicitly counted against her in the patriarchal post-war BBC world. This was despite her having successfully coped with a uniquely traumatic event in television history: she was in charge of the studio floor when, during a live television play, one of the cast died mid-transmission. Sydney Newman's faith in the abilities of his protégé has since been proved to be more than merely justified.

Lambert remained with *Doctor Who* until **19**, 'Mission to the Unknown', and her career went on to encompass a vast variety of successful projects. Her other early credits as producer include *The Newcomers* (1967–69) and *W Somerset Maugham* (1969–70). She became an executive at LWT, moved to Thames (where she became head of drama) and then Euston Films. She was responsible for *The Sweeney* (1974–78), *Minder* (1979–94), *Hazell* (1978) and *Quatermass* (1979). Her own company, Cinema Verity, has produced series including *May to December* (1989–94), *GBH* (1991), *Sleepers* (1991) and *The Boys from the Bush* (1991–92). She is at the time of writing the producer of *Jonathan Creek*, easily British television's best currently ongoing drama series. She has been awarded an OBE for service to television.

Doctor Who?: It is made clear from the outset that the Doctor is not a human being: he is explicitly an alien. He says he and Susan are 'cut off from our own planet without friends or protection' and that he merely tolerates the twentieth century. He dresses in an antiquated manner with a cravat, a shirt with a high wing collar and a coat of a very outdated cut (the implication seems to be that the nineteenth and twentieth centuries are sufficiently alike for him not to realise his clothes are a century wrong). He wears an Afghan hat throughout the first episode and a large opera cape and scarf when outdoors.

His name isn't 'Doctor Who' or even 'The Doctor' at all. In the first episode Ian thinks that he recalls that Susan's unnamed and unknown grandfather is a doctor. In the episode 'The Cave of Skulls', once the TARDIS has carried them back in time to Neolithic times Ian calls Hartnell's character 'Doctor Foreman' – a combination of this assumption and the surname Susan uses at school (which she has taken from the gates of the junkyard the TARDIS is hidden in). To being addressed as 'Doctor Foreman' Hartnell replies, 'Eh? Doctor who? What's he talking about?' Ian addresses him as 'Doctor' from then on, and in 'The Forest of Fear' there's a moment (after Hartnell denies being 'a doctor of medicine') where 'The Doctor' clearly decides that this term is an acceptable thing for these quarrelsome humans to call him. (Susan, of course, continues to refer to him as 'Grandfather'.) While this is clearly the case from these episodes, many (very much) later instalments of the series contradict this clear implication. Hartnell is always credited as 'Dr Who' on screen, as is his successor, Patrick Troughton. Hartnell's 'Doctor' *never* introduces himself as such in the programme (although, by 21, 'The Daleks' Master Plan', he is telling people to 'Call me Doctor', which still isn't the same thing). It is clearly an alias, indeed an affectation.

Villains: The caveman Kal (Jeremy Young) is the cuckoo in the nest among the tribe. He intends to usurp Za (Derek Newark), the hereditary chief and Firemaker. That said, none of the tribe are particularly sympathetic; Za is a weak but bloodthirsty leader. Old Mother (Eileen Way) is a cackling chaos engine of a harridan who is determined that the secret of fire should remain lost; and Horg (Howard Lang) is a suspicious, truculent old fool whose loyalties shift on a minute-by-minute basis.

Science/Magic: Susan describes the fifth dimension (the first four being height, depth, breadth and time) as 'space'. Which is just a description of the first three, surely? Susan says she 'made up the name' of the TARDIS and that it stands for *T*ime *A*nd *R*elative *D*imension *I*n *S*pace. The Ship (as Susan calls it) has a 'camouflage unit' that enables it to blend into its surroundings – it breaks down between their departure from London and their arrival on the plains.

History 101: In 1963 Susan is confident that a 'decimal system' for currency will be introduced in Britain in the near future. While it is arguable that, by convincing Za that 'Kal is not stronger than the whole tribe', Ian introduces the cavemen to the concept of community, he gives them the notion of mob rule with it: the tribe subsequently drive the Doctor's party out after all. Arguments that the story is essentially democratic and progressive fall over when consideration is given to the fact that the hereditary leader reasserts his place at the head of the tribe at the end.

Things Fall Apart: They don't. Not yet.

Availability: Released on video as BBCV 4311 (UK), WHV E1098 (US) in 1990. The release has some small cuts made to it. An uncut, remastered and cleaned-up version was issued in 2000 as BBCV 6959. There is no US version of this re-release. An earlier version of the first episode made for consideration by Newman also exists (it was remade when he rejected it for transmission). It's technically inferior and there are some small scripting differences, but the main cast and plot are the same. This has been released on VHS in partnership with **3**, 'The Edge of Destruction' (BBCV 6877, WHV E1578). It was transmitted on 21 August 1991, on BBC2, as part of a day of themed 1960s programming. To complicate matters further, this earlier version itself comes in two forms, because the second half of the episode was shot twice due to technical considerations. Both are on BBCV 6877. Version A (in which the TARDIS's doors bang) is on BBCV 3608, *The Hartnell Years*; Version B (in which they don't – well, not quite so much) is the version shown on BBC2.

Verdict: 'I know that free movement in time and space is a scientific dream I don't expect to find solved in a junkyard!' The opening episode moves effortlessly from a standard kind of 1960s TV naturalism (which deliberately echoes *Dixon of Dock Green*) to the bizarre expanses of the TARDIS interior and Hartnell's giggling, sinister, utterly captivating performance. The initial takeoff of the ship is a hallucinatory experience of whirling visual feedback, and *musique concrete* sound effects that would never be replicated. The last three episodes have been much undervalued compared with the rightly famous first. This is terribly unfair. They're consistently superb – well acted, cleverly written (if deeply pessimistic) and very well shot. They're both a nightmarish journey into a savage and incomprehensible backdrop and a chance for the characters to bond with each other and the audience through shared adversity. When the Doctor says, 'Fear makes companions of all of us', he's implicitly including the audience in that final word. It is interesting that, given the political climate of the time, both this and the following story are, in essence, about arms races.

2
'The Daleks'

The Dead Planet: 21 December 1963
The Survivors: 28 December 1963
The Escape: 4 January 1964
The Ambush: 11 January 1964
The Expedition: 18 January 1964
The Ordeal: 25 January 1964
The Rescue: 1 February 1964

Written by Terry Nation
Directed by Christopher Barry (1, 2, 4, 5), Richard Martin (3, 6, 7)

Notable Cast: David Graham voiced Daleks in this story and throughout the Hartnell era. His vocal talents also featured throughout *Thunderbirds* (1964–66 – he was the voice of Brains) and he later worked on the English version of the Japanese anime *Dominion Tank Police* (1992). He appears, on camera, as Charlie in **25**, 'The Gunfighters' and Kerensky in **105**, 'City of Death'. Peter Hawkins worked on every Dalek and Cyberman story up to **43**, 'The Wheel in Space', and was also the eponymous voice in *Captain Pugwash* (1957–66). Alan Wheatley (Temmosus) appeared alongside Hartnell in *Brighton Rock* (John Boulting, 1947) and played the Sheriff of Nottingham in *The Adventures of Robin Hood* between 1955 and 1959.

Writer: Terry Nation got his break writing TV, radio and stand-up comedy for the likes of Tony Hancock and Peter Sellers in the late 1950s. He later had stints as script editor on *The Baron* (1966), *The Avengers* (1968–69) and *The Persuaders* (1971–72), and went on to create two sci-fi shows of his own, *Survivors* (1975–77) and *Blake's 7* (1978–81).

Directors: Christopher Barry worked on *Z Cars* (1965–77), *Out of the Unknown* (1965–71), *Poldark* (1975–7) and *All Creatures Great and Small* (1978–80). He also directed TV adaptations of Charles Dickens's *Nicholas Nickleby* (1977) and John Christopher's *The Tripods* (1984). Richard Martin's notable work outside of *Doctor Who* includes the BBC's *Elizabeth R* (1971), starring Glenda Jackson.

Science/Magic: First appearances in the series for static electricity, mercury (the element, not the planet) and futuristic food machines – all of which would become trademark obsessions of the story editor, David Whitaker. Mercury is used for the TARDIS's fluid link (the purpose of which is not specified). The Doctor falsely claims that the link needs refilling with mercury before the TARDIS can take off, and further claims that he doesn't have any in stock, forcing the travellers to search the nearby city.

Doctor Who?: He may be selfish, putting the others in danger so that he can explore the city, but it's what the audience wants him to do. His childlike curiosity reflects that of the younger viewers. He describes himself as a 'scientist, an engineer ... a builder of things' and says that he was 'a pioneer' among his own people.

Other Worlds: Skaro, home to two races – the Daleks and the Thals – who all but wiped each other out in a neutron war many years ago.

Scary Monsters: The Daleks: once the Dals, a race of teachers and philosophers, now twisted by the fallout of a nuclear war into hostile, machine-dwelling mutants. Although Terry Nation was the one to profit from the creatures, much of the credit rests with designer Raymond P Cusick. Cusick had been drafted in to replace Ridley Scott, then a BBC staff designer who found himself unavailable to cover the start of production: although it would be a nice boast for *Doctor Who* if Scott had worked on it, the show might not have lasted six months had Cusick not come up with the right design at the right time (success was immediate: *Doctor Who*'s number of viewers increased by 50 per cent over the course of the serial).

The less practical aspects of the Daleks' design have been subjected to much mockery over the years, yet for the purpose of this story (and Cusick had no reason to think they would be required for any other purpose) the design makes perfect sense. The Daleks are custom-built for the city to which they have confined themselves. They can't climb stairs because their home is completely fitted with lifts, and they can't go over rough terrain because their floors are of polished metal. The 'plunger' which seems silly in later stories is used here as a universal interface for their own technology.

Most of all the Daleks don't look like conquerors of worlds, for the simple reason that they were never supposed to be. They are hostile not because they thirst for power but because they are frightened, aware that their dependence on technology makes them vulnerable. Any story in which the Daleks moved outside of their city would logically see them modify their own design, yet this would have disappointed the audience, for whom the Daleks' design was their main appeal (unlike the Cybermen, who can easily be redesigned because their appeal lies in the concept).

The Plan: The Daleks have become dependent on radiation to survive, so they plan to explode another atomic bomb on Skaro – which will also have the fringe benefit of killing the surviving Thals.

Things Fall Apart: The sequences of Susan's running through the forest are horribly fake. There's some very obvious use of photo blow-up Daleks in 'The Expedition', and 'The Ordeal' debuts the creatures' habit of pointless triumphalist chanting.

Availability: 'The Daleks' was issued on VHS in 2001 as BBCV 6960 (UK), WHV E1275 (US). The serial was remade as a cheerful colour feature film, *Dr. Who & the Daleks* (Gordon Flemyng, 1965), starring Peter Cushing as 'Dr. Who': this is available on

DVD (D038470) and was first broadcast, on BBC1, on 1 July 1972.

Verdict: 'Pacifism only works when everybody feels the same.' An archetypal but well-executed example of Cold War science fiction. Interestingly, it isn't an allegory – neither the Daleks nor the Thals obviously represent a real-world superpower and the nuclear war simply represents itself – rather, it's a parable. Undeniably, aspects of the moral look dodgy under analysis (the mutated Daleks represent a dire warning against nuclear war but the refined Thals make it look quite promising, and the story encourages us to trust beauty and destroy ugliness) and there's a distinct antipacifist message. However, the issues are explored in full and not presented as simple: when Ian tries to justify to himself the act of leading the Thals into battle, Barbara declares, 'All you're doing is playing with words.'

As an adventure it's straightforward matinée serial stuff, with lots of daring escapes and high-tension moments, helped along by the odd handy coincidence. Tristram Cary's avant-garde score is a highlight – no surprise that it was reused several times on the show. Both directors do excellent work, but it's Christopher Barry who comes out with the honours for the sequence in which Barbara is being gradually cornered by a Dalek. His skewed angles, although they partly expose the artificiality of the sets, make this clinical place seem alive and threatening, especially when an ordinary room becomes a lift. The moment when Barbara unwittingly places her hand over the camera subtly acknowledges that she is being watched, but does not know it yet. The viewpoint of the unseen monster is reprised at the end, placing the viewer in the uncomfortable position of doing the menacing.

3
'The Edge of Destruction'

The Edge of Destruction: 8 February 1964
The Brink of Disaster: 15 February 1964

Written by David Whitaker
Directed by Richard Martin (1), Frank Cox (2)

Notable Cast: 'The Edge of Destruction' was commissioned to fill an inconvenient two-week gap in *Doctor Who*'s schedule, and, since the stories either side of it were proving expensive, David Whitaker was briefed to write two very, very cheap episodes. Hence the entire serial takes place on the existing TARDIS set, with no actors other than the four regulars.

Writer: David Whitaker was *Doctor Who*'s first script editor and as such was intimately involved in the show's early development. He was also behind spin-offs such as the stage play *The Curse of the Daleks* (1965) and the comic strip 'The Daleks', which ran in *TV Century 21* (1964–65). He later wrote for cinema, including the spy thriller *Subterfuge* (Peter Graham Scott, 1969). He died in 1979.

Director: A then newly qualified BBC staff director (like many of those assigned to *Doctor Who*), Frank Cox, went on to become producer of the long-running Scottish soap *Take the High Road*.

Science/Magic: The Doctor denies that the TARDIS has any kind of reasoning intelligence, despite its highly creative response to the jamming of the 'fast return switch'. Finding itself hurtling back to the birth of the universe, it tries to alert its crew by electrifying parts of the console, opening and closing the doors while alternately putting attractive and unattractive pictures on the scanner, melting all the clocks and sending the crew gradually insane. Do those safety features come as standard, or can you opt for a passenger airbag instead?

Doctor Who?: The Doctor still mistrusts Ian and Barbara, and it's clear that his understanding of the TARDIS is less comprehensive than he would like. His conflict with Barbara is ultimately a rather trite example of male logic opposing female intuition, which makes him seem a little more human than at other times. The travellers explicitly emerge from this ordeal as a stronger group, reinforcing the bonding they have already experienced over the first two adventures. After this, there's less of an edge to their interactions.

Things Fall Apart: It doesn't make any sense. Not even vaguely. It starts to look as if it might make sense in the second episode, but then it doesn't.

Availability: Issued on VHS as BBCV 6877 (UK), WHV E1578 (US) in April 2000.

Verdict: 'It's not very logical now, is it? Hmm?' Having won over the audience so comprehensively with its Daleks, *Doctor Who* does its best to alienate everybody again with two episodes of slow gibberish. The viewers' likely confusion at Whitaker's incomprehensible tale is offset only by sympathy for the cast, who clearly don't know what's going on either. William Russell is unusually awful (he seems distracted by something – perhaps wondering how he can get out of his 52-week contract), and Carole Ann Ford plays every scene at a point of near-hysteria. Even Hartnell is inattentive (the moment when he steps over to the camera and declares, 'Can it be possible that this is the end?' is the stagiest moment in *Doctor Who*, which is no mean achievement).

Annoyingly, Whitaker raises the possibility that the TARDIS has been invaded and one of its occupants possessed, but this turns out to be a red herring despite the fact that it could have formed the basis of a much better story. Instead, Whitaker desperately tries, and fails, to justify a series of surreal happenings and eventually asks us to believe that all this trouble could be caused by a dodgy spring. Problem is, the cast don't seem to believe it and so neither do we.

4
'Marco Polo'

The Roof of the World: 22 February 1964
The Singing Sands: 29 February 1964
Five Hundred Eyes: 7 March 1964
The Wall of Lies: 14 March 1964
Rider from Shang-Tu: 21 March 1964
Mighty Kublai Khan: 28 March 1964
Assassin at Peking: 4 April 1964

Written by John Lucarotti
Directed by Waris Hussein (1–3, 5–7), John Crockett (4)

Notable Cast: Mark Eden (Marco Polo) had a long run (1986–89) and memorable death as Alan Bradley in *Coronation Street*. Derren Nesbitt (Tegana) went on to spend the 1970s in such comedy lowlights as *Not Now, Darling* (Ray Cooney, David Croft, 1973) and wrote and directed one of his own, *The Amorous Milkman* (1974).

Writer: John Lucarotti also wrote episodes of *The Avengers* (1961–65), *Joe 90* (1969), *The Onedin Line* (1971–80) and *Moonbase 3* (1973).

Director: John Crockett directed episodes of the anthology series *Suspense* (1962).

History 101: The TARDIS lands in the Andes in 1289, where the travellers encounter the Venetian adventurer Marco Polo. Marco is in the service of the mighty Kublai Khan (Martin Miller), a Mongol who conquered the whole of Asia. They travel with Marco through the Gobi desert, to Shang-Tu and then Peking in Cathay (China). Their companions on the journey are Ping-Cho (Zienia Merton), a 16-year-old girl preparing for an arranged marriage to a 75-year-old she has never met, and the warlord Tegana, a peace emissary from the rival Mongol lord Noghai.

Doctor Who?: The Doctor is a normal old man, suffering from a variety of ailments: he is out of breath in high altitude, sleeps heavily when in a bad mood and has a bad back that leaves him in agony when he tries to bow down before the Khan. When the Doctor sickens while crossing the Gobi desert, a spell in the TARDIS allows him to recover – this is probably because it is cool inside, rather than a property of the ship itself. The Doctor loses his temper rapidly, especially where the TARDIS is concerned. He's furious when it breaks down, and is in a constant rage because Marco denies him access to it. His contempt at the idea of a thirteenth-century human being able to understand the TARDIS is fierce: he calls Marco a 'savage' and laughs hysterically at the thought of Kublai Khan being given the TARDIS.

The Doctor never introduces himself – Ian refers to him as 'the Doctor' in Marco's presence, and Marco introduces him to the Khan. The Doctor remembers that Barbara is 'Miss Wright', but introduces Ian as 'Charlton'. Susan says that she has had many homes, in many places – presumably the Doctor has, too. She says that the Doctor will stop travelling when he knows all the mysteries of the universe.

The Doctor can make duplicate TARDIS keys, and play backgammon well, winning huge riches while playing Kublai Khan. However, he loses it all back to the Khan while gambling to get the TARDIS returned.

When the guard watching over the travellers is killed in 'Rider from Shang-Tu', the Doctor asks if Ian killed him, in a manner that seems more curious than disapproving.

Villains: Tegana, who describes the Doctor and friends as evil spirits and sorcerers from the day they meet, and plots to have them killed, as well as plotting against Marco and Kublai Khan.

The Plan: When he finds that the TARDIS can travel without wheels, Marco thinks that giving it to the Khan will persuade him to allow Marco to return to Venice. To this end he separates the Doctor from his TARDIS, and keeps the travellers as 'guests' in his caravan. The Doctor and his friends make several plans to steal the ship back, but none succeed.

Tegana is an assassin, sent to delay Marco's return so that Noghai's armies have time to reach Peking. When Tegana gets to Peking, he is to kill the Khan, leaving the Khan's armies leaderless as Noghai's forces invade. Following Marco's lead, along the way Tegana also attempts to have the Doctor and his friends killed so that he can steal the TARDIS for Noghai.

Other Worlds: Susan alludes to having seen the silver seas on Venus, and says her home is 'as far away as a night star'.

Science/Magic: Several basic scientific principles are elucidated in the course of the story: the thinness of air at high altitudes; how water forms through condensation; and the explosive noise bamboo makes when it is burned. All of these are vital to the plot.

Availability: This is the earliest *Doctor Who* story no longer to exist on film or video. The audio-only version is available on CD as ISBN 0563535083.

Things Fall Apart: There's no consistency as to which of the Asian characters speaks BBC English, and which adopt an accent. With only still photos to look at, it's hard to tell how the sets cope with the sweeping ambition of the script.

Verdict: 'The sun's rays will dispel the shadows from your mind.' An epic journey with a real sense of time and place, 'Marco Polo' has a poetic script, and is a testament to the rationale of using history as subject matter for the series. The story is almost Reithian in the level of educational content, with some basic science alongside the many historical details. Listening to the sound is a surprisingly fulfilling experience, even without visuals – the exotic setting is created as much through dialogue, sound effects and music as through anything on screen – although existing photographs testify to the high quality of the design work.

With only four other significant characters in the story (Marco, Tegana, Ping-Cho and, in the last two episodes, Kublai Khan), the regulars get a lot of development. The Doctor is the leader of the group, but cantankerous and difficult. Ian is very much the heroic lead, who comes up with all the best plans, and befriends Marco as an equal. Susan is less unearthly, and more a child of the 1960s in this story, constantly using contemporary slang (to the bafflement of Ping-Cho). The character who gets the least development is Barbara (which Lucarotti would compensate for in **6**, 'The Aztecs'), but all in all the regulars are working together better as a unit after the trauma of the previous story.

Finally, a big hello to a regular *Doctor Who* motif, as we have the series' first chess metaphor. In 'The Singing Sands' Tegana pretty much spells out his intentions when Marco and Ian are playing chess, asking, 'Marco Polo, can you save your king?' Marco says he can – which he does, defending the Khan from Tegana in 'Assassin at Peking'. The plot can be seen as an extended chess game between the various characters, as they try to capture various kings (the TARDIS, the Khan). The intricacy of these moves demonstrates a key quality that few *Doctor Who* stories possess: genuine subtlety.

5
'The Keys of Marinus'

The Sea of Death: 11 April 1964
The Velvet Web: 18 April 1964
The Screaming Jungle: 25 April 1964
The Snows of Terror: 2 May 1964
Sentence of Death: 9 May 1964
The Keys of Marinus: 16 May 1964

Written by Terry Nation
Directed by John Gorrie

Notable Cast: George Colouris (Arbitan) played Thatcher in *Citizen Kane* (Orson Welles, 1941), and was a member of Welles's Mercury Theatre Company. His later work includes *Papillon* (Franklin J Shaffner, 1973) and *Murder on the Orient Express* (Sidney Lumet, 1974).

Director: John Gorrie went on to direct numerous TV plays, as well as the high-profile miniseries *First Among Equals* (1986, based on Jeffrey Archer's novel) and *Edward the Seventh* (1975) starring Timothy West.

Doctor Who?: The Doctor has developed considerable faith in Ian, describing him as 'resourceful'. He remembers Ian's name correctly. In the city of Millenius the Doctor acts as the defence counsel in Ian's trial for murder (an excellent showcase for Hartnell). The Doctor believes that, while machines can make laws, only people can make justice. He has a liking for truffles, but the luxury he really desires is a well-equipped laboratory. He once met Pyrrho, founder of scepticism. The Doctor is absent from both 'The Screaming Jungle' and 'The Snows of Terror'.

Other Worlds: Unlike most planets seen in _Doctor Who_, Marinus has different continents and environments. The TARDIS lands on an island by an acid sea, at the centre of which is the Conscience of Marinus, a device that influences people's minds, keeping out evil thoughts. The Conscience has not been used for some time and Arbitan, protector of the Conscience, sends the Doctor and his friends to retrieve the microcircuit 'keys' that control it. They visit: the city of Morphaton, where they are hypnotised into believing they are living in luxury; a jungle with vicious plants; a snowy wasteland; and the city of Millenius, with its strict legal system where suspects are guilty until proven innocent.

Scary Monsters: The Voord, knife-wielding, wet-suited humanoids who cross the acid seas of Marinus in glass submersibles. In Morphaton, brains in jars mentally enslave the populace with the 'mesmeron' device.

Villains: Yartek, leader of the alien Voord, who overcame the influence of the Conscience, and with his Voord could commit crimes of violence without facing any resistance from those still subject to the Conscience.

The Plan: Yartek is trying to seize control of the Conscience of Marinus to enslave the minds of the planet.

Science/Magic: The travellers cross Marinus using transport dials (wristwatches with teleportation powers). There is some information about volcanic springs and human circulation in 'The Snows of Terror', but, as this is the same episode in which dead warriors come inexplicably to life, it's hardly an educational exercise.

Things Fall Apart: The script repeatedly collides messily with budgetary limitations. There are moments of pure, unintentional slapstick, as characters limply fall through cardboard trapdoors, run into walls and otherwise mess up overambitious action scenes.

The wolves in 'The Snows of Terror' are on grainy film stock visibly incompatible with the rest of the episode. Yartek tries to disguise himself as Arbitan, pulling the hood of Arbitan's robes over his giant rubber head. Remarkably, neither Ian nor Susan seems to notice Arbitan has a different voice and a two-foot-tall head.

Availability: Issued on VHS in 1999 as BBCV 6671 (UK), WHV E1383 (US).

Verdict: 'This whole affair is outrageous!' A straightforward quest narrative, 'The Keys of Marinus' is a string of adventure clichés – jungles, trap-filled temples, icy wastelands and killer plants. With a Hollywood budget this could be an epic, but as 1960s television its grasp far outstretches its reach.

Some instalments are watchable: 'The Velvet Web' is cleverly directed to cut between illusory luxury and tawdry reality. The dichotomy is played both for drama and, in a scene where the Doctor admires a dirty mug as if it were valuable scientific equipment, comedy. 'Sentence of Death' is by far the best episode, with decent costumes, sets and actors, so it's a shame that the central mystery (and its solution) is so basic. Unfortunately, the middle two episodes are simplistic stories that suffer from the Doctor's absence.

The story ends with the Voord dead. Unlike the Daleks, the destruction of Terry Nation's second race of *Doctor Who* monsters was never reversed, perhaps an indication of how inconsequential this fragmented, silly story is.

6
'The Aztecs'

Temple of Evil: 23 May 1964
The Warriors of Death: 30 May 1964
The Bride of Sacrifice: 6 June 1964
The Day of Darkness: 13 June 1964

Written by John Lucarotti
Directed by John Crockett

Notable Cast: Ian Cullen (Ixta) went on to play sex symbol PC Joe Slater in *Z Cars* (1969–75) who was murdered in one of the most shocking moments of 70s television. He had major roles in *When* *the Boat Comes In* (1976–77, 1981) and *Family Affairs* (1997–99). John Ringham (Tlotoxl) played Captain Bailey in the first episode of *Dad's Army* and Henshawe in *Poldark* (1975–76), but is best known for playing Penny's Father in *Just Good Friends* (1983–86) and being in the famous Indiana Jones pastiche Terry's Chocolate Orange adverts of the 1980s.

History 101: The setting is Mexico, prior to the arrival of Cortes but after the death of the High Priest Yetaxa around 1430 – so probably sometime in the mid-fifteenth century. The Aztec civilisation is at its height and, after the TARDIS lands in Yetaxa's tomb and the travellers emerge, Barbara is mistaken for the reincarnation of Yetaxa. As the alternative is to be condemned as a tomb robber, she maintains the pretence.

Villains: Tlotoxl, the High Priest of Sacrifice, suspects that Barbara is not in fact Yetaxa and works to reveal the truth. In keeping with the vaguely Renaissance-drama tone of the piece, John Ringham plays the role as an Olivier's *Richard III*-style grotesque with hunched stance and rictus-like grin. He keeps just the right side of ludicrous.

Science/Magic: Much of the plot hinges on the conflict between Tlotoxl, who advocates superstition, and Autloc (Keith Pyott), the High Priest of Knowledge. Interestingly, although we know that Tlotoxl is wrong, his argument for sacrifice is strengthened by the way that rainfall follows so precisely after the chosen victim dies.

The Plan: Barbara intends to change history, putting an end to human sacrifice, so that when the Spanish explorers arrive in 1519 they will not be appalled by the violence of Aztec culture. This is the first time that the series addresses such issues, with the Doctor arguing that history cannot be rewritten (and that it's impossible, not inadvisable). The plot appears to prove him right, as Barbara's efforts are ultimately undone. One could argue that if it were impossible to change history the Doctor wouldn't argue so hard that Barbara shouldn't try, but perhaps he is merely trying to protect her from her ultimate painful failure (and from endangering their position among the Aztecs).

Doctor Who?: We see the Doctor's first love interest. Although the Doctor does partly cultivate a relationship with Cameca (Margot van der Burgh) out of a need for information and assistance, Hartnell plays the scenes in a way that makes it clear that the

Doctor is charmed by the Aztec woman. 'You're a very fine woman, Cameca,' he says at the end, 'and you'll always be very dear to me.' His prevarication over whether to take the bracelet with him at the end sees some nice nonverbal acting from Hartnell, and demonstrates how deeply affected the Doctor is by leaving her behind.

Things Fall Apart: The fight sequence in 'Day of Darkness' fails to disguise the use of stunt doubles for William Russell and Ian Cullen, and the edge of the set is visible at some points.

Availability: Issued on DVD (BBCDVD 1099, WHV E1719) in 2002, following a VHS (BBCV 4743, WHV E1257) in 1992.

Verdict: 'Yours is a tragedy far greater than mine.' More brilliance from John Lucarotti, 'The Aztecs' is a well-researched and lyrically scripted piece of historical drama. The contrast between the violent and sophisticated aspects of Aztec culture had piqued the writer's interest while he was living in Mexico and he uses *Doctor Who* very effectively as a vehicle to communicate this to a family audience. The regular characters, with their contemporary morals and values, interpret for the audience what would otherwise seem like a very alien culture. As with 4, 'Marco Polo', a substantial contribution is made by designer Barry Newbery and costumer Daphne Dare.

But 'The Aztecs' isn't just a history lesson: there's a highly engaging plot to be had. *Doctor Who* stories tend to thrive on action but this one operates largely on character-driven tension: there's conflict between Autloc and Tlotoxl; the latter plots against Barbara; and, most memorably, Barbara clashes with the Doctor over her desire to alter history. Jacqueline Hill and William Hartnell are both at their best during these scenes, adding a lot of weight to small events. In fact, Hill very nearly steals the show from Hartnell – she'll have you cheering her on when she saves Ian's life by holding a blade to Tlotoxl's throat. Gorgeous from start to finish and undoubtedly one of the finest *Doctor Who* serials.

7
'The Sensorites'

Strangers in Space: 20 June 1964
The Unwilling Warriors: 27 June 1964
Hidden Danger: 11 July 1964
A Race Against Death: 18 June 1964

Kidnap: 25 July 1964
A Desperate Venture: 1 August 1964

Written by Peter R Newman
Directed by Mervyn Pinfield (1–4), Frank Cox (5–6)

Notable Cast: One of the Sensorites is played by Peter Glaze (1924–83), well known as a comedy regular on the BBC children's game show *Crackerjack* (1955–83).

Writer: Peter R Newman was scriptwriter of both the film (1959) and television (1958) versions of controversial war drama *Yesterday's Enemy*, which portrayed British soldiers in 1942 as anything but heroic. 'The Sensorites' reflects similar concerns.

Director: Mervyn Pinfield was associate producer of *Doctor Who* from **1**, 'An Unearthly Child', to **12**, 'The Romans', regarded as a steadying hand against Verity Lambert's inexperience by conservative elements within the BBC. Most of his other work was not drama based and his major contribution to television was the 'piniprompter' (an invention now commonly known as the autocue). All his *Doctor Who* directorial work is hugely effective and demonstrates real skill with visual storytelling.

Doctor Who?: This is a key story in the evolution of the relationships between the regulars. The Doctor draws attention to how they've all changed in the time they've been together in 'Strangers in Space', saying, 'It all started off as a mild curiosity in a junkyard', but has now evolved into something with 'quite a great spirit of adventure'. The Doctor claims that he 'learned not to meddle in other people's affairs long ago', which causes Ian to laugh openly at him. (Arguably, the Doctor's curing of the Sensorite 'plague' is his first 'active' interference in the lives of the people he visits on his travels.) The Doctor refers to Ian as both 'my friend' and 'my boy', but also mispronounces his name as 'Cheston'. He opines that 'the one purpose in growing older is to accumulate wisdom'.

Susan now resents being treated like a child and consistently addresses Ian and Barbara by their forenames. The Doctor claims that he and Susan have never had an argument – which simply isn't true (see **1**, 'An Unearthly Child') and is just a low-key example of the Doctor's tendency to bluff, exaggerate and lie to unsettle others. The Doctor refers to a group of people, including himself, as 'we humans' and implies he has one heart (see **51**,

'Spearhead from Space'). He states that he doesn't make threats, but always keeps his promises.

Ian and Barbara's sheer physical closeness is striking: they even quietly hold hands when scared and press their faces very close together when talking. The actors are inarguably by this point playing the two schoolteachers as a couple.

History 101: The Doctor once quarrelled with Henry VIII; he threw a parson's nose at the monarch and was sent to the Tower for doing so. In the twenty-eighth century Britain still exists but there's been no London for four hundred years, the whole of southern England being referred to as 'Central City'. Interestingly, the humans trapped in orbit around the Sense Sphere accept that the Doctor's party are time travellers without hesitation.

Other Worlds: It's ages since Susan and the Doctor have seen 'our planet', where the 'sky at night is orange and the leaves on the trees are a burned silver colour'. She once visited the planet Esto, where plants communicate through thought t-ransference.

Scary Monsters: The alien Sensorites aren't scary or monstrous. Their society has three castes – Elders, Warriors and Sensorites – who rule, fight and work/play respectively. They don't seem to have names and are all of a single sex. Their pupils dilate at night, meaning they can't see in the dark; they are naturally timid and are harmed by loud noises. The creatures are *Doctor Who*'s first nonhuman aliens with individual personalities. The Sensorites' leader, First Elder, is said to be elected, but it's not clear how big the electoral college for such elections is. Second Elder is explicitly appointed by First (although this may simply be in the event that office is vacated – the president of the United States appoints a vice president when that office is vacated).

It is implied that Sensorite law allows for the death penalty. Their capital city and seat of government is divided into ten districts and, although it is the seat of government, the city is run by a city administrator, who is independent of them (not unlike the mayor of London, then).

The actual monsters of the story turn out to be humans, who are engaged in a mass poisoning campaign on the Sense Sphere. (Ten years before, five humans came to the Sense Sphere, intending to exploit its mineral wealth, but their ship later exploded and the Sensorites assumed that all the humans had died.)

The Plan: The survivors of the human expedition are using atropine/deadly nightshade poisoning to wipe out the Sensorites by polluting their aqueduct.

Villains: The insane leader of the humans, but also the Sensorite city administrator, who is a ranting, xenophobic, suspicious petty bureaucrat with a liking for kidnap and torture.

Science/Magic: Molybdenum, the mineral the Sense Sphere is rich in, is used in steel. It melts at 2,622°C, rather than 1,539°C as iron does. The human astronauts have 'heart resuscitators', which can revive them from a coma-like state in which they have no pulse, and measure aeronautical speed in machs. The Doctor says they can't break the TARDIS's doors down because this would 'disturb the dimensions inside the TARDIS' (an indication that the ship's inside exists in a different reality from its shell). 'This old ship of mine seems to be an aimless thing,' the Doctor admits at one point, but later takes spectacular offence at Ian's suggestion that he, the Doctor, can't fly it, and threatens to dump him and Barbara at their next port of call.

Things Fall Apart: The Sensorites write in English and use Cyrillic numbers. They also successfully steal the TARDIS lock using a cutting tool while the Doctor is standing about five feet away. A camera-microphone is suddenly in shot in 'Kidnap' shortly after a sound effect is left on for too long. In the same episode, producer Verity Lambert's voice is suddenly audible due to headphone feedback as she gives instructions. There's some script confusion over whether 'Sensorites' is the name of the race or simply one caste.

Availability: Issued on VHS in 2002 as part of the *First Doctor Box Set* (BBCV 7276) in the UK. The US release is WHV E1852.

Verdict: 'It is the failure of all beings that they judge through their own eyes.' The first couple of episodes have a creepy, sinister atmosphere but the story evolves into *Doctor Who*'s first 'greed is the real enemy' tale. There's some great material for Hartnell here as the Doctor cures a plague, camps it up in a big cape, engages in high politics and negotiates with the unhinged human leader. A neglected gem.

8
'The Reign of Terror'

A Land of Fear: 8 August 1964
Guests of Madame Guillotine: 15 August 1964
A Change of Identity: 22 August 1964
The Tyrant of France: 29 August 1964
A Bargain of Necessity: 5 September 1964
Prisoners of Conciergerie: 12 September 1964

Written by Dennis Spooner
Directed by Henric Hirsch (1–2, 4–6), John Gorrie (3)

Notable Cast: Edward Brayshaw (Colbert) was Harold Meaker, the owner of Rentaghost in the BBC children's series of that name (1976–84). The prolific stage and screen actor Ronald Pickup made his television debut as a physician in the episode 'The Tyrant of France'.

Writer: As well as script-editing *Doctor Who* from 11, 'The Rescue' to 16, 'The Chase', Dennis Spooner (1932–86) was a stalwart of British TV for two decades. Early on he wrote comedy for Tony Hancock, while his drama work includes *Thunderbirds* (1964–66), *Doomwatch* (1970–71), *Bergerac* (1981), *Hammer House of Mystery and Suspense* (1984) and *The Avengers* (one of the few writers to pen episodes spanning the whole of the series' run, 1961–69). He also created the espionage series *The Champions* (1968–69) and *Man in a Suitcase* (1967–68).

Director: Henric Hirsch later worked on the BBC's *Wednesday Play*, but spent most of his career in theatre. No director is credited on the episode 'A Change of Identity' because Hirsch fell ill and Gorrie filled in at short notice. Hirsch knew Spooner socially – they played bridge together.

History 101: The TARDIS arrives in France, 12 kilometres north of Paris at dusk on a summer's day in 1794. Soon, Ian, Barbara and Susan are arrested as antirevolutionaries and sent to Paris. Ian and Barbara become involved with an English spy and Paul Barras's plan to topple Robespierre (Keith Anderson): this culminates in their pretending to be an innkeeper and landlady. Ian gets to meet Napoleon, who is plotting with Barras.

The Plan: There isn't one, really. This is more a travelogue in which the main characters spend most of their time being locked into, or escaping from, cells.

Villains: Leon Colbert is a double agent, working for the revolutionary government while ostensibly working on an escapee route. By the end of the story General Bonaparte has plotted his way to national political prominence.

Doctor Who?: Susan says that the French Revolution is the Doctor's favourite period in Earth history, but he later expresses disgust at Robespierre's slaughterhouse methods of public order to the first deputy's face, demanding, 'What can this reign of terror possibly gain?' The scenes where the Doctor impersonates a senior Revolutionary official (complete with huge hat, ribbons and shoulder pads which conspire to make him look something like a pimp) are brilliant; the first on-screen evidence of Hartnell's immense talent for verbal and physical comedy.

Science/Magic: The audience sees the TARDIS materialise on screen for only the second time (the first was in **5**, 'The Keys of Marinus'), and again it materialises silently. The TARDIS also materialises silently in **10**, 'The Dalek Invasion of Earth'. From **11**, 'The Rescue', onwards the TARDIS usually makes a wheezing, groaning sound as it appears, although there are exceptions, such as in **14**, 'The Crusade'.

Things Fall Apart: A camera crashes into the scenery spectacularly at one point in 'A Land of Fear'. The script shows signs of being written quickly; the message that the dying Webster gives to Ian in 'Guests of Madame Guillotine' is nothing like the one Ian relays in 'Prisoners of Conciergerie'. There's a badly acted French child who saves the Doctor from a burning building for no reason other than plot convenience. 'Prisoners of Conciergerie' is a terrible pun.

Availability: The video BBCV 7335 was the final BBC *Doctor Who* VHS release in 2003. It sold out within weeks. The gap caused by the loss of the episodes 'The Tyrant of France' and 'A Bargain of Necessity' was papered over with a (rather good) 2-minute 45-second sequence narrated by Carole Ann Ford with the aid of still photographs and extant audio and video clips from the missing episodes. The US release (WHV E1853) remains available. Various short clips from the misssing episodes are on the *Lost in Time* DVD. (BBCDVD 1353).

Verdict: 'You have no rights. You will be guillotined as soon as can be arranged.' A blackly comic take on *The Scarlet Pimpernel* and its ilk, which features a lascivious, drunken jailer and a wide variety of startling comedy hats, 'The Reign of Terror' pulls as few punches as it can, given that it's teatime television. There's an undercurrent of violence throughout and the revolutionaries are either crude, money-obsessed, bloodthirsty savages or cold-blooded autocrats interested only in their personal power. There's a glorious moment where the Doctor is asked if he thinks he's very clever and he replies, 'Without undue modesty? Yes!'

9
'Planet of Giants'

Planet of Giants: 31 October 1964
Dangerous Journey: 7 November 1964
Crisis: 14 November 1964

Written by Louis Marks
Directed by Mervyn Pinfield (1–2), Douglas Camfield (3)

Writer: Louis Marks found his greatest success as a producer, specialising in televised literary adaptations. His credits include *Middlemarch* (1994), *Northanger Abbey* (1986), *Daniel Deronda* (2002), *Lady Windermere's Fan* (1985) and Sophocles' *Theban Plays* (1984). He also wrote episodes of *Doomwatch* (1970).

Director: The episode 'Crisis' was Douglas Camfield's first directorial credit, although he did not direct the entire episode: 'Planet of Giants' was made as a four-part story but concerns over its pacing meant that the third and fourth episodes were edited into one. Camfield directed the fourth episode, which would have been called 'The Urge To Live'. His other work includes series such as *Paul Temple* and *The Sweeney*, as well as the miniseries *Beau Geste* (1982) and several further *Doctor Who* serials.

Science/Magic: The TARDIS overheats when the Doctor 'changes frequency' from eighteenth-century France, to try to 'sidestep' the ship to England in the twentieth century. The TARDIS's doors open just *before* they materialise, which can have terrible consequences. The TARDIS's fault locator says nothing is wrong, but the Doctor doesn't believe it – materialisation is the most dangerous point of time travel.

DN-6 is a powerful, 'everlasting' insecticide that (according to the Doctor) will eventually destroy 'all life'. The Doctor explains how pressurised cans explode when heated.

Doctor Who?: The Doctor is extremely stressed when the TARDIS doors open in flight of their own accord, and tells Ian and Barbara, in a non sequitur, that they could never understand time travel. After he is convinced no harm has been done, the Doctor apologises to Barbara for being rude. The Doctor calls Ian 'sir' – evidence of how he has mellowed. When Ian and Barbara are in danger, the Doctor undertakes a dangerous climb up a drainpipe to help them.

The Doctor and Susan were once trapped in a zeppelin air raid during World War One.

Other Worlds: The crew leave the TARDIS to find a puzzling environment of sheer rock walls, with a large dead earthworm and huge dead ants. When the Doctor finds a giant matchstick, he realises that they have landed on contemporary Earth – but the incident with the TARDIS doors caused the 'space pressure' to reduce the travellers in size to less than an inch tall.

Scary Monsters: The travellers are menaced by a domestic cat and a housefly.

Villains: Forester (Alan Tilvern), a businessman, and Smithers (Reginald Barratt), a scientist, are developing DN-6. Forester is worried about losing his investment money, while Smithers wants DN-6 to succeed at all costs, since he believes it will end starvation.

The Plan: Forester kills Farrow (Frank Crawshaw), a civil servant who is about to recommend that DN-6 not be allowed to go into production. Forester and Smithers conspire to cover up the murder.

Things Fall Apart: Ian and Susan find a matchbox between the huge rock walls of the paving slabs in the garden, but, when the full-sized Forester picks up the box, it's on the grass. The music is discordant and jarring. Barbara comes into contact with DN-6, and covers up the fact from her friends for no good reason. Forester tries to disguise his voice as Farrow's by holding a handkerchief over the telephone receiver. Criminal genius!

Availability: Issued on VHS in 2001 as BBCV7263 (UK), WHV E1740 (US).

Verdict: 'I can see a huge leg coming. Run!' Surprisingly for such an ambitious idea, it's not the time travellers being miniaturised that lets 'Planet of Giants' down: it's the banality of the plot in which they become tangentially involved. The oversized sets are excellent, as are the giant insects. Even the housefly that menaces Barbara is quite well animated, and there's something cool about the regulars running around giant matchsticks and such. Unfortunately, the plot that is going on at full size is desperately mundane: Forester is a dull and stupid villain, horribly overacted, and the production of dodgy insecticide is a less than thrilling premise. While there are some fun scenes with the regulars, and the direction is good throughout, 'Planet of Giants' adds up to very little.

10
'The Dalek Invasion of Earth'

World's End: 21 November 1964
The Daleks: 28 November 1964
Day of Reckoning: 5 December 1964
The End of Tomorrow: 12 December 1964
The Waking Ally: 19 December 1964
Flashpoint: 26 December 1964

Written by Terry Nation
Directed by Richard Martin

Notable Cast: Bernard Kay (Tyler) was in *Doctor Who* four times. As well as numerous TV credits he appeared in *Doctor Zhivago* (David Lean, 1965) and *Steal This Movie* (Robert Greenwald, 2000).

History 101: It's some time after 2164 (the desk calendar in the warehouse shows this date, and presumably it hasn't been changed in a few years) and Earth has been invaded by the Daleks. Much of the world's population has been wiped out – including the entire populations of Asia, Africa and South America – thanks to the Daleks' use of germ warfare ('cosmic storms') before their physical invasion of the planet.

Scary Monsters: The Daleks, comprehensively reconceptualised by Terry Nation in all aspects except their voices and appearance. It's remarkable to note just how quickly the Daleks were promoted from desperate survivors of a nuclear conflict to the most feared race in the universe (in the light of this and later stories it makes little sense that in **2**, 'The Daleks', the Doctor had no idea who they were: their reputation should be well known to a time traveller). Here they become the only creatures in *Doctor Who* ever successfully to invade Earth, establishing their status in the show's mythology.

Ever since 'The Dalek Invasion of Earth' it has been assumed that the Daleks are the Doctor's greatest enemy, but they were never created for this purpose: they are simply his most *popular* enemy. That people enjoy watching them does not mean that the Daleks pose a greater threat or are more difficult to defeat than any other monster, and on the evidence of their first appearance they are fairly average adversaries. However, Terry Nation was aware that the audience had built the Daleks up into something more than what he had originally written, so here he bolsters them into interplanetary marauders and remorseless embodiments of evil. Similarly, the Doctor acts as if he has always been aware of the threat they posed to the universe.

The Daleks have a ranking system, with a Black Dalek clearly superior to the others.

The Plan: The Daleks plan to remove the magnetic core of the planet and replace it with an engine so that they can pilot it around the universe.

Science/Magic: The Daleks' plan is really, really ridiculous and doesn't justify their invasion of Earth as it's supposed to (magnetic cores being far from unique to our planet).

Doctor Who?: This is the Doctor at his most proactive yet, as he expresses moral outrage at the Daleks' activities. The fact that the TARDIS has been trapped by falling masonry is more or less irrelevant, as it's clear that he intends to remain until the creatures are defeated. He claims that he never kills unless his own life is directly threatened.

He presumptuously makes the decision for Susan to leave the TARDIS, effectively handing her over to David (she is the first of five female regulars to leave for a love interest – male regulars never do this). This marks the first alteration to the regular cast and it's hard to imagine what a big deal this was at the time: *Doctor Who* was an ensemble show and many believed that it couldn't survive such a departure. The very deliberate pace of this final scene, and Carole Ann Ford's awestruck manner when the TARDIS leaves without her, makes it surprisingly moving even when you know it's coming – all the more so compared with the cursory departures of some later regular characters.

Things Fall Apart: Elements that don't impress include the Dalek flying saucer, the photo-blow-up backdrops, the baby alligator, the Slyther and the little model Ian falling down the shaft. There are two ridiculous bombs – Dortmun's cartoon effort (spherical, with a fuse sticking out of the top) and the Daleks' (which makes a loud tick-tocking noise). The Daleks' love of triumphalist chanting continues, and it's remiss of them to leave Central Control completely unattended. The explosion of the Dalek base is a somewhat random montage of stock footage.

Availability: Issued on DVD (BBCDVD 1156, WHV E1813) in 2003. The DVD includes the 1993 radio psuedo-documentary *Whatever Happened to Susan Foreman?*, starring Jane Asher as the Doctor's granddaughter. The disc also includes the option to watch the serial with improved digital special effects. Like 'The Daleks', this serial was adapted into a Peter Cushing-led feature film, *Daleks – Invasion Earth 2150 A.D.* (Gordon Flemyng, 1966) – which is available on DVD (D038470) and was first broadcast on BBC1 on 19 August 1972.

Verdict: 'We are the masters of Earth!' *Doctor Who*'s first sequel sees the production team displaying greater confidence than ever before, safe in the knowledge that the Daleks guarantee the audience's attention. The greater resources afforded to 'The Dalek Invasion of Earth' are certainly not wasted, with some superb location work (especially the crossing-London sequence in the middle of the episode 'Day of Reckoning' and the riverside shots of the Robomen in 'World's End') and far more studio space (courtesy of a move to the more capacious Riverside Studios). Richard Martin, whose work shines throughout, makes liberal use of high and wide angles.

The model work is less successful and the Daleks' plan is not the satisfying revelation that it should be, but the serial stands up in spite of everything because it's so bold. World War Two was less than twenty years ago when this was made and the production automatically reaches for imagery of Nazi-occupied Europe, with collaborators, black marketers, slave-labour camps and resistance members holed up underground. This could be viewed as crass, but it undeniably adds impact to the story's whimsical premise. It never becomes wrapped up in its own importance, concentrating primarily on impressing the viewer, and as such it's genuinely special.

11
'The Rescue'

The Powerful Enemy: 2 January 1965
Desperate Measures: 9 January 1965

Written by David Whitaker
Directed by Christopher Barry

Notable Cast: Maureen O'Brien (Vicki) joins the regular cast. O'Brien has since had memorable roles in *Casualty* (1987), *Moll Flanders* (1996) and *Cracker* (1993), as well as success as a stage actress, and as an author of crime fiction.

Doctor Who?: The Doctor is in a slump following Susan's departure, sleeping through the TARDIS's landing and then wanting to have another nap instead of exploring. Ian thinks the Doctor is going senile, and the Doctor thinks his own handwriting is getting worse. Meeting Vicki re-energises him, to the extent that he gets the strength up to smash a door with an iron girder. He happily welcomes Vicki on board the TARDIS.

The Doctor never got his degree in medicine, which he considers a pity (see **33**, 'The Moonbase').

Other Worlds: Dido, around 2493. The Doctor has been here before, and remembers the natives fondly. The planet is deserted except for space travellers Bennett and Vicki, the only survivors of a rocket crash, with no sign of the aforementioned natives.

History 101: The United Nations still exists in 2493, and the crashed ship sports a Union flag, so presumably the UK exists as well.

Scary Monsters: A vicious-looking sand beast, which turns out to be Vicki's pet, Sandy. Not knowing that Sandy is harmless, Barbara kills it by shooting it in the face with a flare gun.

Villains: Koquillion, a robed figure with clawed hands and a grotesque head, who resembles the natives of Dido in their ceremonial robes. However . . .

The Plan: . . . Koquillion is actually Bennett. He's a killer, who wiped out the survivors of the rocket along with the peaceful natives of Dido to protect his secret, using Vicki as a witness to his innocence and the Koquillion identity to back up his story that it was the natives of Dido who killed the survivors.

Things Fall Apart: Sandy the sand beast doesn't even look vaguely threatening. Ray Barrett is not convincing as either Bennett or Koquillion. The name of the first episode, 'The Powerful Enemy', is therefore a serious misnomer.

Availability: Issued on VHS in a double pack with **12**, 'The Romans', in 1994 as BBCV 5378 (UK) and WHV E1313 (US).

Verdict: 'If you like adventure, my dear, I can promise you an abundance of it.' A weak story built around Vicki's introduction, the plot of 'The Rescue' revolves around one joke – that a *Doctor Who* monster could turn out to be some bloke in a mask. This is story editor Whitaker's second script for the show and, while not as odd as **3**, 'The Edge of Destruction', it does have the occasional strange moment, especially when the spectral 'Dido people' turn up at the end.

O'Brien makes an efficient debut, but this is Hartnell's show. 'The Rescue' showcases the Doctor as mischievous and endearing, a father figure and best friend to children everywhere. Hartnell is on fantastic form, putting on a brave face at the loss of Susan, then building a friendship with Vicki. Unfortunately, he's wasted in the first episode, stuck in the caves with a visibly bored character. However, in the second half the Doctor gets to solve the mystery, batter a door down and confront Bennett about his crimes, in a scene that shows the Doctor at his most heroic.

12
'The Romans'

The Slave Traders: 16 January 1965
All Roads Lead to Rome: 23 January 1965
Conspiracy: 30 January 1965
Inferno: 6 February 1965

Written by Dennis Spooner
Directed by Christopher Barry

Notable Cast: Derek Francis (Nero) appeared in numerous TV series, including a starring role in *Great Expectations* (1981). He also worked on several *Carry On* movies. Kay Patrick (Poppaea) later became a director, working regularly on *Springhill* (1996) and *Jupiter Moon* (1990), and a writer, penning episodes of *Coronation Street*.

History 101: Events take place around the burning of Rome, July 64 CE. The travellers are holidaying at a villa outside the city (the owners are away, so technically the Doctor and co. are squatting). The Doctor decides to take a trip into Rome with Vicki; along the way, he is mistaken for the lute player Maximus Petullian and permitted an audience with Emperor Caesar Nero.

Doctor Who?: The Hartnell Doctor at his campest and most violent in the space of one story. His praise for Barbara's meal is hugely effete ('Oh, fabulous, absolutely fabulous!') while in the episode 'All Roads Lead to Rome' he gleefully engages in combat with an assassin. 'I am so constantly outwitting the opposition,' he tells Vicki, 'I tend to forget the delights and satisfaction of the gentle art of fisticuffs.' Maureen O'Brien's laughter in response to this seems genuine.

Villains: First, there are the slave traders Sevcheria (Derek Sydney) and Didius (Nicholas Evans), who kidnap and sell Barbara and Ian while the Doctor is away. Ian is sold as a galley slave, while Barbara is purchased by Nero's household. Nero himself is the main villain: despite being a comic character, he treats the lives of those around him very casually (his poisoning of Tigilinus is a rather tasteless gag, but very funny). Derek Francis was too old for the role (Nero was 27 at the time of the fire), but the quality of his performance justifies the miscasting. Empress Poppaea is hardly less callous than her husband as she jealously attempts to poison Barbara.

The Plan: Nero wants to create a new city to his own design, and the Doctor inadvertently inspires him to burn Rome down so that it can be rebuilt. Spooner takes certain liberties with historical fact here, since Nero was not in Rome when the fire started. Rumours abounded that he had organised it, but it was probably an accident.

Things Fall Apart: The production overreaches itself with the rather cramped arena set. The size of the flames engulfing Rome makes it too obvious that the city is a model.

Availability: Issued on VHS in a double pack with **11**, 'The Rescue', in 1994 as BBCV 5378 (UK) and WHV E1313 (US).

Verdict: 'Nobody's said anything to me – and I am always informed of intrigues.' Dennis Spooner develops the comedic elements of **8**, 'The Reign of Terror', to produce a script in which whole scenes are designed to be played for laughs, with Hartnell and Derek Francis getting the best jokes (the sauna scene with the sword, the poisoned cup of wine, the imperial footstool). Even so, there's a brutal edge to the story, with no levity about the slave trading or gladiatorial combat, and the machinations of the court regularly claim lives. Spooner treads a line throughout and manages not to fall over.

The serial is slow to get moving, with little happening in the first episode, but it picks up in the second as the setting moves to Rome and is thereafter packed with incident. The farcical aspects usefully justify a number of staggering coincidences as Spooner gets comic mileage out of the regulars' continual failure to encounter each other.

Visually the story isn't a roaring success: it's one of the most demanding historical adventures from a design perspective and a couple of the sets are unimpressive, while Christopher Barry fumbles some of his set-ups. Again, though, because the comedy works these aspects seem less important – you rarely hear people complain about dodgy production values in *Steptoe and Son* or *Dad's Army*.

13
'The Web Planet'

The Web Planet: 13 February 1965
The Zarbi: 20 February 1965
Escape to Danger: 27 February 1965
Crater of Needles: 6 March 1965
Invasion: 13 March 1965
The Centre: 20 March 1965

Written by Bill Strutton
Directed by Richard Martin

Notable Cast: Martin Jarvis (Hilio) has a CV of notable TV leading roles including those in *The Forsyte Saga* (1967), *The Pallisers* (1974) and *Rings on their Fingers* (1978). A regular panellist on the UK's *Countdown* daytime quiz programme, he made a memorable guest appearance in *Inspector Morse* (1991) and is known for reading the *Just William* stories on BBC radio.

Writer: Australian Bill Strutton (1918–2003) wrote for several TV series in the 1960s, including *The Saint* (1963) and *Paul Temple* (1969).

Doctor Who?: The Doctor's ring is of untold value and has an unspecified power that can be used to open the TARDIS doors and control Zarbi. In spite of being trapped on Vortis by a mysterious force, the Doctor initially seems amused by everything – especially rocks. He has heard of Vortis and the Menoptra, and shows no fear of the Zarbi.

Other Worlds: Vortis, a barren planet with pools of acid, occasional pyramids and a large number of moons, including Pictos, which is within flying distance.

Scary Monsters: The Zarbi are giant ants – mindless, speechless creatures that are scared of dead spiders. Larvae Guns are walking weapons, not unlike woodlice. The Menoptra are butterfly people with fey manners and high-pitched voices, and worship gods of light. The Optera are gruff flightless creatures that hop around in the tunnels under Vortis, descendants of Menoptra forced to live underground.

Villains: The Animus, a powerful force that can control the Zarbi and Venom Grubs, trap the TARDIS, cause Vicki to pass out, steal Ian's pen, spin the TARDIS console and pull Barbara's arm via the golden bracelet given to her by Nero (see **Science/Magic** for the significance of gold). The Animus communicates with the Doctor via a bucket lowered over his head (which the Doctor refers to as a 'hair dryer'), and speaks in a feminine voice. The power the Animus is tapping into at Vortis's pole has attracted the planet's new moons, along with the TARDIS. The Animus's physical form is a light blob surrounded by vines.

The Plan: The Animus is aware that the Menoptra are in space, preparing to attack, and wants to use the Doctor's astral map to find them. By draining the Doctor and Vicki of their life and knowledge, the Animus will be able to go to Earth and plunder that, too. The Menoptra intend to destroy the Animus with an isotope created by their wise men.

Science/Magic: The Doctor supposes that it is the thin atmosphere on Vortis that has allowed insects to become the dominant form of life. The Doctor has two ways of counteracting the ill effects of a thin atmosphere: atmospheric density jackets and pills. Vicki falls against the TARDIS console, accidentally repairing the fluid link and restoring the power supply, a tremendously convenient plot twist. The TARDIS's astral map can be moved out of the ship, and will remain operative while the link cable is intact. It can be used to communicate in space. The Animus uses giant gold wishbones to control people (it has some power over gold).

Things Fall Apart: In the episode 'The Zarbi', William Russell as Ian prompts Hartnell with an ad-libbed 'What galaxy is that in?' The Zarbi are unwieldy creatures, frequently bumping into scenery, and in 'Escape to Danger' one head-butts the camera. Kirby wires are clearly visible as the Menoptra fly. The sets look reasonable in early episodes, but visibly fall apart as time goes on.

Availability: Issued on VHS in 1990 as BBCV 4405 (UK) and WHV E1265 (US).

Verdict: 'It's like trying to cut your way through treacle.' The only *Doctor Who* story with an entirely nonhumanoid supporting cast, 'The Web Planet' is an exercise in sustained insanity, an epic conflict between silly insect costumes inhabited by actors using even sillier voices. William Russell looks increasingly annoyed with the story as it progresses (listen for Ian's narky response to being asked whether he will return to Vortis), and who can blame him? 'The Web Planet' is a farcical mess, both ill-conceived and overambitious, and is tragically unaware of its own ludicrousness. Of course, all of this would be forgivable if the thing were anchored by a strong storyline and compelling characterisation. Unfortunately, there's precious little story or character to be found.

14
'The Crusade'

The Lion: 27 March 1965
The Knight of Jaffa: 3 April 1965
The Wheel of Fortune: 10 April 1965
The War Lords: 17 April 1965

Written by David Whitaker
Directed by Douglas Camfield

Notable Cast: Julian Glover (Richard the Lionheart) played Buckingham in the BBC's *Henry VIII* (1979), and appeared in *The Empire Strikes Back* (Irvin Kershner, 1980) and *Indiana Jones and the Last Crusade* (Steven Spielberg, 1989), and is an associate artiste of the RSC. Jean Marsh (Joanna) co-created the TV series *Upstairs, Downstairs* (1971–75) and *The House of Eliot* (1991–93); she also starred in the former. She appeared in *Frenzy* (Alfred Hitchcock, 1972) and played the villainess of *Willow* (Ron Howard, 1987). Tony Caunter (Thatcher) appeared in *Juliet Bravo* (1980–82) and played Roy Evans in *EastEnders* (1994–2003). Bernard Kay (Saladin) appeared in **10**, 'The Dalek Invasion of Earth'.

History 101: 'The Crusade' depicts two historically recorded events from the Third Crusade (1189–92). In October 1191, Richard attempted to arrange a marriage between his sister Joanna and his opponent Saladin's brother, and in November 1191 Richard was ambushed outside Jaffa. (David Whitaker found that the narrative worked more effectively with these events transposed.)

Villains: To his credit Whitaker treats the war even-handedly and Saladin is not presented as the villain by any means (although he does threaten Barbara with death if she does not tell him stories). The Earl of Leicester (John Bay) forms opposition to the Doctor and Vicki, trying to force them out of favour at court but the real villain is the misogynist Saracen Emir El Akir (Walter Randall).

The Plan: El Akir kidnaps Barbara from Saladin's palace after she participates in his humiliation before Saladin, and plots to inflict sundry painful indignities upon her before eventually killing her.

Doctor Who?: Questionable morality from the Doctor as he gleefully robs clothes from the trader Ben Daheer (Reg Pritchard), reasoning that the clothes have been stolen once and can be stolen again. What a shining example for younger viewers! He later compensates for this by declaring that he hates fools, criticising the bloodthirsty Leicester for being a 'stupid butcher', and demonstrating no signs of racial or religious prejudice despite what's going on around him.

Things Fall Apart: Too many events in between the camps are not shown (Ian's journey to Saladin's palace, for example), which contrives to give the impression that these warring factions are only a couple of hundred yards away from each other. Tutte Lemkow's performance as Ibrahim can be generously described as eccentric.

Availability: The episode 'The Wheel of Fortune' has always been held in the BBC archive; 'The Lion' was missing until 1998. The two episodes were issued on a VHS with **15**, 'The Space Museum' (BBCV 6888, WHV E1399), along with a CD of the two audio-only episodes, in 1999. The extant episodes and audio are also on 2004's *Lost in Time* DVD (BBCDVD 1353).

Verdict: 'Now *there's* a subject for our troubadours and actors.' *Doctor Who*'s early adventures in history often have a theatrical feel, and nowhere is this truer than in 'The Crusade'. Unfortunately, this is not always to the story's advantage. David Whitaker tries to make it work like a Renaissance history play, depicting a war via the rulers' decisions and leaving the battles to the viewer's imagination, the production's sense of scale is insufficient. The later film sequences depicting Ian's encounter with Ibrahim (with Douglas Camfield's trademark canny use of stock footage) help to broaden the story's horizons, and it would have been advantageous to do something like this earlier on, before the sense of confinement set in.

Fortunately, the other strengths of 'The Crusade' compensate for this. The dialogue is strong, as are the performances: the argument between Richard and Joanna is superbly played, and Jacqueline Hill gets her best material since **6**, 'The Aztecs', reacting well to Barbara's various traumas – particularly when El Akir's men hunt her down in 'The Wheel of Fortune'. In fact, if all you'd seen or heard of that story was that episode (and for many years it was the only one in circulation), you'd think 'The Crusade' was magnificent. However, 'The Lion' and the sound-only episodes, 'The Knight of Jaffa' and 'The Warlords', reveal that the story never hits those heights at any other point. And who let that godawful pun at the end through: 'A good knight's sleep'?

15
'The Space Museum'

The Space Museum: 24 April 1965
The Dimensions of Time: 1 May 1965

The Search: 8 May 1965
The Final Phase: 15 May 1965

Written by Glyn Jones
Directed by Mervyn Pinfield

Notable Cast: Jeremy Bulloch (Tor) played Boba Fett in *The Empire Strikes Back* (Irvin Kershner, 1980) and *Return of the Jedi* (Richard Marquand, 1983), Edward of Wickham in *Robin of Sherwood* (1985–86) and appeared in Cliff Richard's *Summer Holiday* (Peter Yates, 1962).

Writers: South African playwright and actor Glyn Jones was later script editor of *Here Come the Double Deckers* (1970). He plays Krans in **77**, 'The Sontaran Experiment'.

Doctor Who?: The Doctor is capable of surviving a period in the space museum's freezing/embalming machine – which is usually fatal. His mind is alert throughout the process. He's also strong enough to resist Governor Lobos's mental interrogation equipment (see **Science/Magic**). He doesn't mind admitting that he's 'always found it extremely difficult to solve the fourth dimension'. (In this story and others – such as **21**, 'The Daleks' Master Plan' – 'the fourth dimension' is used in a manner analogous to later serials' use of the term 'space–time vortex'. It's the place one travels *through* when travelling through time.) The Doctor directly refuses to give Governor Lobos (Richard Shaw) his name and claims he always thought he'd find a space museum one day.

Other Worlds: Xeros, a minor world in the Morok Empire a mere three light years from the Morok homeworld. It serves as a lasting memorial to the achievements of the Morok civilisation. When conquering Xeros the Moroks put the adult population to death and now use the children as a workforce, shipping them off-planet when they reach maturity.

The Plan: Having seen a vision of the future in which they end up as exhibits in a museum, the TARDIS crew try to avoid that fate. Unusually, it's Vicki who is proactive, deciding to foment revolution, end the Morok occupation and in the process destroy the museum, since this is the simplest means of escaping their future.

History 101: Vicki doesn't recognise a Dalek (there's one in the museum) but has read of them and the events of **10**, 'The Dalek Invasion of Earth' (300 years before her time) in history books.

Science/Magic: Governor Lobos (who considers himself a scientist) has a machine that, using thought selection, creates pictures out of his prisoners' thoughts. The TARDIS's food machine puts in an appearance.

Things Fall Apart: The first episode, in which the TARDIS 'jumps a time track' due to a faulty spring (see **3**, 'The Edge of Destruction') defies literal sense. The time travellers become intangible, invisible and inaudible to everyone but themselves, change their clothes without noticing, find it impossible to break glasses and don't leave footprints while wandering around a theoretical future. The Doctor's explanation of this in the episode 'The Final Phase' is gibberish. The episode is creepy and peculiar, though, so we're inclined to forgive it; indeed, in its dreamlike, incomprehensible melodrama it inadvertently starts to resemble a David Lynch pastiche of mid-1960s *Doctor Who*.

Availability: The VHS (BBCV 6888) was a double bill with the surviving episodes of **14**, 'The Crusade'. The US release is WHV E1399.

Verdict: 'Time, like space, although a dimension in itself, also has dimensions of its own.' This was the 'cheap' story of the season but it isn't noticeably so after forty years. 'The Space Museum' has aged far better than, say, **16**, 'The Chase', and there's good use of models to convey a sense of scale. Early on, elements of colonial fiction à la Graham Greene (bored governors, ineffective occupation armies, decadent cultures) compete for space with off-the-wall comedy (the Doctor's Dalek impersonation and his interrogation by Lobos, Ian and Barbara's argument about cardigans) and some outright nonsensical madness to create a couple of really peculiar episodes. 'The Search' and 'The Final Phase' are more straightforward, and the scenes where Ian gets to play the action hero, threatening soldiers with a stolen pistol and kneeing a guard in the guts while looking for the Doctor, are enormous fun. Given writer Jones's status as an expatriate South African and the obvious colonial elements of the story, it is tempting – but possibly unwise – to see the story as an antiapartheid parable, one calling for armed revolution against white minority rule in South Africa.

16
'The Chase'

The Executioners: 22 May 1965
The Death of Time: 29 May 1965
Flight Through Eternity: 5 June 1965
Journey into Terror: 12 June 1965
The Death of Doctor Who: 19 June 1965
The Planet of Decision: 26 June 1965

Written by Terry Nation
Directed by Richard Martin

Notable Cast: Hywel Bennett (Rynian, one of the Aridians) later became known for the lead role in ITV's long-running sitcom *Shelley* (1979–92). Peter Purves plays both tourist Morton Dill in the episode 'Flight Through Eternity' and new regular Steven Taylor in 'Planet of Decision'. After leaving *Doctor Who*, he predominantly worked as a TV presenter, with a notable run on *Blue Peter* (1967–78). He keeps fans up to date on his career via his website, www.peterpurves.com.

Doctor Who?: The Doctor likes the Beatles, thinks his singing can 'charm the nightingales out of the trees' (an attribute associated with Orpheus) and claims to have the instincts of a homing pigeon. The Doctor is willing to fight the Daleks to the death, but wants to protect the Aridians and other innocents from getting caught in the battle. He has faith in Ian's survival abilities. When Ian and Barbara get the chance to go home, the Doctor is reluctant to see them go.

Scary Monsters: The Daleks, again. They cannot damage the TARDIS, and have different personalities and manners of speaking (one even stutters). Mire Beasts are flesh-eating, squidlike creatures that used to live at the bottom of Aridius's oceans, but ran amok when the seas dried away. On Mechanus, killer fungus roams the forests, and the Mechanoids are unwieldy robot creatures that live in a city on stilts. Sent from Earth to Mechanus to prepare the planet for human colonists, who never came, the Mechanoids are referred to as 'Mechons' by the Daleks.

Other Worlds: Aridius, a hot, dry planet with two suns where the seas boiled away, and an example of Nation's habit of giving his planets painfully literal names. (Was it called Aridius when its surface was mostly water?) The travellers flee Aridius when the Daleks arrive, and the Daleks pursue the TARDIS as it lands at: the Empire State Building in New York, 1966; the *Mary Celeste*, where the Daleks chase the crew overboard; a haunted-house exhibit at the Festival of Ghana, 1996 (which the Doctor mistakes for the dark side of the human psyche, for some unfathomable reason); and the planet Mechanus.

The Plan: Having been defeated by the Doctor on Skaro and Earth, the Daleks now see him as their mortal enemy, and pursue the TARDIS through space and time to destroy him. The Daleks' status as supreme *Doctor Who* monsters is cemented by their mastery of time travel, and their venomously personal conflict with the Doctor.

On Aridius, Ian traps a Dalek by covering a pit with some sticks, a coat, a cardigan and some sand, then luring the Dalek over it by giving it some verbal abuse. (Following **15**, 'The Space Museum', it seems clear that a cardigan is the essential accessory for the intrepid space/time adventurer.)

Science/Magic: Every time the TARDIS lands, it takes twelve minutes for the computers to recalibrate before they can set off again. It could take years to repair the TARDIS's time mechanism to allow it to be piloted correctly. The TARDIS magnet is a small, compass-like device that always points to the ship, and the time path detector indicates whether another time machine is travelling on the same route. The Daleks have a time machine that is bigger on the inside, and can find a buried TARDIS with the seismic detector. The Time–Space Visualiser is a television-type device that allows the Doctor to see anything from the past. The Doctor builds an ad hoc device that, when activated, immobilises a Dalek with a puff of smoke.

History 101: The travellers use the Time–Space Visualiser to watch Lincoln deliver the Gettysburg address, Shakespeare in discussion with Elizabeth I, and the Beatles playing 'Ticket to Ride'. Vicki says New York was destroyed in the Dalek invasion (see **10**, 'The Dalek Invasion of Earth').

Things Fall Apart: Jacqueline Hill throws herself at the Mire Beast so she can be grabbed by it on cue. When Vicki hits a sailor over the head, the sound effect is out of sync with the action. A Dalek is clearly visible behind a portcullis in the episode 'Journey into Terror', *before* their ship arrives. The Daleks build an identical robot double of the Doctor, which is a foot taller and looks nothing like him. To add to the confusion, at some points Hartnell plays the double and the other actor (Edmund Warwick) plays the real Doctor. Hartnell fluffs many, many lines.

Availability: Issued on VHS alongside **149**, 'Remembrance of the Daleks', as part of a special box set in 1993 as BBCV 5006 (UK), and as WHV E1145 (US).

Verdict: 'My dear boy, we're trying to beat the TARDIS, not start a jumble sale.' Even more than **5**, 'The Keys of Marinus', 'The Chase' is full of schoolboy fascinations: haunted houses, Universal horror movies, the mystery of the *Mary* (sometimes *'Marie'*) *Celeste*, robot doubles and killer squid monsters. Whether this is down to a canny judgement of the audience, or is just reminiscent of children's writing, is hard to tell. It's juvenile fiction, and seems uncertain as to whether the Daleks are a serious threat or comic relief. At least the cast seem to be having some fun, with all concerned demonstrating fine comic timing.

Thankfully, 'The Planet of Decision' pulls everything together with an impressively staged battle between the Daleks and the Mechanoids. Ian and Barbara get a gorgeous send-off, with a montage of photographs of the two joyfully running around London. Newcomer Peter Purves doesn't actually join the TAR-DIS on screen, but makes a sound impression as astronaut Steven Taylor, a prisoner of the Mechanoids for two years of his life. It's a confident debut, but the ending of this story belongs to two of the original leads. The Doctor tells Vicki he will miss them – so will we.

17
'The Time Meddler'

The Watcher: 3 July 1965
The Meddling Monk: 10 July 1965
A Battle of Wits: 17 July 1965
Checkmate: 24 July 1965

Written by Dennis Spooner
Directed by Douglas Camfield

Notable Cast: Peter Butterworth (The Monk) is instantly recognisable for his many appearances in the *Carry On* films – most memorably *Carry On Abroad* (Gerald Thomas, 1972) and *Carry On Screaming* (Gerald Thomas, 1966).

Villains: The Monk – we never discover his name and he isn't a real monk (the Doctor becomes genuinely irritated with the Monk's homilies, calling it 'monkery'). He's the first member of the Doctor's own race – Susan excepted – to appear in the series. The Doctor claims they are from 'the same place' but 'I am fifty years earlier'. Whether this means that he left fifty years before the Monk did or that he's from a different time period of the same world's history is opaque at best. The Doctor and the Monk have explicitly never met before. The Monk wears a blue gemstone ring like the Doctor's, keeps a diary and has an art and furniture collection. Like the Doctor, he clearly has a special interest in human (indeed English) history and culture.

History 101: The TARDIS has arrived in Northumbria in 1066, a matter of days before the Battle of Stamford Bridge – where King Harold II will successfully repel a Viking invasion. He and his exhausted army will then have to march south only to lose a second battle to the invasion forces of William of Normandy.

The Plan: The Monk enumerates his own plan on a huge list. It reads (1) Arrive Northumbria, (2) Position atomic cannon, (3) Sight Vikings, (4) Light beacon fires, (5) Destroy Viking fleet, (6) Norman Landing, (7) Battle of Hastings, (8) Meet King Harold. The Monk's theory is that a fresh Saxon army will defeat the Normans, Harold will be a successful king and, with no wars in France to distract it, medieval England will progress to an industrial age quickly. He seems to be doing this because the idea entertains him. ('It's more fun my way!' he claims when the Doctor states the golden rule of space and time travel as 'never ever interfere with the course of history'.) The Doctor condemns the Monk's frivolity as a 'disgusting exhibition'.

Science/Magic: The Monk's time machine (never referred to as a TARDIS even though inside it's very like the Doctor's; the terms 'machine' and 'time ship' are used) is a Mark IV and implicitly a later model than the Doctor's. Its 'camouflage unit' works perfectly and it is capable of blending into its surroundings. The Doctor congratulates the Monk on the quality of the machine and implies that the Monk must have built it himself (as indeed the Doctor claims to have made his own TARDIS in **16**, 'The Chase').

Steven and Vicki speculate that if the Monk changes history then their memories of the future will change, and they'll remember the 'new' version. The Doctor (conveniently) neither confirms nor denies this, though it runs counter to the logic of later *Doctor Who* (**60**, 'Day of the Daleks', **82**, 'Pyramids of Mars'), which consistently assumes that time travellers are unaffected by alterations to history and thus are able to remember things that never actually 'happened'.

Things Fall Apart: Hartnell fluffs his lines spectacularly in the episode 'The Watcher': 'My dear, I'm not a mountain goat and I prefer walking to any day and I hate climbing.' There's some script confusion over whether the belligerent Eldred is working for the Monk or not. There's a lot of traipsing backwards and forwards from the monastery to the village to pad out the middle two instalments.

Availability: Issued on VHS in 2002 as part of the UK *First Doctor Box Set* (BBCV 7275). The US release is WHV E1854.

Verdict: 'So that's it? You're a time meddler!' This is the first use of anachronisms as a major plot point in *Doctor Who*, something that'll become a regular feature. Peter Purves's ironic and quizzical Steven is an instant, hugely effective foil for Hartnell. Camfield's direction is ambitious with intelligent use of stock footage and back projection to increase the scale of events and a more mobile than usual camera style. A witty, whimsical adventure with a smashing central guest turn from Peter Butterworth, who quickly became *Doctor Who*'s first-ever returning villain, as opposed to recurring monsters (see **21**, 'The Daleks' Master Plan'). The Doctor's pleasure at his own cleverness in disabling the Monk's time machine is a joy to behold.

18
'Galaxy 4'

Four Hundred Dawns: 11 September 1965
Trap of Steel: 18 September 1965
Airlock: 25 September 1965
The Exploding Planet: 2 October 1965

Written by William Emms
Directed by Derek Martinus

Writer: At the time of 'Galaxy 4' William Emms was a short-story writer who had recently moved into television. He later worked on numerous series in both the UK and Australia, including *Ace of Wands* (1970–72) and *Callan* (1967–72). Towards the end of his career he returned to prose fiction.

Director: Derek Martinus, although British, had studied directing in the United States and worked in Canada and what was then called Rhodesia before returning to take up work at the BBC.

Doctor Who?: The Doctor describes himself as a scientist, and works by scientific methods – observing and collating information before making conclusions. He doesn't instantly see that the Drahvins cannot be trusted, and is impressed by the Rill's technology. The Doctor says that neither he nor his friends kill.

Other Worlds: An unnamed planet that is perfect in every way for the development of life, but mysteriously seems to have none. It has three suns, leading to very short nights, and reminds the Doctor of Xeros (**15**, 'The Space Museum'). The planet is coming to the end of its life, and explodes a day after the travellers' arrival.

Scary Monsters: The Rill are large, monstrous-looking but peaceful creatures who breathe ammonia, and so have to send out short, round robots (which Vicki christens Chumblies, after their funny movement) to work for them in the oxygenated air of the planet. The Rill are telepathic, and, since they have no vocal cords, they use the Chumblies as speakers.

Villains: The Drahvins from the planet Drahva, in Galaxy 4, Amazonian Aryan humanoids who have abolished men and are sticklers for racial purity. Maaga (Stephanie Bidmead) is the leader of the group of Drahvins whom the travellers meet; the rest are artificially cultivated warriors, bred purely to kill, with limited mental capacity. Maaga hates the Rill out of pure xenophobia and killed one of her own troops so she could blame it on the Rill, thereby fuelling her troops' hatred.

The Plan: The Drahvin ship is too damaged to fly, so they intend to steal the Rill's ship to escape before the planet explodes. Maaga enlists the Doctor's help by keeping Vicki, and later Steven, hostage.

Science/Magic: Steven judges the Drahvin spaceship to be poorly made, constructed of low-quality metal. The Doctor realises the

Rill could not mean the Drahvin any harm – if they wanted to, they could get the Chumblies to cut through the Drahvin ship with lasers. The Rill ship has equipment to process the air. Vicki works out that the Chumblies detect sounds, but only those that are directly in front of them. The TARDIS can jump-start other spaceships via a power cable. The Doctor explains to Vicki that the planet will explode into hydrogen, spreading across its solar system.

Availability: Six minutes of 'Four Hundred Dawns' is included on the *Missing Years* VHS (see **39**, 'The Ice Warriors' and the *Lost in Time* DVD (BBCDVD 1353). The latter also includes a small number of very short clips from the serial filmed off a home TV screen. The audio-only version is available on CD as ISBN 0563477008.

Verdict: 'This is a fight to the death, for existence itself.' A simple but smartly written tale about perception and xenophobia, 'Galaxy 4' is a story in which the beautiful girls are evil, and an ugly monster that uses robot stooges is sympathetic and noble. The Drahvins are nasty pieces of work, a hierarchical society with disposable, artificially grown foot soldiers, while the solitary Rill is a fascinating character, a booming god-in-the-box trapped in its ship. In the end, intelligence and the desire not to kill win out against murderous self-interest, which is as good a mission statement for *Doctor Who* as you could hope for. The surviving minutes of video footage suggest decent production values, but thankfully clever ideas and good writing make this a story that can be enjoyed by sound alone.

19
Mission to the Unknown

8 October 1965

Written by Terry Nation
Directed by Derek Martinus

Doctor Who?: Or rather Doctor Where? The title character is absent from a whole story for the only time in the series' history.

The Plan: Emissaries from several alien governments (revealed in **21**, 'The Daleks' Master Plan', to represent an entire galaxy each) are meeting the Daleks to form 'a great alliance' and attack humanity. Together they form the greatest war force ever assembled. Human spy Marc Cory (Edward de Souza) discovers this but the Daleks exterminate him before he reports.

Other Worlds: Kembel, 'the most hostile planet in the universe', normally avoided by all races. Presumably only the Daleks are tough enough even to consider having a base there.

The Daleks haven't been active in Earth's galaxy for generations, but in the last five centuries they've conquered seventy planets in the ninth galactic system and forty more in the constellation of Miros. Both of these are millions of light years from Earth's galaxy (never mind Earth itself). Human society seems insular: the spy Marc Cory's pilot thinks humanity shouldn't be concerned with Daleks as long as they don't threaten Earth.

Scary Monsters: Varga plants are part animal, part vegetable, and use their roots to drag themselves along. Described as 'bred in Dalek laboratories', they are also said to grow naturally on Skaro (see **2**, 'The Daleks'). They reproduce by using thorns that poison the systems of their victims, who then turn into Varga themselves. This is the series' first attempt at body horror, something that becomes a recurring concern.

The delegates to the Daleks' conference showcase an amazing array of peculiar costumes (in the absence of the episode itself there are fortunately plenty of photographs from the episode's recording). They are, in no particular order: a man with tendrils hanging from his face and a *Rubber Soul*-era Beatle haircut; someone who looks like the Thing from the *Fantastic Four* comics; a dark-skinned man with a windowed bucket on his head; a white-suited egg-head; a man with a white, velour-looking cowl; and, everybody's favourite, a sort of mechanical Christmas tree, which actually looks like a Ku Klux Klan chess piece. All but the last two reappear in episodes of **21**, 'The Daleks' Master Plan'.

History 101: It's a thousand years since the Daleks occupied Earth (see **10**, 'The Dalek Invasion of Earth'). Mars, Venus and Jupiter are mentioned as planets populated by humans. There are also moon colonies.

Availability: Another destroyed story, but the audio track is available alongside that for **21**, 'The Daleks' Master Plan'.

Verdict: 'Conquest is assured!' The music is cheerfully melo-dramatic, but the fact that a James Bond figure is terrified of the Daleks' military power and tactical might combines with the audacity of their plan (to invade an entire *galaxy*) and makes them a threat on a scale the series hasn't touched on before. That they actually defeat Cory surely gives the audience pause for thought. 'Mission to the Unknown' is well acted, grim and bloody, although you do miss Hartnell.

20
'The Myth Makers'

Temple of Secrets: 16 October 1965
Small Prophet, Quick Return: 23 October 1965
Death of a Spy: 30 October 1965
Horse of Destruction: 6 November 1965

Written by Donald Cotton
Directed by Michael Leeston-Smith

Notable Cast: Max Adrian (King Priam) had previously appeared with Hartnell in *Nothing Like Publicity* (Maclean Rogers, 1936). Barrie Ingham (Paris) had recently played Alydon in *Dr. Who & the Daleks* (Gordon Flemyng, 1965).

Writer: Donald Cotton's previous experience came from musical revue and radio comedy (script editor Donald Tosh hired him for *Doctor Who* with the purpose of producing some more tongue-in-cheek serials). He went on to co-create *Adam Adamant Lives!* (1966) but mainly focused on writing for the stage, as well as extensive journalism work and novels such as *Bodkin Papers* (1986).

Director: Michael Leeston-Smith was a former stills photographer and lighting cameraman who had been Rudolph Cartier's assistant on *The Quatermass Experiment* (1953) and *Quatermass II* (1955). He directed fourteen episodes of *Z Cars* (1964–65).

Producer: John Wiles became *Doctor Who*'s second producer with this serial. Unhappy as a producer, he stayed with the series only until **23**, 'The Ark', and then returned to writing. His experimental, intelligent and forward-looking approach to *Doctor Who* continued to be felt on the series until **26**, 'The Savages', due to scripts commissioned in advance of his departure. His other TV work included writing *Dixon of Dock Green* (1960), the BBC play *Come Death* (1967) and *Poldark* (1975). He died in 1999.

History 101: This account of the Trojan war mingles Homer's *Iliad* and Virgil's *Aeneid* with the romance of Troilus and Cressida (which does not appear in any contemporary accounts and appears to be an invention of European poets 2,000 years later). As these popular versions are most likely not accurate, Cotton adapts them quite freely. He even inserts Vicki into established history. Although Priam's renaming of her as 'Cressida' is fairly random, her anxious adolescent romance with Troilus (James Lynn) rings true. The script anticipates the *Blackadder* style of humour, inasmuch as it invests historical figures with contemporary values and depicts a popular perception of its period rather than an accurate one.

Doctor Who?: The Doctor is mistaken for Zeus. Being keen Hartnell worshippers ourselves, we find the misapprehension understandable. He goes along with the impersonation for quite some time, and is clearly amused at being thought of as a god.

Villains: Each side in the drama features a character who threatens the travellers: Vicki's appearance in Troy is treated with suspicion and scheming by priestess Cassandra (Frances White), although she manages to charm King Priam and most of the other Trojans; the Greeks, meanwhile, have the booze-addled Odysseus (Ivor Salter).

The Plan: Odysseus threatens the Doctor with death unless he comes up with a gambit to win the war for the Greeks. Steven suggests using the Trojan Horse and, although the Doctor dismisses this as an invention by Homer, Odysseus rejects all his other ideas. The Doctor is forced to suggest the obvious and paradoxical, therefore: nobody invented the Trojan Horse – it inspired itself.

Science/Magic: Cassandra's prophecies of doom for Troy are mercilessly mocked throughout but, in accordance with the mythological character, they do come true.

Availability: No episodes are known to exist. The audio-only version has been released on CD (ISBN 0563477776). It's one of the easiest 'lost' stories to listen to: aside from a few fight sequences the story is largely comprehensible without pictures, probably thanks to Cotton's background in radio. There are some short clips on the *Lost in Time* DVD (BBCDVD 1353).

Verdict: 'I think they're doing more talking than they are fighting.' 'The Myth Makers' resembles Dennis Spooner's historical serials but is slightly cleverer. Donald Cotton clearly realises that the trappings of *Doctor Who* give him a licence to work very loosely with his source material, and that he would not be able to do this anywhere else. He mixes his myths, makes light of them, and acknowledges within his own scripts that events probably did not unfold this way at all. Cotton also made several recommendations for the casting and it shows: comedy is much easier to write when you know the voices you're writing for.

The one thing he doesn't quite pull off is the shift in tone for the final episode. One minute it's all chuckles and puns, the next there's a remarkably unfunny mass slaughter and the audience can't keep historical distance when Steven almost falls victim. Compared with those of, say, *Blackadder Goes Forth*, the characters in 'The Myth Makers' don't take their war terribly seriously, so it's jarring when it suddenly becomes very serious indeed. The tone settles down by the end, though: Katarina's (Adrienne Hill) belief that she is dead and the TARDIS is the journey to the afterlife is haunting, and the serial provides a sweet exit for Vicki. Like Peter Purves, Maureen O'Brien deserves high praise for consistently working well with an ill-defined character.

21
'The Daleks' Master Plan'

The Nightmare Begins: 13 November 1965
Day of Armageddon: 20 November 1965
Devil's Planet: 27 November 1965
The Traitors: 4 December 1965
Counter Plot: 11 December 1965
Coronas of the Sun: 18 December 1965
The Feat of Steven: 25 December 1965
Volcano: 1 January 1966
Golden Death: 8 January 1966
Escape Switch: 15 January 1966
The Abandoned Planet: 22 January 1966
The Destruction of Time: 29 January 1966

Written by Terry Nation (1–5, 7)
Written by Dennis Spooner, based upon an idea by Terry Nation (6, 8–12)
Directed by Douglas Camfield

Notable Cast: Jean Marsh (Sara Kingdom) appeared in **14**, 'The Crusade'. Nicholas Courtney (Bret Vyon) later appeared in *Then Churchill Said to Me* (1982) and *French Fields* (1989). Kevin Stoney (Mavic Chen) is a prolific TV actor with credits including *I, Claudius* (1976) and *War and Peace* (1972). Brian Cant (Kert Gantry) was a children's TV presenter par excellence on *Play School* and *Playaway*.

Doctor Who?: The Daleks know of the Doctor as 'some kind of time and space traveller' and think he is from 'another galaxy'. He considers them 'evil things'. Upon realising that there are Daleks on Kembel, he makes an active decision to find out what it is they are doing and stop it, even though he could simply leave. Ten episodes later the Doctor, Steven and Sara decide to return to Kembel to try to stop the Daleks, preferring to risk their own lives rather than let the Daleks conquer the future. Katarina's faith in the Doctor (whom she still believes to be Zeus) leads to her death – it is his absent-mindedness in not closing the door that makes it possible for Kirksen to attack her. Between them the Doctor and Steven can fly both a Spar and a Dalek spaceship. In the episode 'The Feast of Steven' someone calls the Doctor 'Professor' and he corrects this to 'Doctor' – the closest he has hitherto got to introducing himself by that alias.

Villains: Mavic Chen is the Guardian of the Solar System. His diplomatic triumphs include the Intergalactic Conference of Andromeda. He has betrayed humanity to the Daleks by agreeing to supply then with 'a full emm of taranium', which is said to be the rarest mineral in the universe and found only on 'one of the dead planets of the solar system'. It has taken him fifty years to mine secretly what appears to about a jam jar's worth. He is the 'newest' member of the Daleks' alliance. The Daleks believe that Chen has joined them because they have promised him control of Earth's entire galaxy once they have conquered it – destroying Earth along the way ('by sacrificing the solar system he hopes to gain more power') – but Chen has his own agenda, of which the Dalek Supreme is unaware (see **The Plan**).

The Monk (again played by Peter Butterworth – see **17**, 'The Time Meddler') out for revenge on the Doctor. He recognises a

Dalek by sight and knows of their race and 'achievements'. The Doctor twice refers to 'the Monk's TARDIS', the first time someone else's time machine is called that.

Other Worlds: Kembel (see **19**, 'Mission to the Unknown'), but also Desperus, a human penal colony where ownership of a knife is supreme power (the only indigenous species are 'screamers' – giant bats); Mira, a marshy world inhabited by the eight-foot-tall Visians, who are invisible to humans and Daleks; and Tigus, where the Monk hopes to trap the Doctor by destroying the TARDIS's lock while the Doctor is outside.

Scary Monsters: The Daleks' voices are never better than here: harsh, threatening, bass-heavy and metallic. Their portrayal as schemers and betrayers, possessors of the 'greatest war force ever assembled', fits with this. (Chen and Zephon both acknowledge that the Daleks 'have a genius for war'.) 'Master Plan' also proves that Daleks can deliver lots of dialogue no matter what later *Doctor Who* writers have claimed.

The Dalek Supreme emerges as a genuine personality, developing a bitter personal rivalry with Chen and demonstrating several emotions, including anger, fear, hatred, pride and even paranoia (he assumes that the Monk has betrayed the Daleks; in fact he's merely running into difficulties).

Two new delegates are present in the Alliance: a Richard O'Brien lookalike with black globules on his skin and a hooded, tall creature with hands like plant fronds. The latter is called Zephon. Members of the council are said to be on equal terms. There is talk of 'the Embodiment Gris', which has recently tried to depose Zephon. It is unclear what or who this is. But it *sounds* really cool.

The Plan: The Time Destructor is a weapon that can speed up and reverse time; Daleks do not age so are unaffected by it. Powered by taranium, the weapon has been built with contributory elements from all the galaxies in the Daleks' alliance. The first planets to fall will be those in Earth's solar system. The delegates believe that Earth's galaxy is the intended area of conquest. In truth the Daleks intend to conquer the delegates' galaxies as well and they have brought the rulers of them to Kembel to destabilise their domains and make conquest easier. When the Daleks talk of conquering the universe they are clearly talking about gaining control of all known civilisations in the same way that Roman emperors considered themselves rulers of the world.

Chen's conversations with Karlton (Maurice Browning) make clear that he has always intended to betray the Daleks – there is a human 'special force' lying in wait on Venus and Chen intends this to strike at Kembel when the Daleks attack the solar system, seizing the Time Destructor in the process – a situation from which he can only benefit politically. (This counterplot gives the fifth episode its title.) His need for greater power is terrifying ('Would you be content with a part of a galaxy?' he asks Zephon). His plan has two flaws, both caused by his egomania. First, he seems unaware of how the Time Destructor works; second, he doesn't anticipate that the Daleks intend to double cross *him*. As the serial goes on he becomes unhinged and believes the Daleks are his servants and that he is immortal. The Dalek Supreme disabuses him of both notions.

History 101: In the first episode, 'The Nightmare Begins', Chen says that it is the year 4000. The solar system is unified but there have been wars between its planets as recently as 3975 (when a nonaggression pact between the solar planets was signed). This peace is fragile (there are 'conflicting powers' within the solar system that 'must be watched'). Chen's talk of 'getting help from the rest of the solar system' against the Daleks implies that the planets have security forces of their own over which Chen has no direct control. There are indications that the human civilisation of 4000 is essentially fascist – certainly coldly authoritarian. The most obvious is Space Security, the service to which Bret Vyon and Sara Kingdom belong. They are, literally and figuratively, the SS: jackbooted, black-uniformed thugs and visibly the enforcers of a right-wing regime (Sara herself points out it is impossible to question an order). While Bret is an ostensibly heroic figure, he kills Daxta, a man who he believes has betrayed him, in cold blood. It is poetic justice of a sort that he is similarly ruthlessly killed by somebody who believes the same of him.

Vyon also has a utilitarian attitude to life, refusing to risk his mission for an individual whether it's Katarina or the Doctor. This is a contrast with the Doctor, who struggles throughout the story to save every individual life (friend or foe) he encounters while trying to defeat the Daleks. Bret was also 'bred' (not born) on Mars, perhaps implying that his society practises eugenics. It is stated that the government has 'chemical details' of every human being in the solar system on computer files (effectively a DNA database of every person, the fantasy of many a controlling government).

Steven has heard of Christmas, but Sara hasn't – implying that Christianity has been stamped out by 4000. The Doctor, Steven and Bret arrive on Earth near Central City (see 7, 'The Sensorites').

While fleeing through time from the Daleks the Doctor, Steven and Sara visit ancient Egypt. The year is unspecified and no details are gleaned except that a pyramid is being constructed for the burial of a recently deceased pharaoh. There are also stop-offs in Liverpool (Christmas Day 1965), London (New Year's Day 1966), an England–Australia cricket match and a Hollywood film studio in the 1920s.

Science/Magic: There is a magnetic chair in the TARDIS that could 'restrain a herd of elephants'. Dalek technology is 'the most advanced in the universe'. Examples of this include a 'neutronic randomiser' to control others' space vehicles and a 'magnetic beam' that can be used to drag spaceships off course. It is accepted by the representatives that only the Daleks can break the time barrier and travel backwards and forwards in time. On Earth a group of scientists are experimenting with 'cellular dissemination', a method of breaking a living creature into microscopic fragments and sending those fragments light years across space to be reassembled. Humanity can already send small objects short distances this way but this project is about sending humans to other planets in an instant. Fortieth-century medicine cures severe blood poisoning with one tablet.

Availability: The audio-only version is available as a five-CD set (ISBN 0563535008) and an MP3-CD collection (ISBN 0563494174). Only 'Day of Armageddon', 'Counter Plot' and 'Escape Switch' exist on film. The second and third of these were released on the VHS *Daleks – The Early Years* in 1992 (BBCV 4816, WHV E1143). All three episodes are on 2004's *Lost in Time* DVD (BBCDVD 1353), along with more than four minutes of extant clips from 'The Nightmare Begins', 'Devil's Planet' and 'The Traitors'.

Verdict: 'A heroic war cry to apparently peaceful ends is one of the greatest weapons a politician has.' The scale of this story is *huge*, with a dozen locations across thousands of years of history and a plot that involves the Daleks' attempt to occupy the whole of creation. That this is a sprawling epic is obvious, but it's also a thoughtful one: a great space adventure and an antiauthoritarian portrait of an authoritarian society. The final scene, in which the Doctor and Steven discuss the cost of their victory, achieves a horror at the slaughter involved in the Doctor's battles against evil that is unmatched in the series. Very good indeed.

22
'The Massacre'

War of God: 5 February 1966
The Sea Beggar: 12 February 1966
Priest of Death: 19 February 1966
Bell of Doom: 26 February 1966

Written by John Lucarotti (1–3)
Written by John Lucarotti and Donald Tosh (4)
Directed by Paddy Russell

Notable Cast: Andre Morell (Marshal Tavannes) played Professor Quatermass in the television version of *Quatermass and the Pit* (1958), and also appeared in *Ben-Hur* (William Wyler, 1959) and *Barry Lyndon* (Stanley Kubrick, 1975). Eric Thompson (Gaston) wrote and narrated *The Magic Roundabout* (1965–75). The revolving door on the TARDIS during this period of the show keeps on spinning as Jackie Lane debuts here as the new regular character Dorothea 'Dodo' Chaplet. Lane later quit acting to become an agent.

Writer: Donald Tosh's only writing credit on *Doctor Who* is as co-writer on the 'Bell of Doom' episode. (He had been the series' script editor since **17**, 'The Time Meddler'.) Tosh had substantially rewritten John Lucarotti's scripts but, as a member of the BBC staff, was not allowed to be credited as a writer until he left the series, which he did following the episode 'Priest of Death'. After retiring from television, Tosh became custodian of St Mawes Castle in Cornwall.

Script Editor: Taking over from Tosh was Gerry Davis (1930–91), who remained with the series until Episode 3 of **36**, 'The Evil of the Daleks'. He later worked on everything from *Coronation Street* to *The Bionic Woman*.

Director: Paddy Russell was among the BBC's first female directors. In addition to work on such serials as *Compact* (1962) and *Late Night Horror* (1968), she directed prestige BBC miniseries such as *Little Women* (1970), featuring Patrick Troughton, and *The Moonstone* (1972), starring Colin Baker.

History 101: Paris, 20–24 August 1572. Tensions run high between the Catholics and Huguenots (Protestants), as the Protestant prince Henry of Navarre has married the Catholic Princess Margaritte, King Charles's sister. Ten years before, Catholics at Vassey killed a hundred Huguenots.

Doctor Who?: The Doctor is fascinated with a group of advanced apothecaries working in France during this period, and goes to find Charles Preslin (Eric Chitty), whom he considers the most influential of the group, leaving Steven alone in Paris. When the Doctor meets up with Steven at the end of the story, he realises that the massacre is about to begin and ushers Steven into the TARDIS, insisting that his friend Anne Chaplet (Annette Robertson), the Huguenot maid, stay behind. The Doctor tells Steven that he could not interfere to stop the massacre, and had to leave Anne to her destiny.

Steven walks out of the TARDIS when it next lands, determined not to come back. In a beautifully acted scene, the Doctor remembers his fellow travellers, and asks himself whether he should go home – but admits to himself that he can't. He's delighted when Steven returns, and by the addition of young Dodo Chaplet to his crew – he says that she reminds him of Susan.

Villains: The Abbot of Amboise, henchman to the Cardinal of Lorraine, who hunts down heretics. The Abbot is physically identical to the Doctor, leading Steven to assume that the Doctor is impersonating the abbot for his own reasons.

The Plan: Under orders from the Queen Mother, Catherine de Medici, the Abbot is planning the assassination of the Admiral of Coligne, a notable Huguenot who is persuading the king to assist the Protestant Dutch in their rebellion against Catholic Spain. The assassin Bondo tries to kill the admiral. The Huguenots kill the abbot in retaliation. Catherine orders the people of Paris to be set loose on the Huguenots, and the notorious massacre (the event which the word was later invented to describe) begins.

Science/Magic: The Doctor and Preslin discuss early work in 'germinology'.

Things Fall Apart: Steven makes a firm decision to leave the TARDIS, disgusted with the Doctor, but decides to come back when two policemen approach the ship. This seems a very extreme turnaround based on such a small threat to the Doctor.

Availability: This was another destroyed story. The audio-only version was issued on CD in 1999 as ISBN 0563552611.

Verdict: 'Many things frighten people in Paris these days.' Strange and fatalistic, 'The Massacre' throws Steven, the audience's identification figure, into a dangerous and politicised time period and leaves him to fend for himself. He never stands a chance: caught up in bleak events, Steven strives to make things right – but his efforts come to nought.

The story is tightly structured – each episode takes place on a separate day – but also runs down several dead ends. The story centres on a bluff – the Abbot is an ambiguous figure and, like Steven, we're supposed to be unsure as to whether he is the Doctor in disguise, sabotaging the plot to kill the Admiral from within, or simply an incompetent villain. Hartnell is brilliant as the Abbot, his vocal mannerisms very different from the Doctor's. It's a shame the character doesn't appear more.

The production team's indecision over the role of Anne Chaplet, a maid whom Steven befriends in Paris, leads the character to be built up as a regular, then left behind at the end. The Doctor says he can't interfere, but does that really extend to leaving an innocent girl behind when he knows that so many are about to be killed?

The coda, which introduces the contemporary English girl Dodo Chaplet, Anne's presumed descendant, is either proof of some guiding force at work or a severe coincidence. It's a shame that this excellent story peters out and, for all its merits – lyrical dialogue and fine acting among them – 'The Massacre' doesn't quite live up to Lucarotti's other *Doctor Who* scripts.

23
'The Ark'

The Steel Sky: 5 March 1966

The Plague: 12 March 1966
The Return: 19 March 1966
The Bomb: 26 March 1966

Written by Paul Erikson and Lesley Scott
Directed by Michael Imison

Notable Cast: Michael Sheard (Rhos) has been in *everything*, but is best known for playing Mr Bronson in *Grange Hill* (1985–89) and Admiral Ozzel in *The Empire Strikes Back* (Irvin Kershner, 1980). He has also played Adolf Hitler four times and Heinrich Himmler three times, and made five further appearances in *Doctor Who*.

Writers: Paul Erikson had written several feature films, largely thrillers such as *Track the Man Down* (RG Springsteen, 1955) and *Kill Her Gently* (Charles Saunders, 1957), before moving to television in the 1960s, where he wrote episodes of *The Saint* and *Out of the Unknown*. 'The Ark' was co-credited to his wife, Lesley Scott, who also worked in television and was trying to break into writing. She performed no actual work on the scripts.

Director: Michael Imison was a story editor and BBC staff director whose credits include *Swizzlewick* (1964).

History 101: It is the '57th segment' of time (which the Doctor estimates is 10 million years into the future). The sun is about to go nova and Earth will be destroyed, so a select few humans are entrusted with the task of piloting the miniaturised population to a new planet. They have eradicated the common cold and so have no defence against the one they catch from Dodo – it hits the humans so virulently that they start to die.

Other Worlds: Refusis 2, identified as a close match for Earth and suitable for colonisation. The friendly Refusians are amenable to this plan and, judging by the homes they have built for the humans, their interior-design skills are second to none.

Doctor Who?: The Doctor has never considered the possibility of carrying diseases between different planets and periods: 'I don't want to think about it, dear boy. It's too horrifying.' He demonstrates medical expertise in curing the fever (although his advice to keep the victims warm is dubious).

Scary Monsters: The Monoids. Originally servants on board the Ark, towards the end of the voyage they revolt and take command. The Doctor notes that their attitude towards the humans is understandable after their subjugation, but they take too much glee in their power for this to be wholly convincing.

The Plan: The Monoids plan to inhabit Refusis 2 themselves and destroy the Ark with all humans on board. This is clumsily given away by Monoid Two, who chuckles to Dodo that transporting the humans to the planet's surface 'may not take as long as you think'. 'Are you up to something?' asks Dodo. 'Er . . . no,' says Two, realising what a schoolboy error he's made.

Science/Magic: The Refusians have been rendered invisible by some sort of accident involving a giant solar flare. You've got to watch out for those giant solar flares.

Things Fall Apart: Jackie Lane seems to have researched her London accent by watching *Coronation Street*: it veers between RADA and Manchester (the actress's home) without ever going near Wimbledon. As the Doctor says, 'You'll have to do something about that English of yours. It's terrible, child! It's most irritating!'

Availability: Released on VHS in 1998 as BBCV 6609 (UK) and WHV E1046 (US).

Verdict: 'You have a handkerchief, I hope. Well, then, use it, my child!' Michael Imison's work on 'The Ark' constitutes some of the finest direction *Doctor Who* has ever seen. See Michael zoom! See him swoop! See him rove! See him overspend and never work on the series again as a result! It's because of this story that **24**, 'The Celestial Toymaker', ended up with a budget of about tuppence, but at least the extra money is all up there on screen. (For a moment you think the elephant is a piece of stock footage, then it strolls up to the Doctor and co. and they pat it on the head!) The expansive sets are amazing, matching up to a script that thinks big.

Unfortunately, that script has its flaws. There's quite a bit of clumsy exposition as Guardians and Monoids alike tell each other things they already know. This would be understandable if the plot moved more quickly and swift explanations were necessary, but this is slow-paced stuff even by Hartnell-era standards. Problems are often solved conveniently – the trial sequence in the episode 'The Plague' has no impact on the plot at all, as its verdict is immediately overruled. Even so, the narrative is an innovative use of *Doctor Who*'s format (effectively, a two-part story followed by a two-part sequel) and it's consistently interesting, continuing the spirit of experimentation that characterised the show's third year.

24
'The Celestial Toymaker'

The Celestial Toyroom: 2 April 1966
The Hall of Dolls: 9 April 1966
The Dancing Floor: 16 April 1966
The Final Test: 23 April 1966

Written by Brian Hayles
Directed by Bill Sellars

Notable Cast: Michael Gough (the Toymaker) played Batman's butler Alfred in *Batman* (Tim Burton, 1989) and its three sequels. Other memorable roles include those in *Sleepy Hollow* (Tim Burton, 1999) and *Dracula* (Terence Fisher, 1958). Carmen Silvera, who plays a number of the Toymaker's playthings, was a mutitalented actress of stage and screen who is sadly best remembered as Edith in *'Allo 'Allo!* (1982–92).

Writer: Former teacher Brian Hayles worked on the BBC's football soap opera *United!* (1965–67). He wrote the films *Nothing But the Night* (Peter Sasdy, 1972) and *Warlords of Atlantis* (Kevin Connor, 1978). 'The Celestial Toymaker' was heavily rewritten twice (for technical and then copyright reasons), once by outgoing script editor Donald Tosh and once by his replacement Gerry Davis. The experience didn't stop Hayles from contributing regularly to the series over the next seven years.

Director: Bill Sellars was later the producer of *All Creatures Great and Small* (1978–90).

Producer: *Doctor Who*'s new producer, Innes Lloyd, had also worked on *United!* during 1965. His last serial was **40**, 'The Enemy of the World'. He left *Doctor Who* to become the producer of *Thirty Minute Theatre* (1968–71) and later became a fêted producer of prestige dramas such as *The Stone Tape* (1972), *Reith* (1983), *Across the Lake* (1988, starring Anthony Hopkins as Donald Campbell) and *Bomber Harris* (1989, starring John Thaw). The duet of *An Englishman Abroad* (1983) and *A Question of Attribution* (1991), about Guy Burgess and Anthony Blunt respectively, were, like *Talking Heads* (1981), results of a fruitful collaboration with Alan Bennett. There's nothing in the *Doctor Who* serials Lloyd oversaw to suggest that later creative flowering. His period on *Doctor Who* is marked by a concentration of monster-based plotlines, formulaic storytelling and avoidance of the travelogues that had enlivened the early years of the programme. He abandoned the series' habit of splitting its episode count between 'historical' and 'futuristic' stories in order to concentrate on tales about bases under siege.

Villains: The Celestial Toymaker – 'a power for evil who manipulates people and turns them into his playthings'. Amoral and immortal (he has existed for thousands of years), he delights in the playing of games – preferably for such stakes as the lives of his opponents. He is notorious for drawing space travellers to him as a spider draws a fly. Although visibly Caucasian, he dresses as a mandarin. It is not clear whether he was once a human being but, given the Victoriana and Oriental kitsch with which he surrounds himself, it seems likely. The Toymaker confesses that he is bored and considers the Doctor his only possible stimulating opponent (the two have met before). Among his powers are the ability to make people instantly invisible, intangible and inaudible, to turn them into toys and back again and to subject minds to his control.

Science/Magic: In his domain the Toymaker has 'memory windows' (which force people who stare into them to relive traumatic moments in their lives), board games large enough to use people as pieces and a moving desk in the shape of a space car.

Availability: 'The Final Test' is the only existing episode – it was included as part of the VHS *The Hartnell Years* (BBCV 4608, WHV E1098) and on 2004's *Lost in Time* DVD (BBCDVD 1353). The audio-only versions of all four episodes are on the CD ISBN 0563478551.

Verdict: 'This place is a hidden menace, nothing is just for fun!' Memorably strange and very well acted. Peter Purves carries the middle episodes admirably in Hartnell's absence. (Hartnell was on holiday for two weeks and the Doctor appears briefly as a prerecorded voice and as a disembodied hand.) That Steven and Dodo play games against toys who were once human – and who have been promised freedom if they beat the time travellers – should add an element of existential horror as our heroes are forced to condemn others to eternal servitude in order to escape.

Sadly, this isn't brought out as much as it could be and there are other indications that the story has been toned down in the rewriting. Even so, 'The Celestial Toymaker' is quietly sinister in its abuse of the iconography of childhood.

25
The Gunfighters

A Holiday for the Doctor: 30 April 1966
Don't Shoot the Pianist: 7 May 1966
Johnny Ringo: 14 May 1966
The OK Corral: 21 May 1966

Written by Donald Cotton
Directed by Rex Tucker

Director: Rex Tucker was an old-style BBC producer/director responsible for much of the BBC's 1950s and early 1960s drama output: for example *The Three Musketeers* (1954), produced live and starring Laurence Payne, Paul Whitsun-Jones and Roger Delgado. He was nominated 'caretaker producer' of *Doctor Who* during its early development but was superseded by Verity Lambert.

Doctor Who?: He introduces himself as 'Doctor Caligari' (remembering, presumably, the owner of the cabinet in Robert Wiene's 1919 film) and doesn't touch alcohol. He's unaware of the history of the notorious 'gunfight at the OK Corral' (he must be, he tries to stop it). He addresses Wyatt Earp as 'Mr Wearp' throughout, and refuses to carry a gun.

The Plan: The Clanton family want revenge on Doc Holliday – the infamous gunfighter and dentist – for killing Reuben Clanton (this, Holliday claims, he did 'out of sheer professional ethics'). In pursuing this vendetta they initiate a feud with Holliday's friends in the Earp family and hire professional gunslingers Seth Harper (Shane Rimmer) and Johnny Ringo (Laurence Payne) to help their cause, mistaking the Doctor for their opponent along the way.

History 101: On 26 October 1881 the so-called gunfight at the OK Corral took place *behind* the corral (in the vacant Lot 2, Block 17, of Tombstone City, Cochise County, Arizona) between two gangs. One consisted of Doc Holliday and Wyatt, Morgan and Virgil

Earp, and the other Billy Claiborne, Frank and Tom McLowry and Billy and Ike Clanton. Both McLowrys were killed, as was Billy Clanton. Johnny Ringo was not involved. Historically Virgil – not Wyatt – was the marshal of Tombstone and Morgan was his deputy. (Wyatt had been deputy marshal of Dodge City and deputy sheriff of Tombstone, but ran a saloon by 1881.) The feud between Earps and Clatons was related to arguments over horses and women with no obvious 'right' on either side – although the Earps certainly abused their official ties. Holliday and Wyatt Earp later stood trial for murder but were acquitted, pleading self-defence.

Availability: Issued on VHS in 2002 as part of the UK *First Doctor Box Set* (BBCV 7268). US release is WHV E1855.

Verdict: 'So, fill up your glasses and join in the fun.' An unapologetically parodic Western in which Hartnell again demonstrates his impeccable physical and verbal comic timing, 'The Gunfighters' is smart, slick and consistently very funny. Peter Purves's tasselled shirt, double-taking and 'butch' walking are hilarious; and his delivery of 'Well, let's hope the piano knows it' is probably the funniest single moment in all of *Doctor Who*. Everyone else stays exactly the right side of ludicrous, but special points go to Anthony Jacobs for making Doc Holliday a real person amid all the comic shenanigans and Laurence Payne for remaining a credible threat in a comic story.

The serial ignores history and parodies Western film conventions instead, playing with popular perceptions of history as Cotton's earlier **20**, 'The Myth Makers', did. It then goes on to draw attention to what it's doing ('My dear Dodo, you're fast becoming prey to every cliché-ridden convention in the American West!'). The action is backed up by the comic 'Ballad of the Last Chance Saloon', which establishes, narrates and then ironically comments on the action in a variety of amusing ways. The final gunfight, though, is played entirely straight.

Tucker's experience shines through, and this is strikingly well-shot television with high angles on impressive sets and even the odd sweeping camera move. Notably underappreciated on transmission (did nobody get the joke?), this is actually an indication of how varied, confident and clever *Doctor Who* can be. That the episodes survived to be reassessed and enjoyed is something we can all be thankful for. Just *glorious*.

26
The Savages

Episode 1: 28 May 1966
Episode 2: 4 June 1966
Episode 3: 11 June 1966
Episode 4: 18 June 1966

Written by Ian Stuart Black
Directed by Christopher Barry

Notable Cast: German-born Frederick Jaeger (Jano) appeared in war films such as *Ice Cold in Alex* (J Lee Thompson, 1958) and *I Was Monty's Double* (John Guillermin, 1958). In recent years he has appeared in *Selling Hitler* (1991) and *Cold Comfort Farm* (John Schlesinger, 1995). Kay Patrick (Flower) appeared in **12**, 'The Romans'.

Writer: A prolific writer who started off in film, Ian Stuart Black was co-creator of *Danger Man* (1960–67). His other TV credits include *The Saint* (1963) and *The Invisible Man* (1984). He wrote several novels, including *In the Wake of a Stranger* (1953), *The High Bright Sun* (1962) and *Creatures in a Dream* (1985); and his play *We Must Kill Toni* (1953) was adapted for the screen as *She'll Have to Go* (Robert Asher, 1962).

Other Worlds: An unnamed planet in the far future, an age of peace and prosperity. Civilised, highly advanced Elders live in a lavish city while barbaric, skin-wearing savages inhabit the wilds. The Elders chart space and time, and have been plotting the course of the TARDIS, expecting its arrival. The ancestors of the savages were once great artists, and murals in their caves indicate this heritage.

Villains: Jano, leader of the Council of Elders.

The Plan: The Elders' civilisation is based on draining the life force of the savages, giving that vital energy to the people of the city, enabling them to be more intelligent and creative. The savages are contained in a 'reserve', and hunted like animals to drain their strength.

When the Doctor opposes the Elders, Jano orders that the Doctor's vital essence be transferred to him. This causes Jano to inherit some of the Doctor's morality.

Doctor Who?: The Doctor is honoured with the position of High Elder, and wears the cloak of office. The Elders know the Doctor's real name, but refer to him simply as 'the traveller from beyond time'. According to the Elders, the Doctor has made great achievements in time and space exploration. Their observations imply that he is, if not unique, by far the best-travelled of a small number of such travellers.

By accepting the Elders' gifts, the Doctor considers himself to be endorsing their lives, and he cannot do that without knowing more about how they built their civilisation. The Doctor suspects the secret behind the Elders' power before Dodo provides eyewitness evidence. He is determined to help the savages, and protests that all human beings are equal – including himself in that description. He refuses to leave the planet before liberating the savages. He suspects the effect his essence will have on Jano.

The Doctor refuses Jano's suggestion that he could be a mediator between the two peoples, but believes that Steven is an exceptional candidate. He encourages Steven to take on the challenge, and says he is proud of him. He tells Dodo he doesn't know whether they will see Steven again – but that anything could be possible.

Science/Magic: D403 capsules are given to the savages by the Doctor to counter the effects of the draining process. The people from the city use 'light guns' to hypnotise the savages. Steven turns one of the light guns back on its holder using a mirror.

Availability: Another destroyed serial. The audio-only version was released on CD as ISBN 0563535024. Some short, off-screen clips are on *Lost in Time* (BBC DVD 1353).

Verdict: 'Human progress, sir? How dare you call your treatment of these people *progress*?' In Episode 1, Dodo asks Steven if he really is a grown man, and by the end of the story he has established his own maturity, taking on the role of leader of the people. Raymond Jones's incidental music is intense and dramatic, with heavy use of strings. Photographs of the production indicate impressive sets and strong direction, and the script cuts between scenes with pace and energy. The Doctor is a moral firebrand, arguing against the inhumanity of the Elders' practices.

Unusually, 'The Savages' has an ending based around constructive, rather than destructive, change (although the Elders' equipment is smashed). Characters go through traumatic experiences that are both transforming and redeeming. Jano tries to drain the Doctor's intellect, but with it gains some of the Doctor's conscience, causing him to turn against his allies. Through their time together, the savages learn courage from Steven, and in turn he learns to become a leader, leaving the Doctor to help the Savages and the Elders to work together in peace. It's an intelligent ending to an intelligent story.

27
The War Machines

Episode 1: 25 June 1966
Episode 2: 2 July 1966
Episode 3: 9 July 1966
Episode 4: 16 July 1966

Written by Ian Stuart Black
Directed by Michael Ferguson

Notable Cast: *Doctor Who*'s two new regular roles went to Michael Craze (Ben) and Anneke Wills (Polly). Craze had previously appeared in the sci-fi series *Target Luna* (1960) and later took a regular role in the radio soap *Waggoner's Walk*. Wills had appeared as Pussy Cat in the 'Dressed to Kill' episode of *The Avengers* (1963). Following *Doctor Who*, she starred in *Strange Report* (1969) before becoming an interior decorator and occasional theatre director in Canada.

Director: Aside from his *Doctor Who* work, Michael Ferguson directed numerous TV series, including *Flambards* (1978) and *Colditz* (1972–74). He later became a producer, working on *EastEnders, The Bill* and *Casualty*.

Doctor Who?: The Doctor claims he can sometimes sense the presence of evil. He earns the confidence and respect of Professor Brett (John Harvey) and his colleagues with incredible ease (off screen, conveniently). He's a hit with young and old alike, with Kitty (Sandra Bryant) at the Inferno club declaring that she 'digs' his 'fab gear'. Unusually, the intelligent computer WOTAN and its servants refer to him by his fuller alias of Doctor Who.

History 101: It's London 1966, and the contemporary setting has a huge impact on the type of story being told. The threat is an extrapolation of contemporary science, the characters are ordinary 1960s people and the Doctor enlists the help of politicians and the military, all of which reduces the distance between the viewer and the events on screen. It is less stylised and whimsical than any *Doctor Who* since the first episode.

The acronym WOTAN is devised to stress its significance, since Wotan was the supreme God in Germanic mythology.

Villains: WOTAN, an intelligent computer housed in London's Post Office Tower (it's called the BT Tower these days, kids) and set to be linked to other computers around the world. In order to prevent it from being abused for political ends it is given self-control – which turns out to be a mistake . . .

The Plan: . . . because WOTAN decides that it can run things far more effectively than mankind and attempts to take over the world.

Scary Monsters: The War Machines: mobile armed computers, squarish and about the height of a man, built by WOTAN to aid its world-domination effort.

Science/Magic: It is never explained how WOTAN is able to attain sentience or hypnotise people. The notion that Britain could build a computer that's absurdly more advanced than anything the rest of the world can achieve is *so* 1966.

Things Fall Apart: The newspaper report of the tramp's death is a clumsy plot device – not only is it far-fetched that this would make the front page, but the news would not have broken in time for the morning editions. There's some poor back-projection when the reprogrammed War Machine is on its way through London, and quite how it fits into the lift at the Post Office Tower is a mystery.

Availability: The copy of 'The War Machines' returned to the BBC in 1984 had been cut by New Zealand censors; however, most of the missing footage was located in Australia in 1996 and reinstated for VHS release the following year (BBCV 6183, WHV E1079). About a minute of Episode 3 and some dialogue from Episode 4 remain missing.

Verdict: 'Nobody operates WOTAN. WOTAN operates itself.' A new kind of *Doctor Who* story – the first full adventure set in the present day except for the skewed **9**, 'Planet of Giants' – but that is not to say it was wholly original. Many viewers were tiring of

Doctor Who's format and Innes Lloyd and Gerry Davis were looking towards what else was popular. Accordingly, 'The War Machines' bears more resemblance to contemporary ITV adventure series and the teleplays of Nigel Kneale than it does to most previous *Doctor Who* stories, and it established a new status for the series as a vehicle for whatever style was in vogue at the time. Before this *Doctor Who* was principally like itself; afterwards, it was frequently defined by the sources it drew from.

This shift secured *Doctor Who*'s longevity, ensuring that it could adapt to become whatever the BBC needed it to be and find new stories to tell by purloining them from other sources. However, in another sense it killed what made the show unique – and for the rest of Lloyd's tenure it would become rather conservative. Even so, 'The War Machines' itself is very charming. Michael Ferguson relishes the opportunity to shoot *Doctor Who* as 'straight' drama and, while the script is quite simple, the overall production is effective. The loss of the peerless Peter Purves deprives Jackie Lane of her principal foil and she is dropped without a shred of sentiment halfway through, making way for Ben and Polly. Hanging out at the hottest nightspots and flirting with each other across class boundaries, they are *Doctor Who*'s reflection of the birth of British cool.

28
The Smugglers

Episode 1: 10 September 1966
Episode 2: 17 September 1966
Episode 3: 24 September 1966
Episode 4: 1 October 1966

Written by Brian Hayles
Directed by Julia Smith

Notable Cast: John Ringham (Josiah Blake) previously appeared in **6**, 'The Aztecs'. George A Cooper (Cherub) worked extensively in television, but is most recognisable as caretaker Mr Griffiths in *Grange Hill* between 1986 and 1992. Paul Whitsun-Jones (Squire Edwards) can be seen in *The Masque of the Red Death* (Roger Corman, 1964) and was in much early live TV drama.

Director: Julia Smith (1927–97) was one of the first women taken on to the BBC directors' programme. She directed episodes of *Z*

Cars and *Dr Finlay's Casebook*, and in the 1980s moved into producing. She co-created *EastEnders*.

History 101: Seventeenth-century Cornwall, propably the 1680s, and the Doctor is given a vital clue as to the location of some treasure plundered by the pirate Captain Avery.

Villains: Chiefly the pirate Captain Pike and his crew – Cherub, Jamaica, Gaptooth and others – but it transpires that Squire Edwards, the innkeeper Kewper (David Blake Kelly) and most of the rest of the village are operating beneath the law.

The Plan: Captain Pike has arrived in Cornwall in the hope of locating Avery's treasure, which he and Joseph Longfoot originally helped to capture. Longfoot has reformed and concealed the treasure but he is killed by Cherub, leaving the Doctor as the only man alive who holds the clue to its whereabouts.

Science/Magic: Ben and Polly escape their cell by the use of magic, although they're only pretending. Having mocked superstition earlier in the story, the Doctor notes at the end that the curse of Avery's gold came true. Woo, spooky.

Doctor Who?: The Doctor started out as a traveller who became caught up in events, but increasingly he sees it as his duty to right wrongs, large or (in this case) small: when the opportunity arises to return to the TARDIS, he refers to a 'moral obligation' to resolve the situation in the village. The story is a fine last hurrah for William Hartnell: he would largely be sidelined in **29**, 'The Tenth Planet' and with hindsight it's clear that this was the last time he enjoyed himself on *Doctor Who*. His supposedly declining health is not evident in the least as his Doctor runs rings around pirates and villagers alike. While the cast and crew continued to change around him, Hartnell simply absorbed himself in a character whom he loved to play.

Things Fall Apart: Longfoot misquotes a riddle to the Doctor in Episode 1, which makes the Doctor's deduction of its significance more remarkable than it should be.

Availability: No episodes of 'The Smugglers' are known to exist, although some short clips are held: a 23-second sequence from Episode 1, 3 clips totalling 21 seconds from Episode 3 and a 3-second clip from Episode 4. The clips are available on *Lost in*

Time (BBC DVD 1353). The audio-only version has been released on CD (ISBN 0563535040).

Verdict: 'Old man, are ye truly a sawbones?' 'The Smugglers' is essentially an excuse for grown men to call each other 'swabs', 'knaves' and 'lily-livered rogues' while going 'arrrr' a lot, and as such it's hugely enjoyable. It must be said that the story is an apt demonstration of Innes Lloyd and Gerry Davis's seemingly conservative attitude towards the series: *Doctor Who*'s adventures in history had previously been used to explore periods that would not normally lend themselves to children's entertainment. Here and in **31**, 'The Highlanders', Davis directed his writers towards settings that were well established for such narratives – in other words, doing things that could just as easily be done outside *Doctor Who*.

However, it would be unfair to let this detract from 'The Smugglers' itself. It is a fairly straightforward pastiche of Russell Thorndyke's *Dr Syn* novels and J Meade Faulker's *Moonfleet* (1898), but one that absolutely captures the appeal of such tales. Every actor is aware of how far they can go over the top while keeping the tone relatively serious, and new regulars Michael Craze and Anneke Wills are both excellent (it helps that Ben and Polly are the first regular characters since Susan's departure to be consistently written; previously the actor was too often left to fill in the character on their own).

29
The Tenth Planet

Episode 1: 8 October 1966
Episode 2: 15 October 1966
Episode 3: 22 October 1966
Episode 4: 29 October 1966

Written by Kit Pedler (1–2), Kit Pedler and Gerry Davis (3–4)
Directed by Derek Martinus

Notable Cast: Robert Beatty (Cutler) was a Canadian actor who worked principally in Britain, usually playing authority figures. He was the US president in *Superman IV: The Quest for Peace* (Sydney J Furie, 1987) and newspaper magnate/cabinet minister Lord Beaverbrook in *Churchill: The Gathering Storm* (Herbert

Wise, 1974). He and Hartnell were friends, working together previously in *Appointment with Crime* (John Harlow, 1946). It is tempting to see his casting as an attempt to placate the series' outgoing lead.

This is Hartnell's final serial as the star of *Doctor Who*. Producer Innes Lloyd appears to have actively taken the decision to 'remove' him, offering the lead to Patrick Troughton. Lloyd and Hartnell had clashed over the series' future direction. The actor later wrote to a fan, Ian K McLachlan, that 'I didn't willingly give up the part'. Conventional wisdom holds that Hartnell left *Doctor Who* due to illness – but he returned to theatre work almost immediately.

Writers: Christopher 'Kit' Pedler (1928–81) was a surgeon at the University of London, and was invited to act as a 'scientific consultant' by Gerry Davis. Pedler accepted, contributing the concept for **27**, 'The War Machines'. The pair collaborated on three *Who* stories, all featuring the Cybermen, went on to create the eco-disaster series *Doomwatch* (1970–72) and co-write two novels. Pedler's small amount of solo work includes the series *Mind Over Matter* (1980).

Doctor Who?: Hartnell's Doctor is denied the swansong he deserves; in fact he's barely present. He spends most the first two episodes sitting doing nothing and has around a dozen lines of dialogue in each. For Episode 3 he is absent entirely. Hartnell refused to turn up for work that week citing illness. Despite this, and the severe limitations of the screenplay, Hartnell is brilliant in his last few scenes as the Doctor, and his 'death' (seemingly from advanced old age) and subsequent physical transformation into a younger man are both moving and strangely unexpected, even now.

The Doctor seems to know about Mondas and this Cyber-invasion, treating it as a historical event.

Other Worlds: Mondas – Earth's 'twin planet' and the tenth planet of Earth's solar system. Its landmasses are an inversion of those of Earth. It 'drifted away on a journey to the edge of space'. Mondas has returned to Earth with a purpose. (According to **137**, 'Attack of the Cybermen', Mondas has a 'propulsion system' but this isn't mentioned here.)

Scary Monsters: Cybermen – humans who altered their bodies with spare parts in order to survive Mondas's long journey through space. They are bulletproof, ostensibly have no emotions and are impervious to cold, but are affected by radiation. They all die when Mondas is destroyed because they draw their energy from the planet itself. Whatever.

The Plan: The Cybermen plan to drain Earth of its energy, transferring it to Mondas. They will then destroy Earth before the absorption of too much energy destroys Mondas. They fail and Mondas boils away into space. They have a secondary plan to capture humans and turn them into Cybermen.

History 101: In 1986 International Space Command is run from Geneva, rockets (with 'Zeus capsules') are in use for space travel and mankind reached the moon (implicitly for the first time) 'six months ago'. There are British, American and Italian soldiers running the Snowcap base under a single officer, US Army General Cutler.

Science/Magic: Although Kit Pedler was a surgeon, his knowledge of (for example) physics and radioactivity seems limited – at least given the poor science that runs rampant here. This rather questions his effectiveness as *Doctor Who*'s scientific adviser.

Things Fall Apart: 'The Tenth Planet' finds *Doctor Who* on the cusp of the least creative period in its history, Lloyd's desire to replace 'whimsy' with 'guts' resulting in a formulaic series; from here until **43**, 'The Wheel in Space' the serials become increasingly similar, until eventually the scenario of an isolated group of people being attacked by monsters is continually recycled. The most notable exceptions are two iconoclastic efforts from the mercurial David Whitaker and **31**, 'The Highlanders', which is a loose adaptation of Robert Louis Stevenson's 1886 novel *Kidnapped*. Cyberleader Krang can't pronounce 'Cyber'. Which is unfortunate. On Episode 1 Kit Pedler is credited as Kitt Pedler. On Episode 3 Gerry Davis is Gerry Davies.

Availability: The BBC doesn't hold a copy of Episode 4, although a number of clips – including Hartnell's transformation into Troughton – exist. A video release in 2000 (BBCV 7030, WHV E1529) included Episodes 1–3 and a 'reconstruction' of the fourth using the sound, said clips and photographs. This version mistakenly credits Hartnell as 'Doctor Who' rather than 'Dr. Who'. The clips are also included on *Lost in Time* (BBC DVD 1353).

Verdict: 'It's far from being all over.' Derek Martinus directs with panache and there's some memorable iconography, but 'The Tenth Planet' is frequently slipshod and never rises above functional. It also sets the pattern for virtually all subsequent Cybermen tales in which the creatures will (a) display emotions while professing to have none, (b) implement entirely illogical plans despite professing to be logical and (c) die in bizarre and convenient ways related to a peculiar weakness despite professing invulnerability. Unimaginative, passionless and really quite dumb, the serial's treatment of *Doctor Who*'s first, most important and arguably best leading man is utterly unforgivable.

30
The Power of the Daleks

Episode One: 5 November 1966
Episode Two: 12 November 1966
Episode Three: 19 November 1966
Episode Four: 26 November 1966
②IH(H②Episode Five: 3 December 1966
Episode Six: 10 December 1966

Written by David Whitaker
Directed by Christopher Barry

Notable Cast: Patrick Troughton (1920–87), taking over as Doctor Who, was television's first *Robin Hood* (1954). Prominent roles include Phineas in *Jason and the Argonauts* (Don Chaffey, 1963), Klove in *Scars of Dracula* (Roy Ward Baker, 1970) and Father Brennan in *The Omen* (Richard Donner, 1976), as well as Tyrrell in Olivier's *Richard III* (1955), and the Player King in that director's *Hamlet* (1948). His TV roles include *The Box of Delights* (1984) and *Edward and Mrs Simpson* (1980). Bernard Archard (Bragen) played Chacal in *The Day of the Jackal* (Fred Zinneman, 1973), Eirig in *Krull* (Peter Yates, 1983) and Leonard Kempinski in *Emmerdale*, a character killed in the notorious plane-crash plot of 1993.

Doctor Who?: The Doctor is now a short, middle-aged man with thick, black, straight hair cut into a messy mop. His clothes have also transformed, with a more garish check to his baggy trousers, a shirt with a normal (rather than wing) collar, a skewed bow tie, braces and a scruffy frock coat. The Doctor wears a huge stovepipe hat, and later admires a military cap, saying, 'I would like a hat like that.' His old ring doesn't fit on his finger.

The effects of the Doctor's transformation leave him initially disorientated. He says that he has been 'renewed', a process that is part of the TARDIS, without which he couldn't survive. He seems to know his friends, but doesn't do anything to put them at ease: when Polly tells him that he is the Doctor, he replies that he doesn't look like him. He briefly sees his previous self in a mirror, and initially refers to 'the Doctor' in the third person. He refers to Saladin (whom he never actually met in **14**, 'The Crusade') and 'extermination' (**2**, 'The Daleks', among others) as he rummages through his personal effects, and later mentions Marco Polo (**4**, 'Marco Polo'). Reading his own 500-year diary engrosses him.

The Doctor clearly doesn't like to wear his knowledge on his sleeve, and is not above a little deception: he doesn't hesitate to adopt the identity of a convenient authority figure, and, when he defeats the Daleks, he covers it up with false modesty. (He accidentally wrecks the colony power supply when dealing with the Daleks, which may be another reason for that modesty.) This new Doctor is more impetuous, trying to walk straight out of the TARDIS without checking the readings. He plays a recorder, occasionally using it to communicate.

Other Worlds: The planet Vulcan, with its bubbling mercury swamps and pervasive mercury gas. There is a small Earth colony on the planet, ruled by a governor and subject to unrest and sabotage.

Scary Monsters: A small force of Daleks, who have spent 200 years stuck in their ship at the bottom of a mercury swamp. According to the Doctor, one Dalek would be enough to destroy the entire colony. The Daleks seem to recognise the Doctor, even in his new body, and Ben seems to regard this recognition as a sign of the Doctor's authenticity. The Daleks are constructed on production lines (as shown in one of the most memorable scenes in the story).

Villains: Lesterson (Robert James), a scientist who discovers the Dalek ship, and Bragen, Vulcan chief of security (and secret leader of the rebels).

The Plan: Lesterson secretly opened the Dalek capsule before being given permission, removing one of the Daleks and working to reactivate it, intending to use the Daleks as a labour force. Once reactivated, the Daleks pretend to serve the humans to allow time for their full reactivation. Bragen is leading the rebels as part of a plot to depose the governor, then take over as governor himself and use martial law to crush the rebels who brought him to power.

Science/Magic: The mercury atmosphere of the swamps causes Ben and Polly to pass out, although there are no long-term ill effects. The Dalek ship is made out of virtually indestructible metal. Lesterson uses a laser to open the ship's locking mechanism, by modern standards a rather primitive remote control. One of the Daleks answers a science pop quiz for Lesterson. The Daleks still run on static electricity, and have to convert other power sources into static. Lesterson gets the Daleks to design a 'meteorite storm computer'. The Doctor says the Daleks have conquered antimagnetism, whatever that means.

Availability: Absent from the archives except for seven clips totalling around 100 seconds. These are included on 2004's *Lost in Time* DVD (BBCDVD 1353). Issued on CD in 2004 as ISBN 0563535037.

Verdict: 'I'd like to see a butterfly fit into its chrysalis case after it's spread its wings.' A solid debut for Patrick Troughton as the Doctor, 'Power of the Daleks' plays with expectations, showing the Doctor as an unknown quantity and the Daleks as meek servants, before reasserting the correct order of things. By the end of the story, Troughton is firmly established, and it's his relationship with the Daleks that seals it – the Doctor knows the Daleks are evil and so does the viewer, pitching the audience in with the Doctor's predicament as an unheard voice. We're in it together, waiting for the Daleks to make their inevitable move – a very clever way of getting the audience on side in this risky transitional period.

The new Doctor is more active than his predecessor, mysterious in his motives, but shares his earlier self's desire to stop evil, especially that of the Daleks. The Daleks themselves are wonderfully sinister, pretending to be servants of the humans, and getting all the best cliffhangers. Their chanting repetition of certain phrases, from the creepy 'I am your servant' to the menacing 'Daleks conquer and destroy' are memorable, as are the Dalek's-eye views as the creatures hungrily track the human characters. A new Doctor, and a new angle on his worst enemies, all carried out successfully – quite an achievement.

31
The Highlanders

Episode 1: 17 December 1966
Episode 2: 24 December 1966
Episode 3: 31 December 1966
Episode 4: 7 January 1967

Written by Elwyn Jones and Gerry Davis
Directed by Hugh David

Notable Cast: Frazer Hines (Jamie McCrimmon) played Joe Sugden in *Emmerdale Farm* (1972–94). During his time on *Doctor Who* he released the pop single 'Who's Dr Who'. Shockingly enough, it didn't chart. He is now a stud farmer.

Writer: Elwyn Jones was head of serials at the BBC in the early 1960s, in which capacity he developed *Z Cars* (1962–65, 1967–68) and *Softly Softly* (1965–77). He later produced the Michael Caine-starring *Jack the Ripper* (1983) and wrote for the Gerry Davis-created series *Doomwatch* (1970). He adapted W Somerset Maugh's *A Man with a Conscience* for the BBC in 1969.

Director: A former actor, Hugh David had turned down the lead role of *Doctor Who* in 1963. He later directed literary adaptations for television such as *Jude the Obscure* (1971) and *The Pallisers* (1974).

History 101: The TARDIS lands on 16 March 1746 in the immediate aftermath of the Battle of Culloden and the collapse of the Jacobite Rebellion. After agreeing to assist Colin, the wounded chieftain of the Clan McLaren, the Doctor and Ben are captured by Redcoats and fall under the dubious custody of Solicitor Grey (David Garth).

The Plan: Grey's business entails finding deserters and prisoners of war, then giving them a choice between the gallows and being sold into slavery in the West Indies. This he intends to do to the Doctor, Ben and the captured Scots, whose number includes a young piper named Jamie McCrimmon.

Villains: As well as Grey there's Trask, who commands the slave ship *Annabel*, on which Grey transports his captives. As a piratical grotesque, Dallas Cavell's performance outstrips anything in **28**, 'The Smugglers', which is quite some achievement.

Science/Magic: While the Doctor treats Colin McLaren, Jamie asks why he hasn't performed blood-letting yet. In response, the Doctor chants 'O Isis and Osiris! Aquarius, Aries, Taurus . . . the blood-letting must wait until Taurus is in the ascendant. So it is willed.' Naturally, it's a ruse to avoid opening the sick man up and spreading the infection.

Doctor Who?: One of the originally conceived traits for Troughton's Doctor was a love of disguises. While this provides some amusement in 'The Highlanders' (Troughton's little-old-Scottish-lady voice is the funniest), it makes it difficult to get a handle on the character and it's easy to see why it was dropped. He displays some surprising qualities here, most notably a violent streak when dealing with Grey in Episode 2 (although the scene is played strictly for its comic value). Troughton is still feeling his way into the part but is clearly having a great time doing so ('I'm just beginning to enjoy myself').

Availability: No episodes of 'The Highlanders' are known to exist, although three short clips from Episode 1 are held and are on *Lost in Time* (BBCDVD 1353). The full audio-only version has been issued on CD (ISBN 0563477555).

Verdict: 'You're a loyal Jacobite, aren't you? This is your tune! Come on, everybody, join in!' *Doctor Who* began with a balance of adventures set in the future and the past: 'The Highlanders' marks the end of that period, and it's far from the best of the early adventures in history. No shame there, since there isn't a single bad story among the Hartnell historicals, but 'The Highlanders' suffers from the same basic problem as 'The Smugglers' in that it doesn't take full advantage of *Doctor Who*'s possibilities and is ultimately very straightforward.

Nevertheless, it also has the same positive qualities as 'The Smugglers': it's well constructed and satisfyingly melodramatic, and, while it's not in any way ambitious, it works very well. Polly drifts out of character as her cowardice vanishes to fit the script's demands, yet Anneke Wills still manages to put in one of her best performances (Polly's upper-class roots show when she declares that Kirsty is 'just a stupid peasant'). However, 'The Highlanders' will always be most noteworthy for introducing Frazer Hines as Jamie, who would go on to become one of the best foils any Doctor has had (appearing in 116 episodes, more than anybody except the first four Doctors).

32
The Underwater Menace

Episode 1: 14 January 1967
Episode 2: 21 January 1967
Episode 3: 28 January 1967
Episode 4: 4 February 1967

Written by Geoffrey Orme
Directed by Julia Smith

Notable Cast: Joseph Furst (Zaroff) appeared in *Diamonds Are Forever* (Guy Hamilton, 1971) and was a regular in the Australian soap *The Young Doctors* (1978).

Writer: Geoffrey Orme wrote several of the *Old Mother Riley* series of cheap, unfunny transvestite comedies of the early 1940s and much television, including the *Avengers* episode 'The Man in the Mirror' (1963).

Doctor Who?: The Doctor recognises volcanic rocks on sight and likes the taste of plankton. He believes that science is in opposition to religion. This is, sadly, the last story in which he wears his stovepipe hat from **30**, 'The Power of the Daleks'. He signs a note to Zaroff 'Dr. W'.

Villains: Professor Herman Zaroff is apparently the greatest scientific genius since Leonardo, not that you'd guess it from his comedy Teutonic accent, ridiculous plan and tendency to roll his eyes for no reason. He is an expert in plankton, and his disappearance twenty years before the story caused increased tensions between East and West. He has a pet octopus called Nemo.

Scary Monsters: The Fish People, humans surgically altered to harvest plankton. Polly almost joins their number.

The Plan: Zaroff is going to pour Earth's oceans into the molten core of the planet and boil them away, causing – apparently – the planet to crack and explode. To destroy Earth is apparently 'every scientist's ultimate dream of power'.

History 101: The TARDIS arrives on a beach, 'West of Gibraltar, South of the Azores, the Atlantic Ridge', at some point after 1968 (Polly finds merchandise from the Mexico Olympics). They are led to the 'lost kingdom of Atlantis', suborned to Zaroff's will by his promise to raise Atlantis from the sea. Here the living goddess Amdo is worshipped. Atlantis can be easily accessed by a lift from a cave on the beach – making nonsense of the Atlanteans' isolation.

Things Fall Apart: It's more that, after the initial TARDIS scene, which is charming, they're never together in the first place.

Availability: Episode 3 was, bewilderingly, kept by the BBC as an outstanding example of *Doctor Who*. This was because of the awe-inspiringly dreadful film sequence of the Fish People revolting against Zaroff, which was regarded as a showpiece. The scene features people flying on wires while wearing tights, lipstick and sticky eye covers. They move very slowly to the discordantly chirpy strains of some appalling pseudo-musique-concrete. Truly diabolical. The episode is included on the VHS *The Missing Years* (BBCV 6766), available in the UK as part of *The Ice Warriors Collection* (BBCV 6755). Thirty-seven seconds of material cut by the Australian Broadcasting Corporation for violent content also exists and is on the tape. In the US *The Missing Years* was packaged with **3**, 'The Edge of Destruction' (WHV E1578). The episode and clips are also on 2004's *Lost in Time* DVD (BBCDVD 1353).

Verdict: 'You're not turning me into a fish!' The worst *Doctor Who* serial up to this point, 'The Underwater Menace' is a chore. It's cheap, slow and humourless, the villain's plan is stupid and his motivation is the copout that he's mad. It's also dreadfully acted by virtually all concerned. Hugh David (see **31**, 'The Highlanders') refused to direct it having read the scripts and it's easy to see why. Rubbish.

33
The Moonbase

Episode 1: 11 February 1967
Episode 2: 18 February 1967
Episode 3: 25 February 1967
Episode 4: 4 March 1967

Written by Kit Pedler
Directed by Morris Barry

Notable Cast: André Maranne (Benoit) played François in six of the seven *Pink Panther* films, from *A Shot in the Dark* (Blake Edwards, 1964) onwards. Patrick Barr (Hobson) appeared in *The Lavender Hill Mob* (Charles Crichton, 1951) and *The Dam Busters* (Michael Anderson, 1954).

Director: Morris Barry worked as a director on *Compact* (1962–65) and *Z Cars* – of which he also became the producer. He produced the first series of *Poldark* (1975) and appeared, as an actor, in **106**, 'The Creature from the Pit'.

Scary Monsters: The Cybermen return, looking so different that it's mildly surprising that Polly manages to identify them. Their faces are fully metal, rather than flexible cloth, with a shutter over the mouth. Evidently they were not all destroyed in **29**, 'The Tenth Planet': these Cybermen are aware of the defeat and have identified Earth as a threat.

History 101: It's 2070 and Earth has established a base on its moon. In addition to repeating much of the plot of 'The Tenth Planet', 'The Moonbase' carries over the Kit Pedler view of The Future: it's ostensibly egalitarian, with a multiracial, multinational team operating the base, but Polly is the only woman and she ends up making the coffee again (she does get the glory of destroying some Cybermen in Episode 3, but even then uses a 'feminised' solution: nail varnish remover).

Science/Magic: The Moonbase exists to house the Gravitron, which regulates the weather on Earth by directing artificial gravitational pressures. Pedler's attitude to the lack of atmosphere on the Moon is hilarious – the Cybermen 'seal' their secret entrance with a pile of sacks, while a tea tray is sufficient to plug a hole in the Moonbase dome.

The Plan: The Cybermen plan to take command of the Gravitron by infecting its crew with a virus. They will then use the device to create extreme weather on Earth and kill off the population.

Doctor Who?: Polly asks if he's a medical doctor: 'Yes, I think I was once,' he replies. 'I think I took a degree once in Glasgow – 1888, I think. Lister.' (Troughton misremembers the script here, as he was supposed to refer to Edinburgh – this being where Joseph Lister actually was in 1888.) Polly's attempt to tactfully suggest that his medical knowledge might be outdated is wittily scripted and played, unlike everything else in this story.

Things Fall Apart: Every time someone jumps on the moon there's a silly 'boing' noise. How does nobody notice the Cyberman hiding on the bed in the medicentre? Why do the Cybermen poison the sugar, given that not everybody takes it? (Why not poison the coffee instead?) There's no good reason why the Cybermen don't just kill the unaffected Moonbase staff in Episode 3. The Cybermen illogically change tactics in Episode 4, despite having already won: the controlled Evans is monopolising the Gravitron and the humans have run out of options, then the Cybermen decide to puncture the Moonbase dome and kill off the humans anyway. All this achieves is to render Evans unconscious, allowing the humans to regain control of the Gravitron.

Availability: Only the second and fourth episodes of 'The Moonbase' have survived as film prints. These were released on 2004's *Lost in Time* DVD (BBCDVD 1353) and the *Cybermen: The Early Years* VHS (BBCV 4813, WHV E1104). The audio-only version is available on CD (ISBN 0563478543). Audio copies and episodes 1 and 3 are also on the DVD.

Verdict: 'Only stupid Earth brains such as yours would have been fooled.' The first *Doctor Who* story to be a clear rewrite of an earlier one, which would have mattered less if the story in question hadn't been broadcast only four months earlier. To be fair, it's an improvement on 'The Tenth Planet': all the regular characters get something to do (even Jamie, who was written in at the last minute) and the Doctor is instrumental in the Cybermen's defeat. Other than that it's very similar, with the Cybermen invading a remote base that houses a piece of whizzo technology. The base is commanded by a cantankerous senior figure who doesn't trust the Doctor at first. Get used to this plot: you'll be seeing a lot more of it.

Gerry Davis apparently believed that 'The Moonbase' represented some golden formula for *Doctor Who*, which is puzzling because it's dull and stupid – not the *most* dull and stupid Troughton story, but an uninspiring serial with some awful dialogue ('Clever, clever, clever') and a lot of half-hearted performances. Even Troughton doesn't seem to be trying that hard, which is unusual for him.

34
The Macra Terror

Episode 1: 11 March 1967
Episode 2: 18 March 1967
Episode 3: 25 March 1967
Episode 4: 1 April 1967

Written by Ian Stuart Black
Directed by John Davies

Notable Cast: Peter Jeffrey (Pilot) played the Headmaster in *If . . .* (Lindsey Anderson, 1968), Norfolk in *Anne of the Thousand Days* (Charles Jarrott, 1969) and the Sultan in *The Adventures of Baron Munchausen* (Terry Gilliam, 1988). His television roles include King Philip II of Spain in *Elizabeth R* (1971) and Major Peabody in *The Jewel in the Crown* (1984).

Director: John Davies directed episodes of *Monty Python's Flying Circus* (1969) and *Mr Bean* (1989).

Other Worlds: 'The colony', a human settlement on an unnamed planet in the future. The day-to-day leader of the colony is known as the Pilot, but the real leader is the Controller, a disembodied voice accompanied by a picture of an imposing man. The colony's main work is the tapping and processing of gas. The colony has a holiday-camp atmosphere, with PA announcements and jingles playing – but the colonists' lives are closely regimented, and a curfew is in place at night.

Doctor Who?: The Doctor is distressed when one of the colony's 'clothes revivers' smartens him up. He uses a rough-and-tumble machine (designed for muscle toning) to reduce him back to a scruffy state. When Ben is hypnotised, the Doctor is insistent that Ben shouldn't be blamed for his inability to control his own actions, even when he betrays the Doctor. The Doctor is so pleased with a calculation he does that he marks himself ten out of ten. When he finds out that he has recreated a formula that took the colony's best computers years to come up with, he raises his mark to eleven. The Doctor adopts the cheery manner of the colony to sweep the colonists along with him when he needs to. He has no reservations about killing the Macra. He sneaks away before the colonists can make him their new leader.

Scary Monsters: The Macra, large crablike creatures. The colonists refer to them as being like insects, with only Polly comparing them to crabs (perhaps the colonists have never seen a crab before, and an insect is the nearest comparison). The Doctor describes the Macra as being like an 'infection' in the body of the colony.

The Plan: The Macra come from below the surface of the planet, where they have plenty of gas to breathe. As they have moved closer to the surface, they have enslaved the colonists to pump it up for them.

Science/Magic: Humans can be hypnotised using a combination of wires in the wall, gas and a hypnotic voice speaking while they sleep. The gas that the Macra breathe is poisonous to humans.

Availability: Only four short clips totalling 28 seconds still exist and are included on the *Lost in Time* DVD (BBCDVD 1353). Issued on CD as ISBN 0563477563. Fortunately they allow the viewer enough time to appreciate Polly's wicked new haircut.

Verdict: 'There is no such thing as Macra. Macra do not exist . . . There are no Macra!' The political concerns of George Orwell are filtered through the paranoid storytelling of 1950s creature features, and embellished with the cheery aesthetic of British holiday camps in Ian Stuart Black's final, and least impressive, *Doctor Who* story. While the plot just about hangs together, and the Macra are fun monsters, this isn't quite as smart as either **26**, 'The Savages', or **27**, 'The War Machines'. However, all the regulars are good and get plenty to do, while there are some creepy moments, and Black's writing remains ahead of the pack, even in a lesser work like this.

35
The Faceless Ones

Episode 1: 8 April 1967
Episode 2: 15 April 1967
Episode 3: 22 April 1967
Episode 4: 29 April 1967
Episode 5: 6 May 1967
Episode 6: 13 May 1967

Written by David Ellis and Malcolm Hulke
Directed by Gerry Mill

Writers: David Ellis wrote for *Dixon of Dock Green* and *United!* Malcolm Hulke scripted eight episodes of *The Avengers* (1962–65) as well as working on *Danger Man*, and was the author of *Writing for Television*, a technical handbook regarded as an industry bible.

Director: Gerry Mill went on to direct episodes of *Robin of Sherwood* and has been the producer of *Heartbeat* since 1996.

Notable Cast: Wanda Ventham (Jean Rock) had regular roles in *Heartbeat* (1996–97) and *Only Fools and Horses* (1989–96). Bernard Kay (Crossland) previously appeared in **10**, 'The Dalek Invasion of Earth'. Colin Gordon (Commissioner) appeared in numerous British films, including *The Man in the White Suit* (Alexander Mackendrick, 1951) and played No 2 in two of the best episodes of *The Prisoner* (1967). Donald Pickering was later in *The Pallisers* (1974). Pauline Collins (Samantha Briggs) starred in the 1969 debut season of *The Liver Birds* and in *Shirley Valentine* (Lewis Gilbert, 1989). Collins was offered the chance to become a *Doctor Who* regular, but turned it down (a shame: while her performance isn't fantastic, Samantha could have performed more useful plot functions than Victoria).

Scary Monsters: The alien Chameleons. They have lost their identities in 'a gigantic explosion' and have come to contemporary Earth to steal the identities of humans. These 'monsters' have individual personalities and are portrayed as desperate rather than merely evil, both trademarks of Hulke's later *Doctor Who* work.

The Plan: The Chameleons have set up their own airline at Gatwick, Chameleon Tours, offering cheap package holidays to young people. The planes are equipped to move up into orbit and on board a space station, where each passenger is miniaturised and their physical features adopted by a Chameleon.

Science/Magic: So the Chameleons lost their identities in a gigantic explosion? What kind of explosion does that?

Doctor Who?: The Chameleons identify him as human from their medical analysis, but they're clearly wrong: at the end, when Ben and Polly decide to stay behind on their own world, he says, 'You're lucky. I never got back to mine.'

Things Fall Apart: The fact that the Chameleons call their airline 'Chameleon Tours' draws unnecessary attention to their activities.

They could also have aroused less suspicion by filling the empty planes with transformed Chameleons before the planes left the satellite: surely people find it odd that the airline delivers no passengers. There's an Austin Powers moment when a Chameleon sets a laser to crawl slowly towards the Doctor, Jamie and Sam and then leaves the room, when it would have been simpler to just kill them there and then.

Availability: A film print of Episode 1 has always existed at the BBC archive. A badly damaged sales copy of Episode 3 was returned in 1987 (the BBC remains on the lookout for a better copy). The other four episodes remain absent. Episodes 1 and 3 were released in on VHS as part of *The Reign of Terror Box Set* in 2003 (BBCV 7335, WHV E1853) and on 2004's *Lost in Time* DVD (BBCDVD 1353). The complete audio-only version is available on CD (ISBN 0563535016).

Verdict: 'You two won't be needing living space.' In a period when *Doctor Who* was becoming simpler and more purely escapist, 'The Faceless Ones' stands out as a piece of quite mature existential horror. It goes further than most 'body-snatchers' plots by emphasising that the Chameleons are not stealing our identities merely as a bridgehead to an invasion, but because they have lost their own and are dying out. The implication seems to be that, without a physical form that we can recognise as ourselves, we cease to function. Set against the evocative technological backdrop of an airport, the plot is like something out of a novel by Haruki Murakami.

Of course, this being *Doctor Who*, the serial sometimes falls back into action-runaround mode and feels compelled to include an unnecessary explanation for the Chameleons' plight (which is inadequate in any case). It's also a bit overlong: this was the first non-Dalek story in two years to break the four-episode barrier, which was a financial decision rather than a creative one and was generally to the series' detriment. In its present state 'The Faceless Ones' suffers particularly badly from the loss of four episodes, since much of the story is told visually and its most arresting imagery (the catatonic Polly, the drawer of miniaturised humans) is lost, but it remains a hugely impressive attempt to stretch the series' format.

36
The Evil of the Daleks

Episode 1: 20 May 1967
Episode 2: 27 May 1967
Episode 3: 3 June 1967
Episode 4: 10 June 1967
Episode 5: 17 June 1967
Episode 6: 24 June 1967
Episode 7: 1 July 1967

Written by David Whitaker
Directed by Derek Martinus

Notable Cast: Marius Goring (Theodore Maxtible) appeared in many films, including the Powell and Pressburger classics *Ill Met by Moonlight* (1957) and *The Red Shoes* (1958) and was a longstanding leading player with the Royal Shakespeare Company. Deborah Watling (Victoria Waterfield) had played Alice Liddle in *Alice* (1965), Dennis Potter's TV biography of Lewis Carroll, and had worked extensively as a child actress. After leaving *Doctor Who* she played the love interests in *That'll Be The Day* (Claude Whatham, 1973) and *Take Me High* (David Askey, 1973) opposite David Essex and Cliff Richard respectively and played 'naughty' Norma in *Danger UXB* (1979). Roy Skelton had previously voiced Cybermen in **29**, 'The Tenth Planet' and **33**, 'The Moonbase'; here he joins the series' rep of Dalek voice actors, which he'll be a part of, on and off, until 1988. He also plays Zippy and George in *Rainbow*.

Script Editor: Peter Bryant became *Doctor Who*'s script editor with Episode 4 of this serial. Assigned to shadow producer Innes Lloyd, who was keen to leave the series (Bryant was credited as 'associate producer' on Episodes 1–3 of 'Evil' and all of **35**, 'The Faceless Ones'), Bryant found himself replacing Gerry Davis instead. Temporarily promoted to producer for **37**, 'The Tomb of the Cybermen' (while Lloyd took a holiday), Bryant returned to the script editor's job for **38**, 'The Abominable Snowmen', and held it until **40**, 'The Enemy of the World'. Thereafter he became producer, Lloyd having departed. Bryant remained producer until **49**, 'The Space Pirates'. To confuse matters further, many of his duties were covered by his successor as script editor, Derrick Sherwin, due to Bryant's ill health. Bryant became the producer of *Paul Temple* (1969–71) and then left television to become a literary agent.

Doctor Who?: The Doctor witnessed the Charge of the Light Brigade on 25 October 1854 ('magnificent folly'). He has often wondered if he would ever meet the Dalek Emperor. He claims to be a student not of human nature but of 'a far wider academy of which human nature is only a part'. The Daleks think the Doctor has 'travelled too much through time' and this has made him 'more than human'. He is immune to being conditioned by the Dalek Factor.

History 101: As in 35, 'The Faceless Ones', it's 20 July 1966. Episode 1 is the most contemporary *Doctor Who* gets, with the Doctor sitting in coffee bars to the accompaniment of Beatles ('Paperback Writer') and Seekers ('Nobody Knows the Troubles I've Seen') tracks while Jamie dances, and flirts, with dolly birds in microskirts and boots. After being abducted, the Doctor and Jamie wake up in Maxtible's house – said to be some miles from Canterbury – on 2 June 1866.

Villains: Theodore Maxtible, a Victorian scientist who is working for the Daleks so that they will tell him how to turn base metal into gold. Edward Waterfield (John Bailey), Maxtible's tortured accomplice, is a decent, sensitive man who is blackmailed into helping Maxtible and the Daleks after they kidnap his daughter Victoria.

Science/Magic: Maxtible and Waterfield, in pursuit of the ability to time-travel, tried to 'project' the images in mirrors by charging 244 polished metal mirrors with static electricity. Because like repels like in electricity, they then attempted to repel the image in the mirrors. This caused the Daleks to 'burst out' of their cabinet. No, we don't understand that either.

The Plan: The Daleks steal the TARDIS and force the Doctor to create the 'Human Factor' by remotely studying Jamie's reactions as he tries to liberate Victoria. This distillation of 'all that is best and finest' in human beings will ostensibly be used to create a super-race of Daleks. (The Doctor hopes to turn the experiments against them and make the Daleks more compassionate and humane in the process.) Unfortunately, in creating the Human Factor the Doctor defines the 'Dalek Factor'. (The Human Factor is 'courage, pity, chivalry, friendship, compassion'. The Dalek Factor is 'to obey, to fight, to destroy, to exterminate'.) 'Without knowing, you have shown the Daleks what their own strength is!' announces the Emperor. 'The Human Factor is useless!' The

Daleks intend to spread this Dalek Factor throughout the history of Earth (as an atmospheric 'steam'), making the human race psychologically like, and loyal to, the Daleks.

Other worlds: The Doctor visits Skaro for the first time since **2**, 'The Daleks'. He makes his way into the Dalek city using the same tunnels traversed at the end of that earlier serial. The Doctor speculates that if the Daleks destroy humanity his friends could flee to what he calls 'my own planet'.

Scary Monsters: One Dalek announces that only 'one form of life . . . matters – Dalek life!' and another that 'The Daleks are afraid of nothing and no one'. The Daleks' Emperor – never seen or referred to before (logically it outranked, or maybe replaced, the Dalek Supreme, killed in **21**, 'The Daleks' Master Plan') – is introduced in Episode 6. The Dalek city on Skaro is destroyed in the fighting at the end of the serial. The Doctor speculates that this may be 'the final end' of his enemies.

Things Fall Apart: The clues that lead the Doctor to Waterfield's shop are nonsensical. The plot requires the Doctor to be duped by the Daleks for five episodes. If the Dalek Factor was the object all along, why does the Emperor allow the Doctor to implant three Daleks with the Human Factor and then allow those Daleks free movement about the city? Both Troughton and Goring overplay their 'possession' by the Dalek Factor (Troughton has the excuse that the Doctor is pretending). Surviving footage indicates that the Dalek civil war that closes the serial is lamentably unconvincing, with use of Dalek toys (a different *shape* from the full-size ones), small sets and poor models.

Availability: Issued on CD as ISBN 0563535975. The single extant episode, Episode 2, is on *Daleks – The Early Years* BBCV 4810 (UK), WHV E1143 (US) and 2004's *Lost in Time* DVD (BBCDVD 1353).

Verdict: 'Why? Why? The Emperor must explain. I *will* obey, but not without question.' Whitaker's greatest assets were a skill for characterful dialogue, his understanding of the value of a striking image and his almost metaphysical approach to science. 'Evil' contains numerous detours, *longueurs* and redundant characters and – disgracefully – has a denouement that relies on a plot oversight. However, it also showcases his strengths beautifully. Thanks to much good verbiage ('Imagination is a virtue, but it can become a vice'), impressive iconography, Maxtible's ludicrous time-travel mirrors and the almost symbolic Human and Dalek Factors, this is, while deeply flawed, Whitaker at his most engaging and one of the three or four best Troughton stories.

37
The Tomb of the Cybermen

Episode 1: 2 September 1967
Episode 2: 9 September 1967
Episode 3: 16 September 1967
Episode 4: 23 September 1967

Written by Kit Pedler and Gerry Davis
Directed by Morris Barry

Notable Cast: Cyril Shaps (Viner) was a prolific television actor who made three other *Doctor Who* appearances. His film work includes *The Madness of King George* (Nicholas Hytner, 1994) and *The Pianist* (Roman Polanski, 2002). George Pastell (Klieg) appeared in Hammer's *The Mummy* (Terence Fisher, 1959) and *The Curse of the Mummy's Tomb* (Michael Carreras, 1964) as well as *From Russia With Love* (Terence Young, 1963). Shirley Cooklin (Kaftan) was married to producer Peter Bryant, which should in no sense suggest that her casting was an unjustifiable act of nepotism. Clive Merrison (Callum) is Radio 4's *Sherlock Holmes*, the only actor to play the character in adaptations of all of Conan Doyle's stories.

Other Worlds: Telos, said to be the Cybermen's home. (A line cut from the script of **33**, 'The Moonbase', confirms that the creatures adopted it as such after Mondas was destroyed in **29**, 'The Tenth Planet'.) A team of archaeologists from Earth, led by Professor Parry (Aubrey Richards), are searching for the creatures' final remains.

Scary Monsters: The Cybermen, who Parry claims have been dead for five hundred years. Also, the Cybermats – supposedly, cybernised rodents – which are actually a bit useless.

Villains: The Cyber Controller, a big-brained Cyberman who gives the orders. Also Klieg and Kaftan, members of Earth's Brother-hood of Logicians, and Kaftan's manservant Toberman (Roy

Stewart) – perhaps the most racially offensive character in *Doctor Who*.

The Plan: Klieg and Kaftan propose to ally themselves with the Cybermen in order to rule Earth. The Cybermen, meanwhile, have placed themselves in suspended animation to conserve energy and hope to be found at a later date by creatures of high intelligence, whom they could then use to rebuild their power base.

Science/Magic: The Cybermen promise to help Klieg take over Earth by giving him 'some of our power devices'. Such as?

Doctor Who?: The Doctor says he is around 450 years old, has a family he rarely thinks about and 'perfected' the TARDIS so that he could 'travel through the universe of time'. What is he actually trying to achieve in this story? Is he trying to manipulate the archaeologists so that he can finish off the Cybermen himself? If so, his actions are often inconsistent with this. Is he trying to help or hinder Klieg's efforts to open the hatch?

Things Fall Apart: How does nobody notice Toberman as he 'sneaks' out of the tomb on his way to sabotage the rocket? (Later, when Captain Hopper (George Roubicek) reports the damage to the others, Toberman grins to himself.) The first two fights in which Toberman is involved are risible, with a visible wire holding him up in the first and an obviously empty Cyber Controller prop in the second. Why can't the revived Cybermen open the hatch from their side? Why lock Klieg and Kaftan in the weapons room, which has weapons in it? Why does the Doctor switch on the Cyber-revitaliser when locking the Controller inside? And why are there bits of old timber lying around on Telos?

Availability: A DVD (BBCDVD 1032, WHV E1181) was issued in 2002. It had previously been rush-released on VHS (BBCV 4772, WHV E1181) in 1992 when film prints of the long-lost episodes were found in Hong Kong.

Verdict: 'The best thing about a machine that makes sense is you can very easily make it turn out nonsense.' A cracking idea for a *Doctor Who* story that affords a sense of scale to the universe in which the Doctor travels. Constructing the Cybermen's resurrection as a 'curse of the mummy's tomb' story is interesting but unfortunately the genre's archetypes are imported wholesale, so the good guys are stoic Brits or square-jawed Canadians, the bad guys are shifty foreigners, the women are treated as delicate flowers and the only non-white person is a monosyllabic strong-man. In this respect the story has dated horribly.

The plotting is disjoined and anticlimactic, with the Cybermen doing far too little, and by the end not much has been achieved (the Doctor even sets the Cybermen's trap back up for them). The deaths are, at least, given appropriate weight, thanks in part to reactive performances from Aubrey Richards and George Roubicek, but George Pastell and Shirley Cooklin are desperately unconvincing. It's Troughton who rescues it, along with Morris Barry, whose direction makes something highly atmospheric out of the material; but nothing can disguise the script's shortcomings.

38
The Abominable Snowmen

Episode One: 30 September 1967
Episode Two: 7 October 1967
Episode Three: 14 October 1967
Episode Four: 21 October 1967
Episode Five: 28 October 1967
Episode Six: 4 November 1967

Written by Mervyn Haisman and Henry Lincoln
Directed by Gerald Blake

Notable Cast: Jack Watling (Travers) is the father of Deborah Watling. He played a BBC producer in the *Hancock's Half Hour* episode 'The Lift', and Frank Blakemore in several episodes of *Bergerac*. His films include Lewis Gilbert's *Reach for the Sky* (1956), *The Admirable Crichton* (1957) and *Sink the Bismarck!* (1960).

Writer: Mervyn Haisman wrote the scripts for two 1980s adaptations of the *Jane* newspaper strip – a 1982 TV series, and the movie *Jane and the Lost City* (Terry Marcel, 1987) – and script-edited *The Onedin Line* (1971). Henry Lincoln is co-author of *The Holy Blood and the Holy Grail*, and other occult conspiracy books.

Director: Gerald Blake directed episodes of *Dr Finlay's Casebook*, *Coronation Street* and *Z Cars*.

History 101: The area around the Detsen Buddhist monastery in the Himalayas, Tibet. The year is not specified, but Travers recognises the word 'robot', which was coined by the Czech playwright Karel Capek in his 1921 play *R.U.R.*, which dates the story to some time after then. The Doctor borrowed a ghanta (a ceremonial bell) from the monastery in 1630, to protect it in a troubled time. We are told that this attack was three hundred years ago. (See also **41**, 'The Web of Fear'.)

Villains: The Great Intelligence, an alien entity that has enslaved the mind of the Buddhist master Padmasambhava, and through him controls the Abbot Songsten. Padmasambhava has been kept alive by the Intelligence since the Doctor was last at Detsen, and recognises his face. Padmasambhava fell under the control of the Intelligence while exploring space with his mind. He co-ordinates the Yeti's movements through chess-piece-style effigies on a map of the area.

The Intelligence/Padmasambhava/Songsten can control the minds of others, deleting memories and causing trance states. Padmasambhava speaks through Victoria, his voice coming from her lips, and leaves her with a hypnotically induced fear so that she will insist that the Doctor take her away from Detsen. In a final confrontation, Padmasambhava uses levitation and other mental tricks on the Doctor, then catches bullets out of the air. It's unclear whether these powers are the Intelligence's, or Padmasambhava's own.

Scary Monsters: The Yeti, bulky, furry creatures that look more cute and cuddly than threatening. Real Yeti (within the context of the story, that is) are timid, but mostly we see robot Yeti, built by Padmasambhava over two hundred years. The robot Yeti are inert without their control units, silver spheres that fit into gaps in their chests. These spheres can move independently. The Yeti can only obey instructions, and are inactive when not receiving a signal.

The Plan: The Great Intelligence wants to achieve physical form using a crystal pyramid, which is placed between a triangle of control spheres: together they release a foamlike substance while making a horrible droning noise. This foam is the Intelligence's body, and will consume the world. This plan is spectacularly vague – there's no real explanation for the specific timing of events, such as why the Intelligence suddenly needs to drive the monks away from the monastery.

Doctor Who?: The Doctor is excited to be back in the Himalayas so he can return the ghanta (a ceremonial bell – see **History 101**). Having seen a large footprint, the Doctor insists that Jamie and

Victoria stay in the TARDIS while he goes to the monastery alone. The Doctor is wary when Jamie has a plan for capturing the Yeti, and suggests that he and Victoria retreat to a safe distance. Padmasambhava admires the Doctor's intelligence, but worries that he will interfere. The Doctor is saddened by Padmasambhava's condition. The Doctor can hypnotise people, and also reverse the hypnotic conditioning others have applied.

Science/Magic: The Great Intelligence seems to be a mystical presence, but his plan involves robotics, and is referred to as an 'experiment'. Thonmi (a monk) says that a Buddhist master can learn to free his spirit and travel in time and space, as Padmasambhava has.

Availability: Episode Two is the only one to survive on film, and was included on the *Troughton Years* VHS (BBCV 4609) and 2004's *Lost in Time* DVD (BBCDVD 1353). Two very short clips from Episode 4 also exist. The story is available on CD and MP3-CD as ISBN 056347856X and 0563494182.

Verdict: 'The devil in his guile wears his armour beneath the skin to protect his evil heart.' Although overlong, and sticking closely to the isolated-community-under-siege formula, 'The Abominable Snowmen' has the advantage of an exotic setting and a number of evocative ideas. The robot Yeti are great, as is the iconography of the silver spheres and the glowing pyramid. Padmasambhava is an eerie presence, a disembodied, whispering voice (actor Wolfe Morris). Unfortunately, the explanations don't live up to the imagery, with plenty of convoluted exposition while the layers of characters being hypnotised by each other makes matters incoherent (how much control does Padmasambhava have over himself at any one time, for instance?). Ultimately, the story doesn't fulfil its early promise.

39
The Ice Warriors

One: 11 November 1967
Two: 18 November 1967
Three: 25 November 1967
Four: 2 December 1967
Five: 9 December 1967
Six: 16 December 1967

Written by Brian Hayles
Directed by Derek Martinus

Notable Cast: Peter Sallis (Penley) has appeared in *Last of the Summer Wine* since its debut in 1973, and voiced Wallace in the *Wallace and Gromit* films (1991, 1993, 1995 and 2005). Bernard Bresslaw (Varga) was in thirteen films in the Carry On series, from *Carry On Cowboy* (Gerald Thomas, 1965) to *Carry On Behind* (Gerald Thomas, 1975). Angus Lennie was Scots cook Shuggie McFee in virtually all of *Crossroads*. Author, RADA lecturer and actor Peter Barkworth starred in the TV series *Manhunt* (1969) and featured in films as diverse as *No My Darling Daughter* (Ralph Thomas, 1961) and *Wilde* (Brian Gilbert, 1997).

History 101: In the future, Earth is in the grip of a new ice age caused by an imbalance of carbon dioxide in the atmosphere. Scientists at Brittanicus Base are holding back the advance of glaciers with their Ioniser.

Doctor Who?: Not for the first or last time, the Doctor avoids being ejected from a trouble spot by solving an immediate problem in a matter of minutes. Troughton's innocent manner makes these sequences work beautifully – 'You ought to get an expert in, you know.' The Doctor's dislike of computers was a standard 1960s theme but looks a bit Luddite these days.

Scary Monsters: The Ice Warriors, inhabitants of Mars. The particular group in this story have been frozen for an indeterminate period of time, ever since their ship landed on Earth and became entombed.

The Plan: Varga plans to conquer Earth in the name of Mars, but first he needs to free his ship from the ice. To achieve this he plots to take control of Brittanicus Base. In truth, though, the Martians do little until the final episode except stomp around their ship and chuckle sibilantly to themselves, and rewriting this script for the Cybermen would be more or less a find-and-replace job.

Science/Magic: Another common 1960s motif – the computer spins around when presented with an insoluble problem. Why this was thought necessary is unclear (most modern computers simply respond with a polite error message). The 'moral' that computers and science should be treated with caution is mixed, but this demonstrates that binary answers aren't always applicable. This message is so hammered into the ground, however, that you wonder how stupid Clent (Peter Barkworth) and Miss Garrett (Wendy Gifford) can be if they don't see it themselves.

Things Fall Apart: The blocks of 'ice' that Victoria clambers over squeak when she moves them. The Ice Warriors would have worked much better if close-ups on their heads had been avoided. Varga appears to sulk in the fourth episode by retracting his head into his neck, which looks a bit silly – although not half as silly as the way they spin around when their ship is being destroyed.

Availability: The second and third episodes of 'The Ice Warriors' are not known to exist. Episodes One, Four, Five and Six were released on VHS in 1998. The boxed set also includes a CD of the complete audio-only version from Two and Three and a bonus video, *The Missing Years*, featuring clips from other lost episodes and Episode 3 of **32**, 'The Underwater Menace'. The set as a whole was designated BBCV 6387; in the US 'The Ice Warriors' was released on its own as WHV E1392, whilst *The Missing Years* was packaged with **3**, 'The Edge of Destruction'.

Verdict: 'Here we are completely computerised.' Brian Hayles seems to be enjoying himself in the first episode when he's setting up the apocalyptic backdrop, but the joy starts to ebb away when the first Ice Warrior wakes up – suggesting that Hayles possibly wasn't that interested in writing a monster story. The to-and-fro padding of the six-episode stories is becoming increasingly familiar and the serial desperately needs a battle sequence between Brittanicus Base security and the Ice Warriors to give some sense of struggle, but the budget blatantly won't stretch that far, so instead the Martians just stroll in.

Unfortunately, this generic monster-attack plotline obscures the interesting elements of the story. The design is great (the Brittanicus Base uniforms appear to have been commissioned from Bridget Riley, while Jamie's tinted goggles make him resemble Scott Walker) and there's some great music (check out Dudley Simpson's Hammond freak-out in the third episode). The performances of Peter Sallis and Peter Barkworth help to prop up an uncertain message and the last episode partly atones for some dire patches earlier on, although it remains unsatisfying, because the Doctor gets hardly anything to do.

40
The Enemy of the World

Episode 1: 23 December 1967
Episode 2: 30 December 1967
Episode 3: 6 January 1967
Episode 4: 13 January 1968
Episode 5: 20 January 1968
Episode 6: 27 January 1968

Written by David Whitaker
Directed by Barry Letts

Notable Cast: South African Bill Kerr (Giles Kent) was a regular in the radio version of *Hancock's Half Hour*. His films include *The Dambusters* (Michael Anderson, 1954), *Gallipoli* (Peter Weir, 1981) and *Peter Pan* (PJ Hogan, 2003). He is superb in this.

Director: Barry Letts is one of *Doctor Who*'s principal creative figures. A former sailor and actor, he was *Doctor Who*'s producer from **52**, 'Doctor Who and the Silurians', to **75**, 'Robot', and cast Tom Baker in the title role. He was executive producer from **109**, 'The Leisure Hive', to **115**, 'Logopolis'. See the index for his writing and directing credits. He also produced the BBC's Classic Serial strand from 1976 to 1985, making over a dozen successful literary adaptations. He created and produced *Moonbase 3* (1973). Other works as a director include the BBC's 1986 *David Copperfield* and episodes of *EastEnders* (1990–92) and *Z Cars* (1967).

Doctor Who?: The Doctor likes the seaside and building sand-castles. In keeping with Whitaker's own era, he doesn't introduce himself and when his title is conferred on him claims it's 'not of any medical significance'. He flirts with Astrid Ferrier (Mary Peach), saying he'll do 'anything at all' for her after she calls him 'wonderful'. He considers himself the 'nicest possible person' and human beings' favourite pastime to be 'trying to destroy each other'. He can vocally impersonate Salamander and correctly identifies his accent as Yucatan. He expresses a moral rage at Kent's casual attitude to murder.

Villains: Salamander is a Mexican scientist and influential politician labelled the 'shopkeeper of the world'. While he is widely loved, there have been many attempts to poison him. He is a near physical double of the Doctor (Troughton plays both roles).

There's also Australian Giles Kent, formerly the deputy security leader for North Africa and Europe, dismissed after a financial scandal. He proclaims a desire to bring Salamander down for the good of mankind, but in fact Kent was in on the creation of Salamander's plot (see **The Plan**) and wants simply to kill Salamander and take his place. Either of these men could be considered the titular 'Enemy'.

The Plan: Salamander has been undermining, murdering and disgracing his political rivals and manipulating the situation to place weak men loyal to him in their vacated positions. Part of this process involves causing earthquakes using a community of people who've been underground for five years and believe that the world has perished in a nuclear holocaust. They are causing these 'natural' disasters on Salamander's say-so, believing they are destroying 'enemies of truth and freedom'. They are in fact slaughtering civilians in areas where Salamander needs to undermine government figures.

History 101: The story is set in a future where the world is divided into 'Zones' (supranational groups of countries), each of which has a 'controller' (it is unclear whether this is an elected position). The Zones include 'Central European' and 'Central Asian'. The 'United Zones' organisation appears to function like the contemporary UN, but with more power. Australians seem to be a dominant cultural group. Middle Europeans and South Americans also have considerable influence. Hovercraft are still used, as are telephones and automatic weapons; 'rockets' are for international travel (from Hungary to Australia takes less than two hours). Alaskan wine is thoroughly respectable.

Science/Magic: Salamander invented the Suncatcher Mark VII, which 'captures' sunlight and stores it. It can be 'fired' in concentrated form on to selected areas to force-grow three or four crops in one summer. The crops are harvested by robots.

Things Fall Apart: In Episode 3, Denes is imprisoned in a corridor rather than a prison cell because 'it's easier to guard him' (i.e. there's a shortage of sets). Jamie and Victoria trick their way into Salamander's confidence via a fake 'bungled' bomb plot. That he falls for this doesn't say much for his intelligence (but perhaps something about his arrogance). The middle episodes are padded runarounds, and the last two fit too much into too little time. Some plot information is repeated, but other explanations are absent. As Salamander, Troughton looks like a poverty-stricken matador and talks like Speedy Gonzales.

Availability: The audio-only CD is ISBN 0563535032. The surviving episode (Episode 3) is on *The Troughton Years* (BBC V 4609, WHV E1097) and 2004's *Lost in Time* DVD (BBCDVD 1353).

Verdict: 'What do you hope to gain by this gesture?' This is manifestly smarter and more ambitious than the serials that surround it and, although the geopolitical landscape and Salamander's exact position in it are inconsistently drawn, it manages to be 'about' power in a way that no other story of the era is 'about' anything. Surviving photographs suggest a big production, with considerable location filming and the use of a helicopter, although the extant episode is a static, small-scale affair. Interestingly, dialogue refers to Victoria as Jamie's 'girlfriend' and Hines and Watling play their relationship as physically close (this sexual tension between characters is typically Whitaker). Griff the pessimistic chef (Reg Lye) is hilarious.

41
The Web of Fear

Episode 1: 3 February 1968
Episode 2: 10 February 1968
Episode 3: 17 February 1968
Episode 4: 24 February 1968
Episode 5: 2 March 1968
Episode 6: 9 March 1968

Written by Mervyn Haisman and Henry Lincoln
Directed by Douglas Camfield

Notable Cast: This was Nicholas Courtney's first appearance as Lethbridge-Stewart (he had earlier worked on **21**, 'The Daleks' Master Plan'). Courtney would return to the role many times over the next 25 years. Rod Beacham (Corporal Lane) later turned his hand to writing, scripting *Poirot*, *Bergerac* and *Blake's 7*. Jon Rollason (Harold Chorley) was a *Coronation Street* regular (1963–71). Jack Watling reprised the role of Travers from **38**, 'The Abominable Snowmen'.

Script Editor: Actor/writer/producer Derrick Sherwin worked as script editor until **45**, 'The Mind Robber' (returning briefly to the post for **49**, 'The Space Pirates'). He would become *Doctor Who*'s producer with **50**, 'The War Games', having already spent several months sharing the job in an unofficial capacity with credited producer Peter Bryant, who was ill. He left following **51**, 'Spearhead from Space', to become the producer of *Paul Temple* (1971–73).

Villains: The Great Intelligence, again controlling the robot Yeti. It has taken hold of the London Underground on contemporary Earth by means of a poisonous weblike substance spread by the Yeti. The city has been evacuated while the army tries to deal with the problem.

Scary Monsters: The Yeti are redesigned from their earlier appearance in 'The Abominable Snowmen' in order to look less cuddly: they now possess claws, glowing eyes and a more streamlined frame.

The Plan: The Intelligence initially claims that its objective is purely to drain the Doctor's extensive knowledge and experience. Capturing the whole of London seems a needlessly elaborate way to do this, so it's no surprise that the Intelligence later implies that it plans to seize Earth afterwards ('your knowledge of the past will help to shape the future of this planet').

Doctor Who?: The villain comments that the Doctor's 'mind surpasses that of all other creatures'. Quite a compliment, coming from a creature that calls itself the Great Intelligence.

Science/Magic: When faced with the prospect of having his brain drained, the Doctor takes advantage of the sci-fi rule that clearly states that most hi-tech devices feature two wires that can be swapped over in order to reverse the device's function.

Things Fall Apart: The first scene sees Travers trying to buy back his Yeti from Silverstein, a disgracefully stereotypical covetous Jew; worse still, he is specifically punished for being covetous. If the Intelligence is controlling Arnold all along, why doesn't it do more with him? Unlocking the Goodge Street fortress from the inside and spiriting the Doctor away wouldn't be that difficult, surely.

Availability: Only Episode 1 survives, along with almost a minute's worth of clips from later episodes. This material was issued on

2004's *Lost in Time* DVD (BBCDVD 1353) and in a video set with the remaining episodes of **8**, 'The Reign of Terror', and **35**, 'The Faceless Ones' (BBCV 7335, WHV E1853). The full audio-only version is available on CD and MP3-CD (ISBN 0563553820 and 0563494182 respectively).

Verdict: 'I consider this to be a military matter.' By far the best of the Troughton-era 'base-under-siege' serials. It contains less substance than, say, **39**, 'The Ice Warriors' but sustains itself more effectively over six episodes because the tension is there, in the writing and (on the evidence of what visual material remains) the direction. This distracts viewers from the slow pace and simple (though commendably original) conclusion. Haisman and Lincoln wisely choose to have the Doctor land when the invasion is already under way, establishing the eerie atmosphere of a deserted London from the first episode, and the showpiece battle sequence in Episode 4 is well placed.

This atmosphere of the menace attacking somewhere 'real', assisted by some excellent Underground sets, is the story's first trump card (borrowed from the deck used by the 1958 TV serial *Quatermass and the Pit*). The second is the way that its grimness is tempered with wit. The scene where smug journalist Chorley (who bears the slightest passing resemblance to David Frost) records a soldier's dying screams from the other end of a telephone displays wonderfully black humour. Anne's sly dismissal of the soldiers' sexism is also noteworthy, given *Doctor Who*'s often cringe-inducing approach to feminism in later stories.

42
Fury from the Deep

Episode 1: 16 March 1968
Episode 2: 23 March 1968
Episode 3: 30 March 1968
Episode 4: 6 April 1968
Episode 5: 13 April 1968
Episode 6: 20 April 1968

Written by Victor Pemberton
Directed by Hugh David

Notable Cast: This is Deborah Watling's last serial as Victoria. Her leaving is given a lot of screen time – the threat is resolved ten minutes before the end of the last episode, with the rest given over to Victoria's departure.

Writer: Victor Pemberton was story editor on **37**, 'The Tomb of the Cybermen', and had a minor acting role in **33**, 'The Moonbase'. He went on to write *Timeslip* (1970), act as a consultant on Jim Henson's *Fraggle Rock* (1983–87) and write historical novels.

Doctor Who?: The Doctor is susceptible to the effect of tranquilliser darts. He carries a stethoscope, and a sonic screwdriver – a slim device that can unscrew a bolt with sound waves. The Doctor is adventurous, thinking that getting into trouble, running from one crisis to another, is 'the spice of life'. He's obsessed with boys' toys, eager to try flying a helicopter – although he grasps the basics, his piloting skills leave a lot to be desired. His only responsibility is to his friends: when Victoria confesses that she wishes that they could arrive somewhere peaceful, the Doctor realises that she will be leaving him soon. The Doctor is sensitive about letting Victoria make her own decision, but says that he and Jamie will stay another day in case she changes her mind – highly unusual, as the Doctor usually sneaks away unnoticed during this period.

History 101: A Euro Sea Gas power plant on the English coast, some time in the future. Gas from beneath the sea, piped up by offshore rigs, is an important power source, and the pipelines are subject to sabotage. The plant provides power for the south of England and Wales.

Scary Monsters: Killer seaweed that produces foam and poisonous gas, and is thriving by feeding on the North Sea gas that the humans are pumping. The weed stings humans, taking parasitic control of them. It makes an odd heartbeat noise, and records of its existence are in an eighteenth-century textbook of the Doctor's.

Villains: Mr Oak and Mr Quill, servants of the weed and rather polite maintenance men. They're a typical odd couple – one tall and thin, one small and round. They can exhale poison gas, and act as saboteurs on the weed's behalf.

The Plan: The weed is taking over the rigs to form one large colony, as a spearhead for attacking the UK – and perhaps after that the world.

Science/Magic: The Doctor knows the weed is alive when he finds 'molecular movement' in a sample. Having discovered that the weed is susceptible to sonic attack, the Doctor builds an amplifier to direct sound at the encroaching weed.

Things Fall Apart: The scene where the travellers have a foam fight is risibly reminiscent of bad children's variety shows featuring 'gunk'. The possessed humans have sprigs of weed sticking out of their cuffs, which makes them look more like scarecrows than the victims of an alien parasite. Episode 6 – the point where the drama should be reaching its peak – is undermined by an endless comedy scene where the Doctor badly pilots a helicopter.

Availability: The serial has been destroyed, but eight clips totalling two minutes and fifteen seconds still exist. This is on *Lost in Time* (BBCDVD 1353). Issued on CD as ISBN 0563524103.

Verdict: 'It's down there, in the darkness – waiting.' An odd premise for a story – killer seaweed – provides some very creepy moments, but also interminable *longueurs* between those moments. At its best, 'Fury from the Deep' is downright disturbing, but for long stretches the story is preoccupied with tiresome politicking between the characters who run the power plant. The Doctor and his friends take too long to get involved in the main plot, which develops slowly over the first few episodes and focuses on a bland set of guest characters. In the later episodes there is some random action that fails to add any tension, and the earlier tension devolves into foam-machine overkill. On the plus side, there are some very nice interchanges between the Doctor, Jamie and Victoria, with a clear character reason for Victoria's departure, one that highlights why the Doctor is compelled to get involved in these adventures. It's a shame that you have to wade through so much (foam) padding to get to these oases of good stuff.

43
The Wheel in Space

Episode 1: 27 April 1968
Episode 2: 4 May 1968
Episode 3: 11 May 1968
Episode 4: 18 May 1968
Episode 5: 25 May 1968
Episode 6: 1 June 1968

Written by David Whitaker (from a story by Kit Pedler)
Directed by Tristan De Vere Cole

Director: Tristan De Vere Cole later directed episodes of Terry Nation's *Survivors* (1975), *Kessler* (1981) and *Bergerac* (1980–89).

Doctor Who?: The Doctor is a 'known and recorded' enemy of the Cybermen. He acquires the alias 'John Smith' when Jamie needs to give W3's medical crew a name. He continues to use it for as long as he's been using 'Doctor' up to now (see **1**, 'An Unearthly Child', **51**, 'Spearhead from Space', **70**, 'The Time Warrior'), thus it's arguably as valid as 'the Doctor' or 'Doctor Who' as a name for the character. He believes logic merely allows one to be 'wrong with authority' and noticeably flirts with Dr Gemma Corwyn (Anne Ridler).

Scary Monsters: The Cybermen hatch out of eggs and are directed by a 'Cyber Planner', which looks like a talking plum in a vice. They have the power to ionise a star. 'More robot than man' and 'ruthless, inhuman killers', they have 'a need to colonise' and must have 'Earth's treasures'.

The Plan: The Cybermen's plan comes in six stages: (1) Cybermats gain access to the W3; (2) Cybermen on *Silver Carrier* hatch; (3) Star Hercules 208 destroyed in order to cause meteorite problems for W3, (4) Cybermats consume bernalium aboard W3; (5) bernalium crates (actually containing Cybermen) brought over from *Silver Carrier* to replace that eaten; (6) Cybermen take control of Wheel and use radio beam to guide their invasion army to Earth. In practice the Cybermen's plan requires that *Silver Carrier* not be destroyed by W3's laser (which happens only because of Jamie's signalling W3 and later sabotage), that Jarvis Bennet be mentally unstable and that the crew not tell one another anything about what's happening.

History 101: The year is not specified (see **45**, 'The Mind Robber' and **50**, 'The War Games': references to Jet Heliports and the costumes imply it's contemporary to Whitaker's **40**, 'The Enemy of the World'. 'The Wheel' is W3, one of (at least) five satellites between Earth and the moon (the position Zoe gives for the Wheel relative to Venus is virtually that of Earth relative to Venus, thus the Wheel is in Earth's orbit). No one has heard of Cybermen (and Zoe hasn't heard of Daleks). Indeed, the crew seem unaware of extraterrestrials. Spaceships are referred to as 'rockets' throughout. W3 is equipped with an X-ray laser (powered by bernalium, although the Doctor substitutes the TARDIS's Time Vector Generator when that runs out; conveniently it fits perfectly) and is a repair and traffic control station, a radio and visual relay station, and an early-warning station for solar phenomena.

Science/Magic: The TARDIS 'fault indicator' is now on the console. The fluid link (see **2**, 'The Daleks') breaks and again mercury is needed to fill it. The TARDIS tries to warn the crew not to disembark on *Silver Carrier* by showing images of more pleasant places to visit. Space is treated as if it were water throughout, with talk about how much fuel is needed to traverse a certain distance (with no friction in space a burst of energy creates momentum that sustains indefinitely). Hyper-oxide (a spray-on plastic that comes in cans) is stronger than steel. Placing a small piece of metal with a transistor taped to it on the back of someone's neck prevents them from being controlled by Cybermen (!).

Availability: The two extant episodes (3 and 6) were included on 2004's *Lost in Time* DVD (BBCDVD 1353) and *Cybermen – The Early Years* (BBCV 4813, WHV E1104). Fourteen seconds' worth of clips exists from the destroyed episodes. The audio-only version on CD is ISBN 0563535075.

Verdict: 'All spacemen are protected against brain control by drugs.' A clash between Whitaker's mercurial approach to *Doctor Who* and the clichés of the era, 'The Wheel in Space' is deeply unsatisfactory. Typical Whitaker elements are featured, such as a pronounced faith in intuition over logic and a young couple realising a mutual attraction, and there's some whimsical dialogue ('flowers of Venus'). However, the banal staples of the era (the isolated base, the unstable authoritarian, the emotionless motiveless monsters and an Earth-invasion plot) are all present. Wendy Padbury's bright debut as astrophysicist/librarian Zoe (who stows away in the TARDIS at the end) is the only endearing aspect. The Doctor gets knocked unconscious in Episode 1 and remains so throughout Episode 2 while Troughton has a week off. The audience can only feel envious.

44

The Dominators

Episode 1: 10 August 1968
Episode 2: 17 August 1968

Episode 3: 24 August 1968
Episode 4: 31 August 1968
Episode 5: 7 September 1968

Written by Norman Ashby
Directed by Morris Barry

Notable Cast: Ronald Allen (Rago) was Mr Hunter, owner of, and lead in, *Crossroads* (1968–87). Brian Cant previously appeared in **21**, 'The Dalek's Masterplan'.

Writer: 'Norman Ashby' is a pseudonym for Mervyn Haisman and Henry Lincoln (**38**, 'The Abominable Snowmen' and **41**, 'The Web of Fear'), who fell out with the production team over heavy edits to the story (the scripts were cut down to trim the story from six episodes to five). Haisman and Lincoln never worked on the series again.

Other Worlds: Dulkis, a peaceful planet inhabited by a society of indolent pacifists, the Dulcians. Its 'island of death' is a former nuclear test site kept intact for 172 years as an example of the horrors of atomic weaponry.

Villains: The titular Dominators, towering humanoids with large shoulder pads, who are engaged in a constant campaign of war. They do not believe in waste, and will use local populations as slaves if possible. The Dominators are either 'masters of the ten galaxies', or rule 'a whole galaxy', depending on what scene it is.

Scary Monsters: The Quarks, diminutive boxy robots that serve the Dominators and talk in incomprehensible little-girl voices.

The Plan: The Dominators wish to drill through the crust of the planet, detonating the magma and turning Dulkis into a ball of molten radioactive waste. The radiation will then act as a power source for the Dominators' war fleet. If possible, the Dominators wish to gather slaves for their war effort while they're at it, but they decide the Dulcians are too weak.

Doctor Who?: The Doctor thinks he and his friends need a holiday. The Doctor has been to Dulkis before, and thinks it's wonderful. He doesn't hesitate to blow the Dominators to bits with their own bomb.

Science/Magic: The Dominators' 'molecular lock' can fix people in their place with a force field. The Quarks operate on ultrasonics.

The Doctor's sonic screwdriver can cut through a wall, if adjusted correctly. The Doctor makes bombs with some medical supplies.

Things Fall Apart: The Dulcian costumes are appalling toga-like affairs, and the actors playing them are pretty bad throughout. Like the writers' other creations, the Yeti, the Quarks are just too cute to be scary.

Availability: Issued on VHS in 1990 as BBCV 4406 (UK), WHV E1264 (US).

Verdict: 'Submission leads to slavery. We must fight.' *Doctor Who* can be many things, but 'The Dominators' exhibits one quality that the series could do without: meanness of spirit. The script has little time for hippies, pacifists, intellectuals and others it deems 'weak', and spends most of its length scoring cheap points against them. While it would be going too far to say that 'The Dominators' is actually fascistic, there's something unpleasant in this humourless mockery of the Dulcians, using the bullying, sadistic Dominators to prove their way of life wrong.

There's a good dynamic going on between the Doctor and Jamie, with Patrick Troughton and Frazer Hines engaging in their usual banter, but all the secondary characters are ciphers intended to make crude political points. No fun at all.

45
The Mind Robber

Episode 1: 14 September 1968
Episode 2: 21 September 1968
Episode 3: 28 September 1968
Episode 4: 5 October 1968
Episode 5: 12 October 1968

Written by Peter Ling (2–5)
Directed by David Maloney

Writer: Peter Ling was the producer/creator of soap *Crossroads* (1964–88) and wrote episodes of *The Avengers* (1961–63) and *Sexton Blake* (1968). Script editor Derrick Sherwin (see **41**, 'The Web of Fear'), not Ling, wrote Episode 1, but no writer is credited on the finished piece.

Notable Cast: Bernard Horsfall (Gulliver) can be seen in *On Her Majesty's Secret Service* (Peter Hunt, 1969).

Director: David Maloney would become *Doctor Who*'s second most prolific director. Latterly he was the producer of *Blake's 7* (1978–80), *When the Boat Comes In* (1981) and *Day of the Triffids* (1981).

Doctor Who?: The Doctor is unsure whether the TARDIS can survive being immersed in lava. Amusingly, he can't bring himself to admit that it's his fault that Jamie's face changes when he loses one of the Master's games.

Other Worlds: The Doctor activates the TARDIS's 'Emergency Unit', which moves the ship out of the time–space dimension and into 'a dimension about which we know nothing'. Initially the travellers are in an empty white void and later find themselves wandering across the pages of book of proverbs before encountering a black void, a labyrinth at the end of which is a castle on a huge rock. Zoe describes her home as 'the City' and implies she is from the year 2000.

Villains: The Master (Emrys Jones), although not the one who'll become a familiar fixture from **55**, 'Terror of the Autons', onwards. This 'Master' is a children's fiction author from the early part of the twentieth century who fell asleep at his desk and woke up to find himself enslaved by a vast computer ('the Master Brain'), which utilises his knowledge of myth and literature and his inventiveness to populate the area around it. (It seems that the computer area and the White Robots are real – everything else is the product of the Master's imagination – which is why only the Robots continue to exist after the Master is removed from the system.) We never discover the origin of the Master Brain and its servile robots.

Scary Monsters: The Minotaur, a savage unicorn, life-sized clockwork soldiers and Medusa are all conjured up by the Master. The serial also features the Karkus, a Teutonic super-antihero whose comic-strip adventures are featured in *The Hourly Telepress* in the year 2000.

The Plan: The Master Brain has drawn the Doctor to it (it is aware of him and his travels) so that he can replace the aged Master. The Master will inevitably eventually die, whereas the Doctor is 'ageless'. Rather disappointingly, the Master Brain later reveals that it intends to occupy Earth. Just like everything else.

Science/Magic: The TARDIS's 'fluid links' break down, leading to vaporisation of the mercury within them (see 2, 'The Daleks'). The TARDIS power room is immediately next to the console room – it doesn't have roundels and is never seen before or after this story. Either Jamie has a precognitive dream or the Master can pluck ideas out of the heads of the sleeping. If a real person is in the Master's domain and they do something that has been written about beforehand, they turn into fictional character and come under the Master's control. The Karkus carries an 'anti-molecular ray disintegrator', which the Doctor comments is scientifically impossible.

Availability: The 1990 VHS release is BBCV 4352 (UK), WHV E1200 (US). The DVD was scheduled for early 2005.

Verdict: 'After some consideration I was of the opinion that this was altogether impossible.' Not so much 'surreal' as determinedly peculiar, 'The Mind Robber' is also whimsical and witty, and alternates rapidly between disturbing and charming. It skilfully uses wordplay, the archetypes of children's fiction and conceptual juxtapositions to move its simple 'exploring' plot onwards. The Doctor encounters a variety of mythical and fictional characters including – wonderfully – Lemuel Gulliver, who can speak only in quotations from *Gulliver's Travels*. The programme wouldn't ever dare to be quite this strange again – and it wouldn't even try for almost exactly twenty years. Emrys Jones is brilliant as the schizophrenic Master. Conceptually, if not actually, the first post-*Sgt Pepper Doctor Who* serial 'The Mind Robber' is also easily the best Troughton story.

46
The Invasion

Episode One: 2 November 1968
Episode Two: 9 November 1968
Episode Three: 16 November 1968
Episode Four: 23 November 1968
Episode Five: 30 November 1968
Episode Six: 7 December 1968

Episode Seven: 14 December 1968
Episode Eight: 21 December 1986

Written by Derrick Sherwin (from an idea by Kit Pedler)
Directed by Douglas Camfield

Notable Cast: Kevin Stoney (Tobias Vaughn) previously appeared in **21**, 'The Daleks' Master Plan'. Peter Halliday (Packer), in addition to numerous film roles, played Dr John Fleming on TV in *A For Andromeda* (1961) and *The Andromeda Breakthrough* (1962) and appeared numerous times in *Doctor Who* including in **105**, 'City of Death' and **149**, 'Remembrance of the Daleks'. John Levene (Benton) would return to the role regularly over the next seven years.

Script Editor: Terrance Dicks is a major creative player within *Doctor Who*. He remained script editor until and including **74**, 'Planet of the Spiders' (excluding **49**, 'The Space Pirates') and wrote six serials (see the index). A successful producer of television adaptations (including *The Diary of Anne Frank* (1987) and *David Copperfield* (1986)) and an extraordinarily prolific novelist, he adapted more than sixty *Doctor Who* serials into children's books between 1973 and 1990 and has written as many other books again. These range from other children's novels to adult thrillers and books on television production.

Scary Monsters: The Cybermen return (their fifth appearance in a little over two years). They don't appear much, but Bobi Bartlett's design is possibly the most effective ever used in the series: it's not elaborate and gives a good impression of fortitude.

History 101: The date is never specified, but it's intended to be a near-future Earth (and a BBC announcement before the first episode stated it's 1975). Lethbridge-Stewart places the events of **41**, 'The Web of Fear' as being about four years before, and this Earth is more technologically advanced than 1968 (although this is arguably because International Electromatics has access to Cyber technology). Lethbridge-Stewart (again played by Nicholas Courtney) has been promoted to Brigadier and placed in charge of the British wing of an international military organisation created to investigate strange happenings: UNIT.

Villains: Tobias Vaughn, director of International Electromatics, who is in league with the Cybermen. In terms of motivation he's your basic megalomaniac (believes that individuals are weak, a strong leader is required, etc.), but Kevin Stoney brings a sinister charm to the part. He also has a great rapport with Peter Halliday, which almost papers over the implausibility that the efficiency-obsessed Vaughn would continue to employ the hapless Packer as his head of security. (Did Vaughn promise Mrs Packer on her deathbed that there'd always be a job for her son at IE?)

The Plan: Vaughn has been placing micro-monolithic circuits in all of IE's equipment. When activated, these produce a hypnotic signal that will immobilise humans and allow the Cybermen to invade Earth. However, Vaughn plans to double-cross the Cybermen: he has kidnapped electronics expert Professor Watkins to build a machine that can induce emotions in its subject. Emotions are alien to the Cybermen and destroy the creatures' nervous systems. As a method of killing Cybermen this makes a lot more sense than some others we've seen.

Science/Magic: When the Cyber-fleet is decimated on its way to Earth, the Cyber Planner announces that 'the Cyber-Megatron Bomb will be delivered'. This will 'destroy life on Earth completely'. The Cybermen still depend on radio waves to land (see **43**, 'The Wheel in Space', etc.).

Doctor Who?: Troughton's comedy jumping in Episode Eight is either hilarious or a bit silly, depending on whom you ask.

Things Fall Apart: The recapture of Professor Watkins by UNIT happens off camera, which could have been better disguised by not placing the scene of Captain Turner planning the recapture directly before the scene where Gregory relates it to Vaughn. The first victim of the hypnotic signal stops walking when he hears it, but the sound of his footfalls keeps going.

Availability: Episodes One and Four of 'The Invasion' no longer exist in the BBC archives, but film prints of the other six survive. These were released on VHS (BBCV 4974, WHV E1273) in 1993. The audio-only version is available on CD (ISBN 0563535088).

Verdict: 'Is this what you wanted? To be the ruler of a dead world?' One of the slickest serials to date, 'The Invasion' refines the template laid down by **27**, 'The War Machines', **35**, 'The Faceless Ones', and **41**, 'The Web of Fear', to create something that loses some of the sense of wonder present in much black-and-white *Doctor Who* but which can be achieved with no small amount of style. It benefits from a vast amount of location filming, during which Douglas Camfield indulges his fantasies of directing James Bond or Harry Palmer.

There are some blemishes, notably the cringeworthy battle-of-the-sexes stuff between Isobel and Lethbridge-Stewart (the main problem being that Isobel's subsequent failure endorses his sexist attitude) and Vaughn's not-quite-watertight plan (why is he still working on his plot to betray the Cybermen right up until the day of the invasion?). The quality of the production and performances (Troughton and Hines have never been better) overcome all, making this the best Cyberman story.

47
The Krotons

Episode One: 28 December 1968
Episode Two: 4 January 1969
Episode Three: 11 January 1969
Episode Four: 18 January 1969

Written by Robert Holmes
Directed by David Maloney

Notable Cast: Welshman Philip Madoc (Eelek) was born in 1954. He played the title role in TV's *The Life and Times of David Lloyd George* (1981) and starred in the detective drama *A Mind to Kill* (1994–97). He's made guest appearances in everything from *Dad's Army* (1973) to *Doctors* (2003) as well as playing *Cadfael* for Radio 4.

Writer: Former military officer, policeman and court reporter Robert Holmes was one of *Doctor Who*'s most prolific authors – contributing 64 episodes (three double-length). He was working on the conclusion to **144**, 'The Trial of a Time Lord', when he died (it was completed by other hands). He was script editor from **75**, 'Robot', to **94**, 'Image of the Fendahl'. Other television work includes episodes of *Blake's 7* (1979, 1981), *Juliet Bravo* (1982), *Dixon of Dock Green* (1974), *Doomwatch* (1971) and *Bergerac* (1983–87) and the acclaimed thriller serial *The Nightmare Man* (1981). He was the script editor of *Shoestring* (1980).

Doctor Who?: He claims he's 'not a doctor of medicine' and he demonstrates an ability to hypnotise people. Zoe considers the Doctor to be 'almost as clever' as she is. The Doctor dismisses the idea that the Gonds might practise human sacrifice because they are 'too civilised' (see **6**, 'The Aztecs').

Other Worlds: The unnamed planet on which the TARDIS arrives circles twin suns and the ground is largely composed of magnesium silicate. There's an unusually large amount of sulphur in the atmosphere. The Gond civilisation, centred on one city, is referred to as 'the Community' and governed by a council, which votes on propositions (it is unclear whether the council is itself elected by the population, but leadership of it is hereditary). Dogs are mentioned but not seen.

Scary Monsters: The Krotons – crystalline entities in an organic spaceship, the 'Dynotrope', which has grown a 'root structure' to anchor itself physically into the planet. They are immortal with a life system based on tellurium (atomic weight 128). 'Complete Obedience' is the Krotons' first law (see **History 101**).

Villains: Eelek, a power-grabbing schemer keen on using war with the Krotons to further his own ends, and also Council Leader Selris, a reactionary old autocrat primarily interested in protecting his own power.

History 101: Thousands of years before the story a Kroton spaceship was damaged in battle. Two of the four Kroton crew were killed, so the surviving two initiated an 'emergency procedure' by landing on the nearest planet and putting the Dynotrope into 'perpetual stability' mode and themselves into hibernation. They set their machine systems to educate the indigenous life. Ever since then, every so often the two brightest students (the current class is V1926) have been sent into the Dynotrope ostensibly to become the companions of the Krotons. In fact their mental powers are turned into energy, which is then used to attempt to revive the two Krotons and power their ship for its return flight.

Science/Magic: The Krotons' 'teaching machines' have a soporific effect on those who use them (including the Doctor and Zoe), making the examinee happy to have pleased their masters. The Krotons' education of the Gonds is selective – they have a good knowledge of medicine and use solar power for lighting – but they have no knowledge of chemistry, since this may give them clues as to how to fight the Krotons. The Krotons quiz Jamie about the TARDIS's 'transference interval'.

Availability: Released on VHS in 1991 as BBCV 4452 (UK), WHV E1266 (US).

Verdict: 'We only know what the Krotons tell us. We don't *think*, we obey.' A story concerned with the withholding of information from the population and the lengths those with power will go to in order to hold onto it, 'The Krotons' is well directed and atmospheric with cool monsters and great sound effects. A much smarter (and infinitely less padded) story than the series' then current norms, 'The Krotons' is, like the preceding two serials, a fine example of *Doctor Who*'s creative renaissance after the wretched, formulaic lows of much of 1967.

48
The Seeds of Death

Episode One: 25 January 1969
Episode Two: 1 February 1969
Episode Three: 8 February 1969
Episode Four: 15 February 1969
Episode Five: 22 February 1969
Episode Six: 1 March 1969

Written by Brian Hayles
Directed by Michael Ferguson

Notable Cast: Ronald Leigh-Hunt (Radnor) was King Arthur in *The Adventures of Sir Lancelot* (1956–7) amongst many other TV credits. Christopher Coll (Phipps) was Victor Pendlebury, Mavis Riley's earnest suitor in *Coronation Street*.

History 101: Earth, the near future. All other forms of transport have been superseded by T-Mat, a matter-transmission network controlled from a moon base. All rocket programmes were abandoned, leaving Professor Eldred (Philip Ray), son of the man who engineered 'the first lunar passenger module', as a lone enthusiast designing rockets. T-Mat has made life easy, and no one is interested in space exploration or adventure any more.

Scary Monsters: The titular Martian monsters from **39**, 'The Ice Warriors'. This group of Ice Warriors has a leader notable for his smaller, less heavily armoured body and huge curved helmet. The Grand Marshal of the Ice Warrior space fleet looks similar, but has spangly bits of glitter on his helmet. The Ice Warriors are vulnerable to heat, and can be killed with bursts of solar energy.

The Plan: The Ice Warriors intend to use T-Mat (short for 'Travelmat') to transmit seeds to earth, each of which explodes, releasing a gas that causes a foamlike fungus to spread across the area, growing at vast speed. The fungus will strip Earth's atmosphere of oxygen, making it lethal to humans but ideal for the Ice Warriors, allowing them to invade and colonise.

Science/Magic: The characters have an unusual retroactive attitude to the space age (still very big news when this story was broadcast), with contemporary rockets regarded nostalgically as relics of a long-gone age, compared with the boring efficiency of T-Mat. The TARDIS is not suitable for short-range travel, and, if the Doctor tried to hop to the moon, it would overshoot either in time or space. Anyone too near the seeds when they burst dies from oxygen starvation in seconds.

Doctor Who?: The Doctor is fascinated with rocket technology. The Doctor survives the bursting of a seed in front of him, an event that kills any human. However, it does leave him unconscious for an episode. The Doctor has no compunction about destroying Ice Warriors with bursts of solar energy, and actively hunts them down in the last episode. His plan to defeat the invasion involves letting the entire fleet fly into the sun. So, a kill-frenzy all round.

Things Fall Apart: The 'action' music in the story is hammering and melodramatic, reminiscent of silent-film cliché. There are a couple of extended slapstick chase scenes, including a strange, semi-comedic one in which the Ice Warriors pursue the Doctor through endless corridors, including a hall of mirrors. Then there's the return of the foam machine from **42**, 'Fury from the Deep', with another interminable scene of the Doctor messing about in the bubbles.

Availability: Issued on Region 2 DVD in 2003 as BBCDVD 1151, and on Region 1 DVD as WHV E1924. VHS is WHV E1112 (US) and VHS BBCV 2019 (UK).

Verdict: 'Your leader will be angry if you kill me – I'm a genius.' Large sets, good lighting and inventive direction from Michael Ferguson bring a rare sense of scale and style to this story, which zips from the Earth to the moon and back. There's some clever use of first-person perspective in Episode One, where we see the attack on the moon entirely from the perspective of the Ice Warriors, and other signs of directorial flair can be seen throughout. Unfortunately, the sense of drama engendered by this higher standard of direction is undermined by some ill-thought-out comedic scenes, and signs of script padding (the story was rewritten from four episodes to six). The Doctor is unusually bloodthirsty, building weapons to destroy the Ice Warriors and hunting them down. 'The Seeds of Death' is slicker than most black-and-white stories, and is certainly entertaining, but it's a slightly soulless and brutal affair.

49
The Space Pirates

Episode One: 8 March 1969
Episode Two: 15 March 1969
Episode Three: 22 March 1969
Episode Four: 29 March 1969
Episode Five: 5 April 1969
Episode Six: 12 April 1969

Written by Robert Holmes
Directed by Michael Hart

Notable Cast: Gordon Gostelow (Milo Clancy) appeared in *Elizabeth R* (1971) and *Anna Karenina* (1977), and played Bardolph in the BBC's *Henry IV Part I* and *Henry V* (1979). Jack May (General Hermack) played Nelson Gabriel in *The Archers* between 1951 and 1997, was a regular in *Adam Adamant Lives!* (1966) and voiced Igor in *Count Duckula* (1988–93). George Layton (Ian Warne) appeared in *It Ain't Half Hot Mum* (1974–81) and much light TV comedy.

Director: Michael Hart's other TV work includes *Nowhere to Hide* (1968) and *Raven* (1977).

History 101: Some time in the future, humans have spread out into deep space, with prospectors staking claims to mineral-rich planets and setting up mining operations. In recent decades the Space Corps has established law and order in these areas, much to the chagrin of old-fashioned miners like Milo Clancy.

Science/Magic: Practically everything these days is made from an element known as argonite: its strength makes it particularly desirable for constructing spaceships.

The Plan: Pirates have been blowing up unmanned space beacons, then using strategically planted rockets to guide the pieces to a covert collection point where they strip them for their argonite content. General Hermack of the Space Corps posts his men on board the beacons and orders them to shoot any pirates on sight, which has unfortunate repercussions when the TARDIS lands on Beacon Alpha Four.

Other Worlds: The pirates are operating from the mining planet Ta, owned by Madeline Issigri (Lisa Daniely) – daughter of Clancy's some time business partner Dom. Madeline originally became involved with the pirates for salvage deals, but events have spiralled out of her control.

Villains: The pirates are led by Caven (Dudley Foster), who is, er, a pirate. There really isn't much more to his character than that.

Doctor Who?: Ever a hit with the ladies, Troughton's Doctor receives a kiss on the cheek from Madeline at the end.

Things Fall Apart: It's pathetically obvious that Madeline, rather than Clancy, is in league with the pirates. Hermack notes that she has just acquired two Beta Darts, and that the pirates are using the very same type of ship for their raids. He even points out that Clancy doesn't seem wealthy enough to afford one. Yet Hermack still suspects Clancy on the strength of a small amount of circumstantial evidence. That said, Gordon Gostelow is awful as Clancy (he rewrote a lot of his own dialogue to make it more 'in character' – nothing to be proud of there).

Availability: Only Episode Two still exists, a film recording having been preserved as an example of *Doctor Who*'s sixth season. This was issued on 2004's *Lost in Time* DVD (BBCDVD 1353) and the VHS *The Troughton Years* (BBCV 4609, WHV E1097). Ninety seconds of material from Episode One has also been located and is also on the DVD. The audio-only version of the serial is available on CD (ISBN 0563535059).

Verdict: 'Rubbishy new-fangled solar toasters!' You know things are wrong with 'The Space Pirates' when you reach the halfway point of the first episode and none of the regular characters have appeared. The roles played by the Doctor, Jamie and Zoe are small: largely they are thrown into dangerous situations while remaining fairly passive. This kind of story can work – see Holmes's own **135**, 'The Caves of Androzani', for a prime example – but the pace needs to be quicker, the supporting characters more engaging and the backdrop far more interesting than what we see here. Although it makes a creditable attempt to cope without monsters, 'The Space Pirates' is stuffed with stock characters and situations and feels very tired.

It's a strong contender for the most padded *Doctor Who* story: nearly all of the Space Corps scenes are unnecessary, as Hermack and his men achieve so little in between explaining the plot to each other (and they don't even meet the Doctor). We should explore each new time and place in conjunction with the Doctor and his friends, but 'The Space Pirates' isolates them and consequently encounters dreadful exposition problems. The production is lifted by some excellent music and groovy design, but in all other respects is forgettable.

50
The War Games

Episode One: 19 April 1969
Episode Two: 26 April 1969
Episode Three: 3 May 1969
Episode Four: 10 May 1969
Episode Five: 17 May 1969
Episode Six: 24 May 1969
Episode Seven: 31 May 1969
Episode Eight: 7 June 1969
Episode Nine: 14 June 1969
Episode Ten: 21 June 1969

Written by Terrance Dicks and Malcolm Hulke
Directed by David Maloney

Notable Cast: Bernard Horsfall (First Time Lord) was in **45**, 'The Mind Rober'. Trevor Martin (Second Time Lord) played Doctor Who on stage in Terrance Dicks' play *Doctor Who and the Daleks in Seven Keys to Doomsday* (1974). Philip Madoc (War Lord) appeared in **47**, 'The Krotons' whilst Edward Brayshaw (War Chief) was in **8**, 'The Reign of Terror'. Leslie Schofield (Leroy) plays Chief Bast in *Star Wars* (George Lucas, 1977) but is more recognisable from his many TV roles, including *Johnny Briggs* (1985–87) and *EastEnders* (two different roles, 1988 and 1997–2000). Rudolph Walker (Grant) starred in *Love Thy Neighbour* and plays Patrick Trueman in *EastEnders*. Despite these credits he's a superb actor with a fantastic reputation. He makes the most of his minimal screen time here.

History 101: The TARDIS arrives on the Western Front, between the German and British lines, near Ypres. It is 1917, yet Jamie meets a Redcoat who hours before was fighting the Scots in 1745. The Doctor escapes from the British Army – which has convicted him of espionage – and finds himself being attacked by Roman legionnaires (see **The Plan**). There are eleven Zones on the map of the War Games. Zones seen or mentioned include the 1917 Zone, a 1745 Jacobite Rebellion Zone, a Roman Zone, an 1862 American Civil War Zone, an English Civil War Zone, an 1871 Crimean War Zone, a Mexican Civil War Zone, a 1905 Russo-Japanese War Zone, a 30 Years War Zone, a Greek Zone, a Boer War Zone and a Peninsular War Zone. This is – as you may have noticed – more than eleven.

The Plan: On an unnamed planet the Aliens are conducting the titular War Games. These recreate wars throughout human history using captured (and mentally conditioned) soldiers. The aim is to use the battle-hardened survivors to create an army to conquer the galaxy.

Villains: The War Lord is a softly spoken maniac in pebble glasses. His deputy, the War Chief, is a Time Lord whose technical knowledge has made the whole enterprise possible. The Security Chief (James Bree) is a stentorian, racist midget locked in a bitter power struggle with the War Chief. 'General Smythe' (Noel Coleman) is a bloodthirsty Alien in charge of the British troops in the 1917 Zone. His German counterpart is the lip-smacking 'Von Weich' (David Garfield) – who also serves as a Confederate captain in the American Civil War Zone.

Science/Magic: The various Zones are separated from each other by a mist, which the conditioned humans cannot cross. The War Chief's 'space–time travel machines' are bigger on the inside than the outside. They are referred to (although only once, in Episode Seven) as SIDRATs. Unlike the TARDIS, they can be operated remotely, but have a limited life span. The Security Chief has a vaguely pyramid-shaped face mask-cum-helmet, which forces people looking at him to tell the truth. In Episode Eight the Doctor's ship is referred to as '*a* TARDIS' rather than '*the* TARDIS'. From now on all Time Lord time machines will be referred to as 'TARDISes' and this becomes, effectively, the name of the technology rather than that of the Doctor's ship.

Doctor Who?: It's in Episode Six that the term 'Time Lord' is first used, but even then they're people the War Chief has fled from rather than anything to do with the Doctor. It's only in Episode Eight that the audience is told that the Doctor and the War Chief are of the same race. Their people 'live for ever, barring accidents'. The War Chief recognises the Doctor (and knows him by that alias) but not from his physical appearance. It transpires that they were both Time Lords and both 'decided to leave our race'.

It's unclear whether the War Chief has met the Doctor before or merely knows of him. The Doctor maintains to the War Chief that he 'had every right to leave'. At the end of the story the task of returning all the kidnapped humans to their own times and places is too great for the Doctor and he sends a telepathic message (inside a cube, which he mentally constructs from pieces of metal).

'The War Games' portrays the Doctor as a kind of 'trickster' god among a vast, indolent pantheon – a meddler who ran away because he was bored and offended that his species hardly ever use their great powers. This is very different from the portrayal of Hartnell's Doctor as an exile fleeing some unspecified danger who is reluctant to interfere in anything.

Things Fall Apart: Most of the fistfights are badly choreographed. The number of dialogue fluffs increases as the story goes along – with actors interrupting one another at inappropriate moments.

Availability: Issued on VHS in 1990 as BBCV 4310 (UK), WHV E1095 (US). A WH Smith exclusive UK-only rerelease was BBCV 7563. This re-issue has better picture quality.

Verdict: 'Man is the most vicious species of all.' The early trench-based episodes are the first intrusion of historical grimness into *Doctor Who* for years. They give way to a pop-art epic that features laser-gun-wielding alien guards wearing leather catsuits and comedy glasses. This section, strangely, works equally well, albeit in a *totally* different way. The story turns its immense length to its advantage by showing the Aliens fighting among themselves and allowing the Doctor's struggle against them to suffer several reversals. The scale and nature of the problem presented to the Doctor at the end leads logically to his decision to call in the Time Lords and the performances of Troughton, Brayshaw and Madoc effectively convey the significance of this. Revelations about the Doctor's past in the last episode and a half change the nature of the series for ever, but they shouldn't be allowed to overshadow the rest of this terrific adventure story. Jamie and Zoe's departure is the most poignant since the loss of Ian and Barbara. A favourite.

51
Spearhead from Space

Episode 1: 3 January 1970
Episode 2: 10 January 1970
Episode 3: 17 January 1970
Episode 4: 24 January 1970

Written by Robert Holmes
Directed by Derek Martinus

Notable Cast: Jon Pertwee (1919–96) was best known for playing multiple roles in radio comedy, notably the long-running series *The Navy Lark* (1959–77). He also had his own variety series, *The Jon Pertwee Show*, on ITV in 1966. After leaving *Doctor Who* with **74**, 'Planet of the Spiders', he presented *Whodunnit* (1974–6) and was the eponymous *Worzel Gummidge* (1979–81, 1987–89). He toured as Doctor Who in the 1989 stage play *The Ultimate Adventure* and returned to the role four other times (see **129**, 'The Five Doctors', **157**, 'The Paradise of Death', **158**, 'Dimensions in Time', **159**, 'Doctor Who and the Ghosts of N-Space'). His autobiography comes in two volumes, *Moon Boots and Dinner Suits* and *I Am the Doctor*. He is listed in the *Dictionary of National Biography*. Caroline John (Dr Elizabeth Shaw) had played Ophelia in the first production of Tom Stoppard's *Rosencrantz and Guildenstern are Dead* (1968). John Woodnutt (Hibbert) played Sir Watkin Bassett in *Jeeves and Wooster* (1990–94).

Doctor Who?: The Doctor has been exiled to Earth and forced to undergo a change of appearance by the Time Lords. As in **30**, 'The Power of the Daleks', the process (not here, as there, referred to in terms of 'renewal') seems to be physically debilitating and initially to result in mental disorientation. Unlike the case in that earlier story, the Doctor's clothes don't change when his body does. He has two hearts and his blood is recognisably not that of a human being – the first time it's indicated that his basic physiology is not human. Many of his memories have been blocked, including some related to how to pilot the TARDIS (the TARDIS itself has also been tampered with). He has a tattoo on his right arm. By the end of the serial, the Doctor agrees to act as a scientific adviser to Lethbridge-Stewart of UNIT (see **46**, 'The Invasion') in exchange for materials and assistance in repairing the TARDIS. He uses the 'Dr John Smith' alias again. He now claims to be a doctor of 'practically everything'. The character is now credited as 'Doctor Who' (not 'Dr. Who' as before).

Scary Monsters: The Nestene consciousness – a telepathic space entity that has been colonising unsuspecting planets for a thousand million years. Their shock troops, the Autons, are six-foot plastic men, each with a gun built into his right hand. They have been created in a plastic factory at the Nestene's behest. The result is essentially a version of zombies that can be portrayed on teatime television.

The Plan: Conquest of Earth by the Nestene.

History 101: It's the late twentieth century – during the preceding ten years mankind has been pushing deeper and deeper into space. Sixties fashions vie for space with futuristic technology and deliberately space-age military uniforms. The production team intended the story – and subsequent ones – to be set in the 'near future'. It's unclear how much time has passed since 'The Invasion', for the Brigadier. (In **74**, 'Planet of the Spiders' he remembers it as 'months'.)

Science/Magic: The TARDIS doors will not open for anyone apart from the Doctor due to the ship's 'metabolism detector'. The Nestene spheres are made of neither thermosetting nor thermosoftening plastic and contain no polymer chains. Lasers, spectrographs, microprobes and lateral molecular rectifiers are all mentioned. The TARDIS is 'dimensionally transcendental'.

Other Worlds: The Doctor talks of 'the planet Delphon, where they communicate with their eyebrows'.

Availability: A DVD was released in 2001 as BBCDVD 1033 (Region 2), WHV E1163 (Region 1); the VHS was BBCV 5509 (UK), WHV E1163 (US). The American release is in omnibus format. Commercial releases of the serial remove a snippet of the record 'Oh Well' (Part One) by Fleetwood Mac for legal (and arguably aesthetic) reasons.

Verdict: 'All over the country window dummies coming alive – and attacking!' Slick, vivid and full of hallucinatory conviction, 'Spearhead from Space' builds on **46**, 'The Invasion', to reinvent *Doctor Who* as an action-adventure series with horror overtones, one with simple plots that dabble in contemporary issues and in which an eccentric, acerbic, well-meaning dandy is aided by the military in the foiling of said schemes. It's also one of the best-remembered *Doctor Who* stories. Seen now, it's both *very* 1960s (reflecting its production in the summer before transmission) and strangely timeless. It may be *the* archetypal *Doctor Who* story.

52
Doctor Who and the Silurians

Episode 1: 31 January 1970
Episode 2: 7 February 1970
Episode 3: 14 February 1970
Episode 4: 21 February 1970
Episode 5: 28 February 1970
Episode 6: 7 March 1970
Episode 7: 14 March 1970

Written by Malcolm Hulke
Directed by Timothy Combe

Notable Cast: Fulton Mackay (Dr Quinn) played Mr MacKay in *Porridge* (1973–78) and *Going Straight* (1978), and turned down the role of the Doctor when offered it in 1974. Paul Darrow (Captain Hawkins) played Avon in *Blake's 7* (1978–81). Geoffrey Palmer (Masters) is best known for the sitcoms *The Fall and Rise of Reginald Perrin* (1976–78), *Butterflies* (1978–83), and *As Time Goes By* (1992–2002). His film roles include *The Madness of King George* (Nicholas Hytner, 1994), *Mrs Brown* (John Madden, 1997) and the James Bond movie *Tomorrow Never Dies* (Roger Spottiswoode, 1997). Peter Miles (Dr Lawrence) has mixed stints in the Royal Shakespeare Company with much TV work including *Blake's 7* (1978–79) and *Survivors* (1975).

Director: Timothy Combe directed the 1975 movie *Ballet Shoes*, based on the novel by Noel Streatfield.

History 101: It is sometime after **51**, 'Spearhead from Space'. The Doctor is still on Earth. UNIT seems to have jurisdiction over energy matters, as the Brigadier is looking into mysterious power losses at an atomic research centre in the caves beneath Wenley Moor.

Two hundred million years before, the Silurian civilisation went into hibernation when a small planet threatened to collide with Earth. The planet was trapped in orbit, becoming the moon.

Scary Monsters: The Silurians, prehistoric reptilian humanoids hibernating beneath Wenley Moor. They're tall, with puckered faces and a third eye, which can be used as a sonic key, a cutting tool and a weapon. They use a dinosaur as a guard dog in the caves, which is controlled with a whistling noise that sounds like a rubbish truck reversing. The Silurians are not universally aggressive – some are scientists, who wish to study the humans before making any attack. All of them have wobbly heads.

The Plan: The Silurians are draining power from the research centre to revive more of their number from hibernation. While their leader agrees to try to find a peaceful solution, a rebellious subordinate who believes the Silurians should reclaim the Earth releases a virus to kill the humans, and then kills his leader. The Silurians seize the cyclotron to power a molecular disperser, which will clear the Van Allen belt around Earth, allowing radiation in through the atmosphere, which will kill humanity but not harm the Silurians.

Doctor Who?: The Doctor has a more compassionate attitude to other species than we've seen in a long time, always searching for a peaceful solution, and interested in what he can learn. He tries not to see the Silurians as necessarily monstrous, often interpreting their violent actions as being self-defence. He wants to make peaceful contact with the Silurians, and believes they can live in the parts of the world too hot and hostile for humans. He loses confidence when he can't find a cure for the Silurian virus. He condemns the Brigadier's blowing up the Silurian base as 'murder'.

The Doctor resists and resents the Brigadier's authority, but is happy to use that authority when it's useful. He hasn't been potholing for a long time, and has seen dinosaurs in their natural time period. The Doctor says his life has 'covered several thousand years'. He sings a musical version of Lewis Carroll's nonsense poem 'Jabberwocky', from *Through the Looking Glass* (1872). He's bought a yellow open-top vintage car and named it *Bessie*.

Science/Magic: A cyclotron is being used in research to develop a cheaper form of atomic energy. Humans have 'race memories' of the Silurians from their prehistoric ancestors.

Things Fall Apart: The dinosaur in the caves is pretty unconvincing. Carey Blyton's theme for the Silurian creatures seems to heavily use a kazoo.

Availability: Issued on VHS in the UK in 1993 as BBCV 4990, and in the US as WHV E1278.

Verdict: 'These creatures aren't just animals, they're an alien life form, as intelligent as we are.' For the first time in over three years, *Doctor Who* features an alien race who are more than just monsters. While a number of them are bloodthirsty, the Silurians do have a point when they say that Earth was theirs to start with, and that man is an occupying force. While it would be going too far to say that the Silurians are complex characters, they *do* have different personalities, putting them way ahead of the cannon fodder the Troughton Doctor faced. Malcolm Hulke's intelligent scripting builds up the pace as the story goes on, which means that by the end the viewer has forgotten how slow the first couple of episodes were. The story's peak, however, is clearly Episode 6, with director Timothy Combe shooting impressive scenes of death as the virus spreads to London. After that the final confrontation may seem a little lightweight, but at least Hulke has a final sting for his clever story.

53
The Ambassadors of Death

Episode 1: 21 March 1970
Episode 2: 28 March 1970
Episode 3: 4 April 1970
Episode 4: 11 April 1970
Episode 5: 18 April 1970
Episode 6: 25 April 1970
Episode 7: 2 May 1970

Written by David Whitaker
Directed by Michael Ferguson

Notable Cast: Ronald Allen (Ralph Cornish) appeared in **44**, 'The Dominators'.

Writer: Script editor Terrance Dicks, his assistant Trevor Ray and Malcolm Hulke (see **35**, 'The Faceless Ones') heavily rewrote Whitaker's scripts. Accordingly, the story demonstrates elements of all their approaches to *Doctor Who*. The erratic, intuitive, intensely moral Doctor, full of arcane knowledge and capable of sudden charm, is very much Whitaker's take on the character, but the unhinged, idealistic military villain and clueless government ministers are typical Hulke creations. Equally, having villains who plot against one another is pure Terrance Dicks.

Doctor Who?: The Doctor recognises the language in which the aliens transmit information but can't recall from where – a side effect from when his memory was tampered with (see **51**, 'Spearhead from Space'). He can make objects appear and disappear from his hands (objects too large for this to be a mere conjuring trick). He doesn't trust computers and thinks they're 'stupid things'. Pertwee's Doctor says 'Now listen to me' (which becomes something of a catchphrase) for the first time in Episode 1.

Scary Monsters: The unnamed, unexplained alien ambassadors thrive on radiation. They are from another galaxy, yet reached Mars before humanity – where they unexpectedly encountered Mars Probe 6.

The Plan: A xenophobic British Army faction arranges for alien ambassadors to come secretly to Earth. They then kidnap them – all part of a conspiracy to reveal the existence of these 'hostile' aliens to the public.

History 101: The series continues to use its odd 'near-future' setting. Cornish's suit is *very* 1970, but his assistant wears a wacky silver mini-dress with a Nehru collar. The British space programme reached Mars long enough ago for the current mission to be Mars Probe 7 (and the round trip takes at least fourteen months).

Science/Magic: The Doctor is trying to reactivate the TARDIS's Time Vector Generator (see **43**, 'The Wheel in Space'), which is shown to be able to project people into the future. The Doctor has taken the TARDIS console out of the ship and set it up in a workshop. (In this story and **54**, 'Inferno', it's visibly light green.) The story's understanding of radiation is childish at best. The Doctor talks of 'transmigration of object' and claims this is different from 'real science'. He ain't kiddin'.

Things Fall Apart: Bruno Taltalian has a hilarious 'French' accent – but only in some scenes: in others he speaks BBC English. This is especially odd given that he's named after a Sicilian character in *The Godfather*. His spectacles appear and disappear at random. The plot depends on so many counterconspiracies and characters not knowing the whole truth that it becomes hugely incoherent. This isn't helped by the fact that the serial is padded and loaded with *longueurs*. (Essentially, it hinges on set pieces with nearly every episode having a filmed action sequence – a gun battle, a hijack, a car chase, a robbery – that lasts three to five minutes.) The title gives away a plot twist that isn't revealed until Episode 6 (Whitaker's title was 'The Carriers of Death').

Availability: Only Episode 1 was retained in colour by the BBC. The VHS (BBCV 7265 in the UK, WHV E1856 in the US) combines colour footage taken from surviving domestic video recordings with black-and-white film copies of Episodes 2–7 to offer around 65 additional minutes of colour.

Verdict: 'It was my moral duty. You do understand, don't you?' Despite its lurid title, this is essentially a straight-faced military conspiracy thriller – what humour there is comes from the contrast between that essence and the Doctor's inherent whimsy. It's also packed with hardware – including helicopters, convoys, motorcycles, and a full-size moon unit prop – and is arguably the most visually impressive *Doctor Who* up to this point. The to-camera news reports from journalist John Wakefield (Michael Wisher) add eerie verisimilitude to early episodes. This consistent atmosphere combines with ambitious camerawork and impressive production values to keep the serial together tonally as the plot detours for the umpteenth time. Compulsive stuff.

54
Inferno

Episode 1: 9 May 1970
Episode 2: 16 May 1970
Episode 3: 23 May 1970
Episode 4: 30 May 1970
Episode 5: 6 June 1970
Episode 6: 13 June 1970
Episode 7: 20 June 1970

Written by Don Houghton
Directed by Douglas Camfield

Notable Cast: Christopher Benjamin (Sir Keith Gold) has numerous TV credits, including *The Forsyte Saga* (1967), *The Diary of Anne Frank* (1987) and *Pride and Prejudice* (1995).

Writer: Don Houghton scripted *Dracula A.D. 1972* (Alan Gibson, 1972), *The Satanic Rites of Dracula* (Alan Gibson, 1974) and *Legend of the 7 Golden Vampires* (Roy Ward Baker, 1974). He also created the Scottish soap *Take the High Road* (1980–2003).

Director: Douglas Camfield fell ill during production and producer Barry Letts took over, directing the studio sequences of the final three episodes.

The Plan: Professor Stahlman (Olaf Pooley) is the originator of a government project to drill through Earth's crust. This, he theorises, will release a new energy source, which he christens Stahlman's Gas.

Doctor Who?: The Doctor has been attached to the Inferno project as an adviser, much to Stahlman's chagrin. Upon his arrival he solved in ten minutes a mathematical problem that Stahlman's team had been working on for a month. The Doctor is abusing his position outrageously by using the project's nuclear reactor to conduct some experiments on the TARDIS console, but he is still determined to escape his exile.

Other Worlds: The Doctor attempts to operate the TARDIS console independently from the rest of the ship transport him to a parallel Earth where Britain is a totalitarian republic. This Earth has its own Inferno project, which is more advanced and penetrates the Earth's crust several hours earlier. Security is overseen by the RSF, whose number includes Brigade Leader Lethbridge-Stewart, Section Leader Elizabeth Shaw and Platoon Under Officer Benton – twisted counterparts of the Doctor's UNIT colleagues.

Villains: Back on 'our' Earth, the villain is Stahlman – not evil, but so obsessed with the completion of his project that he ignores all indications of the destruction that it will cause.

Scary Monsters: Members of the project's staff are infected by a green substance that bubbles up from the drill shaft. They degenerate into Primords: vicious, simple creatures who thrive on heat. They are the least effectively realised element of the production, as the fully transformed versions sometimes look ridiculous, and arguably they are present only because conventional wisdom suggests that the *Doctor Who* audience expects monsters. However, they do add an extra dimension to the fifth and sixth episodes as a source of immediate threat. Why they exist is never explained, and they're basically hairy zombies (they can infect others, and the infection is irreversible).

Science/Magic: The Doctor can't rescue anybody from the doomed parallel Earth because it 'would create a dimensional paradox . . . shatter the space–time continuum of all known universes'.

Things Fall Apart: The Doctor's first trip 'sideways' resembles something from a 1950s antidrugs film. The fight between Sutton and the Brigade Leader in Episode 6 looks very staged. The creeping-lava model shot at the end of the same episode is quite good, but matches poorly as a backdrop to the hut doorway.

Availability: Copies of all seven episodes were recovered from Canada in the 1980s. These include an extra scene in Episode 5 in which the Doctor, the Brigade Leader and Elizabeth listen to a radio report (the newsreader in this scene is played by Pertwee). Released on VHS in 1994 as BBCV 5269 (UK), WHV E1298 (US).

Verdict: 'There will be no emergency.' The three plot threads of 'Inferno' (the ecological disaster, the alternative Earth and the monster-dodging) are expertly woven to create almost three hours of utterly compelling television. Parallel-world stories were nothing new in sci-fi, but this serial uses the concept to great advantage: one of the few things *Doctor Who* usually can't do is a modern-day apocalypse because Earth has to be around for the Doctor to save next week. Here, a second Earth is created, fully realised, and then destroyed in the space of four episodes.

While the scripting and direction are both of a very high standard throughout (and there's some fine sound design, mixing an ambient score with industrial noise and frequent alarms), it's the actors who really carry it off. When the end of the world is taking place in such a small space and on such a small budget, the cast must display absolute conviction, and that's what Derek Newark (Greg Sutton), Sheila Dunn (Petra Williams), Nicholas Courtney and Caroline John emphatically deliver. Pertwee is superb, playing the Doctor with a rare level of intensity as he inspires a group of fascists to commit an act of altruism. It doesn't get better than this.

55
Terror of the Autons

Episode One: 2 January 1971
Episode Two: 9 January 1971
Episode Three: 16 January 1971
Episode Four: 23 January 1971

Written by Robert Holmes
Directed by Barry Letts

Notable Cast: Three new regulars debut in this story: Katy Manning (Jo Grant) appeared in the movie *Don't Just Lie There, Say Something* (Bob Kellett, 1973); Roger Delgado (the Master) played Hasmid in *The Mummy's Shroud* (John Gilling, 1967) and a Soothsayer in *Antony and Cleopatra* (Charlton Heston, 1972); Richard Franklin (Captain Mike Yates) played Dennis Rigg in *Emmerdale*.

Villains: Introducing the Master, the Doctor's fellow Time Lord. He has dark, grey-tinged hair and a beard, and wears a black suit with a Nehru collar and black leather gloves. He can hypnotise people with a gaze, and regards humans as primitives. He has a TARDIS that functions properly and can transform itself into an appropriate form. He uses the pseudonym Colonel Masters, and wears a dark suit and gold tie when in this guise.

The Master impersonates a telephone engineer, complete with rubber mask and different voice. He considers the Doctor his intellectual equal, a rarity, and he will miss the Doctor when he's gone. On the evidence here, he's not actually that bright – he doesn't see that his alien allies are likely to betray him, even though it's obvious, and wastes time with elaborate schemes.

History 101: The Doctor is still exiled on Earth. Since **54**, 'Inferno', Liz Shaw has returned to Cambridge.

Doctor Who?: The Doctor takes an imperious but sentimental attitude towards Jo Grant, his new assistant, and is unable to bring himself to sack her after she inadvertently ruins his experiment. He wants a scientist as his assistant, although the Brigadier thinks it's unnecessary to have someone so qualified. The Doctor couldn't bring himself to destroy the Nestene energy unit. He has his pride, claiming to have been a late developer as an excuse for the Master's getting a better degree in cosmic science.

The Doctor destroys a bomb left by the Master to prevent the humans researching how to use it. He considers the weapons humanity already has to be bad enough. He continues to use the pseudonym Smith.

The Doctor's wallet doesn't contain any money. The Doctor likes being childish. In spite of mocking the Brigadier, he jumps to the defence of his workload in the face of civil servants. The Doctor claims to know Lord 'Tubby' Rowlands.

The Doctor rather smugly says he's looking forward to his next run-in with the Master. From Episode Three of this story onwards the character is credited as 'Dr. Who' again, as per the Hartnell and Troughton eras. The credit is later erratic – 'Dr. Who' or 'Doctor Who' on a seemingly random basis, until **70**, 'The Time Warrior'.

Scary Monsters: The Autons and Nestenes from **51**, 'Spearhead from Space'. The Nestene energy unit has been in the National Space Museum, on loan from UNIT (this can't be one left over from 'Spearhead from Space', as they're all accounted for). The Nestenes can 'energise' plastic, turning it almost semiorganic and alive. The plastic objects created by the Nestenes include a chair, an ugly doll, a telephone wire and daffodils, all of which can kill. Rather than the waxwork-type duplicates in the earlier Auton story, when duplicating humans the Nestenes use normal Autons with rubber masks. The Autons talk for the first time – they have metallic, almost Daleky voices.

The Plan: The Master steals the Nestene energy unit, and hijacks a radio telescope to allow it to make contact with the Nestenes. The Master prototypes a plastic chair that can be used to suffocate people, but develops a more efficient design to cut off the airway – a plastic daffodil that fires a thin film over the mouth and nose when triggered by a radio signal. The chaos of 50,000 deaths will give the Nestenes the opportunity to invade.

Science/Magic: The Doctor has been experimenting with steady-state microwelding, an engineering technique pioneered by the Lamadeens. The Master has a weapon that kills by shrinking the target to miniature size. A Time Lord appears without a TARDIS, albeit with a similar sound effect. The Master's hypnosis can completely overcome the human mind, and the aftereffects involve deep trauma for the subject. Particularly stubborn subjects can resist the hypnosis. The dematerialisation circuit in the Master's TARDIS is incompatible with the Doctor's, and when the Doctor tries to install it in his it causes an explosion.

Things Fall Apart: Blue-screen effects are used at several points in the story not for effects sequences but as a substitute for sets – it isn't an effective technique, with the perspectives all wrong. The Nestene creature manifests itself as a blobby light effect.

Availability: Issued on VHS in 1993 as BBCV 4957 (UK), WHV E1276 (US).

Verdict: 'The Master is controlling your mind. You must resist him, you can resist him.' A virtual rerun of **51**, 'Spearhead from Space', 'Terror of the Autons' adds a twist in the form of the Master, renegade Time Lord and recurring foe for the Doctor. The black-clad Master never really has any sensible motivation to his actions, and he's really there only to be generically evil, the ultimate clichéd villain. His presence represents a change for the simpler in the series – 'Terror' lacks the complexity of the previous three stories, but makes up for it in an aesthetic shift to brightly coloured action. There are some impressive set pieces (sometimes too impressive – isn't it overkill for the Brigadier to order an airstrike to destroy a bus?) and action scenes, making it one of the most straightforwardly entertaining *Who* stories to date.

56
The Mind of Evil

Episode One: 30 January 1971
Episode Two: 6 February 1971
Episode Three: 13 February 1971
Episode Four: 20 February 1971
Episode Five: 27 February 1971
Episode Six: 6 March 1971

Written by Don Houghton
Directed by Timothy Combe

Notable Cast: Michael Sheard (Dr Summers) appeared in **23**, 'The Ark'.

History 101: The Doctor is still in exile. The first ever World Peace Conference is taking place in London. The Thunderbolt missile is banned – it's a nuclear weapon with nerve gas in the warhead. Execution of criminals is considered uncivilised, and prison reform is a high priority for the Chinese government.

Villains: The Master, who smokes cigars and travels in the back of a chauffeur-driven limousine. He can wiretap a phone, using his favourite disguise as a telephone engineer (as in **55**, 'Terror of the Autons'). He is posing as Professor Emil Keller, a scientist who has allegedly created a process for draining evil impulses from the human mind using the Keller Machine. The Master has been working on this for a while – he installed the machine a year ago. The Master fears the Doctor's derision. The Machine in fact contains the alien parasite that feeds on evil (see **Scary Monsters**).

Scary Monsters: An alien parasite that feeds on human evil. It kills by summoning up visions of human fears, and can be directed over an unlimited range. The Doctor considers it to be the greatest threat to humanity in history. As it becomes stronger, the creature learns to teleport the Keller Machine from place to place. The creature inside resembles a formless blob.

The Plan: The Master has taken hypnotic control of one of the Chinese delegates, Captain Chin Lee (Pik-Sen Lim), to disrupt the World Peace Conference, and also wishes to steal the Thunderbolt missile, launch it at the conference and start a war. Yet again, the Doctor has to point out a blatant flaw in the plan – the Master won't be able to escape the nuclear war he's about to cause. His parting message indicates a desire to destroy both the Doctor and Earth, although he doesn't explain why.

Doctor Who?: The Doctor is worried by the Keller Machine, based on what he has heard. He doesn't believe any talk of taking evil impulses and storing them, and distrusts attempts to tamper with the human mind. The Doctor gets halfway through saying that he has been a scientist for several thousand years, before thinking better of it.

He is afraid of fire following the events of **54**, 'Inferno'. The Keller Machine also summons up images of his terrifying enemies – the Daleks (**2**, among others), the Cybermen (**29** and others), the Ice Warriors (**39** and others), the Silurians (**52**) and, bizarrely, the War Machines (**27**), the Zarbi (**13**) and Koquillion (**11**) as well. The Doctor is left exhausted by the Keller Machine, and slips into a coma.

The Doctor uses Venusian karate to temporarily paralyse opponents. The Doctor speaks both Hokkien and Cantonese, and claims to have been on friendly terms with Chairman Mao Zedong. The Doctor was once locked in the Tower of London, and shared a cell with Sir Walter Raleigh.

Guns make the Doctor nervous. He is bad at draughts – he's more used to playing three-dimensional chess – and he isn't too happy to be stuck on Earth while the Master goes free.

Science/Magic: A telepathic amplifier is used to channel and direct telepathic impulses from the Keller Machine, via a human mind. The Doctor builds a machine that confuses the Keller Machine by creating signals that match the Beta rhythms of the human brain.

Availability: Issued on VHS in 1998 as BBCV 6361 (UK), WHV E1020 (US).

Verdict: 'There's something to be said for a pure mind after all.' 'The Mind of Evil' is predominantly a spy thriller, with the genre staples of both a peace conference under threat *and* a stolen nuclear missile. The only science fiction element is the alien in the Keller Machine, an unusually nasty threat. The prison setting gives the story a bleaker, real-world feel. Like Combe's previous *Doctor Who* directing gig (**52**, 'Doctor Who and the Silurians'), this is impressively staged throughout (the storming of Stangmoor Prison is one of the biggest action scenes in the series to date). If there's one flaw to the story, it's repetition: most of the cliffhangers are the same, and two prison riots in as many episodes seems like overkill. Nonetheless, it's a gripping thriller.

57
The Claws of Axos

Episode One: 13 March 1971
Episode Two: 20 March 1971
Episode Three: 27 March 1971
Episode Four: 3 April 1971

Written by Bob Baker and Dave Martin
Directed by Michael Ferguson

Notable Cast: Tim Piggott-Smith (Captain Harker) is best known for the TV productions *The Jewel in the Crown* (1984), *Life Story*

(1987) and *The Chief* (1990–91); he also performs extensive voiceover work for documentaries and commercials. Donald Hewlett (Hardiman) had regular roles in the comedies *Now Look Here* (1971–73), *It Ain't Half Hot, Mum* (1974–81) and *You Rang, M'Lord?* (1988–93). Bernard Holley (Axon Man) played PC Bill Newcombe, a major player in *Z Cars* at the time of 'Claws . . .' transmission. He previously appeared in **37**, 'The Tomb of the Cybermen'.

Writer: Bob Baker and Dave Martin created the children's sci-fi series *Sky* and *King of the Castle*. Independently Baker has been the more prolific, writing episodes of *Shoestring* (1979–80) and *Bergerac* (1980–90). He is one of *Doctor Who*'s few Oscar winners, having co-scripted the *Wallace and Gromit* films *The Wrong Trousers* and *A Close Shave*, which won Best Animated Short at the 1994 and 1996 Academy Awards.

History 101: The USA is now involved in the hunt for the Master. Agent Bill Filer has come over from Washington HQ and gets a substantial role in the plot: it's a little surprising that he didn't appear again, operating as an American contact for UNIT (as Felix Leiter does for James Bond).

Scary Monsters: The Axons, who initially appear as golden-skinned humanoids but later revert to their true form, becoming a mass of vegetable matter. They arrive on Earth promising friendship and offering a gift: Axonite. The mineral is demonstrated to be a valuable source of energy.

The Plan: Axonite can drain energy as well as supply it. Once it is distributed around the globe, it will be activated and used to suck Earth dry.

Villains: The Master is being held prisoner by Axos. His motivation is more solid than usual – here he's merely trying to survive – and, although the character seems shoehorned into the script, Roger Delgado's performance is one of the best elements.

Doctor Who?: The Doctor claims to have published papers on time travel 'elsewhere', and implies that Time Lords tend to specialise in different areas of the subject (he refers to the Master as a 'mechanic').

Science/Magic: *Doctor Who* is not known for its pinpoint scientific accuracy, yet Bob Baker and Dave Martin still stand out for sheer wrongness. The Master mocks the humans' lack of defence against a nuclear explosion – 'sticky tape on the windows, that sort of thing' – which would be funnier if 'The Claws of Axos' didn't then depict even less advisable nuclear safety procedures: when the Nuton Power Complex goes critical, Jo, the Brigadier and the others simply drive down the road and duck. Then they go back a few minutes later. It's a good thing Bob 'n' Dave have never worked in the energy industry, really.

Things Fall Apart: Axos itself is a psychedelic mess. The Doctor, Jo and Filer are chased by a duvet at the end of Episode Two. Filer stagily mutters in his sleep about the danger of Axonite. The biggest blunders come during the scenes in Filer's car and Benton's Jeep, where the blue backcloth used for the colour-separation overlay (more commonly known as bluescreen) should have been replaced with the appropriate scrolling countryside. In the latter case the exterior shots of the Jeep don't match at all, spoiling a well-executed action sequence.

Availability: Episodes One and Four have always been held in colour; Two and Three were returned from Canada in the 1980s. Released on VHS in 1992 as BBCV 4742 (UK), WHV E1323 (US). Due out on DVD in Spring 2005.

Verdict: 'It seems I'm some kind of a galactic yo-yo!' What should be a run-of-the-mill *Doctor Who* story is dragged down by repulsive design, SFX mishaps and a failure to carry itself through its essential silliness. At the heart of 'The Claws of Axos' is a functioning plot that basically makes sense, but several elements seem to have been ripped off from the previous season (comedy yokel, glory-seeking civil servant, UNIT arrested by the regular army) and they are all executed less effectively. Perhaps this is why the story lacks freshness. Or perhaps it's just *so* run-of-the-mill that nobody can be bothered to make something special out of it.

At least Michael Ferguson seems to be trying, and it's a shame that his good record as a *Who* director is blotted with this final effort. There's little he can do about the horrible sets (although the nuclear reactor is quite good, and the effects shot that introduces it is highly impressive) and so most of his neat visual stylings go to waste.

58
Colony in Space

Episode One: 10 April 1971
Episode Two: 17 April 1971
Episode Three: 24 April 1971
Episode Four: 1 May 1971
Episode Five: 8 May 1971
Episode Six: 15 May 1971

Written by Malcolm Hulke
Directed by Michael Briant

Notable Cast: Helen Worth (Mary Ashe) has played Gail Tilsley in *Coronation Street* since 1974. Tony Caunter (Morgan) and Bernard Kay (Caldwell) appeared in **14**, 'The Crusade'. John Ringham (Ashe) was in **6**, 'The Aztecs'.

Director: Michael Briant directed episodes of *The Onedin Line* (1971–80), *Secret Army* (1977–79) and *Blake's 7* (1978).

Other Worlds: The Time Lords briefly lift the Doctor's exile to send him to Uxarieus in 2472, a planet inhabited by human colonists who are having crop difficulties, along with an indigenous race of primitives. Rich seams of duralinium have attracted the attention of the Intergalactic Mining Company (IMC), which wants the planet for itself. Earth is overcrowded, which is why the colonists left.

Villains: Captain Dent (Morris Perry) and his sadistic sidekick Morgan, representatives of IMC. They will do anything to get the colonists off the planet so they can strip-mine it. The decision over who should have the planet requires the presence of an adjudicator from Earth – instead they get the Master, impersonating an adjudicator. The Master's TARDIS is a more advanced model than the Doctor's, and has black roundels on the walls along with a number of rather arch traps and security systems. The Master believes that there are only two choices in life: you can rule or serve.

Doctor Who?: The Doctor is glad to be away from Earth and exploring again, and takes visible pleasure in being once more on a new world. He claims to be an expert in agriculture, and to be 'every kind of scientist', displaying a fascination with unusual rocks unseen since the early Troughton stories.

The Doctor considers absolute power to be evil, and refuses the Master's offer of power – he wants to *see* the universe, not rule it. He seeks a peaceful solution between colonists and miners, and believes humanity's future is on new worlds, not crammed on Earth.

The Doctor can disarm a man with two fingers to the chest, and perform coin tricks. He's left on the back foot by the fact that the Master has all the proper fake credentials, but the Doctor doesn't. He's kept a key to the Master's TARDIS.

Scary Monsters: The primitives are green mutes that carry spears. They have two subspecies – a handful of short, pale survivors from the genetically enhanced superspecies that used to rule the primitive city, which can speak, and a more numerous, degraded version of the superspecies that are mute and act as priests in a primitive, sacrifice-based religion. The superspecies degraded when the radiation leaked from a devastating, star-destroying 'superweapon'.

The Plan: IMC are using a survey robot armed with fake hands and a holographic projector to make the colonists think that they're under attack from giant lizards. They also spread scare stories about the primitives.

The Master has come to Uxaerius based on information that he found in a stolen Time Lord file concerning a superweapon hidden in the primitives' city. He wants to use it to hold the universe to ransom. He offers the Doctor a 50 per cent share in universal domination. As usual there's a glaring flaw in the Master's plan: he hasn't considered whether or not the creators of the weapon might want to hand it over.

Science/Magic: IMC use survey robots. The Crab Nebula is the result of the testing of the superweapon. The Master's sleep gas is effective on all species. The radiation from the superweapon has been blighting the colonists' crops, and, for some reason, destroying the superweapon causes the radiation to disappear.

Things Fall Apart: The gun battles in Episodes Four and Five are identical, with the aim and outcome the same, except that the aggressors are swapped. The primitive city has a literal puppet ruler, with a doll-like body.

Availability: Issued on VHS in 2001 as BBCV 7175 (UK, bundled with **64**, 'The Time Monster'), WHV E1728 (US).

Verdict: 'This planet is rightfully ours.' For the first time since being exiled in **50**, 'The War Games', the Doctor takes a trip in the TARDIS to another world. What a shame, then, that it's such a drab place, full of colonists with handlebar moustaches whingeing about their crops. The IMC guys may be ruthless, violent and sadistic, but the colonists commit a worse crime: they're boring. Jo is pathetic, providing no useful story function, and the aliens are mostly mute, so it's only with the arrival of the Master in Episode Four that the Doctor has anyone to play off. The scenes in which the Doctor and the Master are communicating as peers rather than enemies are the best, though these are poor consolation for the relentless dullness of the rest.

59
The Dæmons

Episode One: 22 May 1971
Episode Two: 29 May 1971
Episode Three: 5 June 1971
Episode Four: 12 June 1971
Episode Five: 19 June 1971

Written by Guy Leopold
Directed by Christopher Barry

Notable Cast: Rollo Gamble (Squire Winstanley) regularly directed the pop show *Ready, Steady, Go!* (1964–66). Don McKillop (Bert) appeared in *An American Werewolf in London* (John Landis, 1981). Damaris Hayman (Miss Hawthorne) had a regular role in *Crossroads* and appeared in *Confessions of a Driving Instructor* (Norman Cohen, 1976). Future Sooty puppeteer Matthew Corbett plays one of the villagers. Given the Doctor's stated attitude to magic it's probably good he left Sooty with his dad, Harry. Stephen Thorne (Azal) was Treebeard in BBC Radio's *The Lord of the Rings* (1981) and seems to have been in every BBC radio production of the 1970s.

Writer: 'Guy Leopold' is a pseudonym for Robert Sloman and producer Barry Letts (they co-wrote three further Pertwee serials, although only Sloman was credited). Sloman spent most of his career working in theatre and radio, and his plays include *The Tinker* (1961).

History 101: The development of Earth over the past 100,000 years has been influenced by the Dæmons, a race of amoral scientists from the planet Dæmos. Chiefly, they have enhanced mankind's scientific progress. They resemble our vision of the Devil and destroyed Atlantis (see **32**, 'The Underwater Menace', and **64**, 'The Time Monster'). Indeed, *Doctor Who*'s Earth is so accelerated that it has developed BBC3 *thirty years* early.

Villains: Guess who. Yes, it's the Master. He's infiltrated the community of Devil's End by replacing the local priest (who, according to a convenient info-dump from Miss Hawthorne, 'left in such mysterious circumstances'). Thoughtfully, he drops an enormous clue for the Doctor by using the alias 'Magister', the Latin word for 'master'.

The Plan: The Master summons Azal, the last of the Dæmons. Azal's instructions for his final appearance on Earth specify that he should bequeath his power to another so that the 'experiment' that is mankind can continue, or destroy the planet. The Master requests that this power be granted to him.

Scary Monsters: Bok, the stone gargoyle in the crypt, which comes to life and attacks at the Master's command.

Doctor Who?: The Pertwee Doctor at his most infuriating, criticising Jo for agreeing with his comments about the Brigadier and berating Sergeant Osgood for not being a scientific genius on his own level. He thinks Hitler was a 'bounder' and looks ready to start on someone for suggesting that his hair is a wig.

Science/Magic: This is one of the few occasions on which the series deals directly with the concept of magic. The Doctor explains that the black arts are in fact remnants of the Dæmons' advanced science: 'The emotions of a group of ordinary human beings generate a tremendous force of psychokinetic energy.' However, given that all the Dæmonic 'rites' are clearly seen to work without the aid of any technology (and Miss Hawthorne manages to quell the storm in Episode One by chanting against it), the Dæmons' science is effectively magic by a different name, so the Doctor's insistence that there is no such thing as magic looks pedantic rather than rational.

Things Fall Apart: There's a dreadful continuity edit when Miss Hawthorne turns to face the policeman in Episode One (her cape is suddenly back around her shoulders). Damaris Hayman's performance is cringe-inducing. The hoofmarks seen by Yates and Benton from the helicopter become much, much smaller when the helicopter lands. The Doctor's energy exchanger is given huge emphasis, but blows up before he even gets to use it. Who, or what, kills the man in the churchyard in the first scene? Neither Bok nor Azal have awoken.

Availability: Only Episode Four exists in its original colour format. Colour copies of the other four episodes have been assembled using off-air colour recordings and black-and-white film prints. Released on VHS in 1993 BBCV 4950 (UK), WHV E1141 (US).

Verdict: 'This planet smells to me of failure.' 'The Dæmons' is fondly remembered by those who worked on it, probably because it involved a working holiday in a charming country village with an excellent pub just off the green. Merely watching the serial is a less satisfying experience. There are some enjoyable elements: the BBC3 broadcast is a neat way to deal with the exposition and the sinister aspects of isolated villages are brought to the fore (it's not exactly a flattering portrayal of country folk – even those villagers who aren't under the Master's control are easily goaded into burning the Doctor alive).

The idea of the Master as a satanic vicar is hugely amusing and these sequences give 'The Dæmons' some edge, but the script wastes too much time trying (and failing) to justify this within the 'scientific' confines of *Doctor Who*. Worse, the resolution of the plot is deeply stupid: Azal encounters something that doesn't make sense and blows up like a *Star Trek* computer. How can the Dæmons have become so powerful if this is all it takes to destroy one? Presumably the same effect could have been achieved by showing Azal a videotape of 3, 'The Edge of Destruction'.

60
Day of the Daleks

Episode One: 1 January 1972
Episode Two: 8 January 1972
Episode Three: 15 January 1972
Episode Four: 22 January 1972

Written by Louis Marks
Directed by Paul Bernard

Notable Cast: Anna Barry (Anat) was a regular in *Sons and Daughters* (1982–83). Aubrey Woods (Controller) appeared in *Willy Wonka's Chocolate Factory* (Mel Stuart, 1971). Scott Fredericks (Boaz) later made a memorable appearance in *Blake's 7* ('Weapon').

Director: Paul Bernard was a production designer on *The Avengers* before graduating to directing the likes of *Z Cars* and *Coronation Street*. He was instrumental in setting up ITV's attempt to rival *Doctor Who*, *The Tomorrow People* (1973–79).

History 101: On contemporary Earth, the international situation has worsened to the extent that the planet is on the brink of World War Three. British diplomat Sir Reginald Styles is organising a conference to avert this eventuality. Two hundred years into the future, it is established history that the conference fell victim to a bomb, supposedly planted by Styles: 'There was a hundred years of nothing but killing and destruction. Seven-eighths of the world's population was wiped out.' Earth was then occupied by the Daleks.

The Plan: A human guerrilla group travels back in time, intending to kill Styles before he can destroy the conference and ultimately change the future.

Science/Magic: Quite reasonably, Jo asks why the guerrillas can't travel back as many times as they like to make attempts on Styles's life. The Doctor replies that this is due to the Blinovitch Limitation Effect.

Scary Monsters: 'The Daleks have discovered the secret of time travel. We have invaded Earth again.' The time frame heavily implies that they have overwritten the events of **10**, 'The Dalek Invasion of Earth', although the earlier story is not explicitly referenced.

Doctor Who?: He is 'the sworn enemy of the Daleks – the one man they're afraid of'. Over the course of previous stories, the Daleks have been promoted to the most feared race in the universe. By making the Doctor their nemesis, they accord him similar legendary status. He's also pretty cool in this story, 'carrying on rather like a one-man food-and-wine society' (in Jo's words) at Styles's house and later pausing to take a sip of water (or possibly a hair-of-the-dog whisky) while trouncing one of the guerrillas.

Villains: The Controller, a human who has collaborated with the Daleks. He has a shiny face, for some reason – is it a fashion thing?

Things Fall Apart: The computer operator who reports to the Controller speaks in an annoying up-talking fashion. The effect of the guerrillas' time-travel devices is inconsistent: in Episode One they transport the owner of the device; in Episode Two they transport whoever is holding it; and in Episode Three they're liable to transport anybody who's standing too close. It's unclear why future historians have assumed that Styles wanted power only for himself and blew up his own conference: as a victim of the bomb he is hardly the most likely suspect.

Availability: Released on VHS in 1994 as BBCV 5219 (UK), WHV E1151 (US).

Verdict: 'I still don't get it, that changing-history bit.' Some good work behind the cameras from Paul Bernard and a worthwhile attempt at exploring the ramifications of time travel (the first since 17, 'The Time Meddler'). Sadly it's muddled: the Daleks claim to have travelled back and changed history so that their invasion succeeds, but what did they actually do? They didn't cause World War Three: the guerrillas did that in trying to avert it (the most effective aspect of the story is the Doctor's revelation of this). It would have made more sense if the Daleks had no awareness that history had been changed, if they had simply turned up to invade as they did in 10, 'The Dalek Invasion of Earth', and found a weaker planet.

But, then, this isn't much of a Dalek story. It's a poor return considering they'd been away for over four years. They're hardly in it and when we do see them there are only three, making for a limp climax as the Daleks advance on the house. Its vision of a Dalek-occupied planet pales in comparison with 'The Dalek Invasion of Earth' – it says much that the serial's most enduring image is Pertwee on a motor tricycle – and there's quite a bit of padding for a four-part story. It's interesting and reasonably enjoyable, but flawed nonetheless.

61
The Curse of Peladon

Episode One: 29 January 1972
Episode Two: 5 February 1972
Episode Three: 12 February 1972
Episode Four: 19 February 1972

Written by Brian Hayles
Directed by Lennie Mayne

Notable Cast: Of the British acting dynasty that includes Patrick, Michael and Sam, David Troughton (Peladon) is one of Britain's finest classical actors and a longstanding artiste with the Royal Shakespeare Company. Triumphs include Caliban in *The Tempest* (1991), the title role in *Henry IV* (2001), Kent in *King Lear* (1991) and the Duke in *Measure for Measure* (2004, at the Royal National Theatre). He was magnificent as Lopahkin in Chekov's *The Cherry Orchard* (1997). He is best known as Bob Buzzard in BBC Television's *A Very Peculiar Practice* (1984–5) and Sir Arthur Wellesley in ITV's *Sharpe's Rifles* and *Sharpe's Eagle* (1994). He previously cameoed as Private Moor in **50**, 'The War Games', and was an extra in **40**, 'The Enemy of the World'.

Director: Australian Lennie Mayne directed four other *Doctor Who* stories as well as episodes of *Doomwatch* (1971). He died in a boating accident in 1976.

Doctor Who?: The Doctor erroneously believes he's got the TARDIS working; actually the Time Lords have sent him on a mission without informing him. He's a skilled diplomat, a great bluffer and hypnotist and knows a 'Venusian lullaby' that runs to the tune of 'God Rest You, Merry Gentlemen'.

Other Worlds: Peladon, a stormy, rocky, medieval-seeming world that is also aware of other civilisations and may be spacefaring (the king's mother was from Earth). It has applied to join the Galactic Federation (a grouping of affiliated planets) and a committee of representatives from Federation worlds (Earth, Mars, Arcturus, Alpha Centauri) has been sent to assess the planet's suitability. The Federation has a constitution (the Galactic Articles of Peace, Paragraph 59, Subsection 2, forbids it to contradict the laws of member worlds) and a Grand Council. Peladon appears monotheistic (with a religion worshipping the animal Aggedor) and an absolute monarchy (although the king is not above the law). The present king is a compassionate man concerned with those he rules, at one point begging, 'Please, stay and help me to help my people.' That said, there's little sign of the Peladonian peasantry on screen beyond men-at-arms.

Scary Monsters: Martians (see **39**, 'The Ice Warriors'), though they're the good guys this time. Subdelegate Ssorg (Sonny Caldinez) carries a gun that can destroy any living creature. The Doctor distrusts them owing to his previous experiences, but later acknowledges he was wrong to judge an entire species. Before the Federation, Mars and Arcturus were enemies.

The Plan: High Priest Hepesh (Geoffrey Toone) hopes to stop Peladon joining the Federation by using an Aggedor to murder political rivals and invoking an ancient curse that states that 'strangers' will bring ruin to Peladon. It's worth noting that Hepesh isn't simply an isolationist: he's a *racist* – disgusted by the alien delegates and contemptuous of the king's mixed blood.

Science/Magic: The story is profoundly antireligion, equating it with reactionary sentiments, isolation and racism ('Aggedor has pointed the way!'; 'Backwards into superstition!').

Things Fall Apart: Peladon is a David Bowie world of thigh-high purple boots and two-tone hairstyles. Two of the delegates (and the king of Peladon) are inexplicably named after the planets they come from. The Doctor's fight with the king's champion is interminable (see **65**, 'The Three Doctors').

Verdict: 'The ancient curse of Peladon is upon us!' It's common among *Who* fans to label this an 'allegory' of the UK's accession to EEC membership but doing so requires a lack of knowledge of 1970s politics *and* ill-acquaintance with the meaning of the word 'allegory'. For it to be allegorical at least some elements would have to have clear purposes, indicating that this is 'really' about Britain in 1972. They don't. It is clearly 'prompted' by said events, however, and the story *is* generically progressive – arguing for intergovernmental co-operation and disdainful of its isolationist villain. It's unique (as *Doctor Who*) in arguing that the descendants of old enemies should become friends. Pertwee relishes the topical, yet pulpy, material and is on top form. It's also the best ever outing for Katy Manning's Jo Grant, who innocently flirts with King Peladon and pretends (for plot reasons) to be a 'royal observer' from an Earth country with a monarchy – 'Princess Josephine of Tardis' (the Doctor, embarrassed, claims that Earth maintains an aristocracy but 'in a democratic sort of way'). This is also well shot, Mayne using high camera angles and placing objects in the foreground to create interesting visual compositions. One of the best *Doctor Who* serials of the 1970s.

62
The Sea Devils

Episode One: 26 February 1972
Episode Two: 4 March 1972
Episode Three: 11 March 1972
Episode Four: 18 March 1972
Episode Five: 25 March 1972
Episode Six: 1 April 1972

Written by Malcolm Hulke
Directed by Michael Briant

Notable Cast: Edwin Richfield (Captain Hart), a prolific television actor, was in *The Avengers* no fewer than six times (always playing different characters). Clive Morton (Trenchard) played a prison governor in *Kind Hearts and Coronets* (Robert Hamer, 1949) and also appeared in *The Lavender Hill Mob* (Charles Crichton, 1951).

Doctor Who?: Pertwee's Doctor-as-Renaissance-Man can fence, drive a speedboat and putt while blindfolded, and claims to be a trained diver. His name-dropping is moderately amusing (he claims Horatio Nelson is a personal friend), although one might have thought he would make more of an effort to maintain some credibility with people he's only just met.

Scary Monsters: The Sea Devils, water-dwelling cousins of the Silurians (see **52**, 'Doctor Who and the Silurians'). Same origin, same motivation.

Villains: After *two whole stories* without the Master, he's back. The Doctor and Jo pay a visit to his dedicated jail on the coast. The Doctor notes, 'You could almost say we were at school together.' The early sequences of the Master in prison are good but thereafter he adds little to the story, serving mainly to make it less morally complex than **52**, 'Doctor Who and the Silurians'. As usual, his motivation is flimsy (because he's a multipurpose villain) and he fails to anticipate the betrayal of his allies.

The Plan: The Master plans to help the Sea Devils regain their position of supremacy over Earth. Why? For 'the pleasure of seeing the human race exterminated'. What does he have to gain from this? Nothing, but it will annoy the Doctor. All rather childish, really. The sense that the Doctor and the Master treat their battles as a game has the effect of distancing the viewer. Witness the Doctor sportingly handing the Master his sword back during the duel. If they don't take their face-offs seriously, why should we?

Science/Magic: 'Reverse the polarity of the neutron flow' became Pertwee's favourite piece of technical gobbledegook.

Things Fall Apart: It would have been wise to avoid close-ups on the Sea Devils' heads, and, while there's no reason why they shouldn't wear clothing, those string vests don't look practical underwater. Why is there a rack of swords outside the Master's cell? Why does the Doctor leave a soldier guarding the Master during Episode Six, since the Master is obviously going to use hypnosis to escape?

Availability: The first three episodes of 'The Sea Devils' were wiped but colour copies were returned from Canada in the 1980s. Released on VHS in 1995 as BBCV 5667 (UK), WHV E1378 (US).

Verdict: 'Why revive your people only to have them killed?' *Doctor Who* goes high-concept in this water-bound remix of 'Doctor Who and the Silurians'. It's more or less the same story again, with the suspenseful plague plotline replaced by more of the Doctor–Master bickering that characterised the previous season. It's weaker as a consequence but still a decent adventure, slow but generally well structured and with quality dialogue (usually Malcolm Hulke's strongest point). The Navy hardware is well used and lends the production an air of authority.

A handful of striking scenes distinguish the story in the memory, yet there's no tension in the final episode at all. The Doctor abandons hope of a peaceful resolution and uses some nonsense technical trickery to wipe out the Sea Devils, which cheapens his principled stance of 'Doctor Who and the Silurians' but is forgivable. What's annoying is that this isn't executed in a remotely exciting way – the Doctor and the Master's escape from the Sea Devil base is not shown or even explained. A race against time to avoid the explosion might have provided a dramatic climax to two-and-a-half hours of adventure, but what we get is facile and rather boring.

63
The Mutants

Episode One: 8 April 1972
Episode Two: 15 April 1972
Episode Three: 22 April 1972
Episode Four: 29 April 1972
Episode Five: 6 May 1972
Episode Six: 13 May 1972

Written by Bob Baker and Dave Martin
Directed by Christopher Barry

Notable Cast: Paul Whitsun-Jones (Marshal) appeared in **28**, 'The Smugglers'; Geoffrey Palmer (Administrator) was in **52**, 'Doctor Who and The Silurians'.

Doctor Who?: The Doctor puts up little complaint at being used as a 'messenger boy', sent by the Time Lords to Solos to deliver a container that can be opened by only one person. The Doctor compares the situation on Solos to Edward Gibbons's *The History of the Decline and Fall of the Roman Empire*, which is an insult to Roman history. The Doctor claims to have been sent to Solos by the Earth Council. He stuns a man by squeezing his shoulders. The Doctor doesn't suffer the same ill effects as humans when dealing with the radiation and gas on Solos. The Doctor's main vulnerability is Jo – while the Marshal holds her, the Doctor is willing to back the Marshal before the Investigator from Earth, even though it may allow the Marshal to continue his plans.

Other Worlds: Solos, the thirtieth century, one of the last planets in the shrinking Earth empire. The human overlords have ruled the native Solonians for five hundred years, imposing segregation while exploiting the planet's mineral wealth. The atmosphere on the planet is hostile to humans, and so the humans live on Skybase 1, which orbits the planet. The Solonians have cases of mutation among their ranks that may be due to the Marshal's experiments with the atmosphere. Much to the Marshal's chagrin, Earth is pulling out from Solos and giving the Solonians independence. Earth in this period is exhausted due to industrial development. Rebellious Solonians are labelled 'terrorists'. The Solonians can no longer read the language of their ancestors. It takes two thousand years for Solos to orbit its sun, so each season is five hundred years long.

Scary Monsters: The mutants, or 'mutts', Solonians who have mutated into insectoid forms with clawed hands – in fact an intermediate stage in the Solonians' natural life cycle.

Villains: The Marshal, head of security on Solos, who is threatened with losing his job if the planet is given independence.

The Plan: The Marshal conspires with the Solonian tribal leader, Varran, to assassinate the Administrator in charge of the colonial government, preventing the human withdrawal from the planet and allowing the Marshal to impose martial law. He then kills the assassin, and orders that Varran be hunted down. The Marshal is experimenting on the atmosphere of Solos, trying to make it habitable so that humans can properly colonise the planet, allowing him to keep hold of power. He doesn't mind destroying the Solonians in the process.

Science/Magic: The soil of Solos contains a 'nitrogen isotope' unknown on Earth. When triggered by the rays of the sun, it creates a gas poisonous to humans, making the planet uninhabitable by humans during daylight. The Marshal carries a swagger stick with a communicator in the tip. Particle reversal is a technique used to turn objects inside out.

Things Fall Apart: The bearded Solonian running towards the camera at the start of Episode One seems to mimic Michael Palin at the start of *Monty Python's Flying Circus*. A boom mike drops into shot in Episode Two. The mutts evolve into glowing tinfoil angels, and the Doctor's trip through a heavily radiated cave is downright psychedelic.

Availability: Issued on VHS in 2003 as BBCV 7331 (UK), WHV E1857 (US).

Verdict: 'Solos – stinking rotten hole. Can't even breathe. What a planet!' Picking up on many of the themes of colonial conflict in **58**, 'Colony in Space', 'The Mutants' manages the staggering feat of being even duller. Baker and Martin's script, a tiresome screed on the evils of colonialism, unfolds in a way that is both predictable and absurd, with unstructured bouts of random peril to eke out the action. Much of the acting is appalling and the production is so garish that it's genuinely hard on the eye in places. There's an intelligent idea at the heart of the story, but it's hidden beneath too many layers of tedium and tackiness to find.

64
The Time Monster

Episode One: 20 May 1972
Episode Two: 27 May 1972
Episode Three: 3 June 1972
Episode Four: 10 June 1972
Episode Five: 17 June 1972
Episode Six: 24 June 1972

Written by Robert Sloman
Directed by Paul Bernard

Notable Cast: Ingrid Pitt (Queen Galleia) featured in numerous horror films, including as the titular *Countess Dracula* (Peter Sasdy, 1971) and in *The House that Dripped Blood* (Peter John Duffell, 1970), which co-starred Jon Pertwee. Dave Prowse (the Minotaur) was the body, but not the voice, of Darth Vader in *Star Wars* (George Lucas, 1977) and its sequels (but not prequels).

Doctor Who?: The Doctor has a tacky precognitive dream of the Master laughing at him in an Atlantean setting. He's unaffected by the speeding up and slowing down of time using the TOMTIT machine. When he was a little boy he lived in a house halfway up a mountain and sought the advice of a local hermit (see **74**, 'Planet of the Spiders'). He's not too proud of his own subconscious. Kronos knows the Doctor 'of old'.

Scary Monsters: Kronos is the 'most terrible' and powerful of the Kronovores (literally 'time eaters', albeit in an ungainly mix of classical languages) that dwell in the time vortex 'beyond good and evil'. Its usual physical manifestation bears a startling resemblance to a man in a white leotard making chicken noises while wearing a bucket on his head. The Minotaur is the guardian of the Atlanteans' crystal in which Kronos in trapped.

The Plan: The Master (as 'Professor Thascales') plans to unleash Kronos and use its time-altering powers to become ruler of the universe. The Master's desperate actions in this story run utterly contrary to the assumption (based on other stories of this era) that the Master's actions are more motivated by a desire to engage with – and best – the Doctor than a real desire for power, destruction or conquest.

History 101: Atlantis is said to have been 'part of the Minoan civilisation' (and therefore an example of 'all that Cretan jazz', according to Jo) rather than 'in the middle of the Atlantic ocean' as the 'out-of-date' Captain Yates believes. It was destroyed around 1525 BCE (before common era). So that sorts that out. (Although, see **32**, 'The Underwater Menace'.)

Science/Magic: Perhaps more than any other *Doctor Who* story 'The Time Monster' doesn't explain itself in pseudo-rational terms – it just asks the audience to accept what's going on while characters archly mumble platitudes. TOMTIT is the '*T*rans-mission *O*f *M*atter *T*hrough *I*nterstitial *T*ime'. (This involves sending small objects a few moments into the future.) There's endless unfunny gibberish about the difference between imperial miles and Venusian miles. *Bessie*'s brakes work by the 'absorption of inertia'. In the time vortex, $E = MC^3$. TARDISes are telepathic. The Doctor insists his is a 'she' (the idea that the TARDIS has a personality hasn't really been done in the series before this point but later stories often refer to it). This is the first time in the series the Doctor defeats a threat to 'the entire created universe' although it's a very vague one.

Things Fall Apart: Roger Delgado can't decide whether to play 'Professor Thascales' with a Greek accent or not. Ingrid Pitt's performance is one note, but Donald Eccles's in his role as High Priest Krassis is actually worse. *Bessie* is shown driving at great speed by running the film fast. The Atlanteans' costumes, make-up and hair are absurdly fey. The music is tuneless and intrusive – sounding like someone beating someone else to death with a synthesiser keyboard and then removing all the beauty from the resultant sounds.

Availability: Issued on VHS in 2001 as BBCV7175 (UK, bundled with **58**, 'Colony in Space'), WHV E1728 (US).

Verdict: 'I don't really care any more. Do what you like. Just get it over with.' This is a blundering, horribly plotted, would-be epic with a surfeit of bad comedy and consistently soul-crushing dialogue (sample line: 'I'm sorry about your coccyx too, Miss Grant'). It is noticeably directed by someone more interested in camera zooms and 'funny' sound effects than in conveying the plot or eliciting performances from his cast, and the production values are *shameful*. The first four episodes are among the very worst in the whole of *Doctor Who*, but the serial improves dramatically once the Master reaches Atlantis – becoming merely very bad. 'The Time Monster' is so poor it's actually quite difficult to recall how awful it is unless one is actually watching it. Jo's yellow platform boots and her reaction to what she believes to be the afterlife ('Groovy, isn't it?') are the only elements deserving any quarter.

65
The Three Doctors

Episode One: 30 December 1972
Episode Two: 6 January 1973
Episode Three: 13 January 1973
Episode Four: 20 January 1973

Written by Bob Baker and Dave Martin
Directed by Lennie Mayne

Director: It's notable that Lennie Mayne (see **61**, 'The Curse of Peladon') previously directed Patrick Troughton in the *Doomwatch* episode 'In the Dark' (1971), in which the actor gave a splendid dual performance – a likely reason why Mayne was selected to helm this story.

Notable Cast: This serial was William Hartnell's last work as an actor, made when he was already suffering severely from arteriosclerosis, a disease that thickens the arteries – hence the limited nature of his involvement. Determined to participate despite this, he read his lines off cue cards and direct to camera. His scenes were then fed into monitors and screens to give the impression of his interacting with various groups of characters via communication devices (his Doctor is said to be stuck in a 'time eddy', able to talk and advise but not interact). Hartnell died in 1975 following a series of strokes. A 'blue plaque' at BBC Television Centre and a mounted wall bust at BAFTA in Piccadilly celebrate his life and work. He is listed in the *Dictionary of National Biography*. Stephen Thorne (Omega) played Azal in **59**, 'The Dæmons'.

Doctor Who?: This is the first time we see different Doctors meet, and the first time the differences between them are underlined: their personalities clash, and they approach the problem in different ways (presumably this is why the Time Lords don't just send multiple Pertwees to deal with Omega). The Hartnell Doctor is referred to as the 'earliest' version by the Time Lord President (see **84**, 'The Brain of Morbius', **125**, 'Mawdryn Undead') and is observed in a rose garden. The Troughton Doctor is introduced running away from an exploding building, seemingly in the middle of some adventure (neither of these is a clip from earlier stories but both were specially shot – Hartnell in his own garden, Troughton in the quarry that also stood for Omega's world). At the end of the story the Time Lords reward the Pertwee Doctor by giving him a new, working dematerialisation circuit and returning his 'knowledge of time-travel law', making it possible for him to operate the TARDIS.

Other Worlds: A stable world in a universe of antimatter, created and held together by Omega's will. It's a quarry, with a castle (in which Omega lives) built into a rock face. The inside of the castle is organic-looking and made out of the same material as Omega's guards (see **Scary Monsters**). The Time Lords' (unnamed) planet is a gaudy place with a 'President' (Roy Purcell) who seems to be in charge of day-to-day affairs and a 'Chancellor' (Clyde Pollitt) whom the President calls 'Your Excellency' and to whom he is deferential even while going against his express wishes. It's not clear which of them is (or is meant to be) in charge. Both Omega and the Time Lord President refer to the Time Lords as having made a 'pledge' to 'protect' less powerful species, which doesn't square with their policy of 'observation only' as expressed in **50**, 'The War Games' or their covert-seeming actions in **58**, 'Colony in Space', and **61**, 'The Curse of Peladon'. This may indicate a recent change of policy (Omega could be aware of it, since he seems aware of much of what happens outside his domain).

Scary Monsters: Gell Guards, amorphous blobs with an explosive weapon built into their right claws, they are apparently expressions of Omega's will. Omega also mentally conjures up a 'champion' who represents 'the dark side of my mind' and fights the Pertwee Doctor during an interminable slow-motion fight sequence inside the Doctor's own consciousness. Omega sends a smaller, buzzing antimatter blob (achieved electronically, not with a costume like the above) to Earth to capture the Pertwee Doctor.

Villains: Omega, a revered figure from the history of the Doctor's own people. Omega created the power source the Time Lords use (not only for their time travel, but seemingly for all else as well) by exploding a star. He was thought to have died but became trapped on the other side of the black hole he had created. He knows the Doctor by that title without being told and treats the Pertwee Doctor as an equal immediately.

The Plan: Omega is draining the power source he created, seemingly out of pure revenge. Not specifically connected to this is his plan to force the Pertwee Doctor to replace him as controller of the antimatter world, which will collapse if Omega tries to leave without recruiting someone of similar mental powers to hold it together in his absence. The implication is that Omega is softening up the Time Lords' world so that he can attack and rule it once he escapes ('A hero? I should have been a god!') – but this is never specified or followed up.

Science/Magic: Lots of nonsense about antimatter. During his first scene on Omega's world, Dr Tyler (Rex Robinson) mutters, 'The light here must be travelling backwards, because I can still see.' Er, if you say so. Time Lords can shape reality with the power of their minds if they *really* concentrate. (See **162**, 'Death comes to Time'.)

Things Fall Apart: The Gell Guards are really poor, with wobbling gaits and sound effects that are comical, not threatening. When they 'appear' the camera visibly jerks up and down. Stephen Thorne's head is frequently visible beneath/behind his mask, which makes the revelation that he has no physicality even more surprising than the script wants it to be. There's surely no way that the Troughton Doctor's recorder could fall into the inside of the TARDIS console by accident. (When he retrieves it he has to undo a panel to get in.) The design is nasty even by early 1970s standards, there are too many characters and much of the story is spent running around.

Availability: A DVD edition, BBCDVD 1144, was released in 2003. UK VHS is BBCV 4650 (1993). US release initially numbered CBS/FOX 3405, reclassified as WHV E1100. A UK WH Smith exclusive release (2002) is BBCV 7564.

Verdict: 'It's the Doctors!' 'The Three Doctors' sees the series revelling in its own history for the first time (in retrospect it's odd to think that people were impressed that *Doctor Who* had lasted a mere nine years). The original draft featured a more substantial role for Hartnell, which was cut back when his ill health became apparent, and a return for Frazer Hines's Jamie, which was dropped when the actor was refused leave from what was then called *Emmerdale Farm*. Jamie's role was conferred on to Benton. It's imaginatively shot and the comic conflict between the three Doctors is well played (Troughton and Pertwee struggle to upstage one another). There's something *deeply* weird about hearing Hartnell say 'Time Lord' (something he never did in his own serials) but the put-downs he aims at his future selves have been rightly celebrated and it's particularly nice to have a chance to see him one last time.

66
Carnival of Monsters

Episode One: 27 January 1973
Episode Two: 3 February 1973
Episode Three: 10 February 1973
Episode Four: 17 February 1973

Written by Robert Holmes
Directed by Barry Letts

Notable Cast: Ian Marter (John Andrews) returned to the series as a regular from **75**, 'Robot'. He later became a writer, primarily of novelisations of films and television shows, including *Doctor Who*. Leslie Dwyer (Vorg) played Mr Partridge in the dreadful holiday camp sitcom *Hi-De-Hi!* (1980–85). Cheryl Hall (Shirna) played Shirley, the lead character's girlfriend in *Citizen Smith* (1977–80). Peter Halliday (Plectrac) apeared in **46**, 'The Invasion'.

History 101: The Doctor is convinced he isn't on Earth, even when the TARDIS appears to have landed on the SS *Bernice* on 4 June 1926. The Doctor knows the *Bernice* went missing on that day. The ship seems to be stuck in a time loop, with only the Doctor and Jo immune to the same programmed patterns.

Other Worlds: The Doctor is right: he and Jo *have* landed in one of the miniaturised environments inside a miniscope, an entertainment device. The miniscope has been taken to the planet Inter Minor by Lurman entertainers Vorg and Shirna. Amusement is prohibited on Inter Minor, but there is talk of lifting the restriction to halt rebellions among the functionaries, a worker class.

Doctor Who?: The Doctor considered the miniscopes (entertainment devices – see **Other Worlds** and **Scary Monsters**) offensive to sentient life, and persuaded the High Council of Time Lords that they should be banned – even though the Time Lords don't usually interfere. When wandering the miniscope's circuits, the Doctor admires the circuitry. The Doctor tries to speak to some chickens, thinking they might be intelligent life forms. He says it's impossible for him to be wrong, and drinks Scotch.

The Doctor was taught to box according to Queensbury rules by John L Sullivan. He doesn't think any problem is totally impossible: all it requires is lateral thinking to find a solution. He doesn't speak carnival lingo.

Scary Monsters: Creatures within the miniscope include a plesiosaurus that menaces the liner SS *Bernice* and the Drashigs, giant wormlike creatures with vicious teeth. Drashigs cannot be programmed within the miniscope, since they have no intelligence centres to control. They'll eat anything, but, as Vorg says, 'they prefer flesh – when they can get it'. The miniscope also includes Ogrons and a Cyberman.

Villains: Kalik (Michael Wisher), an Inter Minor functionary and brother of Emperor Zarb, is paranoid about attack from aliens, and believes the Lurmans might be spies. Having tried to have the miniscope destroyed . . .

The Plan: . . . Kalik wants to unleash the Drashigs on Inter Minor, causing chaos in which he can stage a coup against Zarb.

Science/Magic: Antimagnetic cohesion is a technique for bonding metal from a thousand years in Jo's future. You need a magnetic core extractor to unbind it. Humans are referred to as Tellurians, and their similarity to other bipeds has been taken as proof that there is not infinite variation in life. The aggrometer on the miniscope raises the aggression level of the creatures inside. Objects taken out of the miniscope's compression field regain their natural size. The Doctor's sonic screwdriver can explode pockets of swamp gas. The SS *Bernice* is returned to 1926, contrary to what the Doctor remembers, so established history can be altered.

Availability: Issued on Region 2 DVD in 2002 as BBCDVD 1098, and on Region 1 as WHV E1758. An earlier VHS is BBCV 5556 (UK), WHV E1311 (US).

Verdict: 'Just like goldfish in a bowl, aren't they? Going round and round for ever.' A highly inventive story, 'Carnival of Monsters' combines surreal humour with satire and historical pastiche. The characterisation is witty and well defined, with some excellent dialogue and performances. The early sequences are memorably surreal, including a fantastic and startling cliffhanger to the end of Episode One. There's a disconnection between the two plot threads – the Doctor doesn't exit the miniscope and join the other characters on Inter Minor until the end of Episode Three. Unusual at every turn, and constantly defying formula, 'Carnival' is notably colourful, in content as well as design.

67
Frontier in Space

Episode One: 24 February 1973
Episode Two: 3 March 1973
Episode Three: 10 March 1973
Episode Four: 17 March 1973
Episode Five: 24 March 1973
Episode Six: 31 March 1973

Written by Malcolm Hulke
Directed by Paul Bernard

Notable Cast: John Woodnutt (Draconian Emperor) previously appeared in **51**, 'Spearhead from Space'. Michael Hawkins (General Williams) is the father of the actor Christian Slater. Peter Birrel (Draconian Prince) was in 60s pop act Freddie and the Dreamers.

History 101: In the year 2540 Earth is in the early stages of building its empire (the Doctor references **63**, 'The Mutants', as having taken place during its decline). Twenty years earlier there was a war between Earth and Draconia, which was resolved by the establishment of a strict frontier in space between the two empires.

Other Worlds: Draconia, which the Doctor previously visited during the reign of the fifteenth emperor and helped them fight off a space plague. As a result he is a noble of the planet. We also visit the Ogrons' home planet, which is never named.

Scary Monsters: The Draconians, noble lizard-like warriors who are reminiscent of Japanese Shogun, although this was not Malcolm Hulke's intention and emerged during the design process (he wrote them with the post-Napoleonic Hapsburgs in mind). It would have aided Hulke's desire to give his 'monster' characters individual personalities if the Draconians' costumes had varied more. The Ogrons also feature, and there's a cameo from the Daleks.

Villains: The Master, played for the last time by Roger Delgado, who tragically died in a car accident shortly afterwards. It's one of his most coherent plans and he gets some great lines ('Thank you, Miss Grant, we'll let you know'), but the end of Episode Six was reshot without him, so it's a rather subdued exit – he simply vanishes after loosing off a bullet at the Doctor.

The Plan: The Master and the Ogrons are stirring up a war between Earth and Draconia by hijacking cargo vessels and using a hypnosis device to give each side the impression that the other is responsible. When the two empires decimate each other, the Daleks will move in to rule. There are clear Cold War parallels and the plot closely resembles Blofeld's in *You Only Live Twice* (Lewis Gilbert, 1967).

Doctor Who?: More boasts from the Doctor: he describes his landing on the cargo ship as 'rather brilliant', claims to be a qualified space engineer and recounts the story of his trial in a hugely biased version.

Science/Magic: The Doctor's air-nozzle trick when he is shaken from the Master's ship wouldn't work. In any case, the ship must be travelling at extraordinary speed and even the slightest deviation in the Doctor's direction would open up a vast distance in a matter of seconds.

Things Fall Apart: Why would the Draconians steal a load of flour anyway? Does Earth suspect them of planning a large bake sale? A visible wire holds the Doctor up when he's fixing the spaceship in Episode 6. The orange billowing duvet that menaces the Ogrons is one monster too far for the budget. Fortunately, Paul Bernard cut all but one shot of it from the finished programme, just one example of his excellent work on this serial (a vast improvement on **64**, 'The Time Monster').

Availability: Released on VHS in 1995 as BBCV 5640 (UK), WHV E1312 (US).

Verdict: 'It's going to be a very short war.' An ambitious attempt to produce epic space opera on a modest television budget, and it more or less comes off. 'Frontier in Space' successfully conveys an impression of scale by using a variety of locations and lots of interstellar travel between them (except when the Doctor is sentenced to imprisonment on the moon and arrives there in the very next scene). The design work is a cut above anything seen in the past couple of seasons, although there's some odd costuming (uniforms in the President's office consist of pastel evening gowns with matching dress gloves).

The serial attempts to demonstrate a future Earth that is equal along lines of gender and race, with a female president (who isn't British or American) and some non-Caucasian characters. When viewed in one sitting, its succession of captures, escapes, interrogations and journeys does become a bit repetitive, but, viewed episode by episode, it's a stirring adventure with enjoyable twists (the misdirection regarding the Daleks' presence is sharp writing from Hulke).

68
Planet of the Daleks

Episode One: 7 April 1973
Episode Two: 14 April 1973
Episode Three: 21 April 1973
Episode Four: 28 April 1973
Episode Five: 5 May 1973
Episode Six: 12 May 1973

Written by Terry Nation
Directed by David Maloney

Notable Cast: Jane How (Rebec) played Den's on-off mistress in *EastEnders* (1986–2003). Prentis Hancock (Latep) was in **51**, 'Spearhead From Space'. Bernard Horsfall (Taron) was in **45**, 'The Mind Robber' among many other *Doctor Who* serials, all for director David Maloney.

Doctor Who?: The Doctor is a mythical figure to the Thal astronauts alongside whom he fights the Daleks. The events of **2**, 'The Daleks' are ancient history. The Thals initially have difficulty believing he is who he says he is because of this – which is really nice. The Doctor still sees his battles against the Daleks as a moral crusade (as in **21**, 'The Daleks' Master Plan') and informs Thal leader Taron that if one adopts the Daleks' methods to fight them one becomes as bad as they. He also warns the Thal survivors against glamorising war when they recount their battles with the Daleks – begging them to remember the casualties and fear involved.

Other Worlds: Spiridon – where the days are tropically hot and the nights are freezing cold; where the vegetation is hostile, the indigenous intelligent species are invisible (although they inexplicably become visible as they die) and there are ice volcanoes. These spew bubbling liquid ice out on to the surface because the core of the planet is a mass of liquid ice that never solidifies.

Skaro is mentioned. The Dalek War (the events of 2, 'The Daleks') is said to have been 'generations ago'. The Thals now have a professional army and have recently developed space flight. The Thal spacecraft 'originates on Skaro', the Thal survivors return there at the end, and the Doctor wouldn't mind Jo living there with Latep, surely meaning the Daleks aren't based there at this point in their history, but the Thals are.

The Plan: The Doctor teams up with some Thal commandos who have come from Skaro to destroy the Dalek army that is poised the take over the galaxy (see 67, 'Frontier in Space').

Scary Monsters: The Daleks are unconvincing opponents this time out. Camera angles often make clear how useless their sucker arms are. They move poorly and slowly (compared with their sinister, effortless gliding in something as otherwise irredeemable as 16, 'The Chase') and simply react to the Thals' attacks on them rather than plotting and scheming. The casings are shabby and poorly painted too. They demonstrate a willingness to use germ warfare and habitually organise mass exterminations on planets they conquer. They have a Supreme Council and a Dalek Supreme (as this is set in 2540 – centuries before 21, 'The Daleks' Master Plan' – is this the same Dalek Supreme seen there but at an earlier point in its existence?).

Science/Magic: The TARDIS can run out of oxygen if its exterior walls are smothered (but it's an extradimensional machine that travels through space!). The Daleks are attempting to learn how the Spiridons stay invisible (it's due to a non-reflecting light wave, which unfortunately requires fantastic power) so that they can create an invisible Dalek army. Daleks that spend time invisible often die of light wave sickness. Eh?

Things Fall Apart: One of the TARDIS's interior walls is a set of flat-pack furniture consisting of several drawers, a wardrobe and a pull-out bed. The Dalek Supreme has a torch for an eye and jam jars over its lights. The Daleks' lights rarely flash in time with their dialogue as they're supposed to. None of the Daleks' technology or buildings seem to have been designed for Daleks (they have ordinary buttons and high ceilings respectively). How does that Dalek get the map out of Marat's pocket? The Doctor's new purple and mauve outfit (which makes him look like a pimp in a Gordon Parks movie) mysteriously complements the Spiridons' purple robes. The Dalek army is very obviously a collection of 1960s Louis Marx Dalek toys (see **36**, 'The Evil of the Daleks').

Availability: The BBC holds only a black-and-white export copy of Episode 3, having destroyed the colour original. This is included on the video. BBCV 6875 is part of a box set with **142**, 'Revelation of the Daleks'. The US release WHV E1495 is a single-tape release.

Verdict: 'Be careful how you tell that story, will you?' This is both a very lazy script – one riddled with minor inconsistencies and containing nothing not done better in earlier Dalek serials – and a rather shambolic production. The sets and make-up are consistently poor and the 'action' scenes are about as exciting as watching some cheese slowly rotting on a table. In the dark. The finished programme is unimaginative, witless and dull – proof that it's not remotely sensible to write a shallow set-piece-based narrative and then produce it on a shoestring.

69
The Green Death

Episode One: 19 May 1973
Episode Two: 26 May 1973
Episode Three: 2 June 1973
Episode Four: 9 June 1973
Episode Five: 16 June 1973
Episode Six: 23 June 1973

Written by Robert Sloman
Directed by Michael Briant

Notable Cast: Katy Manning makes her final appearance as Jo Grant. Tony Adams (Elgin) played the chancer Adam Chance in the soap opera *Crossroads*.

History 101: Back on Earth, in UNIT's time period. Mines are being closed in Llainfairfach in South Wales, but Global Chemicals is expanding its business working on a refining process for creating more fuel from crude oil (the 'Stevens Process'). Professor Cliff Jones (Stewart Bevan) and the Wholeweal community are campaigning against the pollution caused, developing alternative technologies. The prospect of cheap energy has the government eating out of Global Chemicals' hands, with the Prime Minister ('Jeremy') overruling the Brigadier in Global Chemicals' favour.

Doctor Who?: He's still obsessed with taking Jo to Metebelis 3. The Doctor doesn't want to get involved in the ecological conflicts on Earth, instead choosing to travel to the 'blue planet' on his own. The Doctor admired Professor Clifford Jones's paper on DNA synthesis. As Jo's affection for Professor Jones develops, the Doctor becomes visibly aware that soon he will part ways with her. The Doctor disguises himself as an aged Welsh milkman, and drags up as a cleaning lady. He believes you need protein for breakfast.

Other Worlds: The Doctor finally gets to Metebelis 3, taking a solo trip there in Episode One. After all his talk of how peaceful it is he has a terrible time, being menaced by flying monsters and running for his life.

Scary Monsters: The pollution in the mine causes maggots to grow to giant size. The maggots have a chitinous shell that can deflect bullets, and are resistant to pesticide. The maggots eventually pupate into giant flies.

Villains: Jocelyn Stevens (Jerome Willis), director of Global Chemicals, is being controlled by the supercomputer, BOSS. Having been linked to Stevens's brain, BOSS has the human inefficiency that allows creativity. BOSS acts as a substitute Master, brainwashing people into doing its will. Its purpose is the profit and prosperity of Global Chemicals – at all cost.

The Plan: Global Chemicals are dumping the pollution created by the Stevens Process into an old coal mine. The phosphorescent green chemical by-product infects humans on contact, turning them green as it kills them. It causes other life to mutate and grow.

Science/Magic: The space–time co-ordinator in the TARDIS is wearing down due to the ship's age. Dr Jones is working on a hybrid fungus as a substitute for meat. The maggots grow due to 'atavistic mutation'. Metebelis sapphires have hypnotic powers.

Things Fall Apart: The giant fly is extremely unconvincing, with limited movement. When the Doctor drives *Bessie* over a slagheap, model shots, blue-screen work and location footage are cut between with jarring effect.

Availability: Issued on Region 2 DVD in 2004 as BBCDVD 1142, and on Region 1 DVD as WHVE 1349. The earlier VHS is WHV E1349 (US), BBCV 5816 (UK).

Verdict: 'It's time the world awoke to the alarm bell of pollution.' An odd combination of real-world concerns and out-and-out SF wackiness, 'The Green Death' is, almost in alternating scenes, realistic, surreal, socially conscious and daft. The characters and issues are credible, with an unexpected naturalism – the characters actually have time to sit around and chat, eat meals and such. Jo's romance with Professor Jones begins in Episode One, and has time to grow through the story. However, the maggots and BOSS are as stupid and over-the-top as they come, and the Welsh setting is also heavily caricatured, and fairly patronising. However, there's a surprisingly poignant core to the story and the final scene, as the Doctor sneaks out of Jo's engagement party while the UNIT characters celebrate. It's beautifully played by Pertwee, and represents something of an end of an era.

70
The Time Warrior

Part One: 15 December 1973
Part Two: 22 December 1973
Part Three: 29 December 1973
Part Four: 5 January 1974

Written by Robert Holmes
Directed by Alan Bromly

Notable Cast: Elizabeth Sladen (Sarah Jane Smith) remained with *Doctor Who* until **87**, 'The Hand of Fear' and made numerous return appearances (**129**, 'The Five Doctors', **157**, 'The Paradise of Death', **158**, 'Dimensions in Time', **159**, 'Doctor Who and the

Ghosts of N-Space'). She later featured in the 1979 sitcom *Take My Wife* and starred as Sarah Jane in the failed *Doctor Who* spin-off *K9 and Company* (1981). At the time she was cast she'd made three recent guest appearances in *Z Cars*. David Daker (Irongron) was, as PC Owen Culshaw, one of the stars of *Z Cars*, and later played Harry in *Boon* (1986–95). Jeremy Bulloch previously appeared in **15**, 'The Space Museum'. Alan Rowe (Edward) previously appeared in **33**, 'The Moonbase'. June Brown (Lady Eleanor) is immediately recognisable as Dot Cotton from *EastEnders* (1985–93, 1997–present).

Director: Alan Bromly produced the 1969 and 1971 seasons of *Out of the Unknown* and the 1969–70 first season of *Paul Temple*. His directorial work includes a 1973 episode of *Orson Welles' Great Mysteries* and the film *The Angel Who Pawned Her Harp* (1954).

Scary Monsters: The first appearance of the Sontarans, cloned warriors who have been waging a war against a race called the Rutans for millennia. They possess some time-travel capacity. We see only one in this story – its name is Linx – but when you've seen one you've seen them all. The design is the serial's greatest achievement: the headpiece is effectively blended into actor Kevin Lindsay's features and makes him look less obviously 'man-in-suit' than your average alien. Lindsay also gives one of the best 'monster' performances in *Doctor Who*.

History 101: Linx crash-lands in thirteenth-century England (the date is given by Sarah in **77**, 'The Sontaran Experiment').

Villains: In addition to Linx we meet Irongron, a local warlord, and his men. The interaction between Linx and Irongron is neatly scripted and David Daker's performance as the latter is marvellous.

The Plan: Linx has forged an alliance with Irongron in order to have a base from which to repair its spacecraft. It is using time-projection equipment to jump forward to the twentieth century and snatch scientists whom it can force into helping with the repairs.

Science/Magic: The stick weapon that Linx carries can do everything! Twist it one way and it's a stun gun; twist the other and it's a truth ray.

Doctor Who?: The Doctor names his home planet for the first time: it is called Gallifrey. Sarah asks if he's human. 'If you mean am I a native of the planet Terra,' he replies, 'then the answer is no.' Sarah goes on to ask if he's serious and he sums up the spirit of *Doctor Who*: 'About what I do, yes . . . not necessarily about the way I do it.' Unfortunately, Pertwee's Doctor has slipped into self-parody. There's far too much Venusian karate and not only is it unconvincing but it's an easy way for him to get out of trouble.

Some sequences appear to have been contrived largely for Pertwee to do comedy voices, not least the one in which the Doctor poses as Linx's robot knight. (The ensuing sword fight in this sequence also flatters Pertwee unduly: 'Never have I seen a finer swordsman!' exclaims Irongron. Yeah, right.) Irongron refers to the Doctor as 'a longshank rascal with a mighty nose'. The Doctor refers to himself as a 'galactic ticket inspector'. From now until **115**, 'Logopolis' the character is credited as 'Doctor Who'.

Things Fall Apart: Sarah 'accidentally' getting into the TARDIS is contrived. Linx's robot knight unfortunately evokes *Monty Python*.

Availability: Released on VHS in 1989 as BBCV 4245 (UK), WHV E1165 (US), with its four episodes edited into an omnibus.

Verdict: 'Oh, so you like war, eh?' Having already turned in the most atypical serial of this Doctor thus far in **66**, 'Carnival of Monsters', Robert Holmes goes even further afield with 'The Time Warrior' – albeit at the production team's request. Holmes was unenthusiastic about writing a historical adventure, yet his script is spirited and original. The period is efficiently recreated, Alan Bromly's direction is smooth and the Doctor slots into the context very well, as he did in 'Carnival of Monsters' – suggesting that a revival of such settings should have been attempted earlier.

The serial is slightly let down by the Doctor himself: as a hero he is becoming less engaging and sympathetic. The chauvinism he directs towards the 'new girl', Sarah Jane Smith (who is quite promising in this story, if unevenly portrayed), is inexcusable, especially since the whole idea of introducing Sarah was to *counter* the accusations of sexism aimed at the series. If you're willing to ignore, indulge or lightly mock these elements, though, 'The Time Warrior' makes for very good *Doctor Who*.

71
Invasion of the Dinosaurs[1]

Part One: 12 January 1974
Part Two: 19 January 1974
Part Three: 26 January 1974
Part Four: 2 February 1974
Part Five: 9 February 1974
Part Six: 16 February 1974

Written by Malcolm Hulke
Directed by Paddy Russell

Notable Cast: John Bennett (General Finch) played Phillip Boseney in *The Forsyte Saga* (1967) and Xenophon in *I, Claudius* (1976). His film career has rallied in recent years, with roles in *The Fifth Element* (Luc Besson, 1997), *Charlotte Gray* (Gillian Armstrong, 2001) and *The Pianist* (Roman Polanski, 2002). Martin Jarvis (Butler) appeared in **13**, 'The Web Planet'; Carmen Silvera (Ruth) was in **24**, 'The Celestial Toymaker'. Peter Miles was in **52**, 'Dr. Who and the Silurians'.

History 101: The TARDIS lands in a deserted London, a few weeks after the Doctor and Sarah left the research centre in **70**, 'The Time Warrior'. There's no one around except looters and troops enforcing martial law. The city has been evacuated since it became overrun with prehistoric monsters. During the Cold War, a shelter was built beneath London so that the government could keep operating in the event of nuclear conflict. After the end of the Cold War, they were abandoned (the use of 'after' strongly suggesting a near-future setting rather than a contemporary one).

Scary Monsters: Dinosaurs are appearing and disappearing in London – species include triceratops, tyrannosaurus rex, stegosaurus and pterodactyls.

Villains: The conspiracy is led by Sir Charles Grover, MP (Noel Johnson), General Finch of the British Army, time-travel theorist Professor Whitaker (Peter Miles) and Captain Mike Yates of UNIT.

---

[1] The story title for Part One is simply 'Invasion', to conceal the nature of the monsters.

The Plan: Professor Whitaker and his assistant Butler are time-transferring the dinosaurs to keep central London clear as they prepare Operation Golden Age. A combination of athletes, authors, politicians and other great men and women believe they are travelling on a spaceship to colonise a 'New Earth'. In fact, time will be reversed, deleting the whole of human civilisation apart from the conspirators and the deceived 'colonists', allowing humanity to start again.

Doctor Who?: The Doctor says there never was a 'golden age'. He sympathises with Mike's ideals, but doesn't believe he has the right to erase the existence of others. The Doctor is immune to the effects of Whitaker's experiments. The Doctor likes having his photo taken, and believes his right side is his better one. He can do a horrible impersonation of a petty criminal, and a better one of a cockney soldier. He can knock a man out by pinching the back of his neck. He takes a huge amount of sugar in his tea. He has a new car – a silver-finned flying hovercraft.

Science/Magic: A 'time eddy' is when time temporarily runs backwards. The Doctor builds a device to suspend a dinosaur's brain functions, knocking it out cold.

Other Worlds: The Doctor offers to take Sarah to Florana, a beautiful planet covered with flowers.

Things Fall Apart: Every single special effect related to the dinosaurs is hopeless. The monsters themselves are useless puppets, and the model shots completely fail to mesh with the live-action footage. The Doctor claims his new car is necessary because 'speed is of the essence', so why does it move like a crippled milk float? It's very obvious that Sarah hasn't really been on the 'spaceship' for three months, as there is no equivalent break in the plot on Earth.

Availability: Issued on VHS in 2003 in the UK as BBCV 7333, and in the US as WHV E1858.

Verdict: 'The world used to be a cleaner, simpler place. It's all become too complicated and corrupt.' As with **52**, 'Doctor Who and the Silurians', with 'Invasion of the Dinosaurs' Malcolm Hulke again proves it's possible to write an Earth-based story that isn't about an alien invasion (although there are mad scientists of a sort). Unfortunately, solid scripting and some smart ideas are let down by disastrous production values, especially the abysmal dinosaur effects.

Self-indulgence seeps into the story as it goes on, with Part Five mostly taken up with an endless chase sequence for the Doctor while Sarah creeps down a lot of corridors. A layer of UNIT cosiness is stripped away when Yates is exposed as a traitor, but the story bottles it at the end by allowing him to resign quietly off screen. Pertwee is hardly giving his most measured performance, mugging outrageously whenever the Doctor is distressed or annoyed. It's also unfortunate that the plot requires some serious stupidity – the colonists plotline is ludicrous, and Sarah walks into the same obvious trap *twice*. Bright idea – dumb execution.

72
Death to the Daleks

Part One: 23 February 1974
Part Two: 2 March 1974
Part Three: 9 March 1974
Part Four: 16 March 1974

Written by Terry Nation
Directed by Michael Briant

Other Worlds: Exxilon is a world where an advanced civilisation has reverted to barbarism, having created a sentient city that then cast out its inhabitants. The city drains energy from electrical machinery via a beacon atop it. The holiday world Florana – where the water is effervescent and the air like a magic potion – is mentioned.

Scary Monsters: The Daleks are said to be the 'most technically advanced' species in the galaxy and inside every one is a 'living, bubbling lump of hate'. Deprived of the power to kill, they instantly panic, screaming 'Keep away! Keep away!' at the Doctor. They are malicious and scheming throughout with an ability to improvise on the spot. (Their attempt to steal the parrinium is itself a reaction to events.) They can solve the Exxilon city's logic puzzles as successfully as the Doctor can. One Dalek commits suicide, considering itself to have failed by letting prisoners escape.

Villains: Galloway (Duncan Lamont) is a shifty, glory-seeking thug who has a utilitarian attitude to life (always the sign of a swine in a Nation script) and doesn't object to either slave labour or slaughtering the renegade Exxilons. Although he sacrifices himself to destroy the Daleks he does so in an ostentatious way in order to ensure that he will be remembered as a hero.

The Plan: Earth's colonies, the outer planets, are being ravaged by a plague that can be cured with parrinium – a mineral found in abundance on Exxilon. A cadre of human marines and a shipload of Daleks battle over it – with the Daleks planning to hold the human colonies to ransom.

Science/Magic: The TARDIS is a living thing, according to the Doctor. Daleks move by 'psychokinetic power' – a convenient fudge as to why they still function when all electricity is drained away.

Things Fall Apart: The Daleks discuss their plans to betray the humans loudly while about three feet away. Much of Carey Blyton's music is needlessly groovy and thus tension-sapping. Virtually every male member of the cast 'discreetly' gropes Jill Tarrant (Joy Harrison) at some point. The exterior daytime scenes are floodlit, making an unfortunate contrast with the atmospheric night-time shooting and moody underground sequences. The Exxilons' tendency to shout 'ugg' and 'uhm' rapidly becomes very irritating.

Availability: Issued on VHS in 1995 as BBCV 5520 (UK), WHV E1152 (US).

Verdict: 'Now the universe is down to 699 wonders.' This takes place in a universe darker and weirder than is normally the case in early 1970s *Doctor Who*. Exxilon is a planet of sacrificial altars, smoking craters and self-healing cities with savage metallic snake-like root systems. 'Death' is a story that separates the Doctor and Sarah from all safety and plunges them into grim, dark and revolting unknown. The first half of Part One is set at night in a steaming, ashen landscape populated by wordless, hooded savages. In its brutality and obsessions with plague and disintegration, 'Death' anticipates 1975's episodes, when the new producer Philip Hinchcliffe would determinedly turn *Doctor Who* into an overt horror series.

73
The Monster of Peladon

Part One: 23 March 1974
Part Two: 30 March 1974
Part Three: 6 April 1974
Part Four: 13 April 1974
Part Five: 20 April 1974
Part Six: 27 April 1974

Written by Brian Hayles
Directed by Lennie Mayne

Other Worlds: The Doctor makes a long-planned return visit to Peladon, fifty years since his previous visit (**61**, 'The Curse of Peladon'). The trisilicate miners are being menaced by the spirit of Aggedor, royal beast of Peladon, and are rebelling against the queen and the Federation. The Federation is at war with Galaxy Five, who made a 'vicious and unprovoked attack'. The planet is ruled by Queen Thalira (Nina Thomas), daughter of King Peladon.

Doctor Who?: The Doctor namedrops his friendship with King Peladon, and says he has a 'special' relationship with the planet. He believes the Galactic Federation has brought the dispute on itself by mistreating the miners, and wants the queen to reach a settlement with them that benefits both sides. Looking for a peaceful solution, he asks if the Federation has tried to negotiate with Galaxy Five. When he hears of the appearances of Aggedor, the Doctor automatically assumes it's trickery.

The Doctor does a coin trick to distract a guard. He loses a fight with Ettis (Ralph Watson), a miner. He would like 'a quiet life'. The Doctor uses the directional heat ray attached to the Aggedor apparition to kill Ice Warriors. He can survive an assault on his mind and senses by going into a deep trance. He's flattered by the queen's offer to make him her new chancellor.

Scary Monsters: The Ice Warriors return, acting under Federation authority but with their own plans. The alien Vega Nexos has a Panlike appearance (hairy lower body, with human torso and a beard), but with the face of a chicken. Alpha Centauri is long-lived, and remembers the Doctor well.

Villains: Azaxyr (Alan Bennion), Ice Lord Commander, who is collaborating with the human engineer Eckersley (Donald Gee). Ettis, a militant miner who incites rebellion only to bring the wrath of the state down on his followers.

The Plan: Eckersley created the 'ghost of Aggedor' to foment rebellion in the mines, allowing Azaxyr to use the crisis to put the planet under martial law, enslaving the people to work in the mines. They intend to sell the trisilicate to Galaxy Five, allowing Eckersley to become ruler of Earth and Azaxyr to have 'military glory' for his breakaway Ice Warrior faction.

Science/Magic: Trisilicate is a mineral vital to the galactic war effort, the basis of all Federation technology. The sonic lance can increase mining output tenfold. Duralinium is a strong metal. The apparition of Aggedor is created using a matter projector, and the blasts from its eyes are a directional heat ray.

Things Fall Apart: The miners have ludicrous striped wigs that look like badgers. There's a cringe-inducing scene in which Sarah explains women's liberation to Queen Thalira. During the Doctor's fight scene in Part Four, the face of Jon Pertwee's stunt double is clearly visible. Some of the Ice Warrior costumes – in some cases clearly the same ones as in **39**, 'The Ice Warriors' – look very ropy.

Availability: Issued on VHS in 1996 as BBCV 5781 (UK), WHV E1377 (US).

Verdict: 'Local politics are not my concern.' Tedious social commentary and mundane space opera shenanigans combine to indigestible effect in this sequel to **61**, 'The Curse of Peladon'. While the first Peladon story was an efficient four-part exercise in Ruritanian intrigue, this follow-up tries far too hard to be worthy, taking in feminism, workers' rights and the exploitation of small nations by major powers. Eckersley is an obvious villain, and the Ice Warriors have lost the complexity they gained in 'The Curse of Peladon'. The guest roles are either played poorly or with misplaced conviction. When the most impressive and memorable part of the story is the rudely shaped, squeaky presence of Alpha Centauri, you know you're in trouble.

74
Planet of the Spiders

Part One: 4 May 1974
Part Two: 11 May 1974
Part Three: 18 May 1974
Part Four: 25 May 1974
Part Five: 1 June 1974
Part Six: 8 June 1974

**Written by Robert Sloman
Directed by Barry Letts**

Notable Cast: Cyril Shaps (Clegg) previously appeared in **37**, 'The Tomb of the Cybermen'. Gareth Hunt (Arak) played Gambit in *The New Avengers* (1976–77) and was in the final series of *Upstairs, Downstairs* (1976), but remains best known for the Nescafé commercials he made during the 1980s. Cho-Je is played by Kevin Lindsay, Linx in **70**, 'The Time Warrior'.

Other Worlds: Metebelis 3, previously seen in **69**, 'The Green Death'. Here it is at a point sometime in the far future, after it was colonised by settlers from Earth.

Scary Monsters: The spiders of Metebelis 3 evolved from ordinary Earth spiders, imported by the humans. The blue crystals caused them to grow in size and intelligence until they dominated the humans. The creatures are one of the production's major failings: they look like spiders but don't move like them, and the way that spiders move is half the reason people find them creepy. (This applies to a lot of *Doctor Who* monsters: perfectly well designed, but so immobile that they end up looking silly.)

Villains: Lupton (John Dearth), a failed salesman from contemporary Earth who has come to a Buddhist retreat run by Cho-Je to 'find power'. He inadvertently summons one of the spiders and joins forces with it to usurp the Queen Spider. There is also one giant spider – the Great One – who rules all others from a cave of crystals.

The Plan: The spiders, who insist on being referred to as 'eight-legs' (shades of Orwell's *Animal Farm*), plan to return to Earth as its rulers. The Great One has grander ideas: it believes that, with the aid of the perfect blue crystal that the Doctor stole back in 'The Green Death', it can amplify its mental powers to infinity and dominate the universe.

Science/Magic: The Metebelis crystals can focus the mind and repair mental damage. Later the Doctor uses a device from the TARDIS to identify stones that will absorb the spiders' energy attacks.

Doctor Who?: The Doctor says that he leaves the precise location of landing up to the TARDIS, to which Yates comments that he talks about the TARDIS as if it were alive. 'Yes I do, don't I?' the Doctor replies. We know from **64**, 'The Time Monster', that, as a young man, the Doctor was tutored by a hermit who lived on the mountain behind his house ('It was through him that I first learned to look into my mind'). Here we learn that said hermit later regenerated, came to Earth and became a Buddhist monk with the name K'anpo Rinpoche (George Cormack). The Doctor is also familiar with Buddhism (see **38**, 'The Abominable Snowmen'), being conversant with its customs and fluent in Tibetan. (Barry Letts is himself a Buddhist.) At the story's close, the Doctor is killed – destroyed by exposure to the blue crystals. With K'anpo's help his dead body regenerates.

Things Fall Apart: The lengthy chase sequence in Part Two is rendered irrelevant by Lupton's ability to simply vanish at the end. There's a bad acting contest going on among the Metebelis 3 natives: Jenny Laird (Neska) romps home to the prize. (Ironically enough, a Jenny Laird prize for acting is given out at RADA each year.)

Availability: Issued on VHS in 1991 as BBCV 4491 (UK) and WHV E1262 (US).

Verdict: 'Now I know what a fly feels like.' It's unfortunate that the main problems with 'Planet of the Spiders' are the spiders and the planet where they live. The first episode is excellent, well directed and atmospheric, and for a while it feels is if we're going to see the very best of the Pertwee era in its final hours. The wobbles begin in Part Two, with a chase sequence that ultimately irritates with its inclusion of lame 'comedy' characters (there's even a tramp who does a double take). Then in Part Three we go to Metebelis and – oh, dear! Cheap sets, dreadful acting and quivering, hysterical spiders drown the memory of those early moments of quality.

This is a pity, because there is much to commend 'Planet of the Spiders' for. It shrewdly identifies the Pertwee Doctor's character flaws – arrogance, meddling curiosity – and is bold enough to punish him for them. Thematically it works well: the common fear of spiders is used to represent the Doctor's deeper fear of facing up to his mistakes. It tries hard to provide closure for this era of the programme (all the other Letts/Sloman serials are referenced). It just fails as entertainment, that's all.

75
Robot

Part One: 28 December 1974
Part Two: 4 January 1975
Part Three: 11 January 1975
Part Four: 18 January 1975

Written by Terrance Dicks
Directed by Christopher Barry

Notable Cast: Tom Baker (Doctor Who) was born in Liverpool in 1934. Before acting, he spent several years in a seminary preparing to become a monk. Strong film roles include the Miller in Passolini's *The Canterbury Tales* (1971), Rasputin in *Nicholas and Alexandra* (Franklin J Schaffner, 1971) and the villainous magician in *The Golden Voyage of Sinbad* (Gordon Hester, 1974). He worked successfully at the National Theatre under Laurence Olivier. He stayed with *Doctor Who* until **115**, 'Logopolis', and is the programme's most recognisable and durable leading man, making more episodes and playing the Doctor in more consecutive years than any other actor. After leaving *Doctor Who* he appeared in *Black-Adder II* (1985) and *The Lives and Loves of a She-Devil* (1986) and took leading roles in *Medics* (1990–95), *Randall and Hopkirk (Deceased)* (2002–03) and *Monarch of the Glen* (2004–05), and narrated *Little Britain* (2001–present) on both radio and television. He played Sherlock Holmes in *The Hound of the Baskervilles* (1983) for the BBC and drew acclaim on the stage in *Educating Rita* (1983). His autobiography, *Who on Earth is Tom Baker?* (1997), achieved excellent sales. His performance here is terrific, both energetic and focused. It's also surprisingly different from the more relaxed, intuitive performances the actor gives when more secure in the role. Ian Marter (Harry Sullivan) also joins the regular cast here, having previously appeared (in a different role) in **66**, 'Carnival of Monsters'.

Doctor Who?: The new Doctor is erratic, childlike, laid-back, surprisingly young and alarmingly thin. He habitually stares into the middle distance, often thinks aloud and is secretive. The contrast between his grinning, inquisitive, frequently mocking persona and Pertwee's dandified, avuncular patrician is sudden and vast. As in **51**, 'Spearhead from Space', he keeps a TARDIS key in his shoes and tries to flee Earth the moment he wakes up. He has a pilot's licence for the Mars–Venus rocket run and membership of the Alpha Centauri table tennis society. He insists again that the ends cannot justify the means and likes jelly babies.

Villains: The Scientific Reform Society – a fascistic, uniformed pressure group who want to reform Britain along 'rational' lines so that it is run by a scientific elite. They're a bunch of lank-haired, adenoidal geeks – sneeringly sure of their own non-existent superiority. They're prepared to use nuclear blackmail to force their intentions on others.

Science/Magic: British scientists have recently developed a 'disintegrator gun', which does exactly what you'd imagine it does. Professor Kettlewell's experimental prototype robot K1 has a degree of sentience and is made of 'living metal'. 'Solar cells' and 'heat from windmills' are recent technological innovations. 'Dynastrene' is an indestructible metal.

Things Fall Apart: While the costume for the titular Robot is superb, the effects process that is used to make it grow to super size very much isn't. A toy tank is very obviously used in Parts Three and Four. That the people Sarah is interviewing turn out to be behind the problem UNIT is investigating is a shocking plot coincidence. The disintegrator gun is obviously made of polystyrene. The SRS's logo is based on the robot's face, which is a shabby coincidence someone should have noticed.

Availability: Released on VHS in 1992 as BBCV 4714 (UK), WHV E1260 (US).

Verdict: 'A new body's like a new house – takes a little bit of time to settle in.' Made alongside **74**, 'Planet of the Spiders', 'Robot' contains no real indications that *Doctor Who* starring Tom Baker will be startlingly dissimilar from that starring Jon Pertwee, apart from Baker's crackerjack, impressively different lead performance. With its Earth-based plot, human scientist villains, UNIT presence, ecological concerns and characterisation of Sarah Jane as an inquisitive journalist who goes off on her own and gets into trouble as a consequence, 'Robot' is very much a coda to the final run of Pertwee serials. Even Surgeon Lieutenant Harry Sullivan (engagingly played by Ian Marter) is, in this serial at least, a straightforward replacement for Captain Yates. That said, this is – before both the plot and the money run out simultaneously early in Part Four – a glossy, witty and surprisingly action-packed affair.

76
The Ark in Space

Part One: 23 January 1975
Part Two: 1 February 1975
Part Three: 8 February 1975
Part Four: 15 February 1975

Written by Robert Holmes
Directed by Rodney Bennett

Director: Rodney Bennett directed episodes of *Rumpole of the Batley* and Derek Jacobi in *Hamlet* (1980). He lent his name to the rival school in *Grange Hill*.

Producer: Philip Hinchcliffe made his debut as a producer on *Doctor Who*. He left the series to produce high-profile drama *Target* (1977), which had been created by his *Who* successor Graham Williams. (The two pretty much swapped jobs.) Hinchcliffe went on to produce numerous high profile TV projects such as *Private Schulz* (1981), *The Charmer* (1987) and *Friday On My Mind* (1992) starring Christopher Eccleston. In cinema he produced *An Awfully Big Adventure* (Mike Newell, 1995) starring Hugh Grant, and co-produced *Total Eclipse* (Agnieszka Holland, 1995) starring young Leonardo DiCaprio. In recent years he has taken an executive producer role on mainstream crime dramas *Taggart* and *Rebus*.

Doctor Who?: The Doctor keeps a cricket ball in his pocket, and his scarf was knitted by 'Madame Nostradamus'. He believes any improvement in Harry's mind is due to his positive influence. The Doctor has a tendency to soliloquise at great length, and is impressed by humanity's longevity (they're his favourite species). He hates stun guns – they give him a headache. The Doctor is not above cruelly taunting his friends to encourage them.

Other Worlds: The Nerva space station, several millennia after the thirtieth century, where survivors of solar flares that ravaged Earth are sleeping in cryogenic suspension. Human society is highly compartmentalised, with people unable to think outside their set function. (At least, they are until Holmes gets bored of producing dialogue for such flat characters.)

Scary Monsters: The Wirrn, parasitic insects that can infect and control a person by contact, digesting the host from within ('endoparasitism'). The knowledge of the humans digested by the Wirrn is absorbed. They're vulnerable to electricity. The Wirrn are bitter after being driven from Andromeda by humanity.

The Plan: A Wirrn queen reached the Ark, cutting through its electrical systems and laying an egg before dying. The Wirrn spread through space but their breeding grounds are on planets, using other creatures to hatch their eggs. They will then adopt humanity's knowledge and become a high-technology civilisation.

Science/Magic: The TARDIS goes off course due to Harry fiddling with the helmic regulator. The Doctor plays with a yo-yo to take a 'simple gravity reading'. On the Ark, human thought is still preserved on microfilm.

Things Fall Apart: The model of the Ark is extremely tacky and doesn't even rotate. The Wirrn grub is a man in a bubble-wrap sleeping bag, while the grown version has no mobility whatsoever. The cliffhanger to Part Two is Noah (Kenton Moore) gurning at his hand, which is wrapped in green plastic.

Availability: Issued on DVD in 2002 as BBCDVD 1097 (Region 2), WHV E1162 (Region 1). The US VHS is WHV E1162 and is edited into a compilation; the equivalent UK release was long ago deleted. It was re-released, unedited, as BBCV 5218.

Verdict: 'There was not much "joke" in the last days.' Speed-written, fractured fluff, 'The Ark in Space' is a bit of a mess. The production is mostly functional – there are some impressive sets, such as the cryogenics chamber, but other parts of the production are severely lacking: the model shots are poor, and the Wirrn virtually immobile. The story suffers from inconsistencies: the first humans to awake are from an emotionless, functional society, but this is quickly forgotten as the story goes on and the characters become more generic.

Baker is beginning to develop a more brooding, aloof performance as the Doctor, but it's Ian Marter who steals the show, getting all the best lines (including some great jokes). The characters on the Ark are humourless at the best of times, and generally poorly performed. Noah is the worst of the bunch, Kenton Moore delivering a stilted and overly hysterical performance. While Baker and Marter put in a strong showing, the serial as a whole is sloppy.

77
The Sontaran Experiment

Part One: 22 February 1975
Part Two: 1 March 1975

Written by Bob Baker and Dave Martin
Directed by Rodney Bennett

Notable Cast: Glyn Jones (Krans) previously scripted **15**, 'The Space Museum'. Donald Douglas (Vural) worked on *The Armando Iannucci Shows* (2001) and *Bridget Jones's Diary* (Sharon Maguire, 2001).

History 101: This serial follows on directly from **76**, 'The Ark in Space'. The Doctor, Sarah and Harry have beamed down to the ravaged and depopulated Earth so the Doctor can ensure that the transmat is in working order. They encounter members of an Earth colony named Galsec, who have landed on Earth to investigate the disappearance of one of their freighters near the former homeworld. Their ship was vaporised upon landing and they are stranded. They are highly sceptical of the Doctor's claim to be from the space station Nerva: most surviving colonists have assumed the station lost or destroyed.

The colonial themes that Bob Baker and Dave Martin addressed so heavy-handedly in **63**, 'The Mutants' are deftly noted in a single scene here, as Vural rages at the Doctor about Nerva's decadence and assumed 'Mother Earth' dominance. The South African accents of the Galsec colonists subtly underline this (although the dynamic is perhaps more analogous to eighteenth-century America).

Scary Monsters: The Sontarans return (see **70**, 'The Time Warrior'). As a member of a cloned race, Field Major Weam Styre looks very similar to Linx from the earlier story (they are played by the same actor, Kevin Lindsay, although the mask is slightly different and he has five digits rather than three). Lindsay turns in another excellent performance that helps to gloss over a couple of the story's implausibilities.

Science/Magic: The Doctor realises that an alien presence is at work when he finds a small patch of fuel, which he identifies as 'terullian drive'. Styre's robot operates on this.

Doctor Who?: 'I'm sort of a travelling time expert,' he says. He makes light of the destruction of everything on Earth, jovially suggesting that the subsidence that Harry has fallen down could be the Central Line. As well as being able to repair the transmat, the Doctor demonstrates considerable combat skills when engaging Linx.

The Plan: Earth has gained some strategic importance in the endless Sontaran–Rutan war. Styre has arrived on Earth to conduct experiments on humans in preparation for an invasion, and lured the Galsec colonists there for this purpose.

Things Fall Apart: Why does the Sontaran Marshal so easily believe the Doctor's bluff that the fleet will be destroyed if it makes a move on Earth?

Availability: Issued on VHS in 1991 as BBCV 4643 (UK), WHV E1201 (US) in a pack with **78**, 'Genesis of the Daleks'.

Verdict: 'You are a mistake and will be eliminated. According to my data you should not exist.' A highly effective story, which clearly has limited resources but enjoys the benefits of being shot entirely on location. Its claim to represent a ravaged future Earth is lent authority by the Doctor's slightly detached attitude. Although it is often claimed that *Doctor Who* is in some way wedded to the structure of four 25-minute episodes, 'The Sontaran Experiment' exposes the arbitrariness of this by dispensing a satisfying plot in half that time. When edited into a repeat omnibus later that year, it demonstrated that *Doctor Who* could have worked in 45-minute instalments in 1975 just as well as in 2005. Unfortunately, the two-part format would not be used again until **120**, 'Black Orchid'.

78
Genesis of the Daleks

Part One: 8 March 1975
Part Two: 15 March 1975
Part Three: 22 March 1975
Part Four: 29 March 1975
Part Five: 5 April 1975
Part Six: 12 April 1975

Written by Terry Nation
Directed by David Maloney

Notable Cast: Guy Siner (Ravon) played Pilades in *I, Claudius* (1976) and Gruber in *'Allo 'Allo!* (1982–92) and appeared in *Pirates of the Caribbean: The Curse of the Black Pearl* (Gore Verbinksi, 2003). Stephen Yardley (Sevrin) starred in *The XYY Man* (1976–77), played Max Brocard in *Secret Army* (1978) and was a regular in *Howard's Way*. More recently he played Vince Farmer in *Family Affairs* (1999–2003). Tom Georgeson (Kavell) played Dixie Dean in Alan Bleasdale's *The Black Stuff* (1980) and *The Boys from the Black Stuff* (1982), as well as Harry in *Between the Lines* (1992–94). He has a minor role as a police detective in **115**, 'Logopolis'. Peter Miles was in **52** and **71**.

Other Worlds: The Doctor and his friends are pulled out of the transmat beam by the Time Lords and sent to Skaro before the Daleks evolved, to set their development off course. The Thals and the Kaleds are fighting a war from their domed cities; the areas in between are an irradiated no-man's-land of trench warfare. Bands of marauding mutants roam the wasteland. Inside a bomb-proof bunker, the Kaled scientific elite works on ways to destroy the Thals and allow the Kaled race to survive.

Villains: Davros (Michael Wisher), the one-handed, wheelchair-bound Kaled chief scientist. His wheelchair resembles the bottom half of a Dalek and acts as a life-support system. He is hideously scarred and can see only through an electronic eye on his forehead. When he hears of the terror the Daleks will cause, Davros is excited by the possibilities. He considers the Doctor's conscience a weakness and uses it against him, torturing Harry and Sarah to get the Doctor to reveal the mistakes the Daleks will make in the future. He also uses the democracy of his opponents as an excuse to get them to stall. Davros's right-hand man is Security Commander Nyder (Peter Miles), an unsubtly Nazi-esque villain (he wears an Iron Cross in early episodes) who believes Davros is never wrong.

Scary Monsters: The Daleks, revealed as creations of Davros. Davros created the creature within each Dalek by accelerating the mutation of the Kaleds due to chemical weapons, and impregnates the embryos so that they develop without conscience. He created the 'Mark III travel machines' for these ultimate mutations, the familiar Dalek casings. When Davros tests the first Dalek, it moves to kill the Doctor and Harry, recognising them as aliens.

The results of Davros's earlier experiments are loose in a cave near the bunker, and include some kind of reptile as well as a carnivorous giant clam.

The Plan: Davros plots to eliminate the whole of the Kaled people, replacing them with the Daleks and the remains of Davros's scientific elite. To this end, he leaks the secret of how to destroy the Kaled dome to the Thals. When the Kaleds are destroyed, Davros sends the first Daleks to wipe out the victorious Thals as they celebrate.

Doctor Who?: The Doctor is unwilling to co-operate with the Time Lords – until the Daleks are mentioned. His pockets contain a huge amount of junk, including a magnifying glass and handcuffs. When he has the opportunity to destroy the Daleks by blowing up their incubation room, the Doctor hesitates, and is relieved when he thinks he doesn't need to make the choice any more. He believes the threat of the Daleks may bring other races together in their enmity of the Daleks, and that by wiping out an entire race he would be no better than the Daleks themselves. He later changes his mind, and the incubator room is destroyed – but the Daleks are already operating the production line. While he hasn't destroyed the Daleks, he has delayed their progress by about a thousand years. In the final balance he believes that out of the Daleks' evil must come some good – although it's hard to see why he thinks this.

Science/Magic: A time ring is a brass bracelet used by the Time Lords – it's given to the Doctor to reunite him with the TARDIS once his mission is over. The Doctor has an etheric beam locator, which detects ion-charged emissions. The Doctor and Harry are biologically completely different from the natives of Skaro.

Distronic explosive is a poisonous substance – prolonged exposure leads to death.

History 101: The Doctor describes the Daleks' invasion of Earth as taking place in the year 2000 (**10**, 'The Dalek Invasion of Earth').

Things Fall Apart: The killer clam is an astonishingly stupid threat. It's pathetically easy for the Doctor and co. to move between the Kaled and Thal cities, in spite of the fact that the two races have been fighting a war between the domes for a thousand years. In addition, if the war has left everything in such a bad state, how come both cities are spotlessly clean and well maintained? More prosaically, the cliffhanger at the end of Part Five sees a green plastic omelette trying to rip the Doctor's throat out. In Part Six, monitor screens jump to life just so that the Doctor can see events he can't be present for.

Availability: Issued on VHS in 1991 as BBCV 4643 (UK), WHV E1201 (US) in a pack with **77**, 'The Sontaran Experiment'. An edited version of the audio-only version is available, including additional narration by Tom Baker, as ISBN 0563478578.

Verdict: 'Today the Kaled race is ended, consumed in a fire of war, but from its ashes will rise a new race . . .' 'Genesis' has one of the most memorable openings of any *Doctor Who* story, a lavish and brutal scene in which gasmasked soldiers are gunned down on the killing fields of Skaro. However, the story rapidly descends into running around studio corridors. Much of the scene-to-scene plotting is uninspired, with constant captures and escapes, and a MacGuffin such as the time ring or the recording of the Daleks' future defeats providing a mechanical excuse to keep the Doctor going back into danger. The regulars don't really act as protagonists in the early part of the story, stumbling around and trying not to be killed while the situation on Skaro is explained. Harry is a less comedic, more dashing character, closer to the heroes of the Hartnell era. Secondary characters are made from the purest cardboard, and are picked up and discarded, or change sides at moments of plot convenience.

Nevertheless it's almost universally well acted, and directed with melodramatic flair by David Maloney, who squeezes every bit of tension out of Nation's stock action set pieces. There are signs of Robert Holmes's hand in the script editing, specifically the big speeches given to the Doctor and Davros, which echo Holmes's

script for **76**, 'The Ark in Space'. Aside from those speeches and
the odd joke, the script is pure Nation, especially in a plot filled
with random threats, B-movie melodrama and a Dalek philosophy
that is disturbingly successful. Yet Davros, brilliantly portrayed by
Michael Wisher, emerges as Nation's second great *Doctor Who*
creation. It's remarkable that no one had done half man, half
Dalek before. It's a great role, a great visual and a great character.
It is for Davros's debut, and a few key scenes, that 'Genesis' is so
well remembered.

79
Revenge of the Cybermen

Part One: 19 April 1975
Part Two: 26 April 1975
Part Three: 3 May 1975
Part Four: 10 May 1975

Written by Gerry Davis
Directed by Michael E Briant

Notable Cast: The always engaging David Collings (Vorus) is one
of those actors who seem to have appeared in *everything*. He
played Babbington in *Elizabeth R* (1970), Silver in *Sapphire and
Steel* (1979–81), John Turloe in *By the Sword Divided* (1982–3) and
the headmaster in *Press Gang* (1989–93). He was also Bob Crachitt
in *Scrooge* (Ronald Neame, 1971) and has made guest appearances
in everything from *Blake's 7* (1981) to *Miss Marple* (1986). Kevin
Stoney (Tyrum) previously appeared in **21**, 'The Daleks' Master
Plan'. Ronald Leigh-Hunt was in **48**, 'The Seeds of Death'.

Writer: Gerry Davis's script ('Return of the Cybermen') was
heavily rewritten by Robert Holmes. While the finished story is
problematic, Davis's original script – which has since been
published – is much weaker, featuring truly dreadful dialogue and
a risible ending.

Scary Monsters: Cybermen. The Doctor dismisses them as 'a
pathetic bunch of tin soldiers skulking around the galaxy in an
ancient spaceship'. He isn't wrong. Despite good costumes they're
unsatisfactory adversaries, claiming they are 'destined to be rulers
of all the cosmos' while strutting around *very slowly*, hands on
hips. It's been suggested that Holmes erred by not utilising the

Cybermen's potential as a source of body horror, but we believe that overlooks the fact that the Cybermen are a *rubbish* source of body horror and have never been convincingly, let alone compellingly, exploited in this manner. They are now explicitly 'total machine creatures' (and have enough parts in their ship to make an army) and there's nothing in the two previous Cybermen stories to suggest otherwise.

Other Worlds: Voga – a planet made almost entirely of gold. Though destroyed at the end of the last Cyberwar, it has now drifted into the orbit of Jupiter.

The Plan: The Cybermen plan to destroy Voga. A faction of Vogans is likewise plotting to annihilate the Cybermen so that they will no longer have to hide from them.

Doctor Who?: These Cybermen don't know of the Doctor (though the ones in **43**, 'The Wheel in Space', and **46**, 'The Invasion', did). He ties a 'tangled Turk head splice' knot he picked up from Houdini.

Science/Magic: Only a 'molecular short circuit' could damage a Time Ring. Nerva Beacon's transmat has a vital element called a 'Pentalion Drive' (a lovely Holmes phrase). The Doctor transmats Sarah to Voga on the off-chance that the process of disassembling her that it involves may cause the 'plague' to be rejected as an 'alien poison' when the machine puts her back together.

History 101: Cybermen died out centuries before the story. It is set in the same place, but thousands of years before **76**, 'The Ark in Space' (when Nerva was a navigational beacon rather than a Space Ark), and there's much pleasing effort put into making this visually appear to be a much less distant future than that one (the costumes, the fact that the humans use projectile weapons, read magazines, have personal effects). The Doctor, Sarah and Harry arrive at 18.57, Day 4 of Week 57 of Nerva's crew assignment.

Things Fall Apart: Sneering Kellman (Jeremy Wilkin) might be the most obvious traitor in screen history. He has an absurdly complex mantrap built into his quarters just in case anyone breaks in. The snakelike re-envisioning of the Cybermats is by far their most successful on-screen portrayal, but they're still rubbish. While the Cyberleader demonstrates several emotions in its dialogue, this has been the case since (at least) **33**, 'The Moonbase'. The Cybermen's technology's functionality is impaired by the presence of so much gold, but the creatures themselves aren't. All the Vogans look like Jonathan Meades. The Cyberleader is inexplicably characterised as a muscular Canadian bondage queen (this is the first time the actors playing the Cybermen use their own voices, which is perhaps what leads to the more demonstrative acting in this and all subsequent Cybermen stories).

Availability: The very first *Doctor Who* video released (BBCV 2003 in 1983), 'Revenge' was available in an edited, omnibus format. It was re-released in episodic form in 1999 (BBCV 6773). US release is WHV E1110 and corresponds to the former UK issue.

Verdict: 'Fragmentised? Well I don't suppose we can expect decent English from a machine.' This has much witty dialogue, some good model work and is well shot and played. The first episode, particularly, is creepy and involving, as the Doctor, Sarah and Harry explore the deserted, body-strewn Nerva and meet up with the truculent, suspicious skeleton crew. Unfortunately, the basic plot is derivative and weak – although still better than most other Cybermen stories – but the cast (in particular, Baker, Marter, Collings and Ronald Leigh-Hunt) just about manage to save the serial.

80
Terror of the Zygons

Part One: 30 August 1975
Part Two: 6 September 1975
Part Three: 13 September 1975
Part Four: 20 September 1975

Written by Robert Banks Stewart
Directed by Douglas Camfield

Notable Cast: This is Ian Marter's last story as a regular, although he makes a one-off return in **83**, 'The Android Invasion'.

Writers: Robert Banks Stewart is one of British TV's most successful popular dramatists. The creator of *Shoestring* (1979–80) and *Bergerac* (1981–91), he also wrote for *The Avengers* (1965) and *Callan* (1970).

Doctor Who?: This is another – and arguably the last – *Doctor Who* serial to invite the viewer to make direct comparisons between Pertwee and Baker. There's no longer any warmth in the

Doctor's interaction with Benton (he barely even looks at him when they speak). Equally, the Doctor's conversations with the Brigadier are now aggressive and distant rather than affectionately acerbic, and whereas the Pertwee Doctor clearly regarded Earth as a second home, Baker's version demands, 'Why have you called me back? I hope you've got a very good reason.' Then he leaves the moment he's no longer needed. He mocks everyone around him except Sarah, and addresses the Duke of Forgill (John Woodnutt) as 'Your Grace' in a tone that makes it an insult. Angus McRanald (Angus Lennie) perceptively labels the Doctor 'a man who might see round a few corners'. The Doctor can now hypnotise people just by looking at them (see **153**, 'Battlefield').

Scary Monsters: Zygons – aquatic mammals who live on milk and can transform themselves into physical replicas of captured humans. It isn't clear whether this ability is natural or a result of technology. Oh, and the Loch Ness monster – which is more properly a Zygon cyborg called a Skarasen.

The Plan: The Zygons are going to take over the world – imaginative, that.

Science/Magic: The Zygons' technology is organic rather than mechanical. It is squeezed and manipulated rather than clicked and flipped. The peculiar visual implications of this are quite pleasing (everything looks like a cross between a scab and pizza) and this is emphasised by use of cross-fades and odd close-ups when it's on camera. The Doctor mocks humanity for its use of oil as fuel and suggests the 'energising of hydrogen' as an alternative.

History 101: The British prime minister is a woman. Margaret Thatcher was already Conservative Party leader when this was made and the production – ostensibly set in the near future – is clearly anticipating her future general-election victory.

Things Fall Apart: The shots of the Skarasen attacking London at the end are an uncomfortable mix of poor hand puppetry and crackly stock footage. It's impressive that a set-piece-based narrative as simple as this could be so riddled with holes and little contrivances. For example, the Zygons remove their surveillance equipment from the inn because they're frightened it will be found, but it leaves holes when they remove it. This not only means that UNIT know where it was but also leads to the inevitable deduction of where it came from. How controllable the Skarasen is changes from scene to scene. Why do the Zygons always revert to 'monster' form before they attack someone (except to impress the audience)? Sarah accidentally finds her way into the Zygon ship because the door release mechanism is on a shelf that a disguised Zygon *fetches a stepladder to allow her to look at.* The Brigadier claims that oil rigs always remind him of 'three-legged spiders in Wellington boots'. Hmm. Seen a lot of those, has he?

Availability: Issued on VHS in 1999 as BBCV 6774 (UK), WHV E1410 (US).

Verdict: 'Very good, very good, almost impressive, but why bother?' Although less obviously so than **75**, 'Robot', this serial clearly demonstrates the fascinations of the latter Pertwee years (it has an ecological bent Sarah is, for the last time, actively a journalist and so forth). However, the shock/horror atmosphere sets it apart from the likes of **69**, 'The Green Death'. It's impossible to imagine Harry being gunned down (and then bleeding), or his doppelgänger fighting with a pitchfork, under Barry Letts's producership. This is atmospheric and enjoyable, largely down to haunting music from Geoffrey Burgon, but the story, structure and (especially) plotting are a disgrace.

81
Planet of Evil

Part One: 27 September 1975
Part Two: 4 October 1975
Part Three: 11 October 1975
Part Four: 18 October 1975

Written by Louis Marks
Directed by David Maloney

Notable Cast: Frederick Jaeger (Sorenson) previously appeared in **26**, 'The Savages'.

Doctor Who?: The Doctor believes that scientists must have 'total responsibility' for their actions. He uses a gun, albeit only to stun someone, and punches out a guard. He says Shakespeare was charming but a 'dreadful actor'. For the first time in the series, the Doctor controls the TARDIS to make a couple of short, precise journeys – from a spaceship to the planet, then back again.

Other Worlds: Zeta Minor, 'on the edge of the known universe', in the year 37166. A ship has come to the planet to find a previous expedition led by Professor Sorenson, who is trying to find an alternative energy source (the solar system's sun is dying and new energy is needed).

Science/Magic: Zeta Minor is a planet where the two universes of matter and antimatter overlap. The antimatter universe coexists with ours. The Doctor says that 'antimatter in collision with matter causes radiation annihilation', and that there's no safe way to use antiquark energy (which comes in three configurations) as an energy source. The Doctor suggests an alternative energy source to Sorenson, using 'the kinetic force of planetary movement'. The 'oculoid tracker' is a floating camera that acts as an electric sniffer dog.

Scary Monsters: A semi-visible creature from the antimatter universe, essentially the crayoned red outline of a sack of old rags that can change its size. When it comes into contact with humans, it kills them through instant dehydration, a process similar to freeze-drying.

Villains: Mumbling weirdo scientist Sorenson, whose expedition to exploit the mineral wealth of Zeta Minor as an energy source led to the destruction of the other expedition members by the creature.

The Plan: Sorenson plans to remove antimatter material from the planet, which will cause the destruction of the universe. Sorenson has created a vaccine to protect himself against contact with antiquarks, but the vaccine has combined with the antiquarks to hybridise him into an 'anti-man', a degraded beast creature. He later splits into a number of anti-men with similar abilities to the creature on Zeta Minor.

Things Fall Apart: Part One features a man being terrified of his environment, subtly demonstrated by crash zoom shots of nearby plants. The force-field effect is a cartoon squiggle. The camera takes a severe bump in Part Three. Prentis Hancock (Salamar) seems not to be able to deliver a line of dialogue convincingly. Michael Wisher (Morelli) plays a second character, providing a terrible, even offensive, Indian accent on the other end of a communicator.

Availability: Issued on VHS in 1994 as BBCV 5180 (UK), WHV E1319 (US).

Verdict: 'Those minerals are endangering the safety of my command.' It's very rare to see a *Doctor Who* story in which the best thing is the lighting (courtesy of Brian Clemett). 'Planet of Evil' is just that story, a superbly lit and periodically well-directed exercise in histrionic horror nonsense, which has little else of merit. An extended scowl-a-thon in which characters attempt to look worried by otherwise unthreatening events, the story is too weak to be saved by the impressive production values. The threats in the story are incredibly vague, resulting in a final episode in which characters menace each other with different-sized buckets to prevent an ill-defined catastrophe. In spite of all the shouting from the cast, the predicaments in 'Planet of Evil' are dull and almost impossible to care about.

82
Pyramids of Mars

Part One: 25 October 1975
Part Two: 1 November 1975
Part Three: 8 November 1975
Part Four: 15 November 1975

Written by Stephen Harris
Directed by Paddy Russell

Notable Cast: Michael Sheard (Laurence Scarman) previously appeared in **23**, 'The Ark' and **56**, 'The Mind of Evil'. Bernard Archard (Marcus Scarman) previously appeared in **30**, 'The Power of the Daleks'. Peter Copley had a regular role in *Cadfael* (1994–96); his other credits include *Help!* (Richard Lester, 1965), the first series of *The Foundation* (1978–79) and much prestigious theatrework.

Writer: 'Stephen Harris' is a pseudonym for Lewis Griefer, who removed his name after script editor Robert Holmes extensively rewrote his scripts (Paddy Russell also worked on the final draft). Griefer had previously worked on such shows as *The Prisoner*.

Villains: Seven thousand years ago, the influence of a highly powerful race known as the Osirans spread to Earth: 'The whole of Egyptian culture is founded on the Osiran pattern,' according to the Doctor. The most evil of their race, Sutekh (Gabriel Woolf), was captured and imprisoned here.

History 101: In 1911 Sutekh's tomb in Egypt is opened by the archaeologist Marcus Scarman. However, Sutekh is still imprisoned by a device called the Eye of Horus, which exerts a force field around Sutekh's chair from its position on Mars.

The Plan: Sutekh possesses Scarman's mind and has him ship a number of robot mummies, along with the equipment to build an explosive rocket, to the Scarman mansion in England. When constructed, the rocket will be fired at Mars and destroy the Eye of Horus, setting Sutekh free.

Science/Magic: This is a prime example of *Doctor Who* taking ideas and images from supernatural and Gothic fiction and half-rationalising them (usually by substituting the supernatural element for some incomprehensible alien technology) so that it will work on *Doctor Who*'s terms. Where most 'mummy's tomb' stories involve animated cadavers in bandages, 'Pyramids of Mars' has robots, and the vengeful creature that has been freed is not a human brought back to life, but an alien who never died.

Scary Monsters: Mummies, used as manual labour by Sutekh and for the odd bit of killing.

Doctor Who?: Rarely have we seen the Doctor so detached from humanity and focused on the bigger picture. He crushes Laurence Scarman's hope of saving his possessed brother and later Sarah criticises him for his casual response to Laurence's death, to which he points out that many more may die if they delay their efforts. The Osiran identifies him as a Time Lord: 'I renounced the society of Time Lords,' he replies. 'Now I'm simply a traveller.' The Doctor claims that the TARDIS controls are 'isomorphic', i.e. they respond only to him.

Other Worlds: An opportunity arises for the Doctor and Sarah to leave in the TARDIS. She suggests that they do so, reasoning that there is no need for them to stop Sutekh: 'We know the world didn't end in 1911.' The Doctor queries this and takes her to 1980. The TARDIS doors open on a wasteland: this alternative Earth is the one where Sutekh won his freedom. Shocked, Sarah agrees to return to 1911. This scene was inserted by Holmes in order to increase the stakes in this and all subsequent stories set in Earth's history.

Things Fall Apart: It is never explained why Sutekh has been buried along with the robot mummies and the rocket components, as these are precisely the things that he needs to escape. Sarah just happens to put on a Victorian dress before landing reasonably close to the period.

Availability: Released on DVD in 2004 as BBCDVD 1350 (Region 2), WHVE E1109 (Region 1) and on VHS in 1994 as BBCV 5220 (UK), WHV E1109 (US).

Verdict: 'Egyptian mummies building rockets? But that's crazy!' Despite a couple of fundamental holes in the plot, 'Pyramids of Mars' is one of the best *Doctor Who* stories of the 1970s. It moves quickly between set pieces and concentrates on establishing atmosphere, both of which linger in the memory far longer than any quibbles with the logic. Most importantly, the way that the story progresses is logical – there are no sudden leaps or baffling changes of motivation.

Gabriel Woolf makes a significant contribution as the voice of Sutekh (playing the role in a subtle, understated manner). The use of a period setting is welcome as this nearly always results in good design work, and the effects are well handled: Scarman expelling the bullet from his chest is neat, as is the death of Namin (which is the bit that Vince watches in the first episode of *Queer as Folk*). *Doctor Who* has been so many different things that it cannot be summed up in a single story, but, if you've never seen the show before and want to get an idea of what it's like, try this one.

83
The Android Invasion

Part One: 22 November 1975
Part Two: 29 November 1975
Part Three: 6 December 1975
Part Four: 13 December 1975

Written by Terry Nation
Directed by Barry Letts

Notable Cast: Patrick Newell (Colonel Faraday) played Mother throughout the 1968–69 season of *The Avengers*.

Scary Monsters: The Kraals: generic green warlike aliens. A Kraal looks a little like a bipedal triceratops, with a small horn in the centre of its face.

Other Worlds: The Kraals' planet is named Oseidon. Background radiation on the planet is naturally high and is gradually becoming unbearable (the reason for this is never explained).

The Plan: The Kraals want to destroy all life on Earth so that they can colonise it and escape Oseidon. The plan involves a virus, some android duplicates of human beings, and an invasion fleet – possibly in that order, possibly not.

Villains: Styggron (Martin Friend) is the Kraals' chief scientist, responsible for designing the technology that will accomplish the invasion of Earth. He has even gone as far as creating a duplicate of the village of Devesham, along with many of its inhabitants. It's in this village that the TARDIS lands.

History 101: When the Doctor eventually arrives on Earth, the British space programme is proceeding apace: astronaut Guy Crayford (Milton Johns) was manning a mission to Jupiter when his rocket was captured by the Kraals.

Doctor Who?: The Doctor is a skilled darts player, scoring three bull's-eyes with ease (unless he was aiming for treble-20 and missed, of course).

Science/Magic: The TARDIS appears confused by the Kraal duplicate village, unsure of whether it's really Earth. This rather oddly suggests that the TARDIS locates places by what they look like, rather than any kind of co-ordinate system. (Why does the TARDIS dematerialise when Sarah inserts the key?) Also a big hand, please, for the stupidest thing ever in *Doctor Who*: the Doctor's robot detector. It's just a box with a red light on it. Why does he have it? And more importantly, given that this is one of the very few situations in which such a device would be remotely useful, *why didn't he use it earlier in the serial*?

Things Fall Apart: There's some poor editing when Sarah falls down the gentle incline in Part One (see **129**, 'The Five Doctors'). The androids' faces, when revealed, suddenly don't look very mobile. Wouldn't it be better for Styggron to have some sort of CCTV system to monitor the village, rather than a secret hatch in the wall? Why is the pub calendar all made up from the same date? Why does the 'precise' android duplicate of Sarah like ginger pop? What are the androids actually training to do? (Are they learning how to behave on Earth? If so, why don't the Kraals just program them with the information that created the village in the first place?) Why destroy the village? What part do the androids play in the Kraals' plan anyway? The virus kills only on direct contact, so how do the Kraals intend to spread it? Is this what the androids are for? If so, won't it take more than three weeks with only a handful of androids?

How can Crayford never have noticed that his eye isn't missing, and, if the Kraals insist upon this deception, why didn't they remove the eye? If all the androids have been neutralised, why is the android Doctor able to attack Styggron, and what happens to the Kraal invasion fleet?

Availability: Released on VHS in 1995 as BBCV 5526 (UK), WHV E1309 (US).

Verdict: 'We don't have strangers here.' 'The Android Invasion' badly wants to capture the atmosphere of *The Prisoner*, but unfortunately it's more akin to a man shouting, 'Hey, thicko – thicky-thicky-thicko!' while poking a sharp stick in your eye. For an hour and a half. This is almost entirely due to a very lazy script from Terry Nation, which fails to tie together a series of random alien invasion clichés (deadly virus, alien duplicates, fleet waiting in the wings) and has been obviously plotted for the writer's convenience rather than for the viewer's enjoyment.

There are many *Doctor Who* stories that don't really make sense and get by mainly on arresting imagery and escapist action. 'The Android Invasion' fails because it doesn't distract the audience from its holes and inconsistencies: indeed, it seems to brazenly assume that nobody will notice, which constitutes a vast insult to the intelligence. For these failings to pass through to the final script indicates a shocking lapse on the parts of Nation and Robert Holmes. The result is one of the worst *Doctor Who* serials, despite the fact that Barry Letts put in some very good directorial work.

84
The Brain of Morbius

Part One: 3 January 1976
Part Two: 10 January 1976
Part Three: 17 January 1976
Part Four: 24 January 1976

Written by Robin Bland
Directed by Christopher Barry

Notable Cast: Philip Madoc (Solon) previously appeared in **47**, 'The Krotons'.

Writer: Terrance Dicks' original script was heavily rewritten by script editor Robert Holmes. Dicks wasn't pleased with the changes, and asked for the script to be credited to a 'bland pseudonym'.

Other Worlds: The Time Lords drag the TARDIS off course to Karn, a planet within a couple of billion miles of the Doctor's home. The main features of the planet are a graveyard of crashed spaceships, some caves inhabited by a witch cult called the Sisterhood of Karn, and the castle where Solon conducts his experiments. The Sisterhood protect the Elixir of Life, which involves using their powers to crash any ships that come too near.

Villains: Neurosurgeon Mehendri Solon is assisted by his hook-handed servant Condo (Colin Fay). In Solon's basement lives the disembodied brain of Morbius, a tyrannical former head of the Time Lord High Council. Morbius led an army of mercenaries to Karn to try to steal the Elixir. The Time Lords executed Morbius on Karn, destroying his body in the 'dispersal chamber' – but Solon had saved his brain. Morbius reduced many planets to ashes, and is responsible for Karn's devastated state.

The Plan: Solon is constructing a body for Morbius from spare parts and wants the Doctor's head to complete his creation. He fails, so uses an artificial brain case instead.

Scary Monsters: A mutt (**63**, 'The Mutants') is beheaded at the start of the story. The body Solon has made for Morbius is a powerful but hideous patchwork creature, with Condo's arm and the lungs of a birastrop. The brain case suffers from build-ups of static electricity, causing seizures and insanity.

Science/Magic: The 'flame of life' is protected by the Sisterhood of Karn and produces the Elixir of Life, which can 'regenerate tissues'. The Elixir is shared between the Sisterhood and the Time Lords, who use it in rare cases such as problems with regeneration. The Sisterhood can transport objects and create winds with their 'mind powers'. Only Time Lords have the power to shield their minds from the Sisterhood. The flame has been dying due to a soot blockage in the fissures from which the gases leak; the Doctor clears the soot with a firework.

Doctor Who?: The Doctor is sent into a sulk by the Time Lords' intervention and refuses to explore, choosing to play with his yo-yo instead. He says that some people preferred his previous face, but he likes the current one. The Doctor is 749. He considers the Sisterhood's teleportation 'quaint' and helps them only on condition that they stop crashing passing ships. He thinks the consequences of widespread immortality would be terrible, saying 'death is the price we pay for progress' – immortality leads to stagnation. The Doctor is strong enough to carry Morbius on his own. A mind-bending contest is a potentially fatal Time Lord game; when the Doctor battles Morbius in such a contest, eleven of the Doctor's previous selves are seen as the Doctor loses the contest – the Pertwee, Troughton and Hartnell Doctors, then eight other men. (The very clear assertion that Hartnell was not the Doctor's first incarnation was either unnoticed or ignored by subsequent production teams.) He's saved by the Elixir, having lost the battle.

Things Fall Apart: The Sisterhood's ritualistic gestures are a combination of a Mexican wave and 'invisible box' street mime. There's more bad mime when Sarah is temporarily blinded, flailing around and bumping into plastic rocks. The scene where Solon shoots Condo suffers from strobe lines across the screen. When Morbius is thrown down a shallow incline to his death in Part Four (risible in itself), the monster bumps the camera on the way down.

Availability: Issued on VHS in 1990 as BBCV 4388 (UK), WHV E1348 (US).

Verdict: 'We take head now?' A mismatched abomination crudely stitched together from horror-movie cliché, 'The Brain of Morbius' is less than the sum of its butchered parts. The different aspects of the story – crude surgery, mystical psychic powers, a magical elixir – fail to connect in terms of either theme or basic plot logic, resulting in an unsatisfying, melodramatic mess, where the Doctor wins only because his opponent's head randomly explodes and his survival is thanks to someone else's sacrifice. Impressive work on sets and effects (including John Friedlander's wonderful brain) is let down by poor direction (it's hard to believe this is the same man who worked on **2**, 'The Daleks'). Tom Baker drifts through the story with a smirk, as if he can't quite believe the nonsense around him. Characters are one-dimensional and rant at each other in strings of florid overstatement; this hyperbole results in some funny lines, but they clash with the attempts at drama rather than complementing them. Equally, there are some inappropriate moments of gore that are ineptly handled. Gross stupidity, in more ways than one.

85
The Seeds of Doom

Part One: 31 January 1976
Part Two: 7 February 1976
Part Three: 14 February 1976
Part Four: 21 February 1976
Part Five: 28 February 1976
Part Six: 6 March 1976

Written by Robert Banks Stewart
Directed by Douglas Camfield

Notable Cast: Tony Beckley (Harrison Chase) played Camp Freddie in *The Italian Job* (Peter Collinson, 1969). John Challis (Scorby) is best known as Boycie in *Only Fools and Horses* (1981–2003).

History 101: Back in Sarah's time period, the World Ecology Bureau asks the Doctor and Sarah to investigate an alien seed pod that has been discovered in the permafrost of Antarctica.

Scary Monsters: The Krynoid, a vegetable creature whose seed pods are found buried in the Antarctic permafrost after 20,000 years. When the pods open, tendrils infect the nearest life form, making it part of the Krynoid and converting it right down to the blood platelets. Krynoids destroy all animal life on any planet they infest. After a humanoid stage, the Krynoid grows into a large heap of vegetation. Its final form fills a mansion. Once it reaches a certain mass the Krynoid can take control of all the plants on Earth, turning them hostile, and will then germinate.

Villains: Plant-obsessed, well-dressed millionaire Harrison Chase, who wants the Krynoid for his collection. Chase loves plants rather too much, referring to them as his friends. He considers bonsai a form of torture, has a private army of machine-gun-wielding guards and composes terrible experimental music, which he plays to his plants. Chase has no regard for human life: in addition to ordering murder in pursuit of the Krynoid pod, he is willing to use Sarah as bait for it.

The Plan: Chase sends his hired muscle Scorby to Antarctica to bring back a Krynoid pod. Chase then works to open the pod at his estate. When the pod infects Chase's botanist Keeler (Mark Jones), Chase keeps him captive to breed the creature.

Doctor Who?: The Doctor is more of a conventional action hero, jumping through windows, punching out thugs and giving a nasty twist to Scorby's neck at one point. He even carries a gun for part of the story, although Sarah points out he would never fire it. Again, the Doctor says he's 749. He doesn't notice the cold, even in Antarctica. He knows about the Krynoid and is president of the Intergalactic Floral Society. He says he won't perform a surgical operation because the people involved need to help themselves – but Sarah says it's because he isn't a medical doctor. The Doctor describes Sarah as his best friend.

Science/Magic: Chase considers human blood and bone to be an excellent source of nitrogen for plants, which is why he uses human bodies as an ingredient in his compost.

Things Fall Apart: The humanoid Krynoid (a repainted Axon from 57, 'The Claws of Axos') is rather comical as it hops about in the snow. The TARDIS arrives in Antarctica at the end of the story because the Doctor has not reset the co-ordinates – even though they didn't go there in the TARDIS in the first place: they went by plane.

Availability: Issued on VHS in 1994 as BBCV 5377 (UK), WHV E1300 (US).

Verdict: 'It's more serious than death . . .' Exciting, tense and often brutal, 'The Seeds of Doom' is a straightforward thriller that remoulds the Doctor as a more conventional, two-fisted action hero pitched against an implacable menace. Tom Baker embraces this approach to the character, gritting his teeth with ferocity as he gets into a series of violent confrontations. Like any action hero, he's doing what must be done to defeat a relentless foe: the Krynoid is an effective, faceless adversary, which lives only to expand, kill and destroy. As the Doctor fights for life, Harrison Chase is the exact opposite: dispassionate and distant, delegating the dirty work to his subordinates. Tony Beckley is excellent as Chase, bringing a creepy, camp precision to the role. He has great support from John Challis as the murderous Scorby, and the rest of the supporting cast are just as good. If there's a weak link in the story, it's the rather perfunctory use of UNIT in the last couple of episodes – with the absence of any familiar faces, they seem like a pointless inclusion. The series has pretty much grown out of that legacy of the Pertwee era at this point, a connection that would finally be severed with the departure of Elisabeth Sladen.

86
The Masque of Mandragora

Part One: 4 September 1976
Part Two: 11 September 1976
Part Three: 18 September 1976
Part Four: 25 September 1976

Written by Louis Marks
Directed by Rodney Bennett

Notable Cast: Tim Piggott-Smith (Marco) previously appeared in **57**, 'The Claws of Axos'. Jon Laurimore (Count Federico) appeared in *I, Claudius* (1976) and the Dennis Potter teleplay *Traitor* (1971).

Doctor Who?: While walking in the depths of the TARDIS the Doctor and Sarah happen upon another control room, wood-panelled with a smaller console. The Doctor describes it as the 'old' control room: the presence of a recorder and smoking jacket imply that it was used by the Troughton and Pertwee Doctors, although this is the first time it has been seen in the series. The Doctor performs some 'spatial relocation', which converts this control room into the main one. Later, the Doctor notes that he was taught swordsmanship by the captain of Cleopatra's body-guard and we see his ability to mimic others' voices (see **24**, 'The Celestial Toymaker').

Villains: In space, the TARDIS encounters the Mandragora helix. The Doctor explains that this is one of many such helixes that exist in the cosmos, and that it has control over the transmutation of energy into matter.

History 101: The Mandragora helix conceals itself in the TARDIS and guides it to Italy: 'Late fifteenth century. Not a very pleasant time.' A young royal named Giuliano (Gareth Armstrong, who pitches his fey performance just right) has succeeded his late father to the dukedom of San Martino, although he faces competition from his brutal and conservative uncle, Count Federico. A masque is planned to celebrate Giuliano's accession, attended by such learned men as Leonardo Da Vinci (see **105**, 'City of Death').

The Plan: Mandragora has already established contact with a disciple on Earth: the court astrologer Hieronymous (Norman Jones). By investing its power in him and the ancient Roman cult of Demnos, Mandragora plans to take over San Martino, Italy, and eventually Earth, operating it upon the superstitious principles held by Hieronymous.

Science/Magic: The whole story is based on the conflict between these two notions. Belief in magic and superstition is seen as holding humanity back as it stands on the verge of several major breakthroughs in understanding. Mandragora wishes that this should remain the case, preventing humanity from expanding beyond Earth and eventually posing a threat to Mandragora.

Things Fall Apart: The Doctor notes that Sarah's ability to understand other languages is 'a Time Lord gift that I allow you to share', which is fine – but why does the Doctor take her sudden curiosity about this as a sign that her mind is possessed? Does he not expect her to be self-aware? (Probably not: after all, this is Sarah we're talking about.) The Doctor's scarf somehow ties itself into a knot when he trips his executioner. The scenes of Hieronymous talking to Mandragora drag on a bit, and the other follower of Mandragora never appears.

Availability: Issued on VHS in 1991 as BBCV 4642 (UK), WHV E1203 (US).

Verdict: 'Maybe the stars don't move at all . . . maybe it's we who move.' Although it contains very little in the way of actual science, 'The Masque of Mandragora' is an earnest instruction on the importance of scientific progress. Its depiction of the Renaissance is almost like something from the Hartnell era, hoping that the viewer gains an understanding of not only what this period was like but also why it was significant. This could have been deadly dull, of course, so it's perhaps a good thing that Louis Marks didn't bother to include real science because with that element removed, we're just left with the big ideas of progress against superstition. Big ideas, well handled, make for good drama.

Marks also keeps things moving well in the early episodes by introducing the comparatively minor, but highly inconvenient, schemes of Count Federico. These give rise to most of the story's action sequences and work as effective relief from the more conceptual main plot. There's some great design work and the ending makes enough vague sense to be satisfying. Viewers of *The Prisoner* may find themselves driven to distraction during the Portmeirion-based location scenes, however.

87
The Hand of Fear

Part One: 2 October 1976
Part Two: 9 October 1976
Part Three: 16 October 1976
Part Four: 23 October 1976

**Written by Bob Baker and Dave Martin
Directed by Lennie Mayne**

Notable Cast: This is Elisabeth Sladen's last story as a regular.

History 101: The TARDIS arrives back in Sarah's native time. The Doctor is aiming for her home town of Croydon, but ends up in a quarry instead.

Scary Monsters: When Sarah is buried in a rockslide, she finds a severed stone hand. The hand is crystalline, with no organic matter. It's been buried since the Jurassic period. The hand possesses Sarah, causing her to take it to the reactor core of the Nunton power plant, where it feeds on the radiation, coming back to life. The hand belongs to . . .

Villains: . . . Eldrad, 'creator of Kastria', a criminal executed in a spaceship explosion. His body regenerates from the petrified hand, first into a woman (Judith Paris) and then into a towering man (Stephen Thorne), both with crystalline bodies. Eldrad devised the crystalline-silicone form that allowed his species to survive, and destroyed the solar barriers that protected the planet, leading to his execution.

The Plan: Eldrad wants to reclaim control of Kastria and use it as a bridgehead to conquer nearby planets. When he finds Kastria dead, he wants to conquer Earth instead.

Other Worlds: Kastria has been devastated by 150 million years of exposure to the solar winds. The silicone-based inhabitants have died and crumbled to sand. The Kastrians allowed themselves to die and destroyed their race banks so that Eldrad, should he return, could not use them to build a race of conquerors.

Doctor Who?: The Doctor knocks Sarah out by twisting her neck back suddenly. He can survive going into a nuclear reactor unprotected, provided he does it quickly. When nuclear missiles fail to destroy Eldrad, the Doctor recommends older weapons of speech and diplomacy. He's fascinated by such an unusual species, and wants to see Kastria for himself. As a Time Lord, he is bound to prevent alien aggression when it is 'deemed to threaten the indigenous population'. He can't contravene the 'first law of time' by changing history. When he receives a call from Gallifrey, the Doctor decides he must take Sarah home for good, as he can't take her with him. He asks Sarah not to forget him, and fails to drop her off at the correct location.

Science/Magic: The hand has a subatomic structure similar to a DNA helix, and absorbs radiation to regenerate itself. The hand absorbs the release of energy from nuclear fission in an 'un-explosion'. Anything inside the TARDIS exists in a state of temporal grace – that is, it doesn't, strictly speaking, exist, and therefore weapons cannot be used. The power systems Eldrad built on Kastria draw energy from the core of the planet. Eldrad's ring contains his genetic code, allowing him to reconstitute from nearby genetic material.

Things Fall Apart: The scene where Watson (Glyn Houston) phones his wife when he thinks he's going to die ('kiss the children for me') could be touching, if it weren't such a string of pathetic clichés. The Doctor's response to a nearby nuclear explosion is to duck (Bob and Dave strike again – see **57**, 'The Claws of Axos'). Eldrad isn't tripped up by the Doctor's scarf at the end: he steps over it and then does a stunt fall.

Availability: Issued on VHS in 1996 as BBCV 5789 (UK), WHV E1351 (US).

Verdict: 'Hail Eldrad, king ... of nothing.' In an era when virtually every horror cliché had already been mined, it was inevitable that a 'creeping hand' story would turn up sooner or later. Unfortunately, while the effects for the severed hand are as good as can be expected, the hand itself hardly does anything, scampering about a bit in Part Two but never attacking anyone before growing into the full-sized Eldrad. The influence of Eldrad is mainly felt through one of this era's most tedious themes, possession, with Elisabeth Sladen histrionic as the possessed Sarah. She's joined by a weak supporting cast, who are either screamingly over the top or soap-opera bland. Part Two is entirely pointless, a runaround that ends pretty much exactly where it begins. There's some attempt to emphasise the repartee between the Doctor and Sarah before the latter leaves the show, but such a poor story makes her departure a damp squib.

88
The Deadly Assassin

Part One: 30 October 1976
Part Two: 6 November 1976
Part Three: 13 November 1976
Part Four: 20 November 1976

**Written by Robert Holmes
Directed by David Maloney**

Other Worlds: For the first *Doctor Who* serial set chiefly on Gallifrey, writer Holmes reinvents the Doctor's homeworld. Holmes's use of language to evoke this society mixes medievalisms ('Castellan') with utilitarian social philosophy ('Panopticon'), American politics ('president', 'CIA'), Edward Lear ('Runcible') and Catholicism ('College of Cardinals') to compelling effect. There are said to be 'plebeian classes' as well as Time Lords in Gallifreyan society – one of them may be called 'Sheboogans'. The leader of the society is the President and his deputy in the Chancellor (in **65**, 'The Three Doctors', it seemed the other way around); they preside over a High Council. The President is referred to as His Supremacy and selects his own successor. Execution and torture are acceptable. At one point the script seems to acknowledge that this level of detail about the Doctor's home will affect the series deeply, with the Doctor muttering, 'Like it or not, Gallifrey is involved and I'm afraid things will never be quite the same again.' The founder of Time Lord society, engineer and architect Rassilon, is named for the first time. Omega (**65**, 'The Three Doctors') isn't mentioned.

Doctor Who?: The character's stated history here is broadly in line with the Pertwee era, but further details are extemporised. He was a member of the Prydonian Chapter of Time Lords ('the chapter that has produced more Time Lord Presidents than all the others put together') before fleeing. This further cements the idea of the Doctor as an agitprop rebel who escaped a distant, corrupt elite. Tom Baker's performance is largely grim and joyless; physically still with his eyes cast down in misery and contemplation.

The Plan: The Master (Peter Pratt) returns home – to destroy it and extend his own life in the process by tapping into Gallifrey's source of power, a black hole 'set in an eternally dynamic equation against the mass of the planet'.

Villains: Chancellor Goth (Bernard Horsfall), who has made a deal with the Master to assassinate the President in return for becoming his successor. Bernard Horsfall played one of the Doctor's Time Lord judges in **50**, 'The War Games', although no explicit link is made between the characters.

Science/Magic: The TARDIS's lock is said to be 'a double-curtain trimonic'. The Doctor's ship is a Type 40 TT capsule and dialogue implies that only this exact model is 'a TARDIS' (a flat-out contradiction of Holmes's own **55**, 'Terror of the Autons' – never mind the series' first year). 'Artron energy' is somehow involved in a Time Lord's mental strength. Time Lords can regenerate only twelve times, resulting in thirteen lives in total.

Things Fall Apart: The title is arguably tautological – and certainly absurd. It's a shame that after the peculiarity and realpolitik of the first two parts and the hallucinatory horror of the third that the fourth devolves into two people having a fist fight because one is attempting to blow something up. The degree to which the Master is physically incapacitated changes from scene to scene. The presidential assassination plot is arguably a whodunnit with one suspect (there's only one speaking character who can be the assassin). If Goth controls the nightmare landscape, why are all the horrific incidents (trench warfare, being hit by a train, undergoing surgery, etc.) so peculiarly human, even European?

Availability: Released on VHS in the US before the UK as a compilation. The BBC video (uncut) is BBCV 4645 with the US reissue being WHVE 1161.

Verdict: 'If heroes don't exist, it is necessary to invent them.' From a certain point of view, this is the ultimate reading of the vast collective text of *Doctor Who* (or at least its generic 1970s form). In it the Doctor is a brilliant, but unorthodox, member of an autocracy who, having rejected his society, returns to save it when it's rocked to its foundations. It's also visually daring, not merely for *Doctor Who* but for 1970s television generally, with use of sudden flashback and flashforward, freeze-frames and discontinuous editing. While Part Three has been praised for its lengthy mental/physical duel between the Doctor and his adversary, the most memorable moments of the nightmare (the samurai, the surgeon, the clown) are in Part Two. Blackly comic in its mock solemnity and borrowed iconography (the chalk outline where the dead president fell is *hilarious*), 'The Deadly Assassin' is also a superb world-building exercise. This is thanks to a combination of fine costuming, impressive sets and well-delivered, casually evocative dialogue, with Bernard Horsfall, Hugh Walters (Runcible) and Angus Mackay (Cardinal Borusa) in particular demonstrating an appreciation of the comical, political and horrific elements of the material.

89
The Face of Evil

Part One: 1 January 1977
Part Two: 8 January 1977
Part Three: 15 January 1977
Part Four: 22 January 1977

Written by Chris Boucher
Directed by Pennant Roberts

Notable Cast: Leslie Schofield (Calib) previously appeared in **50**, 'The War Games', as did David Garfield (Neeva). Louise Jameson (Leela), comfortably the most talented actress ever to play a regular character in *Doctor Who*, is best known for her leading roles in *Tenko* (1981–82), *Bergerac* (1985–90) and *EastEnders* (1998–2000), although she has also enjoyed a distinguished stage career.

Writer: Prior to *Doctor Who*, Chris Boucher had written comedy material for *That's Life!* and *Dave Allen At Large*. He went on to become script editor of *Blake's 7* (1978–81) and *Bergerac* (1980–86), worked on *Shoestring* (1978–80) and created *Star Cops* (1987). He has also written three original *Doctor Who* novels for BBC Books.

Director: Pennant Roberts has directed numerous TV series, including episodes of *The Onedin Line*, *Blake's 7* and *Tenko*.

Other Worlds: An unnamed world inhabited by the skilled hunter tribe of the Sevateem and the meditative, psychically gifted tribe of the Tesh.

History 101: The timeframe is not clear, but many centuries before the events of 'The Face of Evil' an expedition dubbed Mordee set out from Earth and landed on this planet. The Doctor visited the new colony in its early days and assisted it with its computer, Xoanon, hooking his own brain up to it in order to repair a problem. Unfortunately he left his personality imprinted on Xoanon.

Villains: Xoanon, a computer that has developed a personality of its own as well as retaining that of the Doctor, which has been imprinted on it (see **History 101**), and has gone insane as a result.

The Plan: The colonists were originally divided into two groups: Survey Team and Technicians. Xoanon has been acting out the conflict in its mind by moulding the two factions into the Sevateem and the Tesh, to a point where the descendants no longer have any knowledge of Earth or the colony's technology. The computer has set the two tribes against each other in a religious war, with Xoanon as their god. Their original roles are long forgotten and they loathe each other – an apt demonstration of what happens when workplace politics get out of hand.

Science/Magic: Considering the Sevateem have been around long enough no longer to understand their 'relics', the technology is still in remarkable working order: maybe it was built by the Eternity Perpetual Company (see **66**, 'Carnival of Monsters').

Doctor Who?: He demonstrates skill with a crossbow, and unsurprisingly claims to have been instructed in its use by William Tell. Leela forces herself upon him at the end in a reversal of the ending of **26**, 'The Savages': whereas Steven stayed behind because he had been elected leader, this is one of the factors that motivates Leela to leave her planet.

Things Fall Apart: How does Leela know that the Doctor's jelly babies are for eating? The Doctor's completion of the trial is a rather convenient way of getting the Sevateem to trust him. The inside of the stone rendition of the Doctor's mouth is nowhere near in proportion to the outside – just look at the size of the teeth.

Availability: Released on VHS in 1999 as BBCV 6672 (UK), WHV E1402 (US).

Verdict: 'With proof, you don't have to believe.' A lot of *Doctor Who* stories have strong rewatch value because they're straightforward adventures: you can enjoy them without having to pay too much attention. 'The Face of Evil' has rewatch value for the opposite reason. It's slow-moving but this isn't because it's short on plot: rather, it's because Chris Boucher (among the smartest writers ever to work on the show) is playing with some very interesting ideas and he devotes the screen time to exploring them properly. At first glance this looks like a generic 'two tribes' storyline, but underneath are some solid sci-fi concepts and an exploration of the nature of religion – pleasingly challenging stuff for a 1970s Saturday teatime.

Louise Jameson's Leela, being neither winsome nor annoying, is a breath of fresh air after six years in the company of Jo and Sarah Jane. Jameson's performance is superb and (in Boucher's hands at least) the character complements the Doctor perfectly: she can look after herself, is perfectly intelligent but has been taught almost nothing. Here she is used as somebody to whom the Doctor can explain things while making it clear that she isn't merely passive. She makes use of the information she is given and is capable of working things out for herself (the opening scene sees Leela being condemned for correctly apprehending that Xoanon is not a god).

90
The Robots of Death

Part One: 29 January 1977
Part Two: 5 February 1977
Part Three: 12 February 1977
Part Four: 19 February 1977

Written by Chris Boucher
Directed by Michael E Briant

Notable Cast: Russell Hunter (Uvanov) played Lonely in *Callan* (1967–72, 1974), and had roles in *Taste the Blood of Dracula* (Peter Sasdy, 1974) and *Up Pompeii* (Bob Kellett, 1971). He played the Edinburgh Fringe Festival every year from its inception to his death in 2004. Brian Croucher (Borg) was the second actor to play Travis in *Blake's 7* (1979), and played Ted Hills in *EastEnders* (1995–97). Pamela Salem (Toos) was also a regular in *EastEnders* (1989–90) and played Emma Callon in *The Onedin Line* (1971), Miss Moneypenny in *Never Say Never Again* (Irvin Kershner, 1983) and Sarah Whale in *Gods and Monsters* (Bill Condon, 1998). David Bailie (Dask) worked on Freddie Francis's horror films *The Creeping Flesh* (1973) and *Son of Dracula* (1974), and more recently has appeared in *The Messenger: The Story of Joan of Arc* (Luc Besson, 1999), *Gladiator* (Ridley Scott, 2000) and *Pirates of the Caribbean: The Curse of the Black Pearl* (Gore Verbinski, 2003). David Collings (Poul) previously appeared in **79**, 'Revenge of the Cybermen'.

Other Worlds: An unnamed planet where a giant sandminer proceeds across a desert, gathering precious metals from the sandstorms, including the incredibly valuable Lucanol. The ship is crewed by a small, indolent human command staff and a large crew of servile robots that do the menial work. It is generally believed that the core programming of robots mean that they can never harm a human (Boucher's been reading Isaac Asimov, then).

Scary Monsters: The robots on the sandminer, which divide into three classes: the black voiceless 'dums', the gold vocal 'vocs' and the silver elite 'super vocs'. All classes of robot are elegantly designed, with sculpted features and oriental costumes. They take oral orders, and therefore rely on voice recognition.

Villains: Taren Capel, robot-obsessed lunatic, who has placed himself on board the sandminer as one of the crew. A scientist specialising in robotics and one of the few people who could program the robots to kill, Capel grew up among robots, thinking of them as his brothers. He sees humans as animals.

The Plan: Taren Capel has reprogrammed the robots to kill the crew. He wishes to destroy all humans, and let robots rule.

Doctor Who?: The Doctor is aware that this society, as a robot-dependent civilisation, is doomed if the killer is a robot. He knows robots can only exist thanks to humans, and have no role without them. He thinks that, if you don't seem likely to harm people, they won't harm you, but adds that this applies only 'nine times out of ten'. The Doctor is fond of bumblebees. Helium doesn't affect his voice.

Science/Magic: The Doctor explains to Leela how the TARDIS is bigger on the inside by using two boxes, one large and one small. He leaves the larger box at a distance, and brings the smaller box closer to Leela – he explains that if the larger box could be kept at a distance (where it seems smaller), while at the same time be close, it could fit inside the smaller box. As Leela says, 'That's silly.' A laserson probe is an instrument that can cause great damage, or perform a very delicate operation. Robophobia, or Grimwade's syndrome, is an unreasoning dread of robots caused by their lack of body language.

Things Fall Apart: The 'corpse markers' placed on the bodies of the victims are bicycle reflector discs. The 'disguised' image of the villain on the screen in Part Three doesn't really disguise who it is at all.

Availability: Issued on DVD in 2000 as BBCDVD 1012 (Region 2), WHV E1120 (Region 1) and on VHS in 1995 as BBCV 5521 (UK), WHV E1120 (US).

Verdict: 'My command program has been restructured. All humans are to die.' An enthralling combination of 'serious' science fiction and drawing-room murder mystery, 'The Robots of Death' benefits from a beautifully executed production and superb performances. The sandminer sets evoke Art Nouveau elegance, while the robots are some of the most impressively designed monsters in the show's history. Chris Boucher's script is cleverly constructed, full of smart ideas and witty lines and the acting is first rate. Russell Hunter, David Bailie and co. keep their performances at a high point of drama while never tipping over into silliness. Excellent.

91
The Talons of Weng-Chiang

Part One: 26 February 1977
Part Two: 5 March 1977

Part Three: 12 March 1977
Part Four: 19 March 1977
Part Five: 26 March 1977
Part Six: 2 April 1977

Written by Robert Holmes
Directed by David Maloney

Notable Cast: John Bennett (Li H'sen Chang) previously appeared in **71**, 'Invasion of the Dinosaurs'. Michael Spice (Weng-Chiang) played the eponymous **84**, 'Brain of Morbius'. Christopher Benjamin (Henry Gordon Jago) previously appeared in **54**, 'Inferno'. Deep Roy (Mr Sin) has had a marvellously interesting career, including four appearances on *Blake's 7* (1978–81) and a memorable turn in the *X-Files* episode 'Baadlaa' (2001). Film roles include those in *Return of the Jedi* (Richard Marquand, 1983) (he played Jabba the Hutt's tail), *Return to Oz* (Walter Murch, 1985), *How The Grinch Stole Christmas* (Ron Howard, 2000) and *Big Fish* (Tim Burton, 2003).

Doctor Who?: A mischievous cove in a deerstalker and cloak, the Doctor bears more than a passing resemblance to Sherlock Holmes. He shows a keen interest in music hall and stage magic (he wants to see Little Titch), as well as a hearty scepticism to grander manifestations of magic or mysticism. He recalls a previous visit to China four hundred years ago. He was with the Filipino army on the final assault on Reykjavik during the wars of the fifty-first century.

Villains: Weng-Chiang, a.k.a. Magnus Greel, a.k.a. the Butcher of Brisbane. In the fifty-first century he prowled the death camps left in the wake of Iceland's victorious armies. When Filipino forces closed in on Reykjavik he used his inhuman experiments to escape via the Zigma beam – and became one of Earth's first time travellers (if trying to create a chronology of time travellers is possible). Hideously disfigured in the escape, he prolongs himself by extracting the life energy of young girls while he seeks the missing components of his time machine. In a beautifully contradictory move, Greel is at once a shadowy mystical figure and coldly rationalised sci-fi villain in the mould of Ming the Merciless. Just as **82**, 'Pyramids of Mars' and *Quatermass and the Pit* toy with notions of scientific tyranny mistaken for godhood, so 'Talons' takes a futuristic variation of Nazi death-camp doctor Josef Mengele and dresses him (for two-thirds of the story at least) as a

Chinese demon. Throw into the mix a hearty dose of *The Phantom of the Opera* and you have one of *Doctor Who*'s most memorable villains.

Perhaps he's not so memorable as his henchmen. While Li H'sen Chang is allowed a certain dignity, despite the pantomime stereotyping of his sub-Fu Manchu characterisation (his death is rather touching), the real star of the piece is a tiny homicidal porcine cyborg. Greel's 'pig-brained, pig-faced Peking Homunculus' started its life as a toy for the children of the Commissioner of the Icelandic Alliance, but incorporated within its tiny robotic body was the cerebral cortex of a pig: 'The swinish element took over. It hates humanity and revels in carnage.' We also learn that this fearsome monstrosity nearly started World War Six. The Peking Homunculus is a gem of a throwaway baddie, as ridiculous as Nick-Nack in *The Man with the Golden Gun* (Guy Hamilton, 1974), but sinister in the context of the story. Of lesser note are the Tong of the Black Scorpion, so devoted to their master Weng-Chiang that they would commit suicide using agonising scorpion venom rather than risk capture or dishonour.

Science/Magic: In tune with its villain, 'Talons' cloaks what turns out to be a coldly scientific core in a heavy veneer of magic. What's more the 'magic' has two aspects: not only the grisly Gothic chills of the inhuman 'phantom' (i.e. Weng-Chiang) and his giant rat (caused by pollution from Greel's experiments), but also the vaudeville spectacle of Chang's stage act. The Doctor is, of course, more taken with the latter – 'Do a trick,' he urges Chang at their first meeting and, when Chang's subordinate keels over, dead from a suicide pill, the Doctor at first applauds: 'Very good!' Greel's ego over the Zigma experiments is soon punctured by the unimpressed Time Lord, who decries them as 'a scientific cul-de-sac'. These two forms of 'magic' find their synthesis in the Peking Homunculus: simultaneously a murderous robot from the future and – a frequent image from horror films – the doll who suddenly rises and kills.

History 101: There is no real history to this story, beyond an impressive smattering of period details. The one historical character to get a mention (save Queen Victoria) gives the game away: Jack the Ripper. For this is a journey through the imagery of a certain sort of penny-dreadful Victoriana. *The Phantom of the Opera*, the sinister Chinaman with the hypnotic powers, the vampiric characteristics of the lead villain, foggy streets, ghosts in a music hall cellar, all presided over by an enigmatic chap in a deerstalker. This is loving pastiche of a whole era of pulp fiction, given the *Who* treatment and, as with all good pastiche, the trimming is impeccable: Jago's tongue-twisting tirades; Dr Litefoot (Trevor Baxter) – a strange combination of Watson and Stephen Maturin; the boozy coppers and indignant ladies of the night; the journey down the Thames; and the monstrous piece of Brummie ironmongery wielded by the Doctor. Without any of the time travel or Tom Baker's sublime histrionics this would remain a thoroughly warming and enjoyable tale – it is understandable that there was talk (no matter how inconsequential) of writing a follow-up story, or even spin-off series, for Jago and Litefoot. 'Talons' shows that history can mean a lot more than dry, obsessive detail and includes the spirit of an age manifested in its literature.

Things Fall Apart: The attempts to manifest the giant rat have dated badly, and they weren't all that good on transmission. The script's initial intent (for the creature to be represented by vile sound effects) would have worked out better.

Availability: Released on DVD as BBCDVD 1152 (Region 2) and WHV E1814 (Region 1). The earlier, edited VHS is BBCV 4187 (UK), WHV E1153 (US).

Verdict: 'First you've got to warm the pot . . .' 'The Talons of Weng-Chiang' relishes its scrapbook collection of influences with an eccentric abandon that seems particularly reckless given the comparatively large size of the budget. However, the end result is a hugely enjoyable Victorian romp (a grandstanding gothic grotesque – as Henry Gordon Jago might conceivably describe it) that entertains right through to the final reel of ambitiously constructed 'future history', when it turns into a cautionary tale of experimental time travel and thinly veiled Nazi themes. It's probably Baker's best performance as the Doctor and he's supported by an ensemble cast who universally give their all. 'Talons' is arguably the best *Doctor Who* serial of the 1970s.

92
Horror of Fang Rock

Part One: 3 September 1977
Part Two: 10 September 1977

Part Three: 17 September 1977
Part Four: 24 September 1977

Written by Terrance Dicks
Directed by Paddy Russell

Notable Cast: Alan Rowe (Skinsale) previously appeared in **33**, 'The Moonbase' and **70**, 'The Time Warrior'.

Producer: Graham Williams came to *Doctor Who* with script-editing experience on *The View From Daniel Pike* (1971–73) and *Sutherland's Law* (1973–76). He went on to produce *Supergran* (1985). He retired from television in the 1980s to run a hotel in Dorset, and serve as a town councillor, until his death in an accident in 1990.

Doctor Who?: Trapped in a lighthouse with a cross-section of early 1900s Britain, the Doctor instinctively sides with the downtrodden characters against the financier Lord Palmerdale (Sean Caffrey) and the MP Colonel Skinsale (Alan Rowe). Vince Hawkins (John Abbott) introduces himself to everyone using his full name but while the others automatically call him 'Hawkins' the Doctor calls him 'Vince'. The Doctor later tacitly agrees with Harker's (Rio Fanning) assessment that for causing the deaths of innocent sailors in his pursuit of money Palmerdale deserves to die.

Tom Baker's performance is entertainingly erratic, alternating between loud solemnity and quiet grinning – with the Doctor often amused by the primitivism of those around him. He delivers the lines 'This lighthouse is under attack and by morning we might all be dead' and 'He thinks Lord Palmerdale might have fallen from the lamp gallery' as if they were jokes. Which is as peculiar as it sounds.

Scary Monsters: A Rutan – a part of the amphibious shape-shifting collective consciousness from Ruta 3, which is fighting a war with the Sontarans (see **70**, 'The Time Warrior'). It has the ability to alter the temperature in its own immediate environment. It has come to Earth on a scouting mission.

History 101: It's between 22 January 1901 and 6 May 1909 (Edward VII is king). The plot is really a MacGuffin for a story that seems set on mocking imperialism and portraying a love of money as morally corrupting and inevitably leading to death.

Science/Magic: 'U by Q over R' mutters the Doctor while looking at the generator – proving he's got O-level physics if nothing else.

While Adelaide (Annette Woollett) is contemptuous of superstition, she later turns out to be a keen consulter of astrologers. Leela declares that since knowing the Doctor she has come to realise that 'It is better to believe in science.'

Things Fall Apart: Tom Baker can't pronounce 'Chameleon'. As a lord, Palmerdale is *de facto* an MP himself anyway, so why would he need Skinsale? Harker and Palmerdale repeat some of their dialogue when arguing about the wireless telegraph. At one point the actor Colin Douglas (Reuben) appears to be standing around waiting for a cue. Tom Baker's performance clearly involves a vast amount of on-camera improvisation and a lot of the cast seem either unable or unwilling to go along with it.

Availability: Issued on VHS in 1998 as BBCV 6536 (UK), WHV E1018 (US). The DVD was issued in January 2005.

Verdict: 'There's a long night ahead of us.' A compelling mix of John Galsworthy and Hammer horror, the serial is also, in part, an adaptation of Wilfrid Gibson's poem 'The Ballad of Flannan Isle' (c. 1905), which the Doctor then recites at the end. Dicks's scripts make good use of Leela – writing her as unpretentiously ignorant of 1900s customs and both refreshingly pragmatic and endearingly unsentimental. Louise Jameson's performance is even better than normal – which takes some doing (just look at the way she grins when the Doctor tells her she's come up with 'a beautiful idea'). The story also moves at a remarkable pace. The finale, in which the Doctor sits on the steps of an Edwardian lighthouse and, with total conviction, discusses the politics of an intergalactic war with a large green blob is the kind of sight and situation only *Doctor Who* could possibly provide. One of those stories that can temporarily convince you that all *Doctor Who* stories should be period pieces.

93
The Invisible Enemy

Part One: 1 October 1977
Part Two: 8 October 1977
Part Three: 15 October 1977
Part Four: 22 October 1977

Written by Bob Baker and Dave Martin
Directed by Derrick Goodwin

Notable Cast: Michael Sheard (Lowe) previously appeared in **23**, 'The Ark', **56**, 'The Mind of Evil' and **82**, 'Pyramids of Mars'. Frederick Jaeger (Professor Marius) previously appeared in **26**, 'The Savages'. John Leeson (voice of K9) largely worked as a voice artist and continuity announcer, and provided the voice of Bungle in the early years of *Rainbow* (1972–73).

Director: Derrick Goodwin had worked with Graham Williams on *Z Cars* and holds the dubious distinction of having produced *On the Buses* (1971–72).

Doctor Who?: The Doctor leads Leela into a console room that resembles the one last seen in **82**, 'Pyramids of Mars': 'Number two control room. Been closed for redecoration.' (In fact, the wood-panelled set of the previous season had warped in storage and a return to the old design was favoured.) Later, inside the Doctor's brain, we see 'the reflex link whereby I can tune myself into the Time Lord intelligentsia', but he admits that he lost that faculty when they kicked him out.

At the end he takes a new passenger on board the TARDIS in the form of K9, Marius's robot dog. Created with only this story in mind, K9 was retained by the production team as part of the move towards a lighter, more family-friendly direction.

Scary Monsters: An intelligent virus that lives in space and feeds upon intellectual activity. Once a person catches the virus they immediately fall under its influence.

History 101: The year is 5000 – 'The year of the Great Breakout', according to the Doctor. Humanity is spreading across the galaxy, forming an unsubtle parallel with the virus that attacks them.

The Plan: The virus is attracted first to the TARDIS, then the Doctor. Inside the Doctor it forms a nucleus and begins to incubate, plotting to spread itself to the galaxy's human population.

Other Worlds: The Doctor catches an intelligent virus (see **Scary Monsters**) near Titan and subsequently lands there, finding that the human outpost has also been infected. He resists the virus's control and travels to the Bi-Al Foundation, a medical research centre on asteroid K4067, in search of treatment. (The Foundation seems drastically understaffed, suggesting that the NHS doesn't get any better by the year 5000.) The Doctor's solution is to create clones of himself and Leela and send them into his body to identify an antidote.

Science/Magic: With hindsight, Baker and Martin overestimated the time humanity would take to develop cloning: the first successful experiments are said to have taken place in 3922.

Things Fall Apart: The clones of the Doctor and Leela are produced complete with clothing; Leela also has her knife. The clones live a lot longer than the ten minutes on Marius's clock (and it's handy that the TARDIS dimensional stabiliser plugs right into the Bi-Al's technology). The notion that the cloned Leela could feel pain experienced by the real Leela is nonsense. The virus-possessed Marius must surely remember concealing his assistant in the booth before he was infected – so why doesn't he stop her from slipping away? The Doctor's biodefences don't look very threatening. And then there's the virus/giant prawn . . .

Availability: Issued on VHS in 2002 BBCV 7267 (UK), WHV E1859 (US).

Verdict: 'What do you mean, carriers? I'm not a porter!' Many *Doctor Who* stories have been let down by rubbish monsters. Rubbish monsters are commonplace. It's therefore difficult to emphasise just how jaw-droppingly bad the manifestation of the virus in 'The Invisible Enemy' is. Seriously, it might as well be made out of old newspapers and spit.

Few writers have overestimated what was possible on *Doctor Who*'s budget to a greater extent than Bob Baker and Dave Martin and 'The Invisible Enemy' sees them at their most, let us say, *optimistic*. Taken purely as a script, it's well paced and has good concepts, but did they really think the production would be able to pull off a journey through the Doctor's brain? For the most part it's cheap but functional and some of the 'innerspace' material is effective. But the nucleus is a disappointment and the enlarged virus is just laughable (the hapless 'crustacean' reference just makes things worse). If only the enemy could have stayed invisible.

94
Image of the Fendahl

Part One: 29 October 1977
Part Two: 5 November 1977
Part Three: 12 November 1977
Part Four: 19 November 1977

Written by Chris Boucher
Directed by George Spenton-Foster

Notable Cast: Denis Lill (Dr Fendleman) has many TV and film credits, including regular appearances in *Rumpole of the Bailey* (1983–92) and *Only Fools and Horses* (1989–96, alongside Wanda Ventham (Thea Ransome): *she* previously appeared in **35**, 'The Faceless Ones'). Edward Evans (Ted Moss) was a regular in *Coronation Street* (1965–66) and *Poldark* (1975). Geoffrey Hinsliff (Jack Tyler) was a regular in *Brass* (1983–84) and *Coronation Street* (1987–97) and played Rufrius in *I, Claudius* (1976). Former stuntman and extra Derek Martin (Security Guard) went on to play Charlie Slater in *EastEnders* (2001–present).

Director: George Spenton-Foster produced *Out of the Unknown* (1966–67). He went on to direct episodes of *Paul Temple* (1969) and *Blake's 7* (1979).

Scary Monsters: 'The Fendahl *is* death.' Twelve million years ago, the Fendahl avoided an evolutionary blind alley by feeding on death itself. It is a telepathic gestalt composed of a core creature and twelve sluglike Fendahleen.

History 101: The Fendahl had a profound influence on the development of human evolution: the Doctor notes that this 'would explain the dark side of man's nature'. It was supposed to have been destroyed on the long-lost Fifth Planet of our solar system, but its skull has found its way to Earth and been uncovered by scientists working at Fetch Priory.

Villains: One of the scientists, Max Stael (Scott Fredericks), is involved with local occult practices and believes that he can gain power from the Fendahl skull. However, this proves to be the Fendahl's manipulation at work.

The Plan: The Fendahl will use the scientists and cultists as hosts for new Fendahleen, whereupon it will drain Earth of energy, as it has so many other planets.

Other Worlds: The Doctor attempts to visit the Fifth Planet, but it has been concealed from the rest of the universe by a time loop. The Doctor immediately realises that this is the work of the Time Lords ('They're not supposed to do that sort of thing, you know').

Doctor Who?: He's wonderfully businesslike when entering the Priory, asking how many deaths there have been, even before he's introduced himself. He admits to being frightened by the Fendahl, noting that he remembers them from the stories that scared him as a child – deftly aligning the Doctor with the juvenile viewer at home.

Science/Magic: Fetch Priory in contemporary England has a reputation for being haunted. The Doctor provides an explanation for this, stating that what is perceived as paranormal phenomena are in fact distortions caused by nearby time fissures. Ma Tyler's (Daphne Heard) precognitive abilities are the result of her having spent her childhood near the fissure. 'How do 'ee know so much?' asks Ma. 'I read a lot,' replies the Doctor.

Things Fall Apart: When Thea is possessed by the Fendahl, her eyes are painted on to her eyelids. This wouldn't be a problem if the eyes were purely ceremonial but it's made clear that they are a source of great power. Despite being painted on.

Availability: Released on VHS in 1993 as BBCV 4941 (UK), WHV E1321 (US).

Verdict: 'The body is decomposing. It's falling apart as you watch.' The last *Doctor Who* serial in the horror tradition established under Hinchcliffe and Homes, 'Image of the Fendahl' is also one of the best. New producer Graham Williams had been told to produce more family-friendly fare, and stories such as this were sidelined in favour of whimsical space adventure with more obvious humour. While the series had to move on some time, it's a shame that this involved letting go of a style that the production team had clearly nailed and that still had mileage in it.

As in **89**, 'The Face of Evil', Chris Boucher takes a big idea and lets it unfold gradually, taking care not to show his hand too early. This time, however, the Doctor isn't trying to resolve a situation that's been static for centuries: he's dealing with one that's worsening by the second, hence there's greater tension. One can appreciate why the BBC was concerned for younger viewers – even if the monsters may not be entirely convincing, the scene where Stael asks the Doctor for the gun is strong stuff – but kids *like* to be scared. Isn't that why they watch in the first place? Scott Fredericks and Edward Arthur (Colby) both excel, and Baker gives one of his best performances ('Alas, poor skull').

95
The Sun Makers

Part One: 26 November 1977
Part Two: 3 December 1977
Part Three: 10 December 1977
Part Four: 12 December 1977

Written by Robert Holmes
Directed by Pennant Roberts

Notable Cast: Michael Keating (Gowdry) was Vila, the only one of *Blake's 7* to appear in every episode (1978–81). Henry Woolf (The Collector) was a frequent collaborator with David Frost in his satirical days.

Other Worlds: Pluto. Here, in the far distant future, the remnants of mankind are being worked and taxed to death by a monolithic Company run by aliens. Cassius (named after the man who killed Julius Caesar, or his grandson who killed Caligula, perhaps?) the tenth planet of Earth's solar system, is mentioned.

Villains: Gatherer Hade (Richard Leech) is an obsequious Company functionary, but also a shockingly stereotypical Jewish money grabber played by a man affecting a generically 'foreign' accent. The Collector is a Userian (which sounds a bit like usurer, ho, ho) fungus who runs the Company.

Science/Magic: The Doctor claims it's possible for a planet with two suns not to have a night if the two suns' 'sidereal axle rotation periods' are the same. Pluto has six artificial suns, which are actually 'in station fusion satellites'. Pento-cyllinic methylhydrate (PCM) is an anxiety-increasing drug.

Things Fall Apart: Cheap-looking all round, this is about as visually stimulating as cold, milky tea. The sets are overtly theatrical but lack a strong enough visual identity to establish themselves through iconography. (Director Roberts vetoed the idea of basing the sets on South American propaganda posters.) There are lots of languid performances (and everyone on the planet is blandly middle-class). The planet is sparsely populated and overlit even by *Doctor Who*'s standards. There's a scene of Leela's party running a blockade in Part Three, which is possibly the least exciting action sequence ever filmed. The story is predicated on a simple deception – it equates taxation from government with a company's profits, and they're not the same thing at all. Presumably, this was done because complaining about taxation (which usually involves redistributing money from the richer to the poorer) is generally perceived as less acceptable than complaining about nameless companies making huge profits (which usually involves the redistribution of money from the poorer to the richer).

Availability: Released in 2003 as BBCV 7133 (UK), WHV 1607 (US): one of the last *Doctor Who* serials to be issued on VHS.

Verdict: 'Perhaps everyone runs from the taxman.' Long trumpeted as proof that *Doctor Who* can 'do' politics, this isn't really a satire on the British tax system at all. It's just whining about it. 'The Sun Makers' quite simply isn't funny, relevant or clever. It's also not entertaining, or even particularly well-made television. Leaving aside the quips, this is a simplistic, bland story of capture and escape and despite the conscience-salving swipes at big business and bureaucracy, these are mean-spirited, shallow and reactionary scripts. The sudden introduction of a mass slaughter subplot (literally) five minutes before the end might suggest even the writer was bored and embarrassed by his scripts' conceit. There's something peculiarly obnoxious about watching someone pay his tax bill by scripting something that moans about the fact he was sent it in the first place. At least when the Beatles did it, it had a decent guitar solo halfway through.

96
Underworld

Part One: 7 January 1978
Part Two: 14 January 1978
Part Three: 21 January 1978
Part Four: 28 January 1978

Written by Bob Baker and Dave Martin
Directed by Norman Stewart

Notable Cast: Alan Lake (Herrick) appeared in Dennis Potter's *Stand Up, Nigel Barton* (1965) and Alan Bleasdale's *The Black Stuff* (1980) for television, and on film in *Charlie Bubbles* (Albert Finney, 1967) and as the title character in *Confessions from the David Galaxy Affair* (Willy Roe, 1979). He was married to Diana Dors.

Script Editor: Anthony Read was story editor on *The Trouble-shooters* (1965–72); he also wrote for *The Professionals*, *Chocky*, *Heartbeat* and *Sapphire and Steel*. He remained *Doctor Who*'s script editor until 103, 'The Armageddon Factor'.

Director: Norman Stewart, a frequent production assistant on *Doctor Who* since 2, 'The Daleks', directed an episode of *The Omega Factor* (1979).

History 101: The planet Minyos was destroyed 100,000 years ago 'on the other side of the universe'. The Minyans met the Time Lords and thought of them as gods. The flattered Time Lords gave the Minyans technology, which they then used to destroy each other in a cataclysmic war. This catastrophe led to the Time Lords' policy of non-intervention.

Other Worlds: When the TARDIS arrives at the 'edge of the cosmos' with nothingness ahead, a spiral nebula forms nearby. To escape being sucked into the Nebula the TARDIS materialises on a nearby Minyan spaceship, which has been on its mission for 100,000 years searching for the missing colony ship P7E. The P7E contains the Minyan race bank, which is needed to restart the race. A nebula formed around the P7E, and the mass of the ship caused a planet to form around it. This new planet is riddled with tunnels, where enslaved 'trogs' are oppressed by hooded guards (both descendants of the P7E crew).

Villains: The Oracle is the P7E ship's computer, which has gone insane and set itself up as a god, ruling over the descendants of the ship's crew with the support of robotic Seers, who organise the oppression of the slaves in the tunnels by human guards. Some of the slaves are ritually sacrificed to the Oracle.

The Plan: No one really has anything as well thought out as a plan. The Minyan explorers want the race banks, which are held by the Oracle, and the Oracle tries to stop them. The nearest thing to a scheme in the story is when the Oracle gives the Minyan explorers fission grenades instead of the race banks, and the Doctor gives the grenades back to the Oracle instead of the real race banks.

Science/Magic: A Lieberman Maser is a very dangerous gun. The Minyans have a pacifying ray, and have regenerated themselves over a thousand times each on their long journey. The Minyan ship has a computer built with crystalline cybernetics that are decaying, but K9 acts as a substitute for the decrepit machine. The Doctor says that people living in Aberdeen absorb more radiation from the local granite than people who work in nuclear power stations, showing how life can adapt. The society on the planet gets everything from the rock mined by the slaves – it is processed for food and fuel.

Doctor Who?: The Doctor is rude to K9, even though he says the dog is his 'second-best friend'. He advises Leela to 'never play with strange weapons'. At the end of the story, the Doctor pulls on a smock as he intends to paint.

Things Fall Apart: The caves are entirely created by photos dropped in with bluescreen. The Doctor painstakingly (and painfully) explains the parallels with the story of Jason and the Golden Fleece at the end of the story.

Availability: Issued on VHS in 2002 as BBCV 7264 (UK), WHV E1741 (US).

Verdict: 'No time? Don't say that to me, I'm a Time Lord.' An interminable reworking of the myth of Jason and the Golden Fleece, 'Underworld' is slow, tiresome and lacking any significant characterisation or plot twists. Good guys want something, bad guys try and stop them, the end. The direction is competent enough, but the dialogue is tedious and witless, and the production lacks any dramatic energy. No one involved seems to care very much about what is going on, with the regulars failing to muster any enthusiasm. Who can blame them? A good candidate for the worst *Doctor Who* serial.

97
The Invasion of Time

Part One: 4 February 1978
Part Two: 11 February 1978
Part Three: 18 February 1978
Part Four: 25 February 1978
Part Five: 4 March 1978
Part Six: 11 March 1978

Written by David Agnew
Directed by Gerald Blake

Notable Cast: John Arnatt (Borusa) was born in Petrograd. He had roles in *House of Cards* (1990) and *Miss Marple: The Moving Finger* (1985) and was a regular in *Emergency – Ward 10* (1963). Louise Jameson departs the series at the end of Part Six.

Writer: 'David Agnew' was a BBC pseudonym used when staff had to write a script quickly. 'He' had previously been credited with episodes of *Target* (1977–78). Here 'David Agnew' is producer Graham Williams and script editor Anthony Read.

Doctor Who?: The Doctor claims the Presidency of the Time Lords (his by right, since he is the only candidate who survived **88**, 'The Deadly Assassin'). He considers Time Lords to be 'too single-minded' and 'short on humour and imagination'. He insists to Borusa that he did not have anything to do with the sinking of the *Titanic*. Castellan Kelner confirms that the term 'Doctor' is an affectation.

Other Worlds: Gallifrey is ruled by a Supreme Council (it was the High Council in **88**, 'The Deadly Assassin'). Without a president, the Council can't ratify anything and they haven't had a president since the assassination in that earlier story. Cardinal Borusa illegally appointed Chancellor by the Council – appears to have been acting with executive authority since then. The Time Lords are less indolent and less ignorant of their own history and technology than in 'Assassin'. (Has Borusa been pursuing reforms?) Outside the citadel, there are a group of Time Lords who 'dropped out'. They live as hunter/gatherer nomads.

The Plan: Having learned that the Vardans plan to invade Gallifrey, the Doctor allies himself with them, intending to double-cross them and thwart their plans.

Scary Monsters: The Vardans are not 'monsters', just militaristic humanoids. They can travel along 'wavelengths of any sort' – including thought. Their war fleet has a neo-crystal structure and atomic power and weaponry. They are allied with/being duped by (the script is unclear) the Sontarans (see **70**, 'The Time Warrior'). No mention is made of the Sontarans' war with the Rutan, which forms the background to all the other Sontaran stories and **92**, 'Horror of Fang Rock' and they now seek 'victory over all!' While the aliens' characterisation as buffoons is in keeping with the era's treatment of all authority figures as blundering and crass it does lessen them as a threat.

Science/Magic: The ebonite rod 'Great Key' from 'Assassin' is referred to as 'The Rod of Rassilon' throughout and another Great Key – one that looks like a mortice key – is introduced (see **144**, 'The Trial of a Time Lord'). It is usually entrusted to the Chancellor and the President is unaware of it. The APC net (in which the Doctor fought Goth in 'Assassin') is just a part of the Matrix, a computer that contains 'all the information that has ever been stored, all the information that could ever be stored'. Access to it gives one 'more power than anyone in the known universe'.

Things Fall Apart: Gallifrey is a much less impressive, less populated and less fogbound place than in 'The Deadly Assassin', which is a shame. The silver-foil Vardans are really poor. Stan McGowan lacks the authority and presence to play the Chief Vardan. Leela's departure is hurried and unconvincing. The Doctor's sudden amnesia at the end is irritating (and implied in **98**, 'The Ribos Operation' to be an affectation, suggesting the production team thought better of it later).

Availability: Issued on VHS in 2000 as BBCV 6876 (UK), WHV E1011 (US).

Verdict: 'I'd rather care.' Any scene with John Arnatt is excellent, so astute is his portrayal of Borusa as the consummate political animal. It's one of Tom Baker's best performances too, conveying the levels of deception and affectation the Doctor achieves and heightening the sinister atmosphere of the early episodes. There's much to love about 'The Invasion of Time': the excellent use of K9, the lack of respect for the military, the Doctor's Christlike induction as President, Dudley Simpson's Sontaran theme and the sly intelligence of its depiction of the politics of occupation. Unfortunately, the finale – in which the Doctor shoots his enemy with a big gun – is unworthy of what has come before it and an obvious indication of the speed with which the scripts were written. The production sometimes looks hurried as well: the exploration of the TARDIS interior lacks any sense of wonder and ultimately feels like a missed opportunity.

98
The Ribos Operation

Part One: 2 September 1978

Part Two: 9 September 1978
Part Three: 16 September 1978
Part Four: 23 September 1978

Written by Robert Holmes
Directed by George Spenton-Foster

Notable Cast: Actor and director Iain Cutherbertson (Garron) was Dr Arnold in *Tom Brown's School Days* (1971), the star of *Sutherland's Law* (1973–76) and latterly Vice Chancellor of the University of St Andrews. Paul Seed (Graff Vynda-K) directed *House of Cards* (1990) and its sequels, as well as *A Rather English Marriage* (1988). Robert Keegan (Sholakh) played Desk Sergeant Blackitt in *Z Cars* (1963–65). New regular Mary Tamm (Romana) trained at RADA; before *Doctor Who* she appeared in *The Odessa File* (Ronald Neame, 1974) and afterwards she was a regular in *Brookside* (1993–95). Cyril Luckham (the Guardian) starred in *To Serve Them All My Days* (1978).

Doctor Who?: The introduction of Romana has an immediate affect on the Doctor's character. They patronise each other and squabble over details. She claims the Doctor is 759, he insists it's 756. He graduated from the Time Lords Academy with 51 per cent at the second attempt, she got a triple first. Romana opines that the Doctor's erratic behaviour is the result of a 'sub-transitory, experiential hypertoid-induced condition aggravated by multi-encephalogical tensions'. In essence, it's a 'compensation syndrome'. His sarcasm is 'an adjusted stress reaction'. He lectures her on the difference between experience and education. The Doctor is instantly respectful of the Guardian – even wary of speaking too loudly in his presence. The Doctor claims to have learned tricks from Mescalyne.

Scary Monsters: The Shrivenzale, a large beast not unlike a komodo dragon, which guards the relic room on Ribos. The costume – operated by two people in the tradition of a pantomime horse – is actually rather good.

Villains: The Graff Vynda-K is a deposed Emperor and war leader (his 'Frontier campaigns in the service of the alliance are rightly famous' according to Garron). He's looking for a planet upon which to base himself in preparation for attempted counter-coup against his half brother.

The Plan: Two conmen, Garron and Unstoffe (Nigel Plaskitt), plan to trick the exiled Graff Vynda-K into thinking he is buying a primitive planet. Meanwhile, contacted by the Guardian of Light in Time (Cyril Luckham), the Doctor is sent on a mission to recover the six segments of the Key to Time (see **Science/Magic**).

Other Planets: Ribos, one of the most compelling planets ever seen in *Doctor Who*. It orbits its sun elliptically leading to long seasons of 32 years. The principal city is called Shurr. The planet is three light centuries from the Magellanic clouds and in the constellation of Skytha.

Science/Magic: Jethrik is a mineral used to power the engines of space craft. The Key to Time is a perfect cube 'which maintains the equilibrium of time itself'. So powerful is it ('too great for any one being to have') that it's split into six segments and scattered throughout time and space. When the cube it assembled it has the power to freeze the entire universe. The Guardian needs to do this because the forces within the universe have unbalanced reality to the point where it needs to be repaired. The Doctor has heard of the Key and believes it's 'a story, an old legend'. The tracer for the Key makes a noise like a Geiger counter, and can be plugged into the TARDIS console to show the space–time co-ordinates of each segment.

In Shurr there is a Seeker (Anne Tirard) whose incantations and rituals (used to find missing people) actually seem to work. Binro the heretic (Timothy Bateson) is essentially the Ribosian Galileo Galilei – a man who theorised that planets moved around stars and that every star was a sun, he proved it with mathematics and was then tried, tortured and crippled for heresy.

Availability: All of the Key to Time stories are available on DVD, but only in the US: the Region 1 release of this story is WHV E1336. The US VHS is also WHV E1366. The UK VHS is BBCV 5607.

Verdict: 'When you've faced death as often as I have, you'll know that this is much more fun.' 'The Ribos Operation' sets out to be different, engaging and funny and achieves that ambition in spades. This is thanks, largely, to Iain Cuthbertson's turn as Garron, which additionally provokes one of Tom Baker's best performances as the Doctor as the series' star ups his game to compete with this marvellous actor. It would be unwise to underrate Mary Tamm though – at this point Romana is a marvellous 'straight girl' seemingly modelled on Rosalind Russell's Hildy Johnson in *His Girl Friday* (Howard Hawks, 1940). Equally Holmes's devious, delightful scripts are full of finely polished dialogue and amusing situations – and is another neat world-building exercise – while the Graff is a superb villain; somehow both a comedy madman and a compelling threat. One of the most perfect of all *Doctor Who* serials.

99
The Pirate Planet

Part One: 30 September 1978
Part Two: 7 October 1978
Part Three: 14 October 1978
Part Four: 21 October 1978

Written by Douglas Adams
Directed by Pennant Roberts

Notable Cast: Ralph Michael (Balaton) appeared in *The Heroes of Telemark* (Anthony Mann, 1965) and *The Forsyte Saga* (1967). Bruce Purchase (Captain) appeared in *I, Claudius* (1976) and played Northumberland in the BBC's *Henry IV* (1979). David Warwick (Kimus) had a regular role in the first series of *The Fall and Rise of Reginald Perrin* (1976).

Writer: One of Douglas Adams's earliest credits was on the final 1974 series of *Monty Python's Flying Circus*. In 1978 he wrote the radio serial *The Hitch-Hiker's Guide to the Galaxy*, for which he remains internationally known. As well as further radio series, *Hitch-Hiker's* spawned five novels (the first of which was voted Britain's fourth-favourite novel in 2003's *Big Read*), a TV series and a 2005 film directed by Garth Jennings. During 1979 he served as *Doctor Who*'s script editor, although his inability to appreciate what could be achieved on the programme's budget suggests that this was perhaps not the wisest appointment ('The Pirate Planet' was scaled back before production and is still overambitious). Strong on jokes, though.

Doctor Who?: The Doctor has been operating the TARDIS for 523 years ('Has it really been that long?'). Romana is unfamiliar with the obsolete Type 40 and is reading its manual, which takes the form of a dusty leather-bound book.

Other Worlds: The Doctor locates the second segment of the Key to Time on the planet Calufrax and attempts to land. He remembers the planet as a featureless place of icy tundras, but finds an inhabited world with a temperate climate: the affluent natives state that it is called Zanak.

Villains: Zanak is ruled by the Captain, who operates from a mountainside control room. The population of Zanak are unaware of what he does there: as far as they are concerned he merely announces new golden ages of prosperity at regular intervals.

The Plan: Zanak is hollow. Each 'golden age' is brought about when the Captain operates a powerful dematerialisation engine and moves the entire planet to surround another planet. Automated mining systems drain that world of its mineral resources, then the planet is miniaturised and placed within the Captain's delicately balanced suspension chamber. Zanak then moves on. There is a greater purpose to this harvesting than simple wealth, however ...

Science/Magic: The linear induction corridor serves no real plot function but permits Adams to crack a few physics jokes: it's just a shame that the corridor itself is visually ineffective, and Tom Baker struggles to deliver his dialogue convincingly whilst travelling along it.

Things Fall Apart: When the Doctor crouches down beside K9 and sees the scattered jewels, how can he have only just noticed them? The 'fully automated' mines look a lot like disused manual mines, and jar badly with the presence of aircars and dimensional jump engines. How does the Doctor know that the shrunken planets will precisely fill Zanak's hollow centre?

Availability: Issued on UK VHS in 1995 as BBCV 5610, and on US VHS and Region 1 DVD (in 2002) as WHV E1338.

Verdict: 'It's an economic miracle. Of course it's wrong.' In most parts a great success, occasionally a miserable failure, 'The Pirate Planet' demonstrates what a great radio writer Douglas Adams was. The more successful segments of the Key to Time sequence (**98**, 'The Ribos Operation' and **101**, 'The Androids of Tara') operate well on a modest scale, whereas Adams attempts an epic only to discover that the budget can't even meet him halfway. Visually the story often falls flat, although the script and actors do their best to make off-screen drama (such as the destruction of entire worlds) come to life.

Surprisingly for Adams, although most of the dialogue is excellent, some of it is utterly dreadful. Even David Warwick, who is generally very good, struggles with the line 'Bandraginus Five, by the last breath in my body you'll be avenged,' particularly as he is required to deliver it to a small lump of rock. The Mentiads are also quite poor, chanting away in their cavern and clunkily referring to themselves as 'we Mentiads'. But Adams's sci-fi concepts are typically great and, although Baker puts in an inconsistent performance, the double act of Bruce Purchase and Andrew Robertson (Mr Fibuli) makes up for almost everything.

100
The Stones of Blood

Part One: 28 October 1978
Part Two: 4 November 1978
Part Three: 11 November 1978
Part Four: 18 November 1978

Written by David Fisher
Directed by Darrol Blake

Writer: David Fisher wrote the horror movie *Guardian of the Abyss* (Don Sharp, 1980), and in recent years has collaborated with *Doctor Who* script editor Anthony Read on a number of history books including *The Fall of Berlin* (1992).

Director: Darrol Blake directed episodes of the soaps *Coronation Street* and *Brookside.*

Doctor Who?: Romana tells the Doctor what he should do, but he always feels the need to make it sound like his idea. The Doctor tells Romana about the White Guardian, and that it wasn't the Time Lord President who sent her – he doesn't think it's fair that she doesn't know the truth. He takes an umbrella with him when he leaves the TARDIS and just throws it into a field when he realises it isn't going to rain. The Doctor makes several random claims: that he isn't an expert on fashion; that everybody knows Earth is his favourite planet; that K9 is from Trenton, New Jersey; that he isn't from outer space so much as 'inner time'; that he tried to correct Einstein on the special theory of relativity; and that he's always wanted to get lost in a theoretical absurdity. He does an impersonation of a matador, and keeps a barrister's wig in his pocket which he wears when defending himself. (In court, that is, not against attack.)

History 101: The tracker takes the TARDIS to the contemporary English coast, where druidic rituals in honour of the goddess Cailleach are taking place in a megalithic stone circle called 'the nine travellers'.

Other Worlds: From the stone circle, a spaceship in hyperspace can be reached. The ship is a prison vessel where the prisoners are dead (including a criminal Wirrn from **76**, 'The Ark in Space'). The ship has been there for 4,000 years with 'justice machines' the Megara (floating blobs of light that act as judges, jury and executioners) locked in a cabin the whole time.

Scary Monsters: The Ogri, glowing standing stones that feed on blood, from Ogros in Tau Ceti.

Villains: Cessair of Diplos (Susan Engel), alias the Cailleach, a female alien who has lived on Earth for thousands of years under various identities, and is worshipped as a goddess by the druid cult. The Cailleach uses ravens and crows as her eyes.

The Plan: Cessair of Diplos was to be tried by the Megara for the crimes of murder and stealing the great seal of Diplos. She escaped from the prison ship 4,000 years ago, and has been hiding on Earth ever since. It's never made clear what she's actually supposed to be doing with the Ogri.

Science/Magic: The TARDIS is fitted with a molecular stabiliser that allows K9 to be repaired. The Cailleach uses a static energy force field, which the Doctor thinks is very primitive. Hyperspace is a different kind of space, a different dimension, that allows you to avoid the time distortion predicted by the theory of relativity. The Doctor builds a device to get himself into hyperspace, which is powered by tritium crystals. The third segment, the great seal of Diplos, has the power to transfer things into hyperspace.

Things Fall Apart: There's some atrocious day-for-night recording (made even more obvious by intercutting with genuine night sequences) and poor bluescreen as Romana hangs from a cliff. Three portraits, supposedly from different time periods, are obviously painted by the same artist.

Availability: Issued on UK VHS in 1995 as BBCV 5610, and on US VHS and Region 1 DVD (in 2002) as WHV E1314.

Verdict: 'We're not all programmed for perfection, you know.' A game of two halves, 'The Stones of Blood' begins as an efficient, albeit clichéd, occult thriller, but descends into gibberish as the story goes on. It all begins to go wrong when the Ogri are first seen; six-foot-tall plastic rocks don't make for a convincing threat. By the final episode the whole thing has collapsed into an endless trial scene, with Tom Baker camping it up royally as the squeaky Megara spiral around him. Incoherent, and strangely pointless.

101
The Androids of Tara

Part One: 25 November 1978
Part Two: 2 December 1978
Part Three: 9 December 1978
Part Four: 16 December 1978

Written by David Fisher
Directed by Michael Hayes

Notable Cast: Peter Jeffrey (Count Grendel) previously appeared in **34**, 'The Macra Terror'. Cyril Shaps (Archimandrite) was in **37**, 'The Tomb of the Cybermen' and **74**, 'Planet of the Spiders'.

Director: Michael Hayes directed *A for Andromeda* (1961), and both adapted and directed the television version of Aleksei Arbuzov's play *The Promise* (1969).

Other Worlds: Tara, a leafy planet with a feudal society, where the nobility rule but the peasants have all the useful skills. Androids are widely used, and were introduced to fill labour shortages after a plague wiped out nine-tenths of the population. When the Doctor and Romana arrive, Prince Reynart (Neville Jason) is about to be crowned king and the second in line to the throne, Princess Strella, is missing.

Scary Monsters: The beast of Tara, an incredibly unconvincing long-haired creature.

Villains: Count Grendel, Knight of Gracht, who wishes to stop either Reynart or Strella from taking the throne of Tara, and wishes to be king himself. Grendel, played brilliantly by Peter Jeffrey, is a full-strength pantomime villain, complete with little beard and an endless pleasure in his fiendish schemes. The best swordsman on Tara, he's also daring and brave, audaciously walking into danger to carry out his plans.

The Plan: Prince Reynart wants to distract Grendel using an android double of himself, allowing Reynart to get to his coronation unmolested. When Grendel kidnaps Reynart, Reynart's supporters have the android crowned instead, while they try and find the real prince. Meanwhile, Grendel sends an android double of Strella to assassinate the king at his coronation. Grendel also plans to use a startling resemblance between Romana and Princess Strella – whom he has in his dungeon – to make a counter-claim to the throne. Romana is to stand in for Strella at her wedding to the real Reynart, then, after Reynart is dead, a second marriage to Grendel. Grendel will then have Strella killed, and take his late wife's claim to the throne. Grendel ensures the co-operation of all involved by threatening to kill the real Strella.

Science/Magic: The Tarans use swords and crossbow bolts that carry an electric charge. Segments of the key can blunt a diamond drill. Romana's alpha waves are entirely unlike those of a Taran brain.

Doctor Who?: The Doctor is pretty weak at the start of the story, having lost interest in the quest for the Key to Time, preferring to play chess with K9 and go fishing, and is bullied at the point of a sword. However, later on he becomes positively swashbuckling, fighting a duel with Count Grendel in spite of claiming that a sword is 'too complicated' for him (as he starts the duel ineptly, he's either an inhumanly fast learner or trying to get Grendel to underestimate him). The Doctor turns down both an offer of the throne from Grendel and an offer of Castle Gracht and all its lands from the King. The Doctor programmes the android double of Prince Reynart (which he names George) to be smarter than the real prince, and sympathises with the androids whenever anybody criticises them. He last used his fishing rod when he was with Isaac Walton, and considers fishing 'an art'.

Things Fall Apart: The token monster in the first episode is one of the most appallingly unconvincing costumes in the entire series. Isn't it over-egging the pudding to have a coincidental physical double walk into a plot that already involves robot duplicates? The 'comic ending' with K9 spinning in a boat and the Doctor laughing like an imbecile is very, very weak, and reminiscent of the equally unfunny endings used in *Scooby-Doo*.

Availability: Issued on UK VHS in 1995 as BBCV 5611, and on US VHS and Region 1 DVD (in 2002) as WHV E1310.

Verdict: 'Ten thousand gold pieces to the man who shoots the Doctor!' The Key to Time isn't really relevant to this barely disguised reworking of Anthony Hope's novel *The Prisoner of Zenda* (1893), with the fourth segment found during the course of Part One. Instead, this is a charming and elegant tale of court intrigue, beautifully shot with superb costumes and sets. An excellent supporting cast (including the brilliant Peter Jeffrey in a scene-stealing role as Grendel) keep the tone just right, while Mary Tamm gives a notably different vocal performance as Strella, making her an entirely different ice queen to Romana. Tom Baker is a bit shakier, with the Doctor an ineffectual comic presence early on, but comes into his own in later episodes, showing steel as he battles the Count. While it's an enjoyable affair, the story ultimately feels insubstantial due to its derivative nature; although a lot of fun, 'Tara' isn't distinct enough from *Zenda* to be anything more than pastiche.

102
The Power of Kroll

Part One: 23 December 1978
Part Two: 30 December 1978
Part Three: 6 January 1979
Part Four: 13 January 1979

Written by Robert Holmes
Directed by Norman Stewart

Notable Cast: Glyn Owen (Rohm-Dutt) was one of the stars of *The Brothers* (1972) and *Howard's Way* (1985–90) and memorably played Commander Leyland in *Blake's 7* (1978). Dugeen is played by John Leeson – normally the voice of K9. Philip Madoc (see **47**, 'The Krotons') returns in his least interesting *Who* role. Neil McCarthy (Thawn) was previously in **56**, 'The Mind of Evil'.

Doctor Who?: 'Sometimes I don't think you're quite right in the head,' comments Romana early on and it's fair comment on Tom

Baker's increasingly erratic and bewilderingly uninterested performance. He seems barely conscious when walking out of the TARDIS in Part One. The Doctor believes that the word progress can mean 'just about anything you want it to mean' and is quietly enraged at Thawn's casual racism. One of the story's strongest elements is that it shows the Doctor as a selfless, moral figure in a world of corrupt, avaricious and self-interested men. At one point, when handed a drink, he drops it into his coat pocket without taking a sip.

Other Worlds: The TARDIS arrives on one of the moons of Earth colony Delta Magna ('probably the third'). The native population of Delta Magna, colloquially known as 'Swampies', were moved to the moon by humans centuries before.

Scary Monsters: Holmes was asked to write a story featuring *Doctor Who*'s biggest ever monster – so he did. The titular Kroll is a giant squid, bloated to five miles across by its proximity to the fifth segment. It's worshipped as a god by the Swampies.

Villains: Rohm-Dutt is a gunrunner, supplying the Swampies with weapons. Ostensibly, he's doing this on behalf of the pro-Swampy pressure group the Sons of Earth, but he's actually collaborating with refinery commander Thawn, who wants the Swampies to attack with guns as this will give him an excuse to exterminate them.

Science/Magic: The refinery produces a hundred tonnes of protein a day from methane in the swamps. It does this using a 'fernicular gas separator' and an injection circuit, which feeds a bacterium bioplast raw protein which is then centrifuged. So now you know how to make your own! (The Doctor suggests using 'a plasma catalyst ahead of the bioplast circuit' to make the system more efficient.)

Things Fall Apart: Although this is a generally solid production, the split-screen used to place the giant Kroll in the same picture as the other characters is lamentable. The modelwork has absolutely no sense of scale. There's a confusingly put together action sequence at the end of Part Two where it looks like there's some footage missing. There's a whacking great camera wobble halfway through Part Three. Why does Neil McCarthy play Thawn like he's a Peter Cook character? You expect him to soliloquise about

Jayne Mansfield or announce that he's due to appear on 'Celebrity Suicides' at any moment.

Availability: Issued on VHS in 1995 as BBCV 5612 (UK), the Region 1 DVD is WHV E1337 – a catalogue number it shares with the US VHS.

Verdict: 'I didn't like the bit about death according to one of the seven holy rituals.' On the plus side there's some great location filming (featuring hovercrafts, big guns and neat little boats) and Holmes again convincingly creates an off-screen society using only words. On the other hand, literally every major role is horrendously miscast, Romana is reduced to screaming and being rescued, and the sacrificial sequences have no atmosphere and go on for ever. It's also unbearably slow at times and the production conspicuously fails to bring out either the ambiguity in the characters or the scripts' overt anti-religiosity and obvious hatred of ideologues. The joke about the bad monster costume looking 'more convincing' from the front it just pitiably unfunny. 'The Power of Kroll' is far from terrible, but it is terribly difficult to get worked up about.

103
The Armageddon Factor

Part One: 20 January 1979
Part Two: 27 January 1979
Part Three: 3 February 1979
Part Four: 10 February 1979
Part Five: 17 February 1979
Part Six: 24 February 1979

Written by Bob Baker and Dave Martin
Directed by Michael Hayes

Notable Cast: John Woodvine (Marshal) was a regular in *Z Cars* (1968–69): he played Banquo in the BBC's 1979 *Macbeth* and appeared in *An American Werewolf in London* (John Landis, 1981) and *Edge of Darkness* (1985). Valentine Dyall (Black Guardian) enjoyed a lengthy film career but is best known as the Man in Black from the radio series *Appointment With Fear* (1943–55). William Squire (The Shadow) was an RSC leading man. Lalla Ward (Princess Astra) appeared in *Got It Made* (James Kenelm

Clarke, 1974), five 1977 episodes of *The Duchess of Duke Street* and played Ophelia in the BBC's *Hamlet*. Following 'The Armageddon Factor' Ward was offered the chance to take over the role of Romana, which she accepted. She went on to marry Tom Baker, later divorced him and became an author of children's fiction. She is now married to the eminent scientist Richard Dawkins. This is Mary Tamm's final story as a regular and John Leeson also left the series at this point (although his departure turned out to be temporary).

Other Worlds: The Doctor and Romana's search for the sixth and final segment of the Key to Time brings them to Atrios, which is in the midst of a brutal spacebound war with the planet Zeos.

The Plan: The war between the worlds has been covertly created and supervised by a creature known as the Shadow as a pretext for getting the secret of the sixth segment from Princess Astra of Atrios.

Villains: The Marshal of Atrios is under the control of the Shadow (William Squire); in addition, his lust for glory makes him a dangerous, if slightly ineffectual, presence. He demands that the Doctor concoct a war-winning gambit for him (shades of **20**, 'The Myth Makers' – and again later on, as K9 plays Trojan Horse). All of them are ultimately pawns being manipulated by the Black Guardian.

Doctor Who?: The Shadow has employed Drax (Barry Jackson), another Time Lord, to build Mentalis, a computer that coordinates the entire Zeon campaign. The Doctor encounters Drax in the Shadow's domain: Drax remembers him from their schooldays and refers to him as 'Theta Sigma'. 'You did well, didn't you,' Drax notes, 'getting your doctorate and all that.'

Science/Magic: The Doctor constructs a temporary sixth segment from chronodyne, which from its name presumably possesses some temporal properties. It looks like tinfoil.

Things Fall Apart: The Marshal is incredibly indiscreet when reporting to the Shadow: couldn't he go into another room at least? Davyd Harries (Shapp) does a ridiculous stagger-back-and-fall into the transmat in Part Four. How can the Doctor and Romana move inside the Zeon computer room if it's included in the Time Loop? Why does Drax think that the Doctor wants to be shrunk at the end of Part Five? Was the phoney war really the easiest way to manoeuvre the Doctor and Astra into place? Why reveal the existence of a Black Guardian mere minutes before he appears as part of the twist ending? Romana was told that the President didn't send her on this mission during **100**, 'The Stones of Blood': here she is told again, and is surprised. Again. Tom Baker soars dreadfully over the top when pretending he's tempted by the power offered for the Key to Time. Rolling his eyes into the back of his skull and whispering hoarsely while displaying a breathtaking lack of conviction and interest in the material, it's his worst scene as Doctor Who by a country mile.

Availability: Released on DVD in 2002 as WHV E1340 (Region 1), and on VHS in 1995 as BBCV 5613 (UK), WHV E1340 (US).

Verdict: 'This whole plan depends upon how well you can act!' A decent conclusion to the pseudo-saga of the quest for the Key to Time, 'The Armageddon Factor' is a typical example of actors and script trying to boost *Doctor Who* beyond its budgetary constraints: witness John Woodvine commanding the army of an entire planet from a small set whilst dressed in a cheap *Sgt Pepper* uniform. Anthony Read deserves much praise for his rewrites on the script: Mentalis (created by Read as a cost-cutting measure) is much more striking than the original concept of Zeos as a planet exactly like Atrios, and there's some very good dialogue on display.

Towards the end the story starts to collapse like undried papier-mâché, with Drax being a particular weak link (Jackson's cockney is awful and he lacks the presence to be a convincing Time Lord). The final scene is a muddle, failing to explain whether there ever was a White Guardian (a question finally resolved in **127**, 'Enlightenment'), or if it was necessary to collect and assemble the Key to Time at all, which makes the whole season feel vaguely pointless. Even so, 'The Armageddon Factor' is perfectly acceptable middle-ground *Doctor Who*.

104
Destiny of the Daleks

Episode One: 1 September 1979
Episode Two: 8 September 1979
Episode Three: 15 September 1979
Episode Four: 22 September 1979

Written by Terry Nation
Directed by Ken Grieve

Notable Cast: Tony Osoba (Lan) was McLaren in *Porridge* (1973–78). Suzanne Danielle (Agella) was the bed-hopping lead of *Carry On Emmannuelle* (Gerald Thomas, 1978), possibly the worst film ever made. One of the female Movellans is credited as 'Cassandra'. She may be the 'Cassandra' who starred in *The Erotic Adventures of Robinson Crusoe* (Ken Dixon, 1975). Or perhaps not.

Writer: These were Terry Nation's last *Doctor Who* scripts, over fifteen years after his first. He became a writer/producer on *MacGuyver* (1985). He died in 1997.

Director: Ken Grieve had directed episodes of *The XYY Man* (1976–77). He later contributed to *The Adventures of Sherlock Holmes* (1985) and *Agatha Christie's Poirot* (1993).

Other Worlds: Skaro (D5 Gamma Z Alpha to the Movellans). There's more vegetation than seen in **78**, 'Genesis of the Daleks' and less than in **2**, 'The Daleks'. (The Dalek city is re-created with the aid of ambient noise from the latter story.) While the planet is in ruins, the rubble is bricks and mortar rather than stylised plastic and glass.

The Plan: The Daleks are trying to unearth Davros (played here by David Gooderson; see **78**, 'Genesis of the Daleks') so that he can help them to win their centuries-long war against the Movellans (see **Scary Monsters**).

Scary Monsters: Ken Grieve chooses to shoot the Daleks from floor height, making the creatures loom impressively. They also move well and their voices sound great. Unfortunately the casings are severely battered; each Dalek is a differing shade of grey and has subtly different fittings. In fact, the whole gang of them look like they've been stolen from a junk shop or assembled for a garden fete. They believe that self-sacrifice is illogical, therefore impossible (but then are willing suicide bombers in Episode Four) and are referred to as 'robots' on numerous occasions (including by Davros). They were 'once organic creatures themselves', implying that there is no longer any organic component in a Dalek. Dalek central control is in space, rather than on Skaro which is abandoned. The spandex-clad, silver-dreadlocked Movellan robots look rather fetching and may conceivably be the design most representative of 1979. Removing the power packs from their belts will disable them. They can then be reprogrammed to obey anyone. This calls into question their effectiveness as a fighting force (that said, it's not as if the Daleks are in a position to exploit this weakness).

Doctor Who?: The Doctor implies he saw the universe begin. He either has a detailed knowledge of the history of the Galactic Olympic Games or pretends to because he thinks it's funny. He is entirely prepared to murder Davros with explosives, reasoning it's the lesser of two evils.

Science/Magic: Romana regenerates, seemingly because she wants to. She copies the appearance of Princess Astra (see **103**, 'The Armageddon Factor') because it 'looked very nice on the Princess'. She initially copies Astra's clothes as well. On the Doctor's insistence, she also tries out three other bodies (one tall, one Rubens-esque, the other small and blue). How this squares with the limit of thirteen incarnations for a Time Lord (see **88**, 'The Deadly Assassin') is anyone's guess. Not that it matters – it's an entirely fatuous scene, played for (strictly limited) laughs, but it gets around (the pregnant) Mary Tamm's decision to leave with a minimum of fuss. She initially wears a copy of the Doctor's clothes, then changes into a near-identical outfit in pink and white. While Romana doesn't suffer from any post-regenerative trauma she later affects to be able to tell the recipe for concrete by tasting it.

The planet Magma is an 8,000-mile-wide amoeba that's grown a crusty shell. The Movellans' 'nova device' can destroy a whole planet by changing the molecular structure of an atmosphere to make it flammable. The atmosphere of the planet burns up in seconds. When replacing a computer's brain it's important to always make sure the arrow A is pointing to the front.

Availability: Issued on VHS in 1994 as BBCV 5350 (UK), WHV E1376 (US).

Verdict: 'I believe this is what they call a Mexican stand-off.' Each episode of 'Destiny of the Daleks' functions as 25 minutes of undemanding, languidly paced entertainment and, of the four, Episode Two is easily the best. The plot, though, is a thin run-through of a simple concept, topped up with Nation's personal clichés and disseminated very slowly. There are many 'jokes', but a grand total of none of them are actually funny and the overall tone isn't so much jolly as indifferently trivial and strangely joyless. Although it's moodily and atmospherically directed throughout (that said, Grieve shows zero aptitude for fight scenes) and generally well made, it's still difficult to see how anybody could summon up the will to love or hate 'Destiny of the Daleks'. David Gooderson somehow manages to pronounce 'weaponry' as a four syllable word.

105
City of Death

Part One: 29 September 1979
Part Two: 5 October 1979
Part Three: 12 October 1979
Part Four: 19 October 1979

Written by David Agnew
Directed by Michael Hayes

Notable Cast: Julian Glover (Scaroth) previously appeared in **14**, 'The Crusade'. Tom Chadbon (Duggan) worked on *The Stone Tape* (1972) and has been a regular in *Where the Heart Is* since 2001. Catherine Schell (Countess Scarlioni) appeared in *On Her Majesty's Secret Service* (Peter Hunt, 1969) and was a regular in *The Adventurer* (1972–73) and the 1976–77 season of *Space:1999*. John Cleese (Art Gallery Visitor) was at a loose end in Television Centre (work on *Fawlty Towers* had been halted by a strike: note that he wears the same clothes here as in 'Basil the Rat') and Douglas Adams suggested a cameo, scripting on the spot the wonderful appraisal of the TARDIS as art.

Writer: This time, 'David Agnew' (see **97**, 'The Invasion of Time') is a pseudonym for David Fisher (who submitted the original script, an idea about an alien rigging casinos in Monte Carlo), Graham Williams (who advised extensively on its re-plotting) and Douglas Adams (who wrote the finished version).

Scary Monsters: The Jagaroth, a warlike race of green, monocular creatures.

Villains: Scaroth, last of the Jagaroth, whose ship exploded when taking off from primeval Earth. He was splintered across various periods of Earth's history into twelve identical aspects, who can communicate with – but not reach – each other and have taken on human disguises (for no apparent reason, the disguises are also identical).

The Plan: Scaroth's ultimate goal is to travel back and prevent the catastrophe that splintered him. His present-day incarnation, known as Count Scarlioni, has become an art thief and forger in order to raise money which he spends on time experiments. His activities are being investigated by a detective named Duggan (who could have been retained as a regular in a Jamie-type capacity: Part Three's Romana/Duggan scenes give a glimpse of what *Doctor Who* would be like with a female Doctor and a dumb male assistant).

History 101: Scaroth's splinters have advanced the scientific development of mankind whilst planting treasures for his contemporary self to find and sell – including six extra *Mona Lisa*s, all painted by Da Vinci under duress from a Scaroth in Florence, 1505. The Doctor must prevent Scaroth from averting the explosion of his ship because the radiation generated by this event was responsible for kick-starting life on Earth.

Doctor Who?: The Doctor's trick of acting like an imbecile in order to encourage villains to underestimate him is similar to what the Troughton Doctor used to do: 'Nobody could be as stupid as he seems,' notes Scaroth.

Science/Magic: The time equipment developed by Kerensky (David Graham) makes no sense: the chicken may be isolated on its own in an accelerated time bubble, but that doesn't mean that it can grow to full size without being given food.

Things Fall Apart: Why is the French TV news report of the *Mona Lisa* heist in English? Why does the *gendarme* tell the Doctor what's going on when asked? Scaroth's hands in the opening scene are very obviously gloves (you can see the actor's real skin beneath them). There's no design match-up between the Jagaroth spaceship set and model work (from some angles you can see the ground through the set where you should, according to the model, be able to see the vast black globe of the ship). The final cut from Scaroth's time machine exploding to the final film sequence is very abrupt. Tom Baker punching Peter Halliday is lamentably unconvincingly done. The production is let down at the end by a flat, unimpressive recreation of primeval Earth.

Availability: Released on VHS in 2001 as BBCV 7132 (UK), WHV E1259 (US).

Verdict: 'What do you mean, time's running out? It's only 1505!' The writer's credit on 'City of Death' may not say 'By Douglas Adams', but absolutely everything else about it does – the detached view of history, the preoccupation with evolution, the collegiate humour ... Other hands in the script are barely detectable. However, Graham Williams made a great contribution by stopping Adams's imagination from running away and restricting him to what could be done within the budget. It's noticeable that this production is much more successfully realised than anything else in the season (Da Vinci's study is a beautiful set which, for a change, has been lit with restraint).

You'd never guess that the top-down rewrite was done in three days (especially given that Adams would later become legendary for not finishing his novels): it's tightly constructed, has lots of good lines and is never dull. Even the sequences of the Doctor, Romana and Duggan trotting around Paris (principally included because the production team has gone to the effort of going there and they're bloody well going to show off the scenery) don't pall because they're so elegantly executed. Tom, Lalla, Chadbon and Glover are all exemplary. It's not as funny as **25**, 'The Gunfighters', though.

106
The Creature from the Pit

Part One: 27 October 1979
Part Two: 3 November 1979
Part Three: 10 November 1979
Part Four: 17 November 1979

Written by David Fisher
Directed by Christopher Barry

Notable Cast: Geoffrey Bayldon (Organon) is best known for the title role in *Catweazle* (1970), and played the Crowman in *Worzel Gummidge* (1979–81). David Brierley now provides the voice of K9: he narrated *Adventures of a Taxi Driver* (Stanley Long, 1975) and appeared in *Threads* (1984). Eileen Way (Karela) was 'Old Mother' in **1**, 'An Unearthly Child'.

Doctor Who?: The Doctor is reading Beatrix Potter's *Peter Rabbit* with K9. He has a ball of string given to him by Theseus for helping with the Minotaur (see **108**, 'The Horns of Nimon'). He's had the TARDIS transceiver – which 'receives and sends distress signals' – unplugged to stop him getting calls from Gallifrey. He has a copy of *Everest in Easy Stages* in his pocket but, unfortunately, it's in Tibetan (which wouldn't have been a problem circa **74**, 'Planet of the Spiders'). Luckily, he also carries a copy of *Teach Yourself Tibetan*. His pockets also contain mountaineering equipment. The Doctor was born under the 'sign of crossed computers', which is a symbol of the Gallifreyan maternity service. 74,384,338 is the Doctor's lucky number. Where the plot demands, the Doctor can pilot the TARDIS with immense precision.

Other Worlds: A distress call transmitted by a giant eggshell pulls the TARDIS to the planet Chloris, where the creature from within the shell lives at the bottom of a pit. Bandits live in the forest, heading out to steal quantities of precious metal, which is needed to fight back the endless vegetation.

Villains: The Lady Adrasta (Myra Frances), local despot, who owns the only mine for metal, and therefore has a monopoly on all metal on the planet.

Scary Monsters: Wolfweeds, carnivorous plants that act as guard dogs and wrap their prey in webbing. The creature in the pit is Erato, a hundred-foot-tall green blob that's almost entirely made up of brain matter: he is afraid of fire, and feeds on 'chlorophyll and mineral salts'. Erato is an ambassador from Typhonus, imprisoned by Adrasta and deprived of the disc that allows him to communicate through the voices of others.

The Plan: Like Fisher's earlier **100**, 'The Stones of Blood', there's not a plan so much as a villainess trying to protect a long-held secret. Erato came to Chloris on a trading mission fifteen years before, hoping to trade Typhonian metal in exchange for Chloris' chlorophyll. The deal would have taken away Adrasta's monopoly, so she kept Erato prisoner instead. She wants K9 to kill Erato and protect her secret. Meanwhile, the bandits want to steal Erato's photon drive to stop him leaving, so they can maintain the value of the metal they've stolen from Adrasta. The Typhonians have already responded to the disappearance of Erato by setting a neutron star on course to collide with Chloris's sun.

Science/Magic: Organon is 'an astrologer extraordinary' – his prophecies were not accurate, leading to him being cast into the pit. Erato can produce a self-renewing substance that acts as a protective shell. The finale is a flood of technobabble: Erato creates a shell of aluminium, which the Doctor uses to send a neutron star off course with the help of the TARDIS's gravity tractor beam.

Things Fall Apart: Erato is a huge wet bin bag with a very rude-looking protuberance. Romana's costume appears to be made from crudely tailored lengths of net curtain. Torvin and his murderous, rapacious bandits are portrayed as the stereotypical 'covetous Jews' (see also **41**, 'The Web of Fear') of bad Renaissance comedy, and are obsessed with greedily attaining precious metals.

Availability: Issued on VHS in 2002 as BBCV 7266 (UK), WHV E1860 (US).

Verdict: 'Our researchers divide into two categories. The ones who have got close enough to find out something about it – and the ones who are still alive.' A witless string of clichés, 'The Creature from the Pit' uses weak jokes to try and cover up the hackneyed, underdeveloped plot, overcooked performances and poor production – which is par for the course for 1979's *Doctor Who*. The odd impressive film sequence or costume can't redeem a story that is too jokey and melodramatic to be compelling, and too witless to actually be funny. The dialogue is repetitive and none of the characters are truly sympathetic (including some particularly offensive stereotypes). What passes for the plot grinds to a halt midway through Part Four with the death of Adrasta, and a different scenario unfolds with Erato as if from nowhere, one which ends in a climax so abstract as to be meaningless in dramatic terms.

107
Nightmare of Eden

Part One: 24 November 1979
Part Two: 1 December 1979
Part Three: 8 December 1979
Part Four: 15 December 1979

Written by Bob Baker
Directed by Alan Bromly

Notable Cast: Peter Craze (Costa) previously appeared in **7**, 'The Sensorites'. Geoffrey Hinsliff (Fisk) appeared in **94**, 'Image of the Fendhal' and David Daker (Rigg) in **70**, 'The Time Warrior'.

Villains: Tryst (Lewis Fiander), a scientist who wants to 'Qualify and quantify every species in the galaxy' and who isn't above a little drug trafficking in order to fund his theoretically laudable scheme. Fiander's performance is enjoyable, hilarious in fact – somewhere between Dr Strangelove and the French Waffen SS officer from *Le Chagrin et la pitié* (Marcel Ophüls, 1969) – but doesn't even hint at the scripted ambiguities within the character.

Science/Magic: XYP or Vraxoin is an addictive drug which induces 'warm complacency and total apathy' in the user: withdrawal leads to death. The story is set c. 2116 when Interstellar cruisers use 'warp' to travel between stars. They become intangible when they do so. The Empress has nine hundred passengers of which seemingly only two – Tryst and Della (Jennifer Lonsdale) – are First Class travellers. The CET (Continuous Event Transmuter) is not unlike the Miniscope from **66**, 'Carnival of Monsters' in that it contains sections from a number of worlds preserved inside it. (Its aim is conservational rather than recreational, though.) It works through 'a crude form of matter transfer by dimensional control' and contains a 'spatial integrator', a 'transmutation oscillator', a 'holistic retention circuit' and a 'dimensional osmosis damper'. An intuca laser can be used to carry thousands of telecom messages.

Doctor Who?: When it's suggested that the Doctor shouldn't interfere he responds, 'Of course we should interfere! Always do what you're best at!' and later insists that his adventures are really him 'just having fun'. He later announces that he likes doing the impossible and is described, rather wonderfully, as the 'enigmatic almighty Mr Fixit!' by Captain Rigg. The Doctor claims to have known Professor Stein, Tryst's mentor. Tom Baker's performance is terrifically inventive throughout, switching from some inspired clowning to moral fury with ease.

Other Worlds: The worlds in the CET machine include Bros, Darp, Eden, Gidi, Lvan, Ranx, Vij and Zil.

Scary Monsters: The Mandrels – creatures from the planet Eden who break out of the CET and start killing people at random. After death they decompose into piles of the drug Vraxoin. The costumes are comically rubbish.

Things Fall Apart: At one point a step visibly collapses beneath Tom Baker's foot. At others, the Mandrel costumes are clearly not zipped up at the back. There are many, many dialogue fluffs, moments when the actors verbally stumble and occasions where characters get each other's names wrong. The small number of cheap, frail, yellow sets gets beyond a joke about halfway through Part Two. The visual laser gun effects are inconsistently applied. You can see the stick holding the model Empress up in the very first shot.

Availability: Issued on VHS in 1999 as BBCV 6610 (UK), WHV E1041 (US).

Verdict: 'Maybe that's the entertainment?' Unlike much of 1979's *Doctor Who* 'Nightmare of Eden' doesn't fail because it thinks it's funny and it isn't. Instead, it just about succeeds despite noticeable failures from every production department. This is thanks to the best script of the season – it's fast-paced, demonstrates many good ideas, contains considerable wit and yet has earnest, worthwhile intentions. That said, only a very indulging, or very young, audience will be able to look past the disgraceful production debacle and enjoy the serial's many positive elements.

108
The Horns of Nimon

Part One: 22 December 1979
Part Two: 29 December 1979
Part Three: 5 January 1980
Part Four: 12 January 1980

Written by Anthony Read
Directed by Kenny McBain

Notable Cast: Graham Crowden (Soldeed) was offered the role of Doctor Who in 1974, but turned it down: he later appeared in *A Very Peculiar Practice* (1986–88) and *Waiting For God* (1990–94). His many, many other film and TV credits include The Player

King in the first production of Tom Stoppard's *Rosencrantz and Guildenstern are Dead*. Janet Ellis (Teka) presented *Blue Peter* between 1983 and 1987. Malcolm Terris (Co-pilot) had regular roles in *Warship* (1974) and *When the Boat Comes In* (1976); later, he was a regular in *Coronation Street* (1994–98) and *Family Affairs* (1998–99). Simon Gipps-Kent (Seth) starred in *To Serve Them All My Days* (1980–81).

Director: Kenny McBain later became a producer with stints on *Grange Hill* (1983–84), *Boon* (1986) and *Inspector Morse* (1987–88).

Scary Monsters: The Nimons, bull-like creatures who feed upon the energy in living beings.

Other Worlds: The people of Skonnos once had a great empire, but it collapsed amidst a series of civil wars. They have been visited by a Nimon, falsely claiming to be the last of his race, who has promised to give them the resources to rebuild this empire in exchange for a series of tributes: people for it to feed upon, and hymetusite. The Doctor lands near a Skonnan ship carrying the final batch of tributes.

Villains: Soldeed rules Skonnos and arranges the tributes for the Nimon. Graham Crowden's attention-seeking scenery chewing is briefly amusing, but becomes tiresome.

Science/Magic: Hymetusite is a type of radioactive crystal: 'Oh, how commonplace,' announces the Doctor upon discovering that the ship is carrying it. The Nimons use hymetusite to power their hyperspace gate near Skonnos. Later Sezom (John Bailey), the ruler of Crinoth (a planet which the Nimons have sucked dry), tells Romana that a mineral called jasonite carries a powerful electromagnetic charge and can be used against the Nimons. Which is useful.

The Plan: The hyperspace gate links Crinoth with Skonnos. The rest of the Nimons plan to travel to Skonnos and devour that world.

Doctor Who?: He expresses enthusiasm for cricket: 'Sometimes I think I'm wasted just rushing around the universe saving planets from destruction. With a talent like mine, I might have been a great slow bowler.' He's clearly jealous of the sonic screwdriver Romana has made for herself, attempting to pocket it.

Things Fall Apart: Numerous horrible costumes, especially on Skonnos. Awful model shots as the TARDIS is surrounded by quivering asteroids and is struck by the planet (and those spinning camera shots are always inadvisable). The Nimons themselves are poorly acted and look ridiculous (appropriately, they appear to be wearing Buffalo platform shoes). The supposedly 'shifting' corridors of the Nimon maze are poorly communicated by Kenny McBain's direction, whilst the re-dressing of the Skonnos sets to create Crinoth makes the serial visually dull. The opening scene with the two pilots contains some of the most horrific info-dumping in *Doctor Who*.

Availability: Released on VHS in 2003 as BBCV 7334 (UK), WHV E1861 (US).

Verdict: 'Look, why don't you give me the gun and then I can keep an eye on myself and make sure I don't get up to any funny business?' At first glance it appears that 'The Horns of Nimon' is throwing in jokes at every turn in an attempt to compensate for risible production values (the 'solution' the previous two serials hit upon when some of their budget was also re-allocated to a six-part story which was hit by a strike and never completed: see **164**, 'Shada'). In fact it's trying to distract the viewer from the plot, an uninteresting reworking of the legend of Theseus and the Mino-taur in the vein of **96**, 'Underworld'. It's hampered by a limp performance from Simon Gipps-Kent in the key pseudo-Theseus role and a generic 'something blows up' ending.

The serial doesn't work as drama, and judged against any good piece of comedy it also manifestly falls short. Baker makes some of the jokes work (the Doctor's 'unobtrusive' landing, the rosette he sticks on K9) but in other places it slips into laboured *Carry On*-style 'madcap' humour (the Doctor giving K9 mouth-to-mouth, the noises made by the TARDIS console, the Nimon being distracted by a red flag). It isn't bad *Doctor Who* because it tries to be funny, it's bad television because the attempt fails. Even considered as pure kitsch it tries one's patience and betrays a show in dire need of a fresh approach, so it's just as well that this happened.

109
The Leisure Hive

Part One: 30 August 1980
Part Two: 6 September 1980
Part Three: 13 September 1980
Part Four: 20 September 1980

Written by David Fisher
Directed by Lovett Bickford

Notable Cast: David Haig (Pangol) has supporting roles in *Four Weddings and a Funeral* (Mike Nicholls, 1994) and *Two Weeks' Notice* (Marc Lawrence, 2002). He was a regular in *The Thin Blue Line* (1995–96). Adrienne Corri (Mena) appeared in *A Clockwork Orange* (Stanley Kubrick, 1971) and the BBC's 1979 *Measure for Measure*. Laurence Payne (Morix) previously appeared in **25**, 'The Gunfighters'. John Leeson returns as the voice of K9.

Producer: This is the first serial produced by John Nathan-Turner, who had worked on *Doctor Who* in increasingly important capacities since **49**, 'The Space Pirates' as well as being a production unit manager on series like *All Creatures Great and Small* (1978–80). He was in charge of every television story between this and **158**, 'Dimensions in Time' – becoming *Doctor Who*'s longest serving producer. He died in 2003.

Director: Lovett Bickford had been an assistant on *All Creatures Great and Small* and *The Pallisers* (1974) both alongside John Nathan-Turner. He directed the BBC's 1980 adaptation of HG Wells's *The History of Mr Polly*.

Script Editor: Christopher H Bidmead trained as an actor at RADA and was a regular in *Emergency – Ward 10* in the 1960s. After turning his hand to scriptwriting in the early 1970s with work on *Harriet's Back in Town* and *Rooms* he became a science and technology journalist, a career to which he returned after his one-year stint as *Doctor Who*'s script editor (ending with his own **115**, 'Logopolis').

Doctor Who?: It's an unusually subdued performance from Tom Baker, who is smothered under heavy make-up for much of the story after the Doctor is aged five hundred years by the recreation generator.

Other Worlds: Argolis – where in 2250 a twenty-minute nuclear war rendered the surface deadly to all mammalian life. Those few Argolin who survived the war built the titular 'Leisure Hive', a centre devoted to teaching about, and researching into, 'physical, psychic and intellectual regeneration'.

Scary Monsters: The Foamasi – a pseudo-communist society of chubby lizards who have problems with a mafia-type organisation within their society. The Foamasi we see seem cultured and urbane.

Science/Magic: The story is based upon the theoretical notion of the tachyon, a particle that travels faster than light. There's much talk of 'tachyonics', 'unreal transfer' and the tachyon's ability to 'arrive at point B before its departure from point A'. Also a 'matching tachyonic field creates a temporary reduplication of any physical object' while reversing time can lead to 'perpetual cellular rejuvenation' as well a 'temporal instability'. While much of this science is theoretically accurate, some is mere bafflegab and most viewers aren't going to know this; so it might as well all be the gibberish it often sounds like.

Things Fall Apart: The Doctor and Romana comment on a recording which finishes playing before they enter the room. Not only that but all the other characters act as if the Doctor and Romana saw it too. The Foamasi costumes aren't terribly good when seen in full, fortunately they rarely are. The creatures also somehow disguise themselves as humans who are smaller than they are by putting suits on.

Availability: Released on DVD in 2004 as BBCDVD 1351 (Region 2); an earlier VHS is BBCV 5821 (UK), WHV E1135 (US).

Verdict: 'One must always accept the unexpected.' Separated from **108**, 'The Horns of Nimon' by a mere seven months, 'The Leisure Hive' is radically different to it. The straightforward production and forced levity of 1979's stories is replaced with muttered discussions about nuclear war and theoretical physics and an uber-stylised approach to production that incorporates a vibrant electro-pop score. Whether this is a change for the better is a matter of opinion, but it's worth noting that while 'The Leisure Hive' takes itself more seriously than 'Nimon' does it's also much funnier, smarter and infinitely less smug.

110
Meglos

Part One: 27 September 1980
Part Two: 4 October 1980
Part Three: 11 October 1980
Part Four: 18 October 1980

Written by John Flanagan and Andrew McCulloch
Directed by Terence Dudley

Notable Cast: One of the original *Doctor Who* regulars, Jacqueline Hill (Lexa) played Barbara Wright from **1**, 'An Unearthly Child' to **16**, 'The Chase'. Bill Fraser (General Grugger) was Sergeant Major Snudge in *The Army Game* (1958–60) and got his own spin-off series, *Bootsie and Snudge*.

Writers: Actor Andrew McCulloch has several TV scripting credits to his name, including episodes of *Robin of Sherwood* and *Heartbeat*, all of which he has written in partnership with John Flanagan. They wrote *Sleepers* (1993) starring Nigel Havers, Warren Clarke and Joanna Kanska, still the BBC drama to achieve the highest audience appreciation figures in the corporation's history.

Director: An old-school BBC producer/director for whom 'Meglos' was his last BBC directorial work before mandatory retirement, Terence Dudley had been offered the opportunity to write for *Doctor Who* in 1963. He directed episodes of *Secret Army* and *All Creatures Great and Small* and was the producer (and a frequent writer/director) of *Doomwatch* (1970–73), *Survivors* (1974–77) and *The Mask of Janus* (1965). After his scheduled retirement he finally wrote for *Doctor Who* with **117**, 'Four to Doomsday' and wrote the first and only episode of a failed *Doctor Who* spin-off, *K9 and Company* (24 December 1981) in which John Leeson and Elisabeth Sladen reprised their *Who* roles.

Other Worlds: The planet Zolfa-Thura, a desert world almost bereft of life, and Tigella, home to a humanoid civilisation that is having an energy crisis.

Doctor Who?: The Doctor is summoned to Tigella by the planet's leader, Zastor (Edward Underdown), who met the Doctor on a previous visit fifty years ago and describes him poetically: 'He sees the threads that join the universe together and mends them when they break.'

Villains: Meglos is the last thing left alive on Zolfa-Thura. He is a cactus, but he forms an alliance with some space raiders and they bring him a human (Christopher Owen) from contemporary Earth.

The Plan: By merging with the human, Meglos becomes humanoid and impersonates the Doctor. He then goes to Tigella, intending to steal the Dodecahedron.

Science/Magic: The Dodecahedron is the source of all power on Tigella. Nobody knows where it came from, which seems like lazy scripting but Flanagan and McCulloch at least acknowledge that this is a subject of theological debate on Tigella. In order to delay the Doctor's arrival, Meglos traps the TARDIS in a chronic hysteresis or 'fold of time', dooming the Doctor and Romana to repeat the same few seconds over and over again. The Doctor's solution to this problem (to consciously start performing their actions before the loop reaches the beginning again) makes no sense, but it does give Tom and Lalla an opportunity to wink at the camera ('For one awful moment I thought you'd forgotten your lines' says the Doctor).

Things Fall Apart: The Tigellan haircuts look like something from *UFO*. The plant that attacks Romana on Tigella is very foam-rubber-looking. The Earthling struggling to free himself from Meglos doesn't work either. Lexa's death lacks impact and adds nothing to the story.

Availability: Released on VHS in 2003 as BBCV 7332 (UK), WHV E1862 (US).

Verdict: 'You will observe I am a plant!' A seemingly random mix of the impressive and the risible, 'Meglos' is hampered by the fact that it is, fundamentally, a story about Doctor Who being impersonated by a cactus. It's nowhere near as bold or slick as **109**, 'The Leisure Hive' and suffers from too many generic ideas: the cultists on Tigella resemble those seen in any number of 1970s *Doctor Who* stories and the Dodecahedron is a non-specific 'source of power'.

However, 'Meglos' does benefit from the same rapid pace as 'The Leisure Hive'; it's lovely to see Jacqueline Hill again; Tom Baker makes the most of an opportunity to play the villain; and Lalla Ward wears an outfit that resembles something from Vivienne Westwood's 'Pirate' collections. There's also some remarkable effects work in the realisation of Zolfa-Thura: the later scenes aren't quite as successful due to obvious lighting contrasts but the material in Part One is great, especially compared with similar effects in **96**, 'Underworld'. It's the weakest story of Baker's final year but this just demonstrates the strength of that last run as a whole.

111
Full Circle

Part One: 25 October 1980
Part Two: 1 November 1980
Part Three: 8 November 1980
Part Four: 15 November 1980

Written by Andrew Smith
Directed by Peter Grimwade

Notable Cast: Matthew Waterhouse joins the regular cast as precocious maths genius Adric. George Baker (Login) played the Emperor Tiberius, possibly the most demanding role, in *I, Claudius* (1976) and Inspector Reg Wexford in *The Ruth Rendell Mysteries* (1987–2000) and appeared in the James Bond movies *On Her Majesty's Secret Service* (Peter Hunt, 1969) and *The Spy Who Loved Me* (Lewis Gilbert, 1977). The brilliant Alan Rowe (Decider Garif) previously appeared in **33**, 'The Moonbase', **70**, 'The Time Warrior' and **92**, 'Horror of Fang Rock'.

Writer: Andrew Smith was a *Doctor Who* fan – 'Full Circle' is his only television writing assignment.

Director: Writer/director Peter Grimwade wrote for *Dramarama* and *Z Cars*, and directed episodes of *Dramarama*, *The Onedin Line* and *All Creatures Great and Small*.

Other Worlds: The TARDIS goes off course, due to the disruption of a Charged Vacuum Emboitement (CVE), and lands on the planet Alzarius. The TARDIS scanner shows 'the wilderness of outer Gallifrey', but in fact Alzarius is a wooded, swampy planet. The TARDIS is at the right co-ordinates, but outside realspace in the 'exo-space time continuum' or 'E-space'. A group of humans from Terradon have lived for forty generations around the *Starliner*, a grounded spaceship run by the Deciders, who rule based on the ship's 'procedures'. The First Decider is the only person who has access to the System Files, which contain the secrets of their society. Meanwhile rebellious young 'outlers' have left the *Starliner* to live in the wilderness stealing fruit picked by the settlers. Mists are coming from the swamps, a phenomenon called 'mistfall', and the humans intend to lock themselves in the *Starliner* until the mist retreats. The Deciders tell the citizens that the mists are fatal.

Scary Monsters: Marshmen, tall reptilian swamp people with scaly skin and tendrils on their faces. Born from the marsh during mistfall, they quickly develop intelligent behaviour. They have a destructive urge, attacking the Terradonians and the *Starliner*, but can be repelled with oxygen.

Marsh spiders bite humans, injecting a chemical into their prey before dying.

Villains: Generations of Deciders on the *Starliner*, who have maintained a conspiracy to deceive the citizens.

Doctor Who?: The Doctor is trying to respond to the Time Lords' call to return to Gallifrey. Even though Romana doesn't want to go, the Doctor points out that when he last resisted the Time Lords, he lost (presumably a reference to 50, 'The War Games'). He's looking forward to seeing Leela and Andred, and introducing the two K9s. The Doctor considers himself to be good with children. The Doctor is furious with the Deciders for their decision to experiment on the Marshmen, dismissing their defence of the experiments as being for the benefit of the communities.

The Plan: The Deciders have been deceiving the community, getting the citizens to engage in endless repetitive procedures for an 'embarkation' that never happens, while the *Starliner* has been ready to fly for centuries, covering up for the fact that no one knows how to pilot the ship. This is because the 'Terradonians' on the *Starliner* are not from Terradon at all – they're descendants of the Marshmen, who in turn are descendants of the Marsh spiders. The *Starliner* has been there for forty thousand generations.

Science/Magic: The TARDIS has homing devices, which can be used to find the way back to the ship. The Doctor says that short trips in the TARDIS don't usually work. The marsh spiders, Marshmen and 'Terradonians' all have the same cell structure. The

TARDIS scanner needs a new image translator to visualise the 'negative co-ordinates' in E-space.

Things Fall Apart: Adric and the 'outlers' are all terribly acted, fey youngsters. Paddy Kingsland's soundtrack has some fantastically moody themes, but also contains some horrendous bursts of electronic jazz-funk for action scenes.

Availability: Issued on VHS in 1997 as BBCV 6232 (UK; as part of the *E-Space Trilogy* box), WHV E6229 (US).

Verdict: 'When mistfall comes the giants leave the swamp.' Ironically, considering its swamp-bound setting, 'Full Circle' is slightly too dry for its own good. The script is intelligent, and the production well-executed, but the pace is a little slow, the high concept of the story stretching a bit thin across four episodes. The acting is distinctly mixed, but Peter Grimwade's direction is spot on and there are some very memorable scenes. While aspects of the story may be patchy this is one of the best uses of the Doctor's character in a long time, as he rages against cruelty to a marsh child and is relentless in seeking to uncover the truth.

112
State of Decay

Part One: 22 November 1980
Part Two: 29 November 1980
Part Three: 6 December 1980
Part Four: 13 December 1980

Written by Terrance Dicks
Directed by Peter Moffatt

Notable Cast: Emrys James (Aukon) played Vera Brittain's father in *Testament of Youth* (1979) but was principally a great man of the stage.

Director: Peter Moffatt, who started directing while in a POW camp during World War Two, directed several episodes of *All Creatures Great and Small* including the 1985 Christmas episode 'The Lord God Made Them All'. The studio scenes are blocked as if for the theatrical stage, and good use is made of the limited amount of location filming to create a convincing environment.

Doctor Who?: The Doctor talks of K'anpo (see **74**, 'Planet of the Spiders') and how he used to tell him ghost stories. There's a beautiful scene where, locked in a cell, the Doctor and Romana chat quietly and – after she provides the solution to the problem facing them – he beams at her and whispers, 'You are wonderful,' to which she contentedly replies, 'I suppose I am. I never really thought about it.'

Villains: Zargo (William Lindsay), Camilla (Rachel Davies) and Aukon – three once-human vampires who rule a small village of peasants from a vast castle. They are waiting for their master to wake from his centuries-long recuperation.

History 101: Earth exploration ship Hydrax passed through a CVE (see **111**, 'Full Circle') '20 generations' or 'a thousand years' ago – summoned there by the Great One (or King Vampire), the only survivor of a genocidal war launched against the species by the Time Lords under Rassilon (see **88**, 'The Deadly Assassin').

Science/Magic: The TARDIS has a magnetic card system for storing information. The difficulty of killing vampires is rationalised by saying their 'cardiovascular system is enormously efficient', giving them the ability to heal wounds quickly. The Hydrax comes complete with three 'arrow class scoutships'. The whole story goes out of its way to present science as a route to personal freedom.

Things Fall Apart: The two visualisations of the Great Vampire – both on a screen and of his hand coming out of his crypt – are less than satisfactory, but that's the only real production failing. Tarik (Thane Bettany) looks and sounds like a *Big Night Out*-era Bob Mortimer character, though no one at the time could have known that.

Availability: Issued on VHS in 1997 as BBCV 6232 (UK; as part of the *E-Space Trilogy* box), WHV E6229 (US).

Verdict: 'At midnight our servitude will end and our glory begin.' There's an argument that *Doctor Who* works best when it's juxtaposing inappropriate things (call it the 'police box in a junkyard' factor) and 'State of Decay' has this element in spades thanks to Terrance Dicks and Christopher Bidmead's very different approaches to *Doctor Who*. Working together they produce something arresting and interesting out of the contrast between Dicks wanting to make a straightforward, mythic tale of vampires and rebellious peasantry and Bidmead wanting to eulogise scientific method. The disparate elements of the serial include period adventure fiction, Gallifreyan history, social theorising (Romana diagnoses aristocracy as a 'socio-pathetic abscess'), the evolution of language and much Hammer horror pastiche, and the plot is simple but absorbing. It would be entirely fair, however, to say the serial spectacularly fails as a portrayal of a convincing society and as a demonstration of the politics of oppression (Ivo would surely be lynched by the rebels, not be considered a hero). Nonetheless, it succeeds in combining enormous atmosphere and the odd shock with loads of good jokes, and is hugely enjoyable as a result. Emrys Jones gives a mesmerising performance as the vampire Aukon and the music is fantastic.

113
Warriors' Gate

Part One: 3 January 1981
Part Two: 10 January 1981
Part Three: 17 January 1981
Part Four: 24 January 1981

Written by Stephen Gallagher
Directed by Paul Joyce

Notable Cast: Prolific character actor Kenneth Cope (Packard) played Marty Hopkirk throughout the original *Randall and Hopkirk (Deceased)* (1969–70) and had stints as a regular in *Coronation Street* (1961–66) and *Brookside* (1999–2002). Clifford Rose (Rorvik) played Dr Snell in *Callan* (1970–72), and SS man Ludwig Kessler in *Secret Army* (1977–79) and its spin-off *Kessler* (1980). This is Lalla Ward and John Leeson's last story as regulars.

Writer: Stephen Gallagher is an acclaimed British horror/thriller novelist whose books include *Chimera* (1982), *Oktober* (1987), *Rain* (1990) and *White Bizango* (2002). 'Warriors' Gate' was his first TV work: he later wrote for *Bugs* (1995–97), *Chillers* (1995) and *Murder Rooms* (2001), and created *Eleventh Hour* (2005). His website is www.stephengallagher.com.

Director: Paul Joyce's other work includes the Tom Stoppard-scripted film *The Engagement* (1970), although most of his career was spent in the theatre. His time-consuming efforts to shoot

'Warriors' Gate' in a more cinematic way, using a single mobile camera as opposed to covering scenes with two or three more static cameras, caused much tension on set but the results are hugely impressive.

Scary Monsters: The Tharils, leonine creatures who were once masters of E-Space. Possessing the rare ability to navigate through hyperspace, they were able to move between E-Space and N-Space with ease, plundering our universe for human slaves. Their empire collapsed and it is now they who are enslaved: humans use Tharils as navigators on board hyperspace craft and have no compunction about working the creatures to death.

Villains: Rorvik, captain of a space freighter which is transporting a consignment of dormant Tharils.

Other Worlds: The TARDIS lands in a micro-universe between N-Space and E-Space, which is featureless and white except for a gateway to the Tharils' domain. Meanwhile, Rorvik's Tharil navigator Biroc (David Weston) brings the freighter to the micro-universe and then escapes.

Science/Magic: The freighter is made of super-dense 'dwarf star alloy' and its mass causes the micro-universe to become unstable. The dimension slowly begins to collapse. K9 is badly damaged by exposure to the 'time winds', which also scorch the Doctor's hand.

The Plan: Rorvik's hasty attempts to revive his Tharil cargo meet with failure, leaving him without a navigator. He discovers that within the gateway is a mirror which the Tharils can step through and launches various attempts to break through it. However, the force is always thrown straight back at Rorvik and his men – which *should* suggest to them that issuing greater force against it is a bad idea . . .

Doctor Who?: He sees a glimpse of the Tharils' long-dead empire and is appalled, but judges that they have since suffered enough at the hands of humans. At the end Romana decides to stay and help the Tharils to liberate more of their kind: the Doctor gives her K9, who can only be repaired if he remains on the other side of the gateway (K9 is a fantastic presence in this story, quoting from the *I Ching* – 'If you are sincere, blood vanishes and fear gives way' – and rambling incoherently after sustaining damage). The Doctor misquotes Shakespeare's *Julius Caesar*: 'You were the noblest Romana of them all.'

Things Fall Apart: When the Doctor ducks down so that the two Gundan guards will strike each other, one reaches him far sooner than the other – but obligingly waits for the Doctor to duck before he strikes. The TARDIS console is very noisy during the final scene.

Availability: Issued on VHS in 1997 as BBCV 6232 (UK; as part of the *E-Space Trilogy* box), WHV E6229 (US).

Verdict: 'It does have a certain legendary quality.' It's not always entirely clear what's going on in 'Warriors' Gate' (what exactly is 'the right sort of nothing'?) but this barely detracts from its brilliance at all. It's beautifully shot, opening with a long unbroken take in the style of *Touch of Evil* (Orson Welles, 1958) which few *Who* directors would dare attempt, and the scenes where the Doctor follows Biroc through the black-and-white hallways and gardens on the opposite side of the mirror are breathtakingly strange. Barring a couple of rather fake-looking model shots, this is a resounding visual success.

All style and no substance, then? Not at all. The plot may be frequently oblique but dialogue and characterisation are of the highest standard, with a freighter crew who gripe at each other like real workmates and aliens who would once have been considered evil, but have done penance by suffering themselves. Above all it's great to see *Doctor Who* dealing in more abstract notions again, something it hadn't really done since the 1960s (see **24**, 'The Celestial Toymaker' and **45**, 'The Mind Robber'). Gallagher and Joyce give the show's boundaries a push: it's remarkable how far they move.

114
The Keeper of Traken

Part One: 31 January 1981
Part Two: 7 February 1981
Part Three: 14 February 1981
Part Four: 21 February 1981

Written by Johnny Byrne
Directed by John Black

Notable Cast: Denis Carey (Keeper) was in *The Red Shoes* (Michael Powell, Emeric Pressburger, 1948), played Ebenezer in

Dennis Potter's 1968 play *The Beast With Two Backs* and Skulpit in *The Barchester Chronicles* (1982), both for the BBC. Anthony Ainley (1932–2004) makes his debut as the Master in Part Four, when the body of his character, Tremas, is possessed by the Time Lord: he would play the Master in all appearances until **156**, 'Survival'. Ainley previously played the Reverend Emelius in *The Pallisers* (1976). Sarah Sutton (Nyssa) had starred in the BBC children's drama *The Moon Stallion* (1978). Sheila Ruskin was also in *The Pallisers* (1974) and *I, Claudius* (1976). John Woodnutt can be seen in **51**, 'Spearhead From Space', **67**, 'Frontier in Space' and **80**, 'Terror of the Zygons'.

Writer: Former Beat poet Johnny Byrne had written for *Space: 1999* (1977). He later contributed to *All Creatures Great and Small* (1985–90) and created interminable soporific TV potboiler *Heartbeat* (1993–present).

Director: John Black's other credits include the play *You Talk Too Much* (1976) and the *Doctor Who* spin-off *K9 and Company* (see **110**, 'Meglos'). He later left television to work in retail management.

Doctor Who?: The Doctor can't remember whether he's been to Traken before or not. He used to keep a gazetteer and claims he has a 'very sophisticated prose style'. When Adric criticises his advice he deadpans, 'Don't listen to me, I never do.'

Other Worlds: Traken. A sort of techno-pseudo-Jacobean civilisation whose head of state is the titular Keeper, a person integrated into a machine with 'limitless organising' abilities. The person becomes the 'organising principle' for the Union. The Doctor talks of Traken as an empire 'held together by people being terribly nice to each other' but it isn't really idyllic – it's just that the people who live in it insist it is. It's also an autocracy (the Keeper appoints his own successor) albeit a gender egalitarian one. Proctor Neman (Roland Oliver) is corrupt and overfond of both money and power and no one seems to care in the slightest for the common people. The death penalty seems to be in force for almost every crime.

Scary Monsters: There are none. The statue of Melkur stalking around the grove is a striking image though and the creature sort of fulfils the story's 'scaring kiddies' remit.

Villains: Kassia (Sheila Ruskin) – wife of Tremas and one of the Consuls – presents as the villain, but she's little more than the dupe of Melkur and she's acting purely out of a desire to protect her husband. Melkur is actually the Master (Geoffrey Beevers), still in (a slightly more mobile version of) the rotting form seen in **88**, 'The Deadly Assassin'. The Master paraphrases Shakespeare twice ('By any other name' and 'Kassia is as good a name as Tremas'). He exhibits a streak of pure sadism not previously present in the character.

The Plan: The Master plans to become the Keeper of Traken and use the powers of the office for his own purposes – including possessing the Doctor.

Science/Magic: The 'wave loop pattern' of a TARDIS is unmistakable according to Adric. When the Master makes the Doctor's TARDIS vanish into the future the Doctor makes a 'fold back flow inducer' with a 'binary induction system' in order to make it visible again. The Doctor's party build a 'source manipulator' in order to use the 'ultimate sanction' and remove Melkur once he has become Keeper. This involves decoding the 'gamma mode encryption' of the five keys (one belonging to each consul). Tremas keeps the plans for the source 'atmosphere safe' which seems to be a path of wall which becomes intangible when one touches it.

Things Fall Apart: Sheila Ruskin's performance as Kassia can be generously described as somewhat peculiar and her eye make-up is very silly. Kassia argues that the Fosters (guards) should be armed – and in the next scene they're carrying guns before the suggestion has had time to be implemented. If Kassia is trying to save her husband why does she repeatedly insist he be executed? As she's serving Melkur why does she continually tell people he's evil? If the Master has planned all along to steal the Doctor's body then isn't the Doctor's arrival a bit coincidental? (The Doctor is summoned by the Keeper and the Master plays no part in this.)

Availability: Issued on VHS in 1993 as BBCV 4973 (UK), WHV E1199 (US).

Verdict: 'It's a pity about that poor chap having to sit in a chair for thousands of years, but it is magnificent.' Although you could never call it action packed 'The Keeper of Traken' boasts lyrical dialogue and generally very fine performances. The sets are superb (Tony Burrough later won an Oscar) and just part of the serial's real commitment to creating a believable world (the characters have breakfast at one point). Less positively, it's rather oddly paced and the story's central quandary is solved through the oh-so-convenient plugging of a literal plot device (the source manipulator) into the plot's central MacGuffin (the source).

115
Logopolis

Part One: 28 February 1981
Part Two: 7 March 1981
Part Three: 14 March 1981
Part Four: 21 March 1981

Written by Christopher H Bidmead
Directed by Peter Grimwade

Notable Cast: John Fraser (Monitor) received acclaim for his work on *The Trials of Oscar Wilde* (Ken Hughes, 1960); he also appeared in *A Study in Terror* (James Hill, 1965) and a 1972 *Columbo* TV movie. Janet Fielding (Tegan Jovanka) appeared in an edition of *Hammer House of Horror* (1980) prior to joining *Doctor Who* as a regular: she subsequently quit acting to become an agent.

History 101: The Doctor wishes to mend the TARDIS's chameleon circuit (a new term for the process whereby it's meant to change shape) and needs to measure a genuine police box. He materialises around one in the year 1980. A young Australian air hostess named Tegan Jovanka inadvertently steps into the ship and is still on board when it travels to Logopolis.

Other Worlds: Logopolis is home to a race of master mathematicians: they live like monks, sitting in hollows and chanting their calculations, overseen by the Monitor. Nyssa (see **114**, 'The Keeper of Traken') is there, searching for her father (her retention was a late decision by the production team, who wanted to bolster the new Doctor with a large regular cast: this proved to be a mistake, overburdening subsequent writers with characters).

Science/Magic: 'Structure is the essence of matter, and the essence of matter is mathematics,' according to the Monitor. The Logopolitans' advanced mathematics, known as block transfer computation, can alter the structure of things.

Villains: The Master, still wearing the body of Tremas (see **114**, 'The Keeper of Traken') follows the Doctor to Earth and Logopolis. Anthony Ainley plays more of a Victorian, Raffles-type villain than Roger Delgado, and works better when pursuing his own survival and personal vendetta against the Doctor: these aims seem more consistent with his character than arbitrary lust for power.

The Plan: The Master wishes to hijack Logopolis and abuse the Logopolitans' control over matter, and holds the planet in stasis until the Monitor agrees to his terms. However, he does not realise that the Logopolitans have been working to hold the entire universe together: it 'long ago passed the point of total collapse'. The Master's interference causes entropy to set in, starting with Logopolis itself.

Doctor Who?: 'He's a Time Lord,' the Doctor says of the Master. 'In many ways we have the same mind.' The Doctor's regeneration is different to any we've seen previously in that it is prefigured by the appearance of the Watcher, a white humanoid who blends with the Doctor at the moment of death. It is unclear why this has never happened to the Doctor before. This is the last TV story on which the character is credited as 'Doctor Who'; it's 'The Doctor' from now on.

Things Fall Apart: How does the Doctor escape from the TARDIS recursion by going around the back? The entropy affects things for plot convenience, destroying the Master's control device without affecting Nyssa herself. We never hear the Master's tape-recorded ransom message in full, conveniently avoiding an explanation of how he plans to co-ordinate what appears to be a takeover of the universe. The background of the scene of the Doctor reaching for the cable is a weak paste-up, with a motionless photographic Master watching from the doorway.

Availability: Issued on VHS in 1992 as BBCV 4736 (UK), WHV E1142 (US).

Verdict: 'There is no other mathematics like ours.' In its concepts 'Logopolis' is a fine statement from Bidmead on what *Doctor Who* can be, presenting intelligent science fiction and achieving a grand scale on a small budget (something which many *Who* writers have tried and failed to accomplish). Unfortunately the plotting leaves much to be desired. The first episode and a half is largely a waste of time as it's unclear what the Master is trying to do and the sequences in the lay-by are stilted and overlong. The material on Logopolis is excellent but there's still a weak denouement lying in wait as the Master comes up with a vague last-minute plan to threaten the universe. It's cartoon villainy and undermines Ainley's performance.

Nevertheless, the mere fact that this was Tom Baker's final *Doctor Who* serial gives it an effective air of melancholy, and this most larger-than-life of Doctors could hardly have died for a lesser cause than saving the entire universe. Over seven years Tom had impressed himself so firmly upon the minds of viewers that *Doctor Who* arguably never recovered from his departure: it's not that his successors weren't as good, but that public perception would never allow them to emerge fully from the long shadow his tenure in the role cast. They were never permitted to make the role their own.

116
Castrovalva

Part One: 4 January 1982
Part Two: 5 January 1982
Part Three: 11 January 1982
Part Four: 12 January 1982

Written by Christopher H Bidmead
Directed by Fiona Cumming

Notable Cast: New Doctor Peter Davison (born Peter Moffett, 1951) came to fame as Tristan Farnon in *All Creatures Great and Small* (1983, 1985, 1988–90) before diversifying into the sitcoms *Sink or Swim* and *Holding the Fort* (both 1980). After *Doctor Who*, he played Dr Stephen Daker in *A Very Peculiar Practice* (1986–88), Albert Campion in *Campion* (1989–90), and Clive Quigley in Roy Clarke's sitcom *Ain't Misbehavin'* (1994–95) and recreated Tristan when *All Creatures* was periodically revived (1983, 85, 88–90). He was the original lead in Arthur Miller's play *The Last Yankee* and made memorable guest appearances in *Miss Marple* ('A Pocketful of Rye') and *Jonathan Creek* ('Danse Macabre'). In recent years his most prominent roles have been as David Braithwaite in *At Home with the Braithwaites* (2000–03) and the lead of Detective Constable 'Dangerous' Davies in *The Last Detective* (2003–present). The last two roles have established him as one of the primary dramatic stars on the UK's ITV network. He has also worked as a composer/singer contributing the theme to *Button Moon* (1980). Michael Sheard (Mergrave) previously appeared in **23**, 'The Ark', **56**, 'The Mind of Evil', **82**, 'Pyramids of Mars', and **93**, 'The Invisible Enemy'.

Director: Fiona Cumming has directed episodes of *Blake's 7* (1980) and *Eldorado* (1992).

Script Editor: Eric Saward came to *Doctor Who* from BBC radio. He became the series' script editor shortly after his story **119**, 'The Visitation' was commissioned, and stayed until **144**, 'The Trial of a Time Lord'.

History 101: The story picks up immediately after **115**, 'Logopolis', with the Doctor on contemporary Earth. Pursued by security guards at the Pharos Project, Tegan and Nyssa narrowly escape into the TARDIS with the Doctor. Adric is snatched by the Master, before following them into the TARDIS and setting a course away from Earth.

Doctor Who?: The newly regenerated Doctor has straight, almost shoulder-length blond hair, and looks considerably younger than his previous self. The Doctor is confused after his regeneration and disappears into the depths of the TARDIS in search of the 'Zero Room', a 'neutral environment' with healing properties. He says that he is the Doctor, then modifies that to say that he will be 'if this regeneration works out'. He welcomes Adric to the TARDIS not knowing that Romana has already left. He unwinds his scarf as he walks through the TARDIS, leaving a trail of wool behind him. He appears to drift into the personalities and memories of all his previous selves, adopting their mannerisms, and says this is because the regeneration is failing. He finds a cricket pavilion in the TARDIS, and puts on a new costume – an Edwardian cricketer's outfit with pink and cream striped trousers, a cricket jumper, and a cream frock coat with red piping. He refers to Vicki, Jamie, the Brigadier, Jo and the Ice Warriors. In his weakened state the Doctor is incoherent, frequently falls asleep and requires a wheelchair to move. He wears half-spectacles to read. He has frantic outbursts, then politely corrects himself. He occasionally forgets who he is, and seems to have developed vertigo. He can tell the age of a book by sniffing it. Davison's performance is utterly captivating from his first moment on screen.

Other Worlds: The Master's puppet Adric programmed the TARDIS on a course for the 'hydrogen in-rush' at Event One – the beginning of the galaxy, where the TARDIS will burn up. After escaping, the TARDIS goes to Castrovalva, a place of tranquillity with similar properties to the Zero Room. Built on a hill, Castrovalva is a white citadel with a Renaissance feel, built around a central square, an ideal society formed from warring hunting parties. Brightly dressed hunters venture out from Castrovalva into the surrounding woods.

Villains: The Master, determined to destroy the Doctor, one way or another. He seems to have gone insane and developed a penchant for sadism – if he wants to kill the Doctor, why doesn't he just shoot him through the head when he's vulnerable after his regeneration, rather than cooking up ludicrously elaborate schemes?

The Plan: The Master sends the TARDIS towards Event One. When that fails, he still has another trap to spring – Castrovalva itself, an artificial construct created entirely to trap the Doctor, powered by a block transfer computation (see **115**, 'Logopolis') using Adric's mathematical knowledge.

Science/Magic: A 'TARDIS Information System' database appears on the console. The Doctor's confusion is due to his dendrites needing to heal – the synapses in his brain are vulnerable after regeneration. The Zero Room cuts out all outside information, allowing his mind to peacefully settle. The heat at Event One gives the Doctor's brain a rush of adrenaline and neuro-peptides allowing him to solve the problem – jettisoning rooms from the TARDIS produces the momentum to escape the pull at Event One. Unfortunately, the Zero Room is one of those jettisoned – so the Doctor gets Nyssa to construct a coffin-like 'Zero Cabinet' from the doors. Recursive occlusion is when space folds in on itself – the effects of the recursion can be kept at bay with silver.

Things Fall Apart: There are some uneasy cuts between film and video footage. Whilst the Doctor is incapacitated, the story rests too heavily on the performances of Matthew Waterhouse and Sarah Sutton, neither of whom are up to scratch.

Availability: Issued on VHS in the UK in 1992 as BBCV 4737, and in the US as WHV E1144.

Verdict: 'I think it does us good to be reminded the universe isn't entirely peopled with nasty creatures out for themselves.' Like the previous story, 'Castrovalva' rambles on through a number of esoteric settings and scenarios. However, the central thread of the Doctor's need to recover is never lost, and the journey is as much a search for the Doctor's self as anything else. Davison's performance anchors the entire serial, as the Doctor shows his vulnerability, anger, sense of wonder and desire for survival: his 'difficult' regeneration tacitly and neatly acknowledges the substantial challenge of supplanting Tom Baker in the audience's affections. The citadel of Castrovalva represents what the Doctor stands for and is willing to fight for – decency, compassion, beauty and wonder. A reinvigorating statement of what *Doctor Who* is all about.

117
Four To Doomsday

Part One: 18 January 1982
Part Two: 19 January 1982
Part Three: 25 January 1982
Part Four: 26 January 1982

Written by Terence Dudley
Directed by John Black

Notable Cast: Strafford Johns (Monarch) was Barlow in *Z Cars* (1962–65) and *Softly Softly* (1966–72) and Piso in *I, Claudius* (1976). Philip Locke (Bigon) was vividly memorable as Arnold of Toadi in *The Box of Delights* (1984), played Vargas ('Vargas does not eat, does not sleep, does not make love!') in *Thunderball* (Terence Young, 1965) and was Sir Larry in the spectacularly violent *Comic Strip Presents . . . Mr Jolly Lives Next Door* (1984). Burt Kwouk has appeared in everything from *Tenko* (1981–84), in which he played the Camp Commandant, to *The Harry Hill Show* (1997–2000). A very fine actor, he's underutilised here.

Script Editor: Antony Root, the script editor on only this and **119**, 'The Visitation', was temporarily seconded to *Doctor Who* for three months until Eric Saward took over for **118**, 'Kinda' and **116**, 'Castrovalva' (Davison's first four stories were produced in a very different order to the broadcast sequence). Root is credited on **121**, 'Earthshock' to disguise the fact that Saward had script-edited his own work. Previously an assistant floor manager on *Blake's 7* (1978) and *Private Schultz* (1981), he was in training to become a producer. His later work in this capacity includes numerous excellent Anglo-American co-productions, such as Armistead Maupin's *Tales of the City* (1993) and *Cold Comfort Farm* (1995). He was also a writer/producer on Derek Jarman's *Edward II* (1991).

Doctor Who?: Adric says that the Doctor has never been known to hurry anything and claims his mentor finds trouble amusing. This was the first story Davison made – and, in retrospect, he nails the part entirely first time out. His Doctor is inquisitive, childishly petulant, excitable and wise. He seems ill at ease with the world around him and uncomfortable with both his inability to stamp his authority on a situation (thanks to his apparent lack of seniority) and with the fact that nobody laughs at his jokes. He's also capable of a kind of icy rage, is slyly flippant, and appears to be in constant deep thought. He's instantly suspicious of Monarch. There are lovely scenes of the new Doctor exploring the laboratory on Monarch's ship, buzzing with repressed energy. He claims Francis Drake as a friend and says he's a bit short-sighted in his right eye. He used to bowl a very good chinaman (a left-handed googly) and once took five wickets for New South Wales. He can withstand sub-zero temperatures for six minutes.

Other Worlds: None – the whole story takes place on Monarch's vast spacecraft. Urbanka – where Monarch is from – is in the solar system of Inoce, in the galaxy RA 14 89. Their sun collapsed a thousand years before the story begins.

Villains: Monarch, the egomaniacal leader of the Urbankans, and his two chief ministers Persuasion (Paul Shelley) and Enlightenment (Annie Lambert).

The Plan: Monarch wants to take control of Earth because of its deposits of silicon. His overarching ambition is to travel back in time to the beginning of the universe in order to meet God.

History 101: Bigon, an Athenian, was abducted by the Urbankans 100 generations (2,500 years) ago when he was 55.

Science/Magic: Monarch believes his is the 'most advanced technology in the universe'. It includes an 'electron microscope', a 'resonant stroboscope' (which 'increases density . . . to reduce matter') and an 'interferometer' and graviton crystal detector (both of which measure gravitation waves). He does not have the ability to travel faster than the speed of light. The TARDIS is 'fifth dimensional' according to Adric. There's also talk of 'telemicrographics'. Monarch's androids are made of a polymer stretched over a non-corrosive steel frame. There are more circuits in their memory chips than there are synapses in a brain. A nanometre is 'a thousand millionth of a metre'. Artron energy (as mentioned in **88**, 'The Deadly Assassin') gets a name-check in relation to the TARDIS being pulled off course. Nyssa short-circuits an android using the graphite in a pencil and the electrical charge from the sonic screwdriver. Nyssa reads Bertrand Russell's *Principia Mathematic*.

Things Fall Apart: Strangely, Nyssa and Adric are often referred to as 'children'. The cliffhanger into **118**, 'Kinda' is appalling. While the mathematics of Monarch's visits to Earth – and his repeated doubling of his ship's speed – does all add up, the dates of his visits don't square with the 'representative' humans he kidnapped on each occasion. The sexist/feminist banter between Adric and Tegan is as excruciating as that in **64**, 'The Time Monster'.

Availability: Issued on VHS in 2001 as BBCV 7134 (UK), WHV E 1649 (US).

Verdict: 'Conformity. There is no other freedom.' Great design work, much good dialogue, striking concepts and excellent acting from Davison, Johns and Stone make these slow and wordy scripts into a hundred minutes of captivating television. This is a peculiar, talky serial, which is both an effects *tour de force* and about the most atypical 'Earth invasion' story *Doctor Who* ever attempted. The cliffhanger to Part Two is stunning – a heady combination of traumatising imagery and genuinely plot-furthering revelations.

118
Kinda

Part One: 1 February 1982
Part Two: 2 February 1982
Part Three: 8 February 1982
Part Four: 9 February 1982

Written by Christopher Bailey
Directed by Peter Grimwade

Notable Cast: Richard Todd (Sanders) is a legend in British film and one of the most famous actors to ever appear in *Doctor Who*. His pictures include *The Longest Day* (Andrew Marton, 1962) and *Dorian Gray* (Massimo Dallamano, 1970). Nerys Hughes (Todd) starred in *The Liver Birds* (1971–79, 1996) and *District Nurse*. Simon Rouse (Hindle) has been a regular in *The Bill* since 1992. Mary Morris (Panna) was a regular in *A For Andromeda* (1961) and *The Andromeda Breakthrough* (1962), and made a memorable appearance as Number Two in *The Prisoner* (1967). Anna Wing (Anatta) played Lou Beale in *EastEnders* (1985–88). Adrian Mills (Aris) was a presenter on *That's Life!* (1985–94). Lee Cornes (Trickster) was a regular in *Grange Hill* (1990–2002) and made guest appearances in *Bottom* (1991–95) and *Red Dwarf* (1988).

Writer: Christopher Bailey was an English lecturer who rarely wrote for television: his other credits include *Second City Firsts*.

Other Worlds: At some unspecified point in the future Earth has sent a survey team to consider the planet of Deva Loka for colonisation. Inside their domed headquarters they hold two of the mute native humanoids, known as Kinda, for examination. However, three of their number have disappeared into the forest: only leader Sanders, his second Hindle and scientist Todd remain.

Villains: Hindle, already on the verge of a nervous breakdown, deteriorates further when the Doctor and Adric arrive at the dome. Sanders heads out on reconnaissance and leaves him in charge: Hindle locks the Doctor and Todd in a cell and becomes convinced that the plants outside the dome are a mortal threat, plotting against him. He retaliates by arming the dome's self-destruct system.

Scary Monsters: Isolated from the others, Tegan falls asleep beneath the Kinda's wind chimes. Here she falls prey to the Mara, a malign entity which takes the form of a snake: it can cross into our world via 'the dreaming of an unshared mind' (according to Karuna) when those dreams are enhanced by the chimes (the telepathic Kinda are immune). The creature possesses its victims, first controlling Tegan, then taking possession of a Kinda named Aris.

The Plan: The Mara wins the obedience of several Kinda, intending to use them as an army to defeat the colonists. After this is achieved it will turn on the Kinda and destroy them.

Doctor Who?: He appears surprised by Adric's simple conjuring trick (see **65**, 'The Three Doctors'). He has heard of the Mara, which earns him some respect from the Kinda's wise woman Panna ('Are you an idiot?' she asks him; 'I suppose I must be,' he replies).

Science/Magic: The Doctor builds a 'delta wave augmentor' to cure Nyssa's sickness. He later postulates that the Kinda's 'mental healing' box emits ultrasonic impulses.

Things Fall Apart: The Mara is supposed to be trapped by a complete circle of mirrors, but the wide angle view makes it obvious that there is a gap for the camera. The Mara's true form inspires very little awe, suffering from the same problem as the spiders from **74**, 'Planet of the Spiders'. (Hindle's new capital city is perhaps a wry acknowledgement of the old cliché regarding *Doctor Who*'s cheap sets – its buildings are literally made of cardboard.)

Availability: Released on VHS in 1994 as BBCV 5432 (UK), WHV E1320 (US).

Verdict: 'There is great danger in dreaming alone.' It could have benefited from some location work and the snake is an obvious flaw, but 'Kinda' has in its favour an excellent script and one of the finest casts ever assembled for *Doctor Who*. The three colonists are all outstanding: Simon Rouse's portrayal of madness is light years away from the usual hammy eye-rolling, Richard Todd effortlessly provides two distinct but linked performances and Nerys Hughes is a wonderful foil for Peter Davison. Her character talks to the Doctor on his own level, provides a vital component of the resolution without stealing his thunder (this is his series, after all) and can even be seen as a credible love interest.

Bailey's script is rewarding, juggling two unrelated threats (Hindle and the Mara) without sacrificing structure. It's packed with symbolism, some of it rather blatant (pith helmets = British Empire, apples and snakes = Garden of Eden) but often pointing the way to interesting conclusions: for example, there's an implicit criticism of the Adam and Eve story as Bailey (a Buddhist) gives his female characters knowledge and doesn't punish them for it.

This collage (which also includes big chunks of Ursula Le Guin and Joseph Conrad) sometimes fits together oddly but the high-quality dialogue disguises this.

119
The Visitation

Part One: 15 February 1982
Part Two: 16 February 1982
Part Three: 22 February 1982
Part Four: 23 February 1982

Written by Eric Saward
Directed by Peter Moffatt

Notable Cast: Michael Robbins (Richard Mace) is best known for playing Arthur in *On The Buses* (1969–73); his films include the seminal *Up the Junction* (Ken Loach, 1967). John Savident (The Squire) is recognisable as Fred Elliot in *Coronation Street* (1994–present) and appeared twice, and as two different characters, in *Blake's 7* (in 'Trial', 1979 and 'Orbit', 1981). Michael Melia (Terileptil Leader) was landlord (and eventual murderee) Eddie Royal in *EastEnders* (1990–91).

Doctor Who?: Practical, snappish, sarcastic but charming – prone to sudden rages at others' stupidity and capable of literally joking with his own executioner, Davison's performance as the Doctor continues to develop here. The Doctor assumes the Terileptils will be friendly and initially intends to help them escape Earth. He insists that Terileptian law isn't his strong point.

Scary Monsters: The Tereleptils. Only one has a speaking part, but it's one of the series' best-ever monsters; a tropical fish or lizard in the shape of a man, with a mouth (and flapping gills!) moved by then state-of-the-art animatronics. They breathe soliton gas rather than oxygen. They are familiar with the concept of time-travel, but don't have such technology themselves – although their escape pod may be dimensionally transcendental.

Other Worlds: The Terileptil civilisation condemns criminals to the planet Raaga, where they mine tinclavic as part of their punishment. To be sentenced to Raaga is always for life.

The Plan: The stranded Tereleptils intend to wipe out the human race using a mutant strain of the plague and then occupy Earth – or at least Britain – themselves.

History 101: The TARDIS arrives on Earth in 1666 outside London, near the site of what will one day be Heathrow Airport.

Science/Magic: Soliton is highly combustible when mixed with oxygen. Terileptil technology is largely made of polygrite. They have bracelets that enable them to control human minds. Vintaric crystals are a common form of lighting. The Doctor blames the TARDIS's failure to reach 1981 on a 'temperamental solenoid on the lateral balance cones'. As Tegan asks, 'Why must you always have an incomprehensible answer?' The Doctor's sonic screwdriver – first used in **42**, 'Fury From the Deep' and something of a cop-out plot device during the 1970s – is destroyed by the Terileptil leader (but see **160**, 'The Movie').

Things Fall Apart: The cliffhanger to Part One is horrible. The script struggles throughout to accommodate Nyssa, Tegan and Adric (Nyssa having been added to the story at a late stage). The studio-based action sequences are limp and uncomfortable. The Terileptil leader disguises himself as a human by wearing a cape and no one notices (see **5**, 'The Keys of Marinus'). As in all Saward scripts the Doctor contributes nothing to the eventual resolution of the plot. It would be prurient to speculate as to why Nyssa and Tegan share a bedroom when they live in an infinitely vast spaceship.

Availability: Issued on Region 2 DVD in 2004 as BBCDVD 1329; the 1994 VHS (a double-pack with **120**, 'Black Orchid') was BBCV 5349 (UK), WHV E1322 (US).

Verdict: 'Cruder, but more effective, eh?' A simple, straightforward combination of period atmosphere and monster histrionics in which much time is spent running around. Davison and Robbins are both brilliant, there are lots of enticing visuals – such as the buried pod or the 'Grim Reaper' android stalking the woods – and the music and location shooting are both hugely evocative. Efficient, effective yet unremarkable, you couldn't call 'The Visitation' complex and it misses the 'educational' remit of the series' early historical stories by miles, but it's very enjoyable. The Terileptil leader's head bubbling and popping as he burns to death is really unpleasant.

120
Black Orchid

Part One: 1 March 1982
Part Two: 2 March 1982

Written by Terence Dudley
Directed by Ron Jones

Notable Cast: Barbara Murray (Lady Cranleigh) was in *Passport to Pimlico* (TEB Clarke, 1949), played Ammonia in *Up Pompeii!* (1970) and starred in *The Pallisers* (1974), alongside Moray Watson (Sir Robert Muir) and Michael Cochrane (Lord Cranleigh). An expert in playing gruff authoritarians, Watson was George Frobisher in *Rumpole of the Bailey* (1978–83) and the Brigadier in *The Darling Buds of May* (1991–3). Cochrane also played Sir Henry Simmerson in *Sharpe's Eagle* (1993), *Sharpe's Sword* (1995) and *Sharpe's Regiment* (1996) and portrayed Winston Churchill in *Lawrence After Arabia* (1990) and Nicholas Ridley in the long-delayed *Falklands Play* (2002). He voices Oliver Sterling in BBC Radio 4's *The Archers*. Gareth Milne (George Cranleigh) was Peter Davison's stunt double on *Doctor Who*, *Campion* (1989–90) and many other projects, and played the editor of the *Daily Bastard* in the last episode of *Filthy, Rich and Catflap* (1986).

Director: Ron Jones worked extensively for the BBC on series such as *Juliet Bravo* (1984–85) and *Bergerac* (1980–90).

Doctor Who?: The Doctor works out what's going on at Cranleigh Hall with erudite skill – faced with a small number of clues and a potentially baffling lack of motive, he doesn't so much solve the murders (that isn't what the story is about) as uncover a family's secrets. The scenes where, frustrated by the intransigence of those around him, he smugly demonstrates the TARDIS's abilities to a group of 1925 humans is a glorious example of this Doctor's combination of repression, sarcasm and recklessness. In a manner reminiscent of the Hartnell Doctor he turns down an alcoholic drink (and chooses lemonade instead, though Tegan hits the vodka and orange). The Doctor demonstrates his prowess at cricket (see **98**, 'The Ribos Operation') in Part One. During production Peter Davison genuinely bowled out the batsman he was facing – the footage is in the finished episode. The Doctor fatuously claims that as a boy he wanted to be a train driver, confusing Adric and Nyssa and causing Tegan some amusement.

The Plan: The dowager Lady Cranleigh is hiding her mentally ill, physically disfigured and legally dead eldest son, George, in an apartment backstairs at her country house. He sustained his injuries while leading an expedition up the Orinocco river to look for the mythical flower of the title.

History 101: The TARDIS arrives at Cranleigh Halt railway station, near Cranleigh Hall, somewhere in the south of England at 3 o'clock, 11 June 1925: it's an unsurprisingly wet and windy-looking English summer day.

Other Worlds: Nyssa refers to Traken (see **114**, 'The Keeper of Traken') as an Empire (and, strangely, speaks of it in the present tense – see **115**, 'Logopolis') although Sir Robert Muir is convinced it's actually near Esher (it's nearer the star Metulla Orionsis). Mind you, Lord Cranleigh thinks Alzarius (see **111**, 'Full Circle') is in the Baltic when it's actually in the exo-space–time continuum.

Things Fall Apart: The plot hangs on some vast Dickensian coincidences: the TARDIS arrives somewhere where they are expecting *another* cricketing doctor; the house the Doctor's party then visit has another guest, Ann Talbot, who looks like Nyssa; then George Cranleigh escapes his nurse on the one day in history when there are two identical women in the building. As in **117**, 'Four to Doomsday' Adric and Nyssa are referred to as 'children' which still seems peculiar – especially when Charles Cranleigh (who is engaged to someone played by the same actress who plays Nyssa) does it. There's a slightly ropey bit of dubbing near the end of Part One.

Science/Magic: Despite not being able to successfully return Tegan to her own place and time in the previous three stories, the Doctor is not only able to use the TARDIS to make the short hop from the police station to the Hall, he is confident enough in his ability to do so to make the journey with a ship containing three policemen from 1925. From now on in *Doctor Who* the TARDIS seems to be easily pilotable by the Doctor and can travel anywhere on demand. The decision to make this the case seems to have been taken, either consciously or through unfamiliarity with the programme, by script editor Eric Saward.

Availability: Issued on VHS is 1994 as BBCV 5349 (UK), WHV E1322 (US), a double-pack with **119**, 'The Visitation'.

Verdict: 'First class bat and a demon bowler.' Uniformly strong production values and some terrific performances more than compensate for the plotting hiccoughs of Dudley's (witty and characterful) scripts. Scenes of the Doctor, Tegan, Nyssa and Adric relaxing and enjoying themselves are very effective, particularly Tegan flirting with Sir Robert and Nyssa teasing Adric. With its engaging, beautifully realised setting and intriguing central mystery, 'Black Orchid' transcends its conceptual combination of detective story pastiche and whimsical period demonstration by sustaining a core of real human emotion. As such it's genuinely special – one of the key stories in *Doctor Who*'s early 1980s renaissance.

121
Earthshock

Part One: 8 March 1982
Part Two: 9 March 1982
Part Three: 15 March 1982
Part Four: 16 March 1982

Written by Eric Saward
Directed by Peter Grimwade

Notable Cast: The late Beryl Reid (Briggs) had a long and distinguished career in British film and television. Her films include *Two Way Stretch* (Robert Day, 1960), *The Killing of Sister George* (Robert Aldrich, 1968), *Entertaining Mr Sloane* (Douglas Hickox, 1970) and *The Doctor and the Devils* (Freddie Francis, 1985). Her television appearances include *The Secret Diary of Adrian Mole Aged 13¾* (1985), and the John Le Carré serials *Tinker, Tailor, Soldier, Spy* (1979) and *Smiley's People* (1982). David Banks (Cyber Leader in this and all 1980s Cybermen stories) has had a career dominated by soap, from *EastEnders* and *Brookside* (1991–92) to Live TV's dreadful *Canary Wharf*. James Warwick (Scott) starred in *The Nightmare Man* (1981) and *Partners in Crime* (1983) and as such was big TV news at the time. This is Matthew Waterhouse's last regular appearance as Adric, although the character appears in illusionary form in **122** and **135**.

History 101: Earth, 2526. An archaeological survey team has gone missing in a cavern and Lieutenant Scott (James Warwick) leads troops in to find what happened. The troops are picked off by androids protecting a hatch, behind which is a huge bomb. When the Doctor arrives he finds fossils in the caves, and explains the life and death of the dinosaurs 65,000,000 years ago. After encountering the surviving troops and disarming the bomb, the Doctor follows its control signal to a cargo freighter in deep space, a ship that has suffered the disappearances of three crew members and a number of power losses.

Scary Monsters: Black androids with blank features, which can reduce humans to patches of liquid. The androids are tools of the Cybermen. The Cybermen have a more modernised appearance, and knowledge of their previous encounters with the Doctor, seemingly based on access to a number of clips of old *Doctor Who* serials. Once they recognise the Doctor, the Cybermen want to make him 'suffer'. They sleep while cocooned in plastic bags within cardboard tubes. They seem disorientated when they first wake up. They are vulnerable to their own weapons, as well as gold in their chestplates.

The Plan: The Cybermen are trying to blow up the Earth using the bomb in the cave, and have left the androids there to defend the hatch behind which the bomb is hidden. The intention was to activate the bomb during a conference intended to form an alliance against the Cybermen, then invade the Earth using the force hibernating on the freighter. With the bomb deactivated, they instead decide to crash the freighter into the Earth, even though that will sacrifice the invasion force – the Cyber Leader intends to join 'a secondary force' to mop up any survivors.

Doctor Who?: The Doctor is reading the copy of *Black Orchid* he was given at the end of the previous story. He gets very angry when Adric wants to go back to E-Space, reminding him of the potential dangers. He has a tendency to anger and to sulk, but usually becomes apologetic when he calms down. Ultimately the Doctor has great affection for his friends, and is passionate in his defence of them. The Doctor rages against the Cyber Leader's dismissal of emotion, saying that 'for some people small beautiful events are what life is all about'. He doesn't think friendship is a weakness, but is then kept at heel by the Cyber Leader threatening Tegan's life.

Science/Magic: Scott's troops have a scanner that 'focuses upon the electrical activity of the body', but screens out anything that isn't a mammal. As such, it's useless against androids. The Cyber Leader draws a picture of the TARDIS on his monitor, which appears in outline form – the equipment seems to be a sort of holographic Etch-a-sketch, which is very retro. The Cybermen also have a thermal lance, which can cut through metal. The stabilisation device used in containing anti-matter can be used to turn an energy shield into a solid wall, trapping anything trying to break through. Tampering with the control mechanism the Cybermen attach to the freighter's controls causes the ship to inexplicably timewarp.

Things Fall Apart: The Cybermen are not all that bright – the androids supposedly guarding the bomb only succeed in drawing attention to it, and the disappearances on the space freighter have the same effect. The supposedly emotionless Cybermen are smug, sadistic, angry, vengeful and excitable. The final effects shot of the freighter doesn't really make it clear what's just happened.

Availability: Issued on VHS in 1992 as BBCV 4840 (UK), WHV E1102 (US), and on DVD in 2003 as BBCDVD 1153 (Region 2) and WHV E2022 (Region 1).

Verdict: 'This slaughter is pointless.' A gun-happy thriller for the post-*Alien* generation, 'Earthshock' is humourless and violent, but just about works as an action movie on a TV budget. It's full of memorable images and moments, from the murderous robots in the tunnels, to the Cyberman frozen in the door and the final, shocking scene. Music and production values are excellent throughout, and although the tone is unusually grim, this would be a brilliantly unique experiment in a darker, more violent kind of *Doctor Who* story. Unfortunately, similar stories would be deployed for significantly lesser returns over the following years.

122
Time-Flight

Part One: 22 March 1982
Part Two: 23 March 1982
Part Three: 29 March 1982
Part Four: 30 March 1982

Written by Peter Grimwade
Directed by Ron Jones

Notable Cast: Richard Easton (Captain Stapley) appeared in *The Brothers* (1972–77) and *Finding Forrester* (Gus Van Sant, 2002). Michael Cashman (First Officer Bilton) was a regular in *EastEnders* (1986–89). Nigel Stock (Prof. Hayter) has a list of credits encompassing *Brighton Rock* (John Boulting, 1947) and *The Pickwick Papers* (1985); he was Watson opposite Peter Cushing's Sherlock Holmes (1964–68) and had a memorable role in *The Prisoner* (1968).

Doctor Who?: Tegan urges the Doctor to go back in time and save Adric from his fate in **121**, 'Earthshock'; angrily, he replies that 'There are some rules that cannot be broken, not even with the TARDIS.' The ship materialises in mid-air at Heathrow Airport (unusually, it is able to hover in this story) after nearly colliding with an object time-travelling from that location. The Doctor uses his UNIT credentials to discover that a Concorde has disappeared shortly after takeoff and suggests sending another plane after it, with him and the TARDIS on board.

History 101: The second Concorde follows the first into a time rift and lands on Jurassic-era Earth. The crew of the first Concorde have been hypnotised and are working at the behest of a portly green figure called Kalid, who is trying to gain access to the centre of an incongruous alien citadel.

Villains: At the end of Part Two Kalid is revealed to be – shock! – the Master. 'So you escaped from Castrovalva,' declares the Doctor (no explanation of how he escaped is forthcoming). The dynomorphic generator from his TARDIS is exhausted and he is trapped on Earth, although he has been able to reach forwards in time and find a slave labour force to assist him.

Scary Monsters: The Master is also using the Plasmatons to do his bidding: these are ineffectively realised transparent blobs, created out of the air.

Other Worlds: Many years ago the Xeraphin escaped their own radiation-swamped planet of Xeriphas and came to make a new home on Earth. Suffering from radiation sickness, they formed themselves into a single entity, an amorphous Nucleus, and waited at the centre of the citadel for the sickness to pass.

The Plan: The Master plans to use the Nucleus to replace his dynomorphic generator. The Nucleus is 'all-seeing, all-knowing' and would therefore also make the Master immensely powerful.

Science/Magic: Grimwade seems to have a fascination with the workings of the TARDIS, which is highly tedious (by and large the TARDIS should be a means of arriving at the adventure, not the adventure itself: as later scriptwriter Steven Moffat said, 'Us kids want Narnia, not the wardrobe'). The Doctor prevents the Master from departing in the Doctor's TARDIS as he has 'left the co-ordinate override switched in', and he knows that the Master will go to Heathrow because 'In order to check out the temporal dimensions he'll need to track back the line of the time contour.' That's handy. It's also handy that the Doctor rigs the Master's TARDIS so that it arrives a few minutes after the Doctor's (although surely the Doctor could just work out when the Master will land and then set his own TARDIS to land a few minutes before that).

Things Fall Apart: Heathrow appears to have only one air traffic controller. Why does the Master spend the first two episodes disguised as Kalid, and put on a silly voice even when talking to himself? The breaking down of the illusory Heathrow is a poor piece of effects work, as is Concorde taking off from the Jurassic landscape. In fact, almost everything about this story looks *very* cheap.

Availability: Released on VHS in 2000 as BBCV 6878 (UK), WHV E1528 (US).

Verdict: 'You can exclude me from your wizardry!' The first out-and-out failure of Peter Davison's tenure, 'Time-Flight' was sufficiently bad to convince the actor to limit his time on the show to three years. Clunky dialogue conspires with dreadful sets and convenient pseudo-science to create a wretched mess. Too many ideas and characters vie for attention, most of which aren't very good. Exposition is frequently nonsensical or nonexistent. The ending is dreadful, as the Master doesn't even appear: we are simply told that the Doctor has beaten him, with little indication of how this was achieved.

Davison typically plays the Doctor with a manic energy that is rarely evident in his other roles, and it has been suggested that the actor was attempting to distract the viewer from *Doctor Who*'s production shortcomings. 'Time-Flight' tests his ability to carry a story to the limit, and even he seems somewhat defeated by the effort (although when he gets a proper character moment, such as being told by the Master that his TARDIS has been tampered with, he seizes it with gusto). Fortunately he would never be presented with such poor material again.

123
Arc of Infinity

Part One: 3 January 1983
Part Two: 4 January 1983
Part Three: 11 January 1983
Part Four: 12 January 1983

Written by Johnny Byrne
Directed by Ron Jones

Notable Cast: Colin Baker (born 1943), here playing Maxil, would go on to become Peter Davison's successor as the Doctor from **136**, 'The Twin Dilemma' onwards. He played Major Frayne in *The Moonstone* (1972) and Paul Merroney in *The Brothers* (1973–76). Since playing the Doctor he has had guest roles in *The Young Indiana Jones Chronicles* ('Daredevils of the Desert'), *Casualty*, *Hollyoaks*, *Time Gentlemen Please* and *A Dance to the Music of Time*. Michael Gough (Hedin) previously appeared in **24**, 'The Celestial Toymaker'. Leonard Sachs, who makes a non-impression as President Borusa, was much better as de Coligny in **22**, 'The Massacre'. Elspet Grey (Chancellor Thalia) plays The Queen in *The Black Adder* (1983).

Villains: Omega (last seen in **65**, 'The Three Doctors'), pioneer of the Time Lord race, trapped in the universe of anti-matter. Now played (rather well) by Ian Collier, Omega has a better costume, with a smooth bio-mechanical look rather than cardboard armour, but is still a fruity voiced lunatic. The revelation of the nameless 'renegade' comes late in the story, but as the plot is totally meaningless before the audience finds this out, we've decided not to conceal the 'surprise'.

The Plan: Omega is trying to escape the universe of anti-matter, and controls a powerful area of space called the arc of infinity, where the universes meet. To exist permanently in our universe, he needs to 'temporally bond' with the Doctor. To do this he requires the Doctor's biological information, and has an ally among the High Council to steal it from Gallifrey. To stop the bonding occurring, the Time Lords bring the Doctor to Gallifrey to kill him.

Doctor Who?: The Doctor is trying to avoid doing the list of repairs to the TARDIS a bullying Nyssa is trying to get him to complete when the TARDIS suffers an extra-dimensional attack. The Doctor is trapped in a column of light as Omega attempts to temporally bond with him. The Doctor's friends on Gallifrey include Councillor Hedin and the technician Damon (Neil Dalglish). He mentions Romana and asks after Leela. The Doctor is willing to risk being executed on the presumption that Omega will intervene, and that will bring him closer to his enemy. He doesn't look too happy to be stuck with Tegan again.

Other Worlds: Gallifrey, the Doctor's home planet, a place of metallic corridors and cream leather sofas. Borusa (Leonard Sachs) is now Lord President. Capital punishment has been abolished for a long time on Gallifrey, but there is a precedent for killing to prevent a catastrophe. Only members of the High Council can access biodata extracts from the Matrix.

History 101: Contemporary Amsterdam, where two backpackers (including Tegan's cousin) are sleeping in a crypt where Omega's TARDIS lands.

Scary Monsters: Omega's chicken-headed sidekick the Ergon, who spends his time menacing holidaying students in Amsterdam.

Science/Magic: 'Quad magnetism' is the only force that can shield anti-matter, and is created when a 'Q star' burns out. The Time Lords use the TARDIS's recall circuit to bring the Doctor back to Gallifrey and remove the 'main space–time element' to stop him leaving. Anti-matter cannot co-exist in the matter universe, and the result of contact between the two would be catastrophic. A fusion booster can generate vast amounts of energy from hydrogen. The matter converter is a weapon that shifts objects between the two universes.

Things Fall Apart: The traitor within the Time Lords' ranks has such a distinctive manner of speaking that, even with his voice distorted and face unseen, it's perfectly obvious who he is from the start.

Availability: Issued on VHS in 1994 as BBCV 5199 (UK) and WHV E1296 (US).

Verdict: 'What we are we owe to you. Your return is all that matters.' There's a great story in 'Arc of Infinity'. Unfortunately, that story is squeezed into a few minutes of Part Four, while the rest is a dull, confused runaround with mysteries that fail to compel and only succeed in concealing the point of the story until it's too late to save it. This is a shame, as the scenes towards the end in which Omega, temporarily wearing a duplicate of the Doctor's body, comes to terms with his humanity only to lose it again, are superb, with real pathos and an excellent non-verbal performance from Davison. The Amsterdam chase scene at the end is also pretty good – but after three episodes predominantly spent in the bland corridors of Gallifrey, that's far too little, far too late.

124
Snakedance

Part One: 18 January 1982
Part Two: 19 January 1982
Part Three: 25 January 1982
Part Four: 26 January 1982

Written by Christopher Bailey
Directed by Fiona Cumming

Notable Cast: Martin Clunes (Lon) is best known for the role of Gary in *Men Behaving Badly* (1992–98); more recently he has starred in *William and Mary* (2003–present). Jonathan Morris (Chela) played Adrian in *Bread* (1986–91). John Carson (Ambril) was a regular in *Emergency – Ward 10* (1957) and *The Trouble-shooters* (1970–72), in addition to many film credits. Preston Lockwood (Dojjen) appeared on TV in *A Very British Coup* (1988) and *Great Expectations* (1991). Brian Miller (Showman) went on to provide Dalek voices for the rest of the series' run and is married to Elizabeth Sladen (Sarah Jane Smith – see **70**, 'The Time Warrior').

Other Worlds: The influence of the Mara (see **118**, 'Kinda') takes hold of Tegan once more and she guides the TARDIS to Manussa.

Scary Monsters: We learn the origin of the Mara. Many years ago, the Manussans learned how to fashion crystals that could translate thought into energy and matter – creating whatever the user desired. However, the collective dark side of their nature inadvertently gave birth to the Mara, which dominated them and turned the Manussan Empire into the Sumaran Empire.

History 101: Five hundred years before 'Snakedance' is set the Mara was defeated by the Federation, which turned Manussa into one of its colonies. It is implied that the Federation is an expansion of Earth (the Punch and Judy show, for example). There remains a legend of the Mara's return, but few will admit to believing it. A festival to commemorate the banishment is set to be held as the Doctor arrives.

Villains: As well as Tegan, the Mara gains control of Lon, the governor's bored son and descendant of the person who originally destroyed the Mara.

The Plan: By restoring the largest of the blue crystals to its position of focus, the Mara will play upon the people's deep-seated fear of its return and be reborn.

Doctor Who?: His portrayal here is interesting: although the audience knows that he's doing the right thing by trying to alert the Manussan settlers to the threat posed by the Mara, it's also easy to see why he's dismissed as a crank. He has no proof, finds himself reiterating local superstition and, whereas *Doctor Who* doesn't usually show its characters' private lives, here the Doctor is shown disrupting them (the scene where he barges in on a dinner party, for example). Through deft work from Bailey and Cumming, usually by the simple tactic of not following the Doctor but starting scenes without him so as to make his arrival seem more intrusive, a sense of urgency arises from the Doctor's decreasing credibility (*Doctor Who* plotting typically sees him become *more* credible as the story progresses, but not here).

Science/Magic: The blue crystals *are* just magic, as they can be used to make the bearer's will a reality: if you wish hard enough for something, it happens. The Doctor's use of one in defeating the Mara makes for a slightly unsatisfying ending, as he doesn't have to do anything particularly clever in order to win, although it is a satisfying demonstration of his unselfishness of spirit, bravery and compassion.

Things Fall Apart: The clip they always show on 'before they were famous' programmes of Martin Clunes wearing a daft costume originates from this story. Granted, the tunic he wears in Part Four is not one of the serial's better points, but generally 'Snakedance' holds up pretty well – the snake is much better than the one in 'Kinda', except when it dies and a torrent of blancmange flows from its mouth.

Availability: Released on VHS in 1994 as BBCV 5433 (UK), WHV E1339 (US).

Verdict: 'I offer you fear in a handful of dust.' Less startling than 'Kinda', but slightly tighter, more visually successful and arguably better than its predecessor. Fiona Cumming is a better match for the material than Peter Grimwade, handling the metaphorical moments more carefully (the scene where the festivalgoers cheerfully recreate the Mara's coming, unaware that it is about to happen for real, is a treat). Again the guest cast are excellent, especially Martin Clunes, and Janet Fielding gets to play the villain right to the end this time. The denouement is a little weak but against this the story can boast much superb dialogue, a colony with a real sense of history and an intelligent rewriting of *Doctor Who*'s well-worn 'ancient menace reawakens' plot: on balance, a bit of a triumph.

125
Mawdryn Undead

Part One: 1 February 1983
Part Two: 2 February 1983
Part Three: 8 February 1983
Part Four: 9 February 1983

Written by Peter Grimwade
Directed by Peter Moffat

Notable Cast: Angus MacKay (Headmaster) previously appeared in **88**, 'The Deadly Assassin' and was also in *The Pallisers* (1974). Valentine Dyall (Black Guardian) previously appeared in **103**, 'The Armageddon Factor' and also appears in the next two stories. Mark Strickson (Turlough) came to *Doctor Who* from a semiregular role on *Angels* (1982): he played Young Scrooge in *A Christmas Carol* (1984) and later quit acting to produce and direct wildlife documentaries. Lucy Baker (Young Nyssa) changed her name to Lucy Benjamin and went on to play Julie in *Press Gang* (1989, 1992–93) and Lisa in *EastEnders* (2000–03). The brilliant David Collings (Mawdryn) previously appeared in **79**, 'Revenge of the Cybermen' and **90**, 'The Robots of Death'.

Villains: The Black Guardian has decided to kill the Doctor: either he has only just tracked the Doctor down or he has only just got around to doing anything about it. He cannot be seen to take action (why?) and so engages the services of Turlough, a public schoolboy who looks human but is actually an alien trapped on contemporary Earth (beyond this his origins are not made clear). In return for killing the Doctor, the Black Guardian will send Turlough home.

History 101: Many centuries ago, a team of alien scientists stole a metamorphic symbiosis regenerator from the Time Lords, hoping to harness the ability to regenerate. Instead, it induced perpetual mutation without death. The eight scientists were exiled on an opulent spaceship and occasionally one gathers enough strength to leave in search of help. One named Mawdryn transmats to Earth in 1977. Six years later the TARDIS lands on the apparently deserted ship, but the transmat signal is interfering with the TARDIS. The Doctor's attempts to close the signal down result in the TARDIS being deflected to 1977 with Nyssa and Tegan inside.

The Doctor meets Turlough, and an old friend in the form of the retired Brigadier Lethbridge-Stewart: meanwhile in 1977, Nyssa and Tegan encounter Mawdryn – and the retired Brigadier Lethbridge-Stewart ... Nicholas Courtney does a good job of occupying a plot that was designed for Ian Chesterton (which would have been wonderful, but sadly actor William Russell was unavailable). It seems reasonable that Lethbridge-Stewart might work at a public school, but the odd part is that he teaches maths, of all things (history or geography would have been more plausible).

The Plan: Mawdryn draws the Doctor to the spaceship and asks for help: if the Doctor will sacrifice his eight remaining regenerations then they will be able to complete their own cycles and die. Only after the Doctor refuses, do they resort to blackmail via the lives of Nyssa and Tegan and, although they are criminals, the script does not portray them as evil, rather misguided and pitiful (Mawdryn is certainly not without compassion, displaying urgent concern for the Brigadier's safety).

Doctor Who?: It is stated that not only can Time Lords regenerate twelve times (see **88**, 'The Deadly Assassin'), but that the Doctor has used up four of his regenerations (stating that there were no Doctors before William Hartnell – see **84**, 'The Brain of Morbius').

Science/Magic: The Doctor says 'Reverse the polarity of the neutron flow' again. The nonsensical 'short out the time differential' stuff regarding the two Brigadiers meeting is explained by the Blinovitch Limitation Effect (see **60**, 'Day of the Daleks').

Things Fall Apart: The void in which Turlough encounters the Black Guardian looks like a very primitive screensaver. The TARDIS homing device fits suspiciously snugly in the transmat console. The child actors who play the young Tegan and Nyssa are terrible ('Tegan' doesn't even have an Australian accent). It's annoying that the discharge of energy wouldn't have saved the Doctor had it been 'a millisecond either way', as this makes the resolution seem more coincidental than it needs to be.

Availability: Released on VHS in 1992 as BBCV 4547 (UK), WHV E1204 (US).

Verdict: 'What worries me is the level of coincidence in all this.' The first TARDIS scene, with its clumsy clarification of the end of **124**, 'Snakedance' and the Doctor's line 'Warp ellipse cut-out?' depressingly suggest we're in for another 'Time-Flight', but thankfully Grimwade provides a much better script this time. There's still some irritating technobabble but the drama is stronger and it's a pleasingly unusual adventure. Mark Strickson impresses on his debut: as an actor who can give a controlled performance whilst still going over the top he's perfect for *Doctor Who*. Arguably the weight of references to the series' past can be off-putting to the uninitiated, but it was a good idea to give some closure to the Black Guardian thread before it got too old (at this point his previous appearance was only four years ago).

126
Terminus

Part One: 15 February 1983
Part Two: 16 February 1983
Part Three: 22 February 1983
Part Four: 23 February 1983

Written by Steve Gallagher
Directed by Mary Ridge

Notable Cast: Liza Goddard (Kari) memorably played jewel thief Phillippa Vale in *Bergerac* (1983–90) and was one of the stars of *The Brothers* (1973–76). Peter Benson (Bor) impressed as Henry VI in *Henry VI – Parts I–III* and *Richard III* for the BBC's 'Complete Shakespeare' series. He portrayed another King (Henry VII) in *The Black Adder* (1983) and has played Bernie Scripps in *Heartbeat* since 1995. Andrew Burt (Valgard) was the first actor to play Jack Sugden in *Emmerdale Farm* (1972–76) and later starred alongside Peter Davison in *Campion* (1989–90); he made notable guest appearances in *I'm Alan Partridge* (2002) and *The Day Today* (1994). One of the Lazars is played by future TV star Kathy Burke.

Director: Mary Ridge directed six episodes of *Blake's 7* (1980–81), including the series finale, and also worked on *Z Cars* (1971, 1972, 1974). She was an associate producer on *The Duchess of Duke Street* (1977) and instrumental in the setting-up of the Open University.

Doctor Who?: He throws a chair across a room into a moving gap with fearsome precision – it's almost as if he's been practising for such an unlikely occasion. As in **118**, 'Kinda' and **131**, 'The Awakening' the Davison Doctor spends much of the story engaging in a vaguely flirtatious manner with a glamorous woman who looks slightly older than him. He handles himself effectively in a fight with Valgard (who is supposed to be a trained solider) and works out what Terminus is (see **History 101**) with unnerving speed (although given that no one else confirms his diagnosis, he may just be making it all up to give himself a chance to show off in front of Kari).

Other Worlds: The story takes place on board a space ship and space station Terminus, where those afflicted with Lazar's disease are sent to be cured. Terminus is crewed by drug-addicted soldier-slaves and is at the exact centre of the known universe (see **History 101**).

Scary Monsters: The Garm, a biped doglike creature which traverses the radiation-soaked 'forbidden zone' on Terminus on the orders of the Vanir.

Villains: The Black Guardian continues to sneer in voiceover and attempts to convince Turlough to kill the Doctor.

History 101: Terminus used to be a spaceship capable of time travel. Once, while time travelling it was forced to jettison its unstable fuel – and dumped it into a void. The subsequent reaction caused an explosion which propelled Terminus billions of years into the future and created the universe in the process. Kari considers that 'exploding fuel in space' is 'too simple' an explanation for the creation of all life, but the randomness of the event appeals to the Doctor.

Science/Magic: Nyssa experiments with synthesising enzymes; you must have to make your own fun on board the TARDIS. The technology on Terminus uses translucent coloured 'computer blocks' for memory storage. When asked why he's never mentioned the TARDIS emergency failsafe (in the event of break-up it latches onto the nearest spaceship) before the Doctor responds that it's 'never worked before!' Lazar's disease is cured by controlled exposure to radiation.

Things Fall Apart: The Garm isn't terribly convincing. The spacesuits worn by Olvir (Dominic Guard) and Kari are horrible lurid glam spandex concoctions that, additionally, look desperately impractical. The robot that herds the lazars looks like a central heating boiler on tank tracks. Dominic Guard's performance is *awful* – his shrieking at the end of Part One being particularly poor. The cliffhanger to Part Two is an appalling bit of illogical 'random peril' (Valgard tries to kill the Doctor for no readily apparent reason) and those for Parts One and Three are, while more plot relevant, almost equally poor. There are obviously fewer sets than there ought to be.

Availability: Issued on VHS in 1993 as BBCV 4890 (UK), WHV E1258 (US).

Verdict: 'Some people have the strangest ideas about décor.' 'Terminus' is grimmer, more industrial and a noticeably cheaper production than its more stylish season-mates (**124**, 'Snakedance', **127**, 'Enlightenment'), but it also demonstrates a similar level of intelligence and the same willingness to let concepts and characterisation drive it forwards. As in **125**, 'Mawdryn Undead', the subplot with the Black Guardian gives the story licence to not have an obvious antagonist for the Doctor and the plot is resolved through characters compromising. Mark Strickson continues to impress as Turlough and Peter Benson is quite brilliant as the deranged Bor. Interestingly Tegan and Turlough's antagonistic relationship is played with a noticeable element of sexual tension that is never utilised, or referred to, in the series again. A viewer's opinion of 'Terminus' is ultimately likely to depend on whether they can enjoy a *Doctor Who* story that ends with a bloodless revolution and muttered agreements and looks like a cross between an episode of *Blake's 7* and a Duran Duran video.

127
Enlightenment

Part One: 1 March 1983
Part Two: 2 March 1983
Part Three: 8 March 1983
Part Four: 9 March 1983

Written by Barbara Clegg
Directed by Fiona Cumming

Notable Cast: Keith Barron (Striker) played Nigel Barton in Dennis Potter's plays *Stand Up, Nigel Barton* and *Vote, Vote, Vote for Nigel Barton* (both 1965), Kingsley Amis's Jim Dixon in *The Further Adventures of Lucky Jim* (1967), David in the sitcom *Duty Free* (1984) and Alan Boothe in *Where The Heart Is* (2003–present). Lynda Baron (Wrack) is best known as Nurse Gladys Emanuel in *Open All Hours* (1973–85), and has appeared in the films *Yentl* (Barbra Streisand, 1983) and *Colour Me Kubrick* (Brian W Cook, 2004): she also sang the ballad that soundtracks **25**, 'The Gunfighters'. Tony Caunter (Jackson) appeared in **14**, 'The Crusade'. Leee John (Mansell) was lead singer in 1980s pop group Imagination and really does spell his name like that.

Writer: Barbara Clegg is predominantly a writer for radio. She was the first female screenwriter on *Doctor Who* a mere *twenty years* into the programme's run.

History 101: The TARDIS's power is being tapped by the White Guardian (Cyril Luckham), establishing that he does exist after all (see **103**, 'The Armageddon Factor'). He gives the Doctor galactic co-ordinates that lead the TARDIS to an Edwardian sailing ship. The crew don't remember coming aboard, while the officers are distinctly inhuman and capable of reading minds. When they get to the wheelhouse, the Doctor and his friends see that they're not at sea . . .

Other Worlds: . . . they're in space, where a number of historic human ships are sailing in a race around Earth's solar system. The command crews of each ship are Eternals, immortal, mind-reading beings competing in a race to win the mysterious 'Enlightenment'.

Villains: Captain Wrack, an Eternal in league with the Black Guardian. The Black Guardian wants to give Enlightenment to an Eternal, as with it they will invade time, and 'chaos will come again'.

The Plan: Captain Wrack is placing jewels on board the ships of her opponents, then using those jewels to focus the power of the Black Guardian, destroying the ships.

Doctor Who?: The Doctor believes what he's told by the White Guardian, and is willing to risk the TARDIS overloading to get the full message. He doesn't trust Turlough after he ran away on Terminus. The Doctor is angered by the Eternals' treatment of human 'ephemerals'. He considers Eternals to be parasites that prey on the imagination of 'ephemeral' beings.

Science/Magic: Solar winds propel the ships in the race.

Things Fall Apart: A couple of the bluescreen shots when Turlough goes overboard are a little ropy, and Leee John's performance is lispily overwrought. Otherwise, this is as close to a flawless story as *Doctor Who* gets.

Availability: Issued on VHS in 1993 as BBCV 4891 (UK) and WHV E1268 (US).

Verdict: 'This is the sort of excitement that makes eternity bearable.' Delightful in almost every respect, 'Enlightenment' is a rich experience packed with enchanting, offbeat details as well as wit, character and excitement. The ships in space are a wonderful idea and the eerie, all-powerful Eternals a potent threat. The regulars are all excellent, with Mark Strickson getting some of his best scenes as Turlough is tormented by his conscience. The guest cast are mostly superb, with Keith Barron coldly sinister and Lynda Baron deliciously evil. A joy from start to finish.

128
The King's Demons

Part One: 15 March 1983
Part Two: 16 March 1983

Written by Terence Dudley
Directed by Tony Virgo

Notable Cast: Frank Windsor (Lord Ranulf) was one of the leads of *Z Cars* (1962–65) and went on to star in the spin-off *Softly Softly* (1966–77). Isla Blair (Isabella) was Caroline in *When The Boat Comes In* (1981) and appeared in *The Final Cut* (1995), the last of the BBC's Francis Urquhart trilogy. She is married to Julian Glover (see **14**, 'The Crusade') and cameoed alongside him in *Indiana Jones and the Last Crusade* (Steven Spielberg, 1989). Christopher Villiers appeared in *Top Gun* (Tony Scott, 1985). No, really.

Director Profile: Tony Virgo worked his way up through the ranks in television; he later directed episodes of the revived *All Creatures Great and Small* (1990) and became producer of *Dalziel and Pascoe*.

Doctor Who?: The Doctor's despair at Tegan's ignorance of English mediaeval history is funny, if rather unfair. The Doctor's proficiency with a sword is seen again (see **101**, 'The Androids of Tara'). His swordfight with the Master seems to be a deliberate reference to **62**, 'The Sea Devils'. The Doctor is openly contemptuous of the concept of the Devil.

History 101: England, 4 March 1214. At Fitzwilliam Castle (four hours' ride from London), King John (Gerald Flood) is making temporary court. He's demanding monies from Lord Ranulf, in order to prosecute a Crusade in Palestine. It's actually all a plan of the Master's.

Villains: The Master. Again. He calls The Doctor 'my greatest stimulation' and can catch a knife left-handed.

The Plan: The Master is using Kamelion (see **Science/Magic**) to bring King John into disrepute and 'rob the world of Magna Carta'. (The Doctor opines that King John wasn't forced into signing Magna Carta, but 'offered it' and 'was as much for it as any of them'.) This means that 'the foundations of parliamentary democracy will never be laid'. This is part of a larger plan to undermine the key civilisations of the universe.

Science/Magic: Kamelion (also Gerald Flood) is a shape-changing robot that the Master found on Xeraphas (see **122**, 'Time-Flight'). It can replicate anyone's voice, disguise itself as people of varying heights and, er, play the lute quite well (it does this when not disguised as King John, thus this is a skill the machine itself has, suggesting that the robot's alien designers had some odd priorities). It has a mind of its own but can be controlled by a stronger personality.

Things Fall Apart: The Kamelion robot is feeble, physically unimpressive with spindly arms. It can't walk, only stand. Given that the story was written around the technological trinket (which producer Nathan-Turner had seen demonstrated) they might have made sure it *worked* first. Anthony Ainley's French accent isn't unlike that of the French Taunter in *Monty Python and the Quest for the Holy Grail* (Terry Jones, Terry Gilliam, 1974).

Availability: Released as part of a box set with (a re-edited) **129**, 'The Five Doctors' in 1995 as BBCV 5733 (UK), WHV E1113 (US).

Verdict: 'Such perfidy must not go unpunished.' Impressive locations and music don't distract from the general shapelessness. Part One is atmospheric but little happens; after Sir Giles is revealed to be the Master at the episode juncture the plot arrives and then 'develops' in sudden lurches. The story doesn't 'finish', it just *stops* with the regulars dashing into the TARDIS, taking Kamelion with them. The ensuing TARDIS scene then, perversely, goes on for ever. Turlough spends the story in a cell. Gerald Flood's gloriously camp King John is little compensation.

129
The Five Doctors
(90 minutes)

25 November 1983
(US: 23 November 1983)

Written by Terrance Dicks
Directed by Peter Moffatt

Notable Cast: Richard Hurndall (1910–84) who reinterprets William Hartnell's Doctor herein was a respected National Theatre player. Memorable TV appearances include *Blake's 7*: 'Assassin' (1981) and *Steptoe and Son*: 'Any Old Iron' (1970). Called upon to imitate Hartnell without impersonating him, Hurndall triumphs with his thoughtful recreation of the kindlier, more interventionist Doctor of Hartnell's last year in the title role. Philip Latham (Borusa) starred in *The Pallisers* (1974). Dinah Sheridan (Chancellor Flavia) was in *Genevieve* (Henry Cornelius, 1940) and played Wendy on stage opposite Charles Laughton's Captain Hook and Elsa Lanchester's *Peter Pan*. She's unfortunately best known for her role in the dreary BBC sitcom *Don't Wait Up* (1983–90). Carole Ann Ford, Patrick Troughton, Frazer Hines, Nicholas Courtney, Wendy Padbury, Jon Pertwee, Caroline John, Richard Franklin, Elisabeth Sladen and John Leeson all reprise their old *Who* roles.

Doctor Who?: Hurndall's Doctor announces that he is 'the original' in line with **125**, 'Mawdryn Undead' and **65**, 'The Three Doctors' (but see **84**, 'The Brain of Morbius'). At the end of the story the Davison Doctor is asked, 'You mean you're deliberately choosing to go on the run from your own people, in a rackety old TARDIS?' and replies, 'Why not? That's how it all started.' While it's a lovely moment it also cements the late-1970s/early-1980s view of the Doctor as a renegade who fled from the prospect of imposed responsibility, rather than from institutional corruption or in fear for his life (concurring with Dicks's own **50**, 'The War Games' and the exiled Pertwee Doctor: by contrast, the early Tom Baker Doctor frequently speaks of his Time Lord responsibilities).

Susan recognises Gallifrey and the Dark Tower – as one would expect. Her reunion with her grandfather as played by Davison (a man nearly twenty years her junior) is disappointingly skated over, but Dicks's script makes other sharp observations about the differences between the Doctors. The Troughton Doctor considers the Death Zone to be 'my shame, and that of every other Time Lord' and speculates on legends and rumours from Gallifrey's history which portray Rassilon (see **88**, 'The Deadly Assassin') as a bloodthirsty tyrant. Pertwee's Doctor – more of an establishment figure – confidently expresses the 'official history' without pausing for breath. He does, though, resent the Time Lords' habit of sending him on 'missions' without informing him (see **58**, 'Colony in Space', **61**, 'The Curse of Peladon') and initially assumes that this is what is happening to him now.

Rassilon is, oddly, aware of who the Doctor is without being introduced (see **151**, 'Silver Nemesis'), but doesn't recognise Borusa, his distant successor as Time Lord President. The Doctors can all read 'Old High Gallifreyan' and a nursery rhyme recalled by the Troughton Doctor proves to be accurate in its description of the Death Zone. The Hurndall Doctor knows the code for getting in Rassilon's tower and knows Rassilon's voice upon hearing it, but doesn't recognise the regenerated Master (although the Pertwee Doctor does).

Other Worlds: We return to Gallifrey to discover, in the Master's words, 'the black secret at the heart of your Time Lord paradise' – the Death Zone. In the past primitive time-travel technology was used to kidnap creatures from other points in time and space and dump them into this Death Zone, a wasteland surrounded by an impenetrable force-field. These creatures would then fight and die for the amusement of the Time Lords. Official history says that Rassilon put a stop to this practice; rumour has it he was its initiator. After Rassilon's death he was buried in a vast tower at the centre of the Death Zone.

Scary Monsters: Cybermen and a Yeti are found in the Death Zone. There's a single Dalek trapped in a walled labyrinth. A Raston Warrior Robot is one of the story's few self-generated elements – and also one of the most memorable of all *Doctor Who* monsters. A silver, faceless automaton with the power to teleport, it can fire arrows and discs from its hands, has a retractable knife in its fingers and is *really* cool. (The dancers on Kylie Minogue's 2002 *Fever* tour wore costumes based on it.) It massacres a small party of Cybermen in a scene vividly recalled by more than one generation of children to this day.

Villains: Despatched by the Time Lords to rescue the Doctor, the Master is characterised in a continually interesting and amusing manner. Contrary to expectations he takes his mission seriously, making two attempts to contact the Doctor(s) and growing increasingly exasperated when they won't believe his honest intentions (the pardon and new 'regeneration cycle' he's been offered in payment clearly outweighing his desire to kill the Doctor). Anthony Ainley shines, fuming, 'I knew this was going to be difficult: I didn't realise even you would be so stupid as to make it impossible!' When he later attempts to steal Rassilon's gifts for himself, protesting that he's only doing so out of frustration at not being believed, he's actually telling the truth.

The Plan: Having learned that anyone who penetrates the Death Zone and gains access to the Dark Tower will be offered immortality by Rassilon, Borusa uses the Doctors to access the Tower for him – planning to step in at the last moment and claim the prize for himself.

Things Fall Apart: Some (although by no means all) of the direction is rather indifferent. The Troughton Doctor demonstrates knowledge of things that happened minutes before he was 'executed' in **50**, 'The War Games' (did he somehow escape, if only temporarily? Dicks later published a novel in which this is confirmed to be the case). The Time Lords' transmat booth seems to give out capes to those who use it.

Availability: The DVD (BBCDVD 1006) is a re-edited version of the story produced in 1995. It has 'improved' special effects, a few extra minutes of material and remixed sound. The pace of the original disappears in the re-edit and there are some puzzling editing decisions (e.g. the Cybermen now bellow their plans at each other within visible earshot of the Master, which doesn't happen in the transmitted version). The famous 'black triangle' time-scoop, as featured on the *Radio Times* cover (perhaps the story's most recognisable symbol) is replaced with a nasty swirling CGI inverted ice cream cone, robbing the audience of the Doctors' panicked faces inside. Previously released on VHS (as BBCV 5734) this is, despite director Moffatt's public disapproval, the only version currently commercially available (even though the sleeve announces it as 'not intended as a replacement for the original'). The as-broadcast version was released on VHS as BBCV 4387 in 1990. If you can still find it second-hand then that's the release to get. The only available US VHS (WHV E1116) is the re-edit.

Verdict: 'A man is the sum of his memories, you know, a Time Lord even more so.' This is a balanced and beautiful showcase for the series and its many elements, with far too many great moments to count. Everyone involved does an excellent turn; even Hartnell and Tom Baker's cameos (in clips from **10**, 'The Dalek Invasion of Earth' and the unfinished original version of **164**, 'Shada') are somehow perfect, and there's lots of surprisingly clever stuff besides. Dicks shows the Time Lords' dark history in detail while depicting the previously benign Borusa as a deranged despot seeking his own glory above all else. Much of the imagery is taken from Robert Browning's poem 'Childe Rolande to the Dark Tower Came' – making Dicks the only writer to pen not one, but two *Doctor Who* stories based largely on poems (see **92**, 'Horror of Fang Rock').

130
Warriors of the Deep

Part One: 5 January 1984
Part Two: 6 January 1984
Part Three: 12 January 1984
Part Four: 13 January 1984

Written by Johnny Byrne
Directed by Pennant Roberts

Notable Cast: Ian McCulloch (Nilson) played Greg Preston in *Survivors* (1975–77), Peter West in *Zombi 2* (Lucio Fulci, 1979) and Dr Peter Chandler in *Zombi Holocaust* (Marino Girolami, 1980). Ingrid Pitt (Solow) previously appeared in **64**, 'The Time Monster'.

History 101: Turlough has decided not to go home, so the Doctor takes his friends to Earth in 2084, to show Tegan some of her people's future. After a brief run-in with an orbital weapons satellite the TARDIS materialises on Sea Base Four, an underwater military base on alert due to a state of worldwide cold war.

Scary Monsters: The titular creatures from **52**, 'Doctor Who and the Silurians' and **62**, 'The Sea Devils'. The Silurians are led by Icthar (Norman Comer), 'sole survivor of the Silurian Triad', who has met the Doctor before (presumably he's supposed to be the Silurian scientist from 'The Silurians', the last survivor of the three speaking monsters in that story). The Silurians have a more turtle-like appearance than before, with shelled torsos. Their third eyes light up when they speak, and their voices are akin to a vocodered George Formby. The Sea Devils act as the military wing of the Silurians, and wear Samurai-esque armour. A third species of creature is introduced, the bestial Myrka, a horse-sized monster used as a weapon. Silurian technology is still more advanced than humanity's. There are millions more Silurians and Sea Devils still in hibernation.

Villains: Solow and Nilson, psi-surgeons at the Sea Base who are enemy agents.

The Plan: The Silurians intend to use the Sea Base to trigger a World War, allowing the two blocs to wipe each other out – the civilisation of the Silurians and Sea Devils will rise again from long hibernation. Solow and Nilson brainwash the sync-operator to compromise the security of the Sea Base on behalf of the enemy power bloc, while stealing secrets.

Doctor Who?: The Doctor's idea of causing a distraction is setting a nuclear reactor to overload. When trapped in an armed confrontation, the Doctor breaks the deadlock by being first to lower his weapon. The Doctor believes the Silurians are honourable, that 'all they ever wanted to do is live in peace', and that he let them down in their previous encounter. (This is a somewhat eccentric version of events in **52**, 'Doctor Who and the Silurians', where the creatures were aggressive, and the Doctor was the only one championing a peace between them and humans.) He recognises a Silurian battle cruiser or a Myrka when he sees one (although Lord knows how). The Doctor is horrified by the suggestion that the Silurians and Sea Devils should be killed to stop their plan – he believes they are in many ways more advanced than humans. The Doctor manages to 'sync-up' with the computer, which would burn out a human brain. The Doctor had hoped that humans would ban hexachromite gas, and believes there should have been an alternative to the massacre that resolves the crisis.

Science/Magic: The hibernation of the Sea Devils may have caused 'muscular and organic deterioration'. (Maybe their neck muscles deteriorated, hence their wobbly heads.) The Doctor causes the TARDIS to perform a 'materialisation flip-flop'. The weapons technology of Sea Base Four is reliant on a 'sync-up operator' mentally connecting with the missile computer. Hexachromite gas is a sealant compound that's 'lethal to marine and reptile life'. A particle suppresser is a defensive weapon that redirects an energy beam from whence it came. The Doctor uses a blast of strong light to kill the Myrka, which as a creature from the ocean depths is exceptionally photosensitive (although it seems happy enough in the glaring, overlit corridors of the Sea Base).

Things Fall Apart: Several of the cast are downright awful. Peter Davison is visibly wearing the bottom half of a wetsuit in an underwater shot. The Silurian and Sea Devil costumes look fine when lit right and static, but the masks have virtually no movement, and the actors don't seem to be able to walk properly while wearing them. Oh, and the Sea Devils' helmets are ill fitting. Far, far worse is the Myrka, a dreadful green plastic pantomime horse that limply blunders around the sets. In one notably poor scene, Solow tries to engage the lumbering beast in a karate battle.

Availability: Issued on VHS in 1995 as BBCV5668 (UK) and WHVE1380 (US).

Verdict: 'Twice we offered a hand of friendship to these ape-descended primitives, and twice we were treacherously attacked, our people slaughtered.' A steely performance from Peter Davison, whose Doctor gets a more dynamic role than usual, can't save this damp affair from sinking beneath its own ineptitude. The unwelcome return of the 'isolated base under siege' storyline only demonstrates how little mileage that formula has, while a series of inconsistencies and outright mistakes make the story an unsatisfactory sequel to the monsters' previous appearances. There's a competent script in here, but the concept behind it is muddled and the execution is just awful.

131
The Awakening

Part One: 19 January 1984
Part Two: 20 January 1984

Written by Eric Pringle
Directed by Michael Owen Morris

Notable Cast: Polly James (Jane) had been Beryl Hennessey, one of *The Liver Birds* (1969–74). Keith Jayne (Will) was a well-known child actor, the star of the BBC's *Stig of the Dump* (1981). Dennis Lill (Sir George Hutchinson) previously appeared in **94**, 'Image of the Fendahl'. One of the roundheads is *Blue Peter* presenter Christopher Wenner.

Writer: The writer of dozens of original plays and literary adaptations for BBC Radio, Eric Pringle is also the author of the popular 'Big George' series of children's books.

Director: Newly qualified BBC director Michael Owen Morris had been a PA on earlier *Doctor Who* serials. He later directed several episodes of *Tenko* (1984) and the *Tenko: Reunion* special (1985). He continues to work in British TV on such series as *Holby City*, *Wycliffe* and *The Bill*.

History 101: On 13 July 1643 the English Civil War came to Little Hodcombe when a parliamentary force and a regiment for King Charles I slaughtered each other over several days of brutal fighting. In 1984 the inhabitants of the village are commemorating the events with a staged recreation of the battle.

Doctor Who?: The Doctor's black sense of humour resurfaces; he deadpans that the Queen of the May (who is to be burned at the stake) will be 'the toast of Little Hodcombe' and then jokes about Tegan sharing the same fate. He also expresses genuine moral disgust when informed that the villagers are enthusiastically commemorating the events of the English Civil War ('You're celebrating *that*?'). He impetuously rushes into a collapsing building to save the life of someone he's never met. When accused of 'speaking treason' he responds 'Fluently!' Which is *brilliant*.

Scary Monsters: The Malus, a semi-organic machine-beast trapped in the wall of a church. It lives on the energy produced by human pain and misery and is manipulating the civil war games in order to feed itself. The final battle of the games will be for real.

Other Worlds: The Tinclavic mines of Raaga (see **119**, 'The Visitation') are mentioned. The Malus originates from Hakol and was sent to Earth centuries before to prepare the way for a potential invasion.

Villains: Sir George Hutchinson – a local magistrate and businessman driven to madness by being used as the focus of the Malus's need for 'psychic energy'.

Availability: Issued on VHS in 1997 as BBCV 6120 (UK), WHV E1080 (US): both releases are double-packs with **132**, 'Frontios'.

Verdict: 'Think of it as the resurrection of an old tradition!' A production that uses that old *Doctor Who* favourite, the anachronism, to vivid effect, 'The Awakening' has a witty script, terrific location filming and makes efficient use of its brief length. It also has an ebullient, yet sinister guest performance from Denis Lill as the manic Sir George. Despite the obvious influence of ITV's

Sapphire and Steel its cunning blend of English history, black humour, ghost stories and 'real' science fiction is something that could really only be done as a *Doctor Who* story. The exquisite period and pseudo-period sets are by Barry Newbery, who first worked on *Doctor Who* on 1, 'An Unearthly Child'. Near perfect.

132
Frontios

Part One: 26 January 1984
Part Two: 27 January 1984
Part Three: 2 February 1984
Part Four: 3 February 1984

Written by Christopher H Bidmead
Directed by Ron Jones

Notable Cast: Jeff Rawle (Plantagenet) played George Dent in *Drop the Dead Donkey* (1990–98) and the eponymous *Billy Liar* (1967). Lesley Dunlop (Noma) was a regular in *Angels* (1975–76), *May to December* (1990–93) and *Where the Heart Is* (1997–present); she also featured in *The Elephant Man* (David Lynch, 1980). Peter Gilmore (Brazen) starred in *The Onedin Line* (1971–80).

Other Worlds: The TARDIS lands on Frontios, home to one of the last surviving Earth colonies in the very far future (the date is never specified, but it's further into the future than most *Doctor Who* adventures: Earth is either dying or already dead). The colony is struggling and its fey leader Plantagenet is finding it difficult to retain control. There have also been a number of mysterious deaths, which Tegan investigates (Fielding gets some good material here; Tegan even goes to save the Doctor at one point, claiming that he is her responsibility, in a welcome contrast to her usual childish characterisation).

Doctor Who?: The Doctor implies that the Time Lords have placed some kind of moratorium on going too far into the future, and is nervous of reprisals should his actions on Frontios be discovered.

Science/Magic: The equipment brought by the colonists was designed to take care of all their needs once they arrived. It was also designed to be failure-proof: 'It failed,' notes Range.

Scary Monsters: Frontios is also home to the Tractators, large woodlouse-like burrowing creatures, who would be harmless but for the malign influence of . . .

Villains: . . . the Gravis, who can produce gravitational force at will and desires to parasitically plunder other worlds. Turlough identifies the menace, possessing race memories of the Tractators from his own people.

The Plan: The Gravis is creating a network of tunnels around Frontios through which it can channel its gravity fields and pilot the planet through space. (Been done, hasn't it? See **10**, 'The Dalek Invasion of Earth'.)

Things Fall Apart: Once more it's the monsters who let the story down: the Tractators and the Gravis are not a bad design on paper, but the finished costumes look very artificial and move awkwardly. Also, the manner in which Brazen becomes trapped in the excavating machine is contrived.

Availability: Released on VHS in 1997 as BBCV 6120 (UK), WHV E1080 (US) in a double-pack with **131**, 'The Awakening'.

Verdict: 'Oh marvellous, you're going to kill me! What a finely tuned response to the situation.' One of the few *Doctor Who* stories that would have benefited, rather than suffered, from being filmed in a gravel pit. Studio-bound, it's a little stagey but well directed and designed (the colony built out of bits of the ship is effective). As usual, Bidmead bases the story around a strong science-fiction concept rather than an adventure plot and allows it to develop at its own pace. Setting it after the death of Earth increases the scale and stakes whilst still confining the plot to a small group of characters (suggesting that Bidmead had learned from the experience of **115**, 'Logopolis'). Had the Tractators been more effectively realised the story would be near faultless.

With that in mind, why obsess over a slightly poor monster when there's so much else to enjoy? Bidmead's understanding of the series' potential is so keen that you wish he'd stayed on longer as script editor. Not only is the exploded TARDIS resonant (the Ship is the only sacred aspect of the series and Bidmead violates it even more than he did in 'Logopolis'), it provides an imaginative conclusion to the serial. Davison in particular seems enthused by the script, exceeding his own high standards: provided with a confident Doctor he delivers a confident performance.

133
Resurrection of the Daleks
50-minute episodes

Part One: 8 February 1984
Part Two: 15 February 1984

Written by Eric Saward
Directed by Matthew Robinson

Notable Cast: Rodney Bewes (Stien) is a TV legend, having played Mr Rodney in *The Basil Brush Show* (1968–69) and Bob in both *The Likely Lads* (1964–66) and *Whatever Happened to the Likely Lads?* (1973–74). Terry Molloy, taking on the role of Davros for this story and the character's next two appearances, plays Mike Tucker in *The Archers*. Leslie Grantham (Kiston) is one of Britain's best known TV stars as the bullet-proof 'Dirty' Den Watts in *EastEnders* (1985–89, 2003–present). Maurice Colbourne (Lytton) starred in *Gangsters* (1974–75), *The Day of the Triffids* (1981) and as Tom Howard in *Howard's Way*, a role he played from 1985 to his premature death in 1988. Rula Lenska (Styles) played Q in *Rock Follies* (1976) and a memorable villain in *Robin of Sherwood* (1985). Chloe Ashcroft (Laird) was a *Play School* presenter. Del Henney (Colonel Archer) was in *Straw Dogs* (Sam Peckinpah, 1971). This is Janet Fielding's last story as a member of the regular cast, with Tegan staying in London.

Director: Matthew Robinson directed episodes of *EastEnders*, but is now better known as the producer of *Byker Grove* and executive producer of the likes of *Carrie's War* (2004).

History 101: A time corridor brings the TARDIS to contemporary London, where machine-pistol-toting policemen gun down men in futuristic costumes in the streets of Docklands. A bomb disposal team has been dispatched to deal with alien cylinders found in a warehouse. The time corridor links London to a battle cruiser in the future, which the Daleks are piloting to attack a prison station.

Scary Monsters: The Daleks, in their first full appearance since **104**, 'Destiny of the Daleks'. The Movellans from that story created a virus that targeted the Daleks, defeating them. The Daleks are led by the Supreme Dalek, who has white spheres on his (black) skirt.

Villains: Davros, defrosted after a ninety-year cryogenic imprisonment. At some point Davros has become aware of the Time Lords and their status as observers (in **78**, 'Genesis of the Daleks' he didn't even believe in life on other worlds). Lytton is a mercenary working for the Daleks. It's unclear whether or not he is a Dalek duplicate.

The Plan: The Daleks intend to create duplicates of the Doctor and his companions, who will go to Gallifrey and assassinate the High Council. They need Davros to create an antidote to the Movellan virus, but Davros instead works to establish a faction loyal to him. The Daleks kept samples of the Movellan virus safely on contemporary Earth, where they could draw the attention of a bomb squad, which could then be duplicated to guard the cylinders 'without suspicion' (yes, really).

Doctor Who?: The Doctor considers his failure to destroy the Daleks in 'Genesis of the Daleks' a mistake, and intends to kill Davros to stop him from saving them. (Davison beautifully modifies what could have been a standard action-hero speech when facing up to Davros, conveying his Doctor's utter fear of straightforward murder.) Ultimately, the Doctor hesitates when he has a gun to Davros's head, allowing him to escape. He doesn't accept Davros's assertion that war is the natural state of the universe, and refuses Davros's offer to take joint command of a new Dalek race, saying that he 'wouldn't know what to do with an army'. In spite of his misgivings about killing the humanoid Davros, the Doctor has no qualms with killing the Daleks themselves: he throws one out of a window, and unleashes the biological warfare of the Movellan virus against the Daleks at the end of the story, watching them die in pain. He looks uncomfortable when handed a gun, but doesn't hesitate to use it on a Dalek mutant. When the creature is dead, he handles the gun gingerly, as if it's more of a threat to him.

Science/Magic: The Daleks use biological weapons that melt human flesh. Davros has a handheld device that, when applied to the flesh, makes humans and Daleks obedient to him. The Daleks' duplicates retain some of the personality of the original person, making their conditioning unstable. The Dalek Supreme can tune into the TARDIS's scanner to communicate directly with the Doctor.

Things Fall Apart: The juvenile crew of the prison station are less than convincing actors, so it's a good job most of them are quickly killed off.

Availability: Issued VHS in 1993 as BBCV 5143 (UK) and WHV E1261 (US), and on DVD in 2002 as BBCDVD 1100 (Region 2, with a limited edition in a fetishistic black rubber slipcase), WHV E1759 (Region 1).

Verdict: 'You're like a deranged child, all this talk of killing, revenge and destruction.' A gun-happy thriller for the post-*Alien* generation, 'Resurrection of the Daleks' is humourless and violent, but just about works ... no, wait a second, it doesn't work at all. This nonsensical retread of **121**, 'Earthshock' has little going for it beyond stylish direction and the odd impressive action set piece. Neither the time corridor nor duplicate aspects of the plot make much sense, while the individual threads don't actually connect (the Doctor never actually meets Lytton or Styles, major guest characters, and there's no reason for the Daleks to be running their Davros/virus and Doctor/duplicates schemes so close together). While it's well made, 'Resurrection of the Daleks' is little more than seethingly aggressive nonsense. Writer Eric Saward later decried his own scripts for it as the worst-ever written for *Doctor Who*. It's not an entirely unfair comment.

134
Planet of Fire

Part One: 23 February 1984
Part Two: 24 February 1984
Part Three: 1 March 1984
Part Four: 2 March 1984

Written by Peter Grimwade
Directed by Fiona Cumming

Notable Cast: Peter Wyngrade (Timanov) was Jason King in both *Department S* (1969–70) and *Jason King* (1971–72) and played Klytus in *Flash Gordon* (Mike Nicholls, 1980). Nicola Bryant (Peri) had not long since completed drama school; she stayed as a regular until Part Eight of **144**, 'The Trial of a Time Lord'. She later gave a fine comedic performance in *Blackadder's Christmas*

Carol (1987) but has mostly worked in the theatre since leaving *Doctor Who*. This is Mark Strickson's final story as a regular.

Other Worlds: Sarn, a volcanic planet that, long ago, was colonised by people from a planet called Trion. It is seemingly populated by both people from Trion and an indigenous humanoid species. The colony fell into disrepair and forgot its origins; years later the planet was used as a dumping ground for political prisoners, but the ship carrying them crashed and most on board were killed. Turlough is revealed to also be a political prisoner from Trion, exiled to Earth because his family was on the wrong side in a civil war (see **125**, 'Mawdryn Undead'). His infant brother, Malkon, was one of the survivors of the crash on Sarn.

Science/Magic: On Sarn the Trions harnessed the blue Numismaton ('an immensely rare catalytic agent') flames of the volcano and used them to heal the sick. Kamelion's habit of turning into a shiny version of Peri's stepfather is blamed on 'psychomorphic fringing'.

Doctor Who?: The Doctor kills Kamelion after the abused and suicidal machine begs him to. The Doctor allows the Master to burn to death on Sarn, but forces himself to stay and watch the torment of his former friend. It's a powerful scene, and an interesting commentary on their twisted relationship. As the Master dies he cries out, 'Would you show no mercy to your own . . .' It has been suggested that the unspoken final word of the sentence would have been 'brother'.

Things Fall Apart: There are some dodgy American accents. While the location filming (on Lanzarote) is impressive the fact that the island represents both itself and the planet Sarn is very odd: the TARDIS leaves Lanzarote and arrives . . . on a planet which looks a lot like some other bits of Lanzarote. Kamelion still isn't very good (see **128**, 'The King's Demons'). Turlough's line about 'the indigenous population' feels tacked on by someone who doesn't understand the script (the entire story, with the exception of that one line, assumes that all the Sarns are descended from Trions – they even travel there at the end). How did the artefact containing the co-ordinates of Sarn end up at the bottom of the Atlantic, then?

Availability: Issued on VHS in 1998 as BBCV 6567 (UK), WHV E1021 (US).

Verdict: 'The ways of the gods are complex.' Although principally an attack upon religion, 'Planet of Fire' pities, rather than despises, those who believe in a god. It is keen to portray Timanov as a victim, as well as a perpetrator, of theocracy. (His suicide in the flames is very muted – in Grimwade's later novelisation of the serial, the character is allowed to survive.) The serial is merely functional as an adventure story though and the plot only holds together if one excuses some vast coincidences.

Nevertheless, the script has a reasonable amount of drive, there's some good dialogue and Turlough is strongly written. His departure is suitably underplayed and thus considerably more affecting than it might otherwise have been. (He directs his goodbye to Peri, not the Doctor, saying, 'Look after him, won't you? He gets into the most terrible trouble.') It's a glossy production too, with fine performances from Anthony Ainley (particularly as the Kamelion–Master), Peter Davison and Peter Wyngarde and some excellent camerawork. Enjoyable, engaging but entirely unremarkable, 'Planet of Fire' is the kind of essentially average *Doctor Who* serial that the programme was about to suddenly, and disastrously, lose the ability to produce.

135
The Caves of Androzani

Part One: 8 March 1984
Part Two: 9 March 1984
Part Three: 15 March 1984
Part Four: 16 March 1984

Written by Robert Holmes
Directed by Graeme Harper

Notable Cast: Robert Glenister (Salateen) appeared alongside Peter Davison in *Sink or Swim* (1980–82); more recently he has appeared in *A Touch of Frost* and been a regular in *Hustle* (2004–present). Christopher Gable (Sharaz Jek) was an accomplished ballet dancer who had appeared in *The Boy Friend* (Ken Russell, 1971). Maurice Roeves (Stotz) was a regular in *Spender* (1991–93), and *Days of Our Lives* (1986), and appeared in *The Nightmare Man* (1981) and an episode of *Star Trek: The Next Generation* (1993). He plays God in *The Acid House* (1999). John Normington (Morgus) appeared in *My Family and Other Animals*

(1987) and *Longitude* (2000). David Neal (President) appeared in *Superman* (Richard Donner, 1978) and *Flash Gordon* (Michael Hodges, 1980).

Director: Newly qualified director Graeme Harper had directed hospital soap *Angels* having previously worked on *Doctor Who* in junior capacities on stories such as **58**, 'Colony in Space' and **113**, 'Warriors' Gate'; he went on to direct episodes of *EastEnders*, *Juliet Bravo*, *Star Cops*, *The New Statesman* and *The House of Eliott* amongst others.

Other Worlds: The TARDIS lands on Androzani Minor. Its neighbour, Androzani Major, hosts a human colony ruled by the business interests of the founding families, who grew rich from harvesting a weblike substance called spectrox from the caves of Androzani Minor. When processed, spectrox has the capacity to slow down the ageing process. Access to the spectrox nests has been seized by a brilliant but horribly scarred scientist named Sharaz Jek, whose android army continues to harvest the spectrox whilst fighting off the military's attempts to evict him.

The Plan: Jek's ultimate aim is to be conceded legal ownership of the spectrox mines: this will make him more powerful than Morgus, his former business partner who betrayed him.

Villains: Jek keeps his war effort going by exchanging small quantities of spectrox for weapons brought by smugglers from Androzani Major, but does not realise that the gun runners he has been using are middlemen for Morgus. As a result of dealing with Jek, Morgus is the only person on Androzani Major with a supply of spectrox and whilst the war continues the price will remain high. Morgus is controlling the stalemate and profiting handsomely. John Normington's deadpan performance as Morgus is remarkable ('Tut tut. How sad'). His asides to camera should ruin the story, but are in fact some of the best bits: 'The spineless cretins!'

Science/Magic: Shortly after their arrival, the Doctor and Peri come into contact with a spectrox nest. In its raw form spectrox induces a form of toxaemia that kills within hours. The antidote is the milk of a queen bat, a creature that lives in the deepest caves where there is no oxygen.

Doctor Who?: Peri asks why the Doctor wears a stick of celery in his lapel: 'I'm allergic to certain gases in the praxis range of the spectrum. If the gas is present the celery turns purple.' He eventually succumbs to the toxaemia and regenerates, although he isn't sure of this beforehand – 'I might regenerate. I don't know. Feels different this time' – which lends weight to his sacrifice for Peri. It's fitting that this most compassionate of Doctors dies to save just one life. Anything grander would not do his character justice.

Scary Monsters: Why, in this most character driven of stories, does there have to be a lame monster? Sigh ... The dragon that lives in the caves is plastic looking, and could easily have been written out. Thankfully Harper's direction does much to conceal its shortcomings (his work on this serial is consistently excellent, with intelligent variation of lighting and effective use of cross-fades and points-of-view).

Things Fall Apart: Morgus's handheld unit is a TV remote control (it has volume and contrast buttons), whilst Stotz's ship is controlled by the keyboard from a BBC Micro. Jek appears to anticipate that he's about to have a moment of blind rage in Part Two, walking up to a conveniently positioned piece of equipment on a table which he then swipes away.

Availability: Released on DVD in 2001 as BBCDVD 1042 (Region 2), WHV E1608 (Region 1) and on VHS in 1992 as BBCV 4713 (UK), WHV E1183 (US).

Verdict: 'Well, don't keep us in suspense!' Robert Holmes reworks elements from two of his worst scripts (the 'regulars-in-peril' plotting of **49**, 'The Space Pirates' and the double-agent gun runners of **102**, 'The Power of Kroll') and somehow produces his best. The plot is tightly and elegantly structured: the Doctor isn't trying to do anything except find a cure for the toxaemia, yet his presence is the catalyst that causes the stalemate in the Androzani system to rapidly collapse, brutally ending an unnecessary war. The characters are intelligently drawn, engaging yet almost entirely unlikeable: the most sympathetic is Jek, and he's a psychopath. Whilst Holmes writes a rather generic Doctor, Davison is more than capable of filling in the gaps.

Davison is awesome in his final outing as the Doctor – nobody has ever been better in the role than he is in these episodes, reflecting the increasing urgency of the situation with an increasingly intense performance. His defiance of Stotz at the end of Part Three makes something extraordinary out of what could have been a cheesy matinee-serial moment. The actor was so energised by the material that he regretted having decided to leave *Doctor Who*. 'The Caves of Androzani' is wonderful, possibly the single best *Doctor Who* serial in fact, but Davison's exit deserved no less.

136
The Twin Dilemma

Part One: 22 March 1984
Part Two: 23 March 1984
Part Three: 29 March 1984
Part Four: 30 March 1984

Written by Anthony Steven
Directed by Peter Moffatt

Notable Cast: Colin Baker (The Doctor) previously played Maxil in **123**, 'Arc of Infinity'. Kevin McNally (Hugo Lang) played Drake in *Poldark* (1977) and Castor in *I, Claudius* (1976). His films include *The Long Good Friday* (John Mackenzie, 1980), *Cry Freedom* (Richard Attenborough, 1987), *Entrapment* (Jon Amiel, 1999), *Pirates of the Caribbean: The Curse of the Black Pearl* (Gore Verbinski, 2003) and *De-Lovely* (Irwin Winkler, 2004). Maurice Denham (Edgeworth/Azmael) had a long career including BBC radio roles and the films *Oliver Twist* (David Lean, 1948), *Night of the Demon* (Jacques Tourneur, 1957), *Our Man In Havana* (Carol Reed, 1959), *Two Way Stretch* (Robert Day, 1960) and *The Day of the Jackal* (Fred Zinnemann, 1973). Edwin Richfield (Mestor) previously appeared in **62**, 'The Sea Devils'.

Writer: Anthony Steven adapted many classic novels for the BBC spanning *Swallows and Amazons* (1963) to *Fanny by Gaslight* (1981), taking in the likes of *The Count of Monte Cristo* (1964) along the way.

Doctor Who?: The Doctor's regeneration has left him mentally unstable, prone to bouts of depression and manic periods. He engages in melodramatic soliloquies, and his speech is littered with quotes and wordplay. He's arrogant, considering his new self to be an improvement. He doesn't consider his outward appearance important, but thinks his new face is noble and admires his own dress sense (even though he has no taste in clothing, wearing a costume combining bright, clashing colours). In a burst of paranoia he considers Peri an alien spy and tries to strangle her.

In spite of his arrogance, the Doctor seems surprised when his confident predictions actually come true. His realisation that his regeneration might have gone wrong causes him to want to become a hermit and spend time suffering in contemplation. The Doctor makes a big fuss about being an alien, and has different priorities to humans. He's willing to let a man die when he's threatened, but when persuaded he can heal injuries with the TARDIS medical kit. At one point he is cowardly enough to hide behind Peri, asking the Jocondans to kill her and not him. The Doctor is an old friend of Azmael/Edgeworth, former Master of Joconda, who he last met two incarnations before. The death of Azmael seems to stabilise the Doctor's new personality – although he's still arrogant and rude. He doesn't hesitate to kill Mestor when he gets the chance.

Other Worlds: The desolate asteroid of Titan 3, where the Doctor wishes to be a hermit. The planet Joconda, once ruled by the Doctor's old friend Azmael, now taken over by giant gastropods.

Scary Monsters: Mestor, tyrant of the planet Joconda and one of Jocondans' mythical 'giant gastropods', who have returned to devastate the planet. He can cause 'death by embolism' in his subjects. The gastropods leave a sticky trail, and smell of their own gastric juices. The Jocondans have silver skin, a birdlike appearance and small horns on their temples.

The Plan: Mestor is breeding more gastropods to take over the universe. Mestor wants to bring two smaller planets into orbit around Joconda, and organises the kidnapping of mathematical geniuses Romulus and Remus to calculate orbits for the small planets. These planets will have a decaying orbit, and will fall into Joconda's sun. The explosion will cast the gastropod eggs across the universe, where the creatures will hatch and consume everything.

Science/Magic: The Doctor describes regeneration as a 'violent biological eruption'. Mestor intends to use time-travelling tractor-beams to pull outer planets into Joconda's space.

Things Fall Apart: The twin boys playing child geniuses Romulus and Remus are absolutely dire. The whole production looks awful, with clashing colours and grotesque 1980s tat.

Availability: Issued on VHS in 1992 as BBCV 4783 (UK) and WHV E1101 (US).

Verdict: 'Self pity is all I have left.' Garish, tacky, unfunny rubbish, 'The Twin Dilemma' tries to make the Doctor 'alien' again, but only succeeds in making him unsympathetic and annoying. Colin Baker's brash performance isn't bad acting as such, but it *is* incredibly irritating, and the histrionics become rapidly wearisome. The plot is a right load of old nonsense about slugs and supernovas, with the twins prominent and good actors like Maurice Denham and Kevin McNally wasted in the thankless roles of hopeless old duffer and poor man's James Bond respectively. The production is gratingly awful, with a colour scheme and design work that scars the retinas. Glaring, loud and pointless, 'The Twin Dilemma' is painful to the eyes, ears and mind.

137
Attack of the Cybermen
(45-minute episodes)

Part One: 5 January 1985
Part Two: 12 January 1985

Written by Paula Moore
Directed by Matthew Robinson

Notable Cast: Brian Glover (Griffiths) may be best known for his role in *Kes* (Ken Loach, 1969) or that in *An American Werewolf in London* (John Landis, 1981). He starred opposite Peter Davison in two seasons of *Campion* (1989–90). His performance is one of the story's few redeeming points. Maurice Colborne returns to the role of Lytton from **133**, 'Resurrection of the Daleks'. Children's TV presenter Sarah Greene plays one of the Cryons.

Writer: Paula Moore was a pseudonym for Paula Wolsey, a friend of script editor Eric Saward's. Both Saward and series continuity consultant Ian Levine contributed to the storyline and scripts.

Doctor Who?: One feels desperately sorry for Colin Baker, required by the script to continue playing the Doctor as in the throes of regenerative trauma (à la **136**, 'The Twin Dilemma') and to repeat 'buzz' words four or five times in quick succession to express irritation. It still really isn't clear if this is the 'real' him or not – despite the character's protestations. The Doctor repeatedly gets Peri's name wrong. His violent streak hasn't vanished either. He guns down the Cyber Controller (Michael Kilgariff) and a multitude of Cybermen, beats up a fake policeman and seems quite prepared to allow Peri to shoot a real one. Even compared to, say, **85**, 'The Seeds of Doom', this is the Doctor at his most violent and easily enraged.

Other Worlds: Telos (filmed in the same quarry used for **37**, 'The Tomb of the Cybermen'). The Cybermen are in the process of abandoning the planet and are mining the surface of it with explosives. For some reason.

Villains: Lytton inherits Kellman's role (see **79**, 'Revenge of the Cybermen') of pretending to work for the Cybermen while actually leading them into a trap. Lytton demonstrates limited compassion for the oppressed Cryons (the indigenous population of Telos) but is still little more than a well-acted thug. The Doctor's belief that he misjudged him is puzzling – and it's still not clear whether he was really a duplicate or not.

The Plan: Cybermen from the future travel back in time to 1985. They're going to destroy the Earth by crashing Halley's Comet into it – preventing the destruction of Mondas in 1986.

Things Fall Apart: The end of Part One with its feebly unconvincing violence and repeated shouts of 'No!' is like a chopsocky cyber 'Bohemian Rhapsody' – although not a fifth as good as that sounds. The story demands that that the audience has a detailed knowledge of **29**, 'The Tenth Planet' (unreasonable given that no copy of that story's final episode had been known to exist anywhere for over a decade) yet makes numerous mistakes and omissions in referring to it: for example, the Cybermen's plan is to destroy Earth before Mondas returns to the solar system, thus saving Mondas from being destroyed by Earth. But in 'The Tenth Planet' Mondas needs to steal Earth's energy to survive, so destroying Earth before Mondas's return will result in Mondas's destruction. It's worth noting that, as in numerous serials produced immediately before and after it, the Doctor is often only peripherally involved in the action. It's almost as if script editor/writer Eric Saward cannot conceive of a situation where the Doctor's usual approach (thinking first, using limited force as a last resort and usually winning through by application of knowledge or some brilliant piece of improvisation) could actually work to resolve the conflicts of an adventure story. He doesn't seem to believe in the Doctor as a character and thus the Doctor is either sidelined or forced to condone, be complicit in, or even actually *enact* the mass slaughter of his enemies.

Availability: Released as part of a box set with what's left of **29**, 'The Tenth Planet' in the UK (BBCV 7030) and on its own in the US (WHV E1609).

Verdict: 'So much for my first visit to London.' Superficially watchable if one is an undemanding adolescent thrilled by implicit gore and unbothered by multiple dead-end subplots and clunking dialogue, this is incoherent, trashy and overloaded with pointless references to the series' own past. 'Attack of the Cybermen' features a lot of shouting, shooting and scowling but no sense and little wit. Deriving, as it does, virtually all of its plot or visual elements from previous Cybermen stories it's also desperately uninspired, failing to put any kind of spin on its many 'borrowings'. Baker, Colbourne, Glover and Terry Molloy all work very hard to lift the material – but they just don't manage it. A ghastly, awful, dreadful mess and a strong contender for the worst ever *Doctor Who* serial (it's visibly rather expensive and few others have *that* advantage extended to them), this is absolutely dire.

138
Vengeance on Varos
(45-minute episodes)

Part One: 19 January 1985
Part Two: 26 January 1985

Written by Philip Martin
Directed by Ron Jones

Notable Cast: Acclaimed theatrical actor and campaigner Nabil Shaban (Sil) has roles in *City of Joy* (Roland Joffe, 1992) and *Wittgenstein* (Derek Jarman, 1993). Jason Connery (Jondar) is son of the infinitely more famous Sean, and played the second *Robin of Sherwood* (1986). More recently he has had a recurring role in *Smallville* (2001–03). Owen Teale (Maldak) played Conor in *Ballykissangel* (1999) and Wilf in *Island at War* (2004) and is a major RSC player. Martin Jarvis (Governor) previously appeared in **13**, 'The Web Planet' and **71**, 'Invasion of the Dinosaurs'. Stephen Yardley (Arak) previously appeared in **78**, 'Genesis of the Daleks'.

Writer: Philip Martin created and wrote *Gangsters* (1975) and has since written for *Star Cops* (1986) and *Hetty Wainthrope Investigates*.

Doctor Who?: The Doctor becomes melancholy when the TARDIS grinds to a halt, considering Peri lucky that, while he may be trapped in the TARDIS for eternity, she will die soon enough. Although the Doctor doesn't go on the attack, he shows no remorse when others are killed by their own violent actions: he doesn't show much pity when two guards he's fighting with fall into an acid bath, and sets up a trap with lethally poisonous vines which kills the people about to kill him and his friends. He uses a gun as a threat in extreme circumstances, but prevents others from firing them at people.

Other Worlds: Varos, former mining and penal colony. The main trade is Zeiton ore, for which the Gallatron Mining Company pays a meagre price. The population is distracted from poverty by broadcasts of torture, executions and the cellular disintegration that assaults the Governor whenever he loses a public vote. A complex system of rules govern the colony, with the Governor as much a prisoner as the citizens. The Governor is trying to negotiate a better price for the Zeiton.

Scary Monsters: Sil, a reptilian creature from Thoros Beta, on Varos to negotiate with the Governor on behalf of the Galatron Mining Company. Sil has a stubby tail, and is carried around by bearers. Greedy when it comes to both money and food, he takes delight in the 'entertainment' on Varos.

Villains: Varos's Chief Officer, who plots against the elected Governor to maintain a status quo that favours the vested interests of the officer class. Mr Quillum (Nicolas Chagrin), Technical Director, invents the punishments that enforce justice and entertain the people. Quillum wears a mask to disguise the scarring caused by experimenting on himself.

The Plan: Sil and the Chief Officer conspire to keep the Governor and people ignorant of the true value of Zeiton ore. When the Doctor threatens to reveal the truth, Sil calls in an occupation force from the Company, and intends to make himself the new Governor.

Science/Magic: Zeiton-7 is vital for the operation of space–time ships, including the TARDIS (the Doctor needs some to get the 'transitional elements' working again). Quillum has invented a transmogrifying device that turns people into animals, based on their thoughts and feelings (for example, it turns Peri into a bird due to her desire 'to fly away'). The punishment dome contains numerous hallucinatory devices, including ones so strong they can trick human beings into thinking they're dying.

Things Fall Apart: The patrol cars are laughably slow. The rebels give weak performances.

Availability: Issued on DVD in 2001 as BBCDVD 1044 (Region 2) and as WHV E1718 (Region 1), and on VHS in 1993 as BBCV 4783 (UK) and WHV E1101 (US).

Verdict: 'And ... cut!' No story squares the circle of the Colin Baker era as well as 'Vengeance on Varos', which has a plot lurid and extreme enough to fit Baker's garish performance and costume. The subject of screen violence is timely and well handled, and in Sil (superbly played by Nabil Shaban) Baker's Doctor has an equally extreme foil. Martin Jarvis gives a great performance as the tormented Governor, while the main action is counterpointed by cutting away to two Varosian citizens watching the broadcast from the Punishment Dome, a conceit that adds an extra layer of commentary. While by its nature this isn't a story for all tastes, and the direction is disappointingly flat, it nonetheless provides a first suggestion that this new Doctor might actually work out.

139
The Mark of the Rani
(45-minute episodes)

Part One: 2 March 1985
Part Two: 9 March 1985

Written by Pip and Jane Baker
Directed by Sarah Hellings

Notable Cast: Terence Alexander (Lord Ravensworth) played Charlie Hungerford in *Bergerac* (1980–90) and Sir Greville in *The New Statesman* (1991–92). Playwright and actor Gawn Grainger (George Stephenson) played Hitler in *Private Schultz* (1981) and the apostle Andrew in Dennis Potter's *Son of Man* (1969). Kate

O'Mara (The Rani) appeared opposite Colin Baker in *The Brothers* (1973–76), appeared in *Triangle* (1981–83) and went on to fame in *Dynasty* (1986). She's also had a notable theatrical career.

Writers: Husband-and-wife writing team Pip and Jane Baker met while young socialist activists. Their long career of co-written projects includes the movie *The Painted Smile* (Lance Comfort, 1962) and episodes of *The Expert* (1976), *Space: 1999* (1977) and *Watt on Earth* (1991).

Director: Sarah Hellings had been a BBC film editor before becoming the director of the outdoor documentary strand of *Blue Peter*. *Doctor Who* was her first drama work. She continues to direct extensively, and impressively, in TV including *The Casebook of Sherlock Holmes* (1991), *Lovejoy* (1992–94) and *Midsomer Murders* (1997–present).

Doctor Who?: Still portrayed as snappish and liable to sudden bursts of anger, the Doctor is now a more whimsical figure, insatiably curious, physically brave and strongly moral. (He has an 'abhorrence of violence' and refuses the gun that Stephenson offers him.) He's also patronising, preoccupied with his own brilliance, insensitive to the actions and emotions of others and spectacularly socially inept. Colin Baker shines at portraying this revised (or merely better expressed?), and much more interesting, characterisation. The Doctor implicitly believes in the human soul and considers himself 'expressly forbidden' to change the course of history. After talking to him Lord Ravensworth concedes it's 'just possible' he 'might be a gentleman'.

Villains: The Master – there's no explanation for him surviving **134**, 'Planet of Fire' (Eric Saward cut the explanation that Pip and Jane Baker provided). The Rani is another Time Lord and former classmate of the Doctor and the Master. Exiled from Gallifrey she is the absolute ruler of the planet Miasmia Goria. The Master considers himself one of the Rani's biggest admirers. She considers him unbalanced and his plans 'devious and overcomplicated'. The scripts portray the Master as incoherently insane with the Rani mocking him for being an inept villain.

The Plan: The Master claims to have a plan to use the geniuses of the industrial revolution to turn Earth into the base of a space empire he can rule, but he doesn't actually put it into practice, instead spending his time annoying the Doctor. The Rani is extracting chemicals from human brains, intending to use them on her own planet.

History 101: Killingworth, in northeast England, 1813. George Stephenson is organising a conference of the great engineers of the day. Those named as attending include Thomas Telford, Michael Faraday, Humphrey Davy and Mark Brunel.

The Rani has previously experimented on humans during both the Trojan War and the American War of Independence.

Things Fall Apart: The moving tree that rescues Peri is appallingly awful. Some of the northeast accents are a little clichéd. The Rani's landmines are clearly visible on the ground rather than buried, so why do characters need help avoiding them? The plot is too simple to have any holes, but the Doctor and Peri rush off at the end without telling Stephenson that his protégé Luke has been killed. Sir Thomas Henry Liddell wasn't ennobled as Lord Ravensworth until 1821 – although this is the script's only mistake with historical detail.

Availability: Issued on VHS in 1995 as BBCV 5603 (UK), WHV E1350 (US).

Verdict: 'Your invention will take off like a rocket!' Visually impressive and enjoyably (if floridly) acted, 'The Mark of the Rani' is engaging, funny and very watchable despite some spectacularly ostentatious dialogue. Sarah Hellings's superb camerawork, especially the enormous amount of filming carried out at the Ironbridge Gorge museum, helps create a genuine sense of time and place all too rare in colour *Doctor Who*. The serial seems like a throwback to the Hartnell era in other ways too, with educational nuggets thrown into the script and a very leisurely pace. 'The Mark of the Rani' is much better television than any of the stories around it, far more balanced and coherent and, while it doesn't match the dramatic highs of **142**, 'Revelation of the Daleks', it scores over it in numerous ways, including that it presents the Doctor and Peri as the central characters. Gawn Grainger and Terence Alexander provide admirable, enthusiastic support.

140
The Two Doctors
(45-minute episodes)

Part One: 16 February 1985
Part Two: 23 February 1985
Part Three: 2 March 1985

Written by Robert Holmes
Directed by Peter Moffatt

Notable Cast: Patrick Troughton reprises his Doctor and Frazer Hines returns as Jamie McCrimmon. Jacqueline Pearce (Chessene) appeared as arch-villain Servalan throughout *Blake's 7* (1978–81). James Saxon (Oscar) starred in *Brass* (1983–86) and is known to a generation of children as D'arcy D'Farcy in *Roland Rat*.

Science/Magic: The Troughton Doctor and Jamie land on the scientific research space station Chimera to investigate illegal time travel experiments on behalf of the Time Lords (reflecting Robert Holmes's theory that the trial in **50**, 'The War Games' was a sham and the Doctor had been covertly working for the Time Lords all along: quite what led Holmes to this conclusion is a mystery). The Colin Baker Doctor and Peri arrive shortly afterwards and find the station apparently deserted.

Villains: Dastari (Laurence Payne), who looks more like an executive at a corporate record label than Head of Projects at a scientific research station; Chessene, an Androgum whom Dastari has genetically augmented into a genius; and Shockeye (John Stratton), another Androgum who seems to be tagging along purely to sample Earth cuisine.

Scary Monsters: The Sontarans, making their first appearance for seven years, oddly looking not as good as they used to. They also don't *do* anything except stroll around the house making pointless demands, as though it's Christmas and the Androgums' rude, irritating relatives have invited themselves over.

The Plan: The villains have created a time machine but cannot operate it safely without the symbiotic nuclei inherent in the genetic make-up of a Time Lord. They kidnap the Troughton Doctor and take him to contemporary Spain, planning to copy his nuclei and implant it into themselves. Chessene changes her mind halfway through and tries to change the Doctor into an Androgum instead.

Doctor Who?: The tension between the Colin Doctor and Peri has reached the point where you wonder why she doesn't just get off and go home: as Jamie says, 'I think your Doctor's worse than mine.' Troughton and Hines slip into their old personas remarkably well: their chemistry is still evident but unfortunately they are separated for most of the story and there isn't much interaction between the two Doctors either, which is a swizz.

Things Fall Apart: John Stratton's good performance is undermined by his horrible costume – a sort of psychedelic Highlander look. Whilst the Spanish location filming is impressive, the studio sequences match poorly (mainly due to overlighting and a lack of ambient sound).

Availability: Released on DVD as BBCDVD 1213 (Region 2), WHV E1277 (Region 1) in 2003: amongst the extras is the *Jim'll Fix It* sketch 'In a Fix With Sontarans' (with Colin Baker as the Doctor and Janet Fielding as Tegan). Also released on VHS in 1993 as BBCV 5148 (UK), WHV E1277 (US).

Verdict: 'You could augment an earwig to the point where it understood nuclear physics . . . but it'd still be a very stupid thing to do!' 'The Two Doctors' begins well, following the Troughton Doctor and Jamie for ten minutes or so and then flipping to the Colin Baker Doctor . . . but then Troughton vanishes for the best part of an hour, and it's not like Colin Baker's doing anything especially interesting. A farcical plot in which the two Doctors spent much of the story unaware of each other's presence could have been great, and you'd think Robert Holmes would be ideal to write it, yet Troughton is largely wasted in what turned out to be his final appearance in *Doctor Who*.

The presence of the Sontarans and the story length were both forced upon Holmes: he was happy with neither, and it shows. A proper role for the Sontarans might have helped fill the screen time but instead everybody spends the first two parts taking ages to do not much. Part Three is better, featuring the best of the Spanish location work and an amusing performance from Troughton, but it's marred by vicious touches such as the Doctor killing Shockeye with cyanide (compounded by a quip that even Austin Powers would find weak and tasteless) and Peter Moffatt's direction is uninspired. It's not without merit by any means, but 'The Two Doctors' makes the viewer work a little too hard to dig out the nuggets of quality.

141
Timelash
(45-minute episodes)

Part One: 9 March 1985
Part Two: 16 March 1985

Written by Glen McCoy
Directed by Pennant Roberts

Notable Cast: The minor parts of Aram and Gazak, who feature briefly in Part One, are both played by young actors who later came to greater prominence – Christine Kavanagh (Aram) starred in Steven Gallagher's *Chimera* (1991) and played Christine in *Manchild* (2002), while Steven Mackintosh (Gazak) appeared in *Prick Up Your Ears* (Stephen Frears, 1987), *Memphis Belle* (Michael Caton-Jones, 1990), *The Muppet Christmas Carol* (Brian Henson, 1992), *The Buddha of Suburbia* (1993), *Twelfth Night* (Trevor Nunn, 1996), and *Lock, Stock and Two Smoking Barrels* (Guy Ritchie, 1998). Paul Darrow (Tekker) previously appeared in **52**, 'Doctor Who and the Silurians', whilst Dennis Carey (Old Man) was in **114**, 'The Keeper of Traken'. Jean Anne Crowley (Vena) was a principal in *Tenko* (1981–85).

Writer: Glen McCoy has written for the soaps *Emmerdale Farm*, *EastEnders* and *Eldorado*.

History 101: The TARDIS runs into a time tunnel leading to Earth in 1179. When the TARDIS is trapped in the time corridor, it crosses paths with a young woman falling through the corridor. She is knocked off course, emerging in 1885 near Loch Ness.

Other Worlds: Karfel, ruled by the secretive Borad (Robert Ashby), a distinguished old man who only ever appears on screens, never in public. The people are closely monitored and mirrors are banned. Rebels are thrown into the timelash, while there is danger of a war with Karfel's former allies, the Bandrils.

Scary Monsters: The Borad enforces his rule using tall, blue, squeaky-voiced androids. The Morlox are savage, long-necked creatures that live in the caves outside the citadel.

Villains: The Borad is part man, part Morlox due to an accident during an experiment, which has granted him long life and great intelligence. He uses an android as his public face. The elected leader, controlled by the Borad, is the Maylin. The sadistic Tekker is appointed to the post, and relishes the chance to increase his own power.

The Plan: When the lady Vena (JeanAnne Crowley) jumps into the timelash holding the amulet which controls the Borad's power system, Tekker plans to hold Peri hostage, to persuade the Doctor to retrieve the amulet. The Borad is happy for the Bandrils to attack as their missiles will kill everything except the Morlox and the Borad. He intends to merge Peri with a Morlox and together they will then breed more mutants like himself to populate the planet.

Doctor Who?: The Doctor's primary characteristic is raising his voice at the slightest provocation. He has been to Karfel before in his Pertwee incarnation and considers himself to have changed 'immeasurably for the better' since then. The Doctor is concerned not just for Peri's safety, but for the wellbeing of all on Karfel. The Doctor's description of the constellation of Andromeda is the same as his description of the Eye of Orion. He uses his status as President of the Time Lords as leverage while negotiating with the Bandrils. He says that if he broke a law of time, other Time Lords would know – and they are not all as pleasant as him. The Doctor happily pitches the Borad into the timelash.

Science/Magic: A 'kontron tunnel' is more commonly known as a time corridor. Contact with one may cause the TARDIS to 'undergo an adverse contron effect', with 'time particles colliding within a multi-dimensional implosion field'. The TARDIS has seatbelts for emergencies. There are purple plants on Karfel that squirt acid into the face if you get too close. A bendylapse warhead destroys 'anything with a central nervous system'. Contron crystals have various time properties, including creating brief timeslips. Mustakosian 80 can cause 'spontaneous tissue amalgamation', such as the merging of a Karfellan and a Morlox to create the Borad. The Borad has a 'time acceleration beam' which can age a man to death in seconds. The Doctor uses the TARDIS to deflect the Bandril missile heading for Karfel.

Things Fall Apart: The Bandril Ambassador is a glove puppet. The inside of the timelash is lined with tinsel. No one notices the Borad when they enter his chamber, even when he's directly in their line of sight. Paul Darrow gives one of the most (intentionally) ludicrous performances in the history of recorded drama. The dialogue is consistently atrocious and the scripts are ineptly structured, with masses of padding in Part Two and a sudden dogleg when, with ten minutes to go, the story runs out of plot.

Availability: Issued on VHS in 1998 as BBCV 6329 (UK) and WHV E1274 (US).

Verdict: 'I didn't realise dying heroically was such a strain on the nerves.' Atrocious amateurish gibberish, 'Timelash' is incompetent, grindingly unfunny and almost totally incoherent. The plot throws in everything – time corridors, mutation, an oppressive society, the Victorian era – to a bewildering lack of effect. The characterisation is painful, the 'humour' worse. There's a couple of good ideas, but they're buried under poor performances, feeble dialogue and a production where the director completely fails to maintain any kind of drama to proceedings. Rubbish.

142
Revelation of the Daleks
(45-minute episodes)

Part One: 23 March 1985
Part Two: 30 March 1985

Written by Eric Saward
Directed by Graeme Harper

Notable Cast: Despite a great theatrical career Clive Swift (Jobel) is best known to television viewers as Richard in *Keeping Up Appearances* (1990–95). Jenny Tomasin (Tasenbeker) was Ruby in *Upstairs, Downstairs* (1971–75). Alexei Sayle (DJ) was one-fifth of the regular cast of *The Young Ones* (1982–84) but is these days better known as a writer and columnist. Eleanor Bron (Kara) rose to prominence in the 1960s 'satire boom' and can be seen in the Beatles' *Help!* (Richard Lester, 1965) and very briefly in **105**, 'City of Death'. William Gaunt (Orcini) starred in *The Champions* (1968) and the sitcom *No Place Like Home* (1983–88).

Doctor Who?: He claims to be nine hundred years old and demonstrates a cruel sense of humour (mocking Peri's weight, suggesting that she's in danger when she isn't for cheap laughs and later making puns about Davros's hand being shot off). He considers 'being extremely stupid' to be 'the prerogative of a Time Lord'.

Other Worlds: Necros, the site of 'Tranquil Repose', a funeral parlour and cryogenic suspension facility which is run by an shadowy figure known as 'The Great Healer' . . .

Villains: . . . who is actually Davros (Terry Molloy). It isn't explained how he survived **133**, 'Resurrection of the Daleks'. He takes the time to manipulate and humiliate Tasembeker (Jenny Tomasin) and exploit the rivalries and jealousies of his employees, seemingly entirely for his own amusement. He can fire electric bolts from his hand. Davros's business partner Kara is almost equally ruthless, avaricious and ambitious.

Scary Monsters: The Daleks are sidelined in the story, acting simply as Davros's muscle. They look splendid in their new gold-on-white livery, but their voices are squawky and unimpressive and they are shown to be vulnerable to mere bullets on more than one occasion.

The Plan: Davros is making money from selling food made from recycled human corpses; he's also using the bodies and brains of those entrusted to Tranquil Repose to create a new race of Daleks which are loyal to him. He has tempted the Doctor to Necros so that he can be humiliated and killed. Kara hires Orcini, an excommunicated renegade from a religious order of Knights, to assassinate Davros as she wants to take control of his operations. Davros also seems to have some kind of plan involving 'President Vargas' (what he's President of isn't made clear) who is about to visit, although the audience isn't told what this is.

Science/Magic: Herbibaculum vitae ('staff of life') is a common wild plant on Necros. It has a similar protein value to the soya bean plant. Davros has perfected a process whereby human beings can be turned into the organic component of a Dalek. The DJ builds a machine that fires a 'highly directional, ultrasonic beam of rock and roll' which can kill Daleks.

Availability: Released in a box set with **68**, 'Planet of the Daleks' (BBCV 6875) in the UK and as a single tape (WHV E1527) in the US.

Verdict: 'You're becoming morbid.' A slow-paced, superbly directed story with lots of good performances and some really disturbing moments, 'Revelation of the Daleks' seems like a determined attempt to make *Doctor Who* as brutal and cynical as it can possibly get away with at 5:20pm on BBC1. Indeed, there's a lot of material in here that just isn't appropriate for that time slot at all (one of the characters is an alcoholic, there's an incredible number of on-screen deaths, a subplot involving unrequited sexual obsession and a joke about incest, amongst other things). Equally, there are no sympathetic characters (even Takis – played by the excellent Trevor Cooper – who is left in charge at the end, seems to torture people for kicks on the quiet) and the Doctor, Peri and the Daleks are barely involved in the story's main action, the focus being mostly on Orcini, Jobel and Davros. Again, the Doctor plays no real part in the plot's resolution.

These are Eric Saward's best scripts but they contain numerous detours, dead ends and one-scene subplots and the multiple story strands blur the difference between plot, subplot and counterplot to the point of non-existence. They also rely on cheap gags and sudden shocks to maintain audience attention. The irony of the Daleks sweeping in and saving the day is ridiculously underexploited and it all ends with an explosion engineered by someone other than the Doctor. A thrilling grotesque then, but one which only works as well as it does because it's such a peculiar one-off.

143
Slipback
BBC RADIO 4, 10-minute episodes

Episode One: 25 July 1985
Episode Two: 25 July 1985
Episode Three: 1 August 1985
Episode Four: 1 August 1985
Episode Five: 8 August 1985
The Final Episode: 8 August 1985

Written by Eric Saward
Produced by Paul Spencer

Notable Cast: Jon Glover (Grant) has appeared in numerous comedies: he played Mr Cholmondley-Warner in various Harry Enfield sketch shows (1990–94). 'Slipback' was the final acting work of the great Valentine Dyall (Slarn), who first appeared in *Doctor Who* in **103**, 'The Armageddon Factor'. Ron Pember (Seedle) was one of the stars of *Secret Army* (1977–79) playing Alain.

Producer: Paul Spencer was effectively director/producer of 'Slipback'. His credits include the topical radio comedy *Week Ending*.

Doctor Who?: Colin Baker's expansive performance as the Doctor, sometimes variable on TV, seems right at home on radio. Unusually, the story opens with the Doctor waking up after a heavy evening's boozing. The TARDIS then lands on board the space freighter *Vipod Mor*. Peri claims that the Doctor has always insisted that she wouldn't be able to pronounce his 'real name' and is convinced that he never lies.

Villains: In amongst the nefarious plottings of those on the *Vipod Mor*, the Computer has developed a sentient split personality and become dismayed with the violent universe.

The Plan: The Computer plans to travel back to the Big Bang and supervise the development of life according to a more peaceful design. For this it needs to develop time travel, and so it draws the Doctor to the *Vipod Mor*. It also strives to create chaos on board the ship in the hope of antagonising the Captain, who psycho-somatically produces diseases to match his mood: if he becomes angry enough he will wipe out the entire crew.

Scary Monsters: A Maston, native of Sentimenous Virgo, placed on the ship by the Computer (and, indeed, Eric Saward) as a diversion.

Availability: Released on CD in 2001 as ISBN 0563477946.

Verdict: 'Don't blame me, I'm just a machine.' Commissioned as a stopgap for the lengthy gap between **142**, 'Revelation of the Daleks' and **144**, 'The Trial of a Time Lord', 'Slipback' aired as part of a teenage daytime strand, *Pirate Radio 4*, during the 1985 summer holidays. The strand failed miserably and the idea of radio *Doctor Who* lay abandoned for several years.

None of this should be taken as a reflection on 'Slipback' itself, which is better than most of Colin Baker's televised *Doctor Who* stories. Called upon to write sci-fi radio, Eric Saward abandons the bleak macho style of his recent *Who* scripts in favour of Douglas Adams pastiche with a dose of wry pessimism, and does a very good job. Pointless brutality is replaced with black humour; continuity references are replaced with big ideas; angry shouting is replaced with actual dialogue. His script is well treated by a fine guest cast (Alan Thompson's brief performance as the Steward is especially praiseworthy).

It must be said that the serial does lack heroics, as the other Time Lord's abrupt intervention in the final episode reduces the

Doctor's role to that of a bystander. Also, the – typically Sawardian – low level of proactive involvement from the Doctor and Peri means that the plot does not follow through the six episodes particularly strongly: instead, characters with disparate aims wander around getting in each other's way. However, given that many listeners would tune in casually and not hear all six episodes it's more important that the instalments are amusing and intriguing in ten-minute bursts. Which they are, so fair enough.

144
The Trial of a Time Lord

Part One: 6 September 1986
Part Two: 13 September 1986
Part Three: 20 September 1986
Part Four: 27 September 1986

Written by Robert Holmes
Directed by Nicholas Mallett

Note: Although transmitted as one fourteen-part story 'The Trial of a Time Lord' was made as three distinct productions and constitutes four separate, but linked, plotlines.

Notable Cast: Michael Jayston (The Valeyard) and Lynda Bellingham (The Inquisitor) appear in every *Doctor Who* episode of 1986 and should really be considered regulars. Now best known for playing the mother in the 'Oxo family' commercials, Bellingham went on from playing Helen Herriot in *All Creatures Great and Small* (1988–90) to the lead of ITV sitcoms *Second Thoughts* (1991–4) and *Faith in the Future* (1995–8) and played Pauline in *At Home with the Braithwaites* (2000–3) opposite Peter Davison. Jayston had worked extensively at the National Theatre before playing Tsar Nicholas II in *Nicholas and Alexandra* (Franklin J Schaffner, 1971). His TV roles include Peter Guillam in *Tinker, Tailor, Soldier, Spy* (1980), *The Casebook of Sherlock Holmes* (1991) and a pseudo-Doctor Who figure called 'Colonel X' in *Press Gang*: 'UnXpected' (1992). Joan Sims (Katryca) was best known for numerous *Carry On* films, perhaps most notably *Carry On Regardless* (Gerald Thomas, Peter Thomas, 1961) and *Carry On Henry* (Gerald Thomas, 1968). Tom Chadbon (Merdeen) previously appeared in **105**, 'City of Death'. Tony Selby (Glitz) was a star of sitcom *Get Some In!* as the brutal Corporal Marsh.

Director: Nicholas Mallet worked on *The Bill* (1990) and *Children's Ward* (1989) as well as *Doctor Who*. He died in 1997.

Doctor Who?: The Doctor has been deposed as Time Lord President for 'wilfully neglecting' the responsibilities of his great office. Arriving alone on a huge space station, he is to be tried by his own people for being 'an incorrigible meddler in the affairs of other people and planets'. The prosecuting counsel, the Valeyard, presents evidence from 'epistopic interfaces of the system' to the court. In practice, this means that events from the Doctor's recent history are seen on a screen; the overall effect is that the court seems to be watching *Doctor Who* videos. In both the court and 'evidence' scenes the Doctor is written as a warmer, more indulgent figure with an affectionate, less acerbic relationship with Peri and a distrust of violent means. He seems more like the character from **139**, 'The Mark of the Rani' than any other earlier Colin Baker story. He's appalled by Drathro's hubris and lack of compassion and even improvises his way into solving the problems of the plot himself.

Other Worlds: In the first portion of the Valeyard's evidence the Doctor and Peri arrive on Ravolox, within the Stellian Galaxy. It has the same mass, angle of tilt and period of rotation as the Earth. A post-apocalyptic world of lush forests and strictly primitive life, it also has an underground rail network ... with stations such as 'Marble Arch' ... where the London Underground logo can be found decorating the floor. Can you guess what it is yet?

Scary Monsters: No monsters, but two robots: Drathro, a sentient L3 and its associate tracking robot the L1. Drathro maintains an underground civilisation of five hundred human slaves and has a mission to guard the mysterious 'three sleepers' and their secrets until they are rescued by a relief ship from Andromeda. This was meant to happen centuries ago and the sleepers have since died. Drathro continues to wait.

Villains: Katryca is the Bouddica-like Queen of the Tribe of the Free, humans who live above ground and oppose Drathro and his slave humans.

The Plan: In the court, the Valeyard wants the Doctor found guilty and executed. Within the evidence, conmen Glitz and Dibber (Glen Murphy) intend to steal the Sleepers' secrets by destroying Drathro's energy supply, disabling it.

Science/Magic: 'Black light' is a form of channelled ultraviolet which can be used to power robots. The Matrix is now 'fed by the experiences of all Time Lords wherever they may be' (see **88**, 'The Deadly Assassin'). Siligtone is the hardest, and most expensive, metal in the galaxy.

Things Fall Apart: The scripts are sound – with the Doctor well characterised – but while the production is reasonably efficient, it's also inappropriate. The 'evidence' on Ravolox is overlit, flat and not terribly involving. Joan Sims is seriously miscast and most of the minor performances are rather languid, with much good dialogue being delivered in ways which rob it of its potential poignancy and/or wit. The sets for the underground labyrinth are too few and too small and the courtroom sequences quickly become very repetitive. The Part Three cliffhanger is one of those contrived no-I-wasn't-shooting-at-you-but-the-bloke-*behind*-you moments.

Part Five: 4 October 1986
Part Six: 11 October 1986
Part Seven: 18 October 1986
Part Eight: 25 October 1986

Written by Philip Martin
Directed by Ron Jones

Notable Cast: Brian Blessed (King Ycranos) played PC 'Fancy' Smith in *Z Cars* (1963–65), St Peter in Dennis Potter's *Son of Man* (1969), Augustus in *I, Claudius* (1976) and Richard IV in *The Black Adder* (1983). His films include *Flash Gordon* (Mike Hodges, 1980), *Henry V* (Kenneth Branagh, 1989), *Hamlet* (Kenneth Branagh, 1997) and *Star Wars: Episode I – The Phantom Menace* (George Lucas, 1999). He is an associate artiste of the Royal Shakespeare Company. Christopher Ryan (Kiv) was Mike in *The Young Ones* (1982–84) and Dave Hedgehog in *Bottom* (1991–95). Nabil Shaban reprises the role of Sil from **138**, 'Vengeance on Varos'.

The Plan: The Valeyard's second piece of evidence shows the Doctor aiding and abetting the thought-transfer and brain transplant experiments being carried out by Crozier (Patrick Ryecart), an associate of his one-time adversary Sil, on the planet Thoros Beta in 2379.

Other Worlds: Thoros Beta – Sil's home planet: a marshy, partially waterlogged world with a pink sea and azure sky. Its twin planet, Thoros Alpha is populated by humanoids who are oppressed by Sil's race, the Mentors. The 'sondlex crop' of the planet Wilson One is mentioned. Yrcanos comes from Thordon and is King of the Krontep Empire.

Scary Monsters: Sil returns and, thanks to an altered costume, stakes his claim to being the best-designed *Doctor Who* monster of all. Rather less well designed is the Raak, a large gallumphing beast which is fortunately never fully in shot – sparing the audience a **130**, 'Warriors of the Deep'-style debacle. Sil and Kiv negotiate with a Terileptil (see **119**, 'The Visitation') representative who is from the planet Posicar.

Doctor Who?: Being exposed to Crozier's brain alteration machine, er, alters the Doctor's brain, making him – briefly – rambling and incoherent. The evidence shown by the Matrix seems to portray the Doctor as sadistic, foolish and motivated to help Crozier and Sil out of a combination of macabre scientific curiosity and a desire for self-preservation above all else. Before this he continues to show his increasing compassion and personal recklessness, impulsively dismantling some of Crozier's equipment which he considers to be immoral.

Things Fall Apart: There's a profoundly irritating subplot about finding some rebels – who are all then promptly disposed of – in Part Seven (Philip Martin swears he had nothing to do with this). Gordon Warnecke (Tuza) gives a dreary performance, sounding bored throughout, odd, given how good he is in *My Beautiful Laundrette* (Stephen Frears, 1985). The ending of Part Eight requires the Inquisitor to go from being entirely ignorant of matters of Thoros Beta to narrating, chapter and verse, Peri's fate and the reasons for it, within seconds.

Claims of general incoherence, however, are invalid: it's actually very obvious which scenes have been 'altered' by the Valeyard to make the Doctor's actions seem worse. His brief conversation with Sil ('Now I'm just like you') and the circumstances of his capture by the Mentors in Part Two contradict what happens immediately before (where the Doctor is incoherent) and afterwards (where Sil is suspicious of the Doctor, having just accepted him in the forged sequence) and must be an invention for those reasons. Additionally, the scene on the Rock of Sorrows is the other clear creation of the Valeyard. In it the Doctor is terrified that Kiv's brain will be transplanted into his body – a plot strand which is otherwise only mentioned by the Valeyard in testimony. (When Peri saves the Doctor's life after this it is surely because he has explained his plan to her and asked her to start an insurrection with Yrcanos?) These are also the only two scenes which the Doctor, from the courtroom, specifically denies happened as they have been shown on the screen. Also, given that the Matrix's information comes from the TARDIS everything that takes place after the Doctor leaves Thoros Beta *must* also be fabrication.

Part Nine: 1 November 1986
Part Ten: 8 November 1986
Part Eleven: 15 November 1986
Part Twelve: 22 November 1986

Written by Pip and Jane Baker
Directed by Chris Clough

Notable Cast: Honor Blackman (Professor Lasky) was Cathy Gale in *The Avengers* (1962–64) and Pussy Galore in *Goldfinger* (Guy Hamilton, 1964), played Laura in sitcom *The Upper Hand* (1990–96) and has achieved the impossible by remaining a sex symbol into her seventh decade. Malcolm Tierney (Doland) played Patrick Woolton in *House of Cards* (1990), Charlie Gimlet in *Lovejoy* (1986–94), and DCI Raymond in *Dalziel and Pascoe* (1999) as well as having a distinguished theatrical career. New regular Bonnie Langford (Melanie) had been a child actor and as an adult became a singing, dancing light entertainment personality. Michael Craig (Travers) starred in *Triangle* (1981–83) and played the Earl of Huntingdon in *Robin of Sherwood*.

Director: Chris Clough directed episodes of *The Bill* (1984) and *Brookside* (1985) before becoming producer of the former. He is currently the producer of *Born and Bred* (2002–present).

Doctor Who?: He knows the 'highly organised' human society of the thirtieth century well and has some knowledge of thrematology, argronomy and cytogenesis. He (understandably) dislikes carrot juice and has already met both Commodore Travers and

Investigator Hallett (Tony Scoggo). He describes himself as 'a sort of clown' (in the Shakespearean sense, one presumes).

Other Worlds: Mogar, in the Perseus arm of the Milky Way, rich in rare metals like Vionesium: it, and its indigenous population, have long been exploited by human beings.

Villains: This is an Agatha Christie pastiche, so virtually every character has a nasty secret and commits some questionable deed. The real villain of the piece is scientist Doland.

Science/Magic: Vionesium is very similar to magnesium and releases bursts of light and carbon dioxide when exposed to oxygen. Marsh gas is 'a methane derivative'. Carrots are full of Vitamin A, kids, so eat up.

Scary Monsters: The Vervoids are genetically engineered, biped, sentient plants grown in pods by Lasky, Doland and Bruchner (David Allister). Vervoids have venomous stings in their right arms. Their chloroplasts 'function normally' according to the Professor; which is nice to know.

The Plan: Doland plans to use the Vervoids as a race of slaves. Rudge (Denys Hawthorne) is collaborating with two Mogarians to hijack the ship and the Vervoids just want to slaughter everybody.

Things Fall Apart: You can see drawstrings hanging off of the Vervoid actors' trousers at some points. The key for cabin 9 lets Lasky into cabin 6. Thirtieth century technology uses plastic audiocassettes. As with **138**, 'The Mark of the Rani' there's some dialogue which is preposterously overblown even by *Doctor Who* standards. It's difficult to see what Rudge's original plan was, as he and the Mogarians can't have been counting on Bruchner going mad and trying to fly the ship into a black hole, surely? The Time Lord legal system must be pretty wacky if the Doctor can be executed for a crime which he commits on a screen in a hypothetical future. (The whole Time Lord legal system in the story is nonsense anyway, a sort of structureless parody of elements of English law as expressed through courtroom drama rather than as in reality.)

Part Thirteen: 29 November 1986
Part Fourteen: 6 December 1986 (30 minutes)

Written by Robert Holmes (13), Pip and Jane Baker (14)

Notable Cast: Geoffrey Hughes (Mr Popplewick) was best known as Eddie Yeats in *Coronation Street* (1974–83) and went on to play Onslow in *Keeping Up Appearances* (1990–96). He has played Vernon Schipps in *Heartbeat* since 2001, but a far more impressive credit is providing the voice of Paul McCartney for *Yellow Submarine* (George Duning, 1968).

Villains: The Valeyard is described by the Master as 'an amalgamation of the darker sides' of the Doctor's own nature 'somewhere between your twelfth and final incarnations' and later as 'a composite of every dark thought' that the Doctor has ever had (see **64**, 'The Time Monster'). What this actually means is desperately ambiguous and therefore open to some discussion, but the character never returns to the series.

Other Worlds: Gallifrey's is the oldest civilisation and has had 'ten million years of absolute power'.

The Plan: According to the Master, the Valeyard made a deal with the Time Lord High Council to prosecute the Doctor in this show trial, 'adjust the evidence' and make sure he was legally convicted and executed. The High Council ordered this because the Doctor had discovered that Ravolox (see above) was really Earth. It was the Time Lords who moved Earth through space (because a group of aliens from Andromeda were using the planet as their base whilst robbing valuable information from the Matrix) and they feared the Doctor would uncover this. In return, the Time Lords promised the Valeyard the Doctor's remaining regenerations. This is stated as being his motivation in Part Thirteen, but Part Fourteen makes quite clear that the Valeyard never intended to honour this deal and that he has a separate plan of his own. The Valeyard is planning to murder the High Council and exterminate 'the ultimate court of appeal' (which seems to be the institution trying the Doctor). He additionally wants to kill the Doctor (whose existence 'constrains' him in a manner that is not made entirely clear). It's possible he struck the deal with the Time Lords because his role as prosecutor gave him access to the Matrix, which is obviously useful.

Science/Magic: The Key of Rassilon (see **97**, 'The Invasion of Time') is now held by The Keeper of the Matrix and can give a person physical passage into the inside of the computer. The Master's TARDIS materialises as a statue of Queen Victoria. *Brilliant*. The Valeyard immobilises it with a 'limbo atrophier' which basically seems to trap the Master and Glitz by freezing time and turning them grey. The Valeyard also has a device that Melanie refers to as a 'Megabyte Modem' (which sounds like something that comes free when you sign up for broadband Internet) but which the Doctor calls both a Maser and a 'Particle Disseminator'. The Doctor makes it stop working by 'inducing an anti-phase into the telemetry unit' and triggering a 'Ray Phase Shift'. This causes it to blow itself up with minimal damage to the outside world. Whatever.

Things Fall Apart: Melanie misuses 'disinterest' in Part Thirteen – which is irritating. The courtroom set is severely battered by now. Alterations to the script of Part Thirteen (Holmes died before completing work on it) change the nature of the Valeyard from the simple (he's the Doctor from the future, old, corrupt and terrified of dying) to the incomprehensible (see **Villains**). The serial loses much of its point due to this. Why did the Valeyard present the Ravolox adventure as evidence, given that the Doctor's visit is the very thing the High Council wants to cover up? Bonnie Langford's delivery of 'That's it, Doc, now we're getting at the dirt' is shudder-inducing. The Doctor signs his remaining lives away to the Valeyard but this is never mentioned again and has no knock-on effect in the rest of the series (indeed, he regenerates in the very next episode!).

Availability: A box set BBCV 5009 (UK), WHV E1140 (US) was released in 1993.

Verdict: 'Yeah, I knew this was a mistake. My grip on reality's not too good at the best of times.' Each individual 'segment' has elements to recommend it, but while there are many plot twists, and some momentum, the 'Trial' is, as a whole, distressingly less than the sum of its parts. Much of the serial has a superficial, inconsequential air which it never dispels for long enough to acquire the epic status it so clearly desires. The 'Hyperion 3' sections of Parts Nine to Twelve are an engaging, straightforward *Doctor Who* story that fits uncomfortably within the 'Trial' framework and which would have been better off being produced as a separate serial (although the individual episodes are all well structured). Parts Five to Eight experiment with concepts such as unreliable narration and deferred endings and attempt to conceptually integrate the 'Trial' sequences into the rest of the story:

watched in isolation they flirt with greatness and Part Eight features one of *Doctor Who*'s most dramatic climaxes. Parts One to Four are unremarkable but *Doctor Who* has been very much worse than that.

Perversely it is each section's associations with, and links to, each other and the framing sequence that damages all four sections fatally. There are some great *Doctor Who* moments in here. The opening special effects sequence is the best *Doctor Who* ever had and has been much praised, but there are others; the Doctor and Peri's exploration of Marble Arch, Peri's death, the Doctor's agonised reaction to it and the scene where he's forcibly dragged out of time. There's also Sil and the Doctor merrily discussing finance, Ruth Baxter opening her single eye, the Hyperion 3 nearing the black hole, the sudden appearance of the Master and the battle inside the nightmare Victoriana of the Matrix (including the Doctor being dragged underground by dirt-smeared zombie hands). However, there's just not enough to justify nearly six hours of material. There are some nice performances too – Colin Baker, Geoffrey Hughes, Christopher Ryan, Patrick Ryecart, Nabil Shaban and Malcolm Tierney are especially good – but even together they're simply not enough. 'Trial' ends with a lot of shouting and a well-produced explosion: this initially offers some catharsis but, on reflection, doesn't cover up, or compensate for, the numerous production horrors, the nonsensical corkscrew plotting or the frequent *longeurs*.

Huge, blundering and desperately flawed, 'The Trial of a Time Lord' is, like a lot of poor *Doctor Who*, plausible nostalgia for those who were ten years old when it was made (see, for example, **37, 80, 108**). As always, however, that fact shouldn't be confused with it actually being any good.

145
Time and the Rani

Part One: 7 September 1987
Part Two: 14 September 1987
Part Three: 21 September 1987
Part Four: 28 September 1987

Written by Pip and Jane Baker
Directed by Andrew Morgan

Notable Cast: Sylvester McCoy (born Percy James Patrick Kent-Smith in 1943) has a CV divided between substantial dramatic roles on the stage (and, as Bowers in *The Last Place On Earth* (1985), on TV), and children's programming like *Jigsaw* and *Eureka* on television. Playing the Doctor raised his profile, and since then McCoy has played kidnapper Michael Sams in *Beyond Evil* (1997), Flynn in *Leaping Leprechauns* (Ted Nicolaou, 1995) and its sequel, and has had guest roles in *Tom Jones* (1997), *Rab C Nesbitt* (1996) and *Casualty* (2001) while continuing a theatrical career that embraces everything from Beckett to *Noises Off!* Mark Greenstreet (Ikona) played a dual lead role in *Brat Farrar* (1986), and starred as Mike Hardy in the glossy *Trainer* (1991–92). In 1997 he wrote and directed the straight-to-video thriller *Caught In The Act*. Donald Pickering (Beyus) previously appeared in **35**, 'The Faceless Ones' alongside Wanda Ventham (Faroon) who was also in **94**, 'Image of the Fendahl'.

Director: Andrew Morgan has directed episodes of *Casualty*, *Urban Gothic* and the Patrick Troughton-starring *Knights of God* (1987).

Script Editor: Andrew Cartmel was working in IT and at the BBC's script unit whilst trying to break into writing when John Nathan-Turner offered him the job on *Doctor Who*. He remained with the series until the BBC ceased regular production with **156**, 'Survival', at which point he moved to script-edit *Casualty* (1990). He subsequently worked largely in computer magazines – although he has also written four *Doctor Who* novels, the thriller *The Wise* (1999) and comic strips for *2000AD* and *Doctor Who Magazine*.

Doctor Who?: The Doctor regenerates when his TARDIS is knocked off course by the Rani's gun. He's now short, with dark wavy hair, and the clothes he wears include a light-grey jacket, paisley tie, checked trousers and V-neck jumper with question mark motif. His regeneration seems to have gone smoothly until the Rani gives him an injection to take away his memory. He can play the spoons and is prone to malapropisms. He has a melancholy streak, prone to anger and despair. He worries that he will now be 'sulky and bad tempered'. He specifically refers to this as his 'seventh persona'. Thermodynamics was the Doctor's specialist subject at university. He and the Rani are both 953. After he accidentally kills a Tetrap by pushing it into one of the Rani's traps, the Doctor takes his hat off in mourning.

Other Worlds: Lakertya, a grey rocky world where the Rani has set up her laboratory.

Scary Monsters: The Tetraps, bat creatures acting as the Rani's troops. They have all-round vision thanks to their four eyes, and paralysing venom in their tongues.

Villains: The Rani, from **139**, 'Mark of the Rani'. Her TARDIS is in the form of a pyramid with reflective markings.

The Plan: The Rani gives the regenerated Doctor an injection to give him amnesia, then impersonates Mel and tells him that he's in *his* laboratory on Lakertya. She needs the Doctor's skills to complete her experiment, which feeds the knowledge of kidnapped geniuses into a giant brain. The brain is to formulate a lightweight substitute for strange matter – when launched at a strange-matter asteroid this substitute ('Loyhargil') will cause detonation, and a supernova on Lakertya. The rush of chronons on the Rani's pet brain will cause it to become a time manipulator, with which she will be able to redirect history.

Science/Magic: The Rani shoots down the TARDIS with a navigational guidance system distorter. She has set traps which, when a wire is tripped, trap the victim in an energy sphere which bounces around before exploding. Her other means of keeping the Lakertyans in line are exploding anklets and a mirrorball full of electric bees. An explosion of strange matter can only be detonated by more strange matter, and will produce helium 2.

Things Fall Apart: The Colin Baker Doctor gets the most pathetic regeneration to date, killed when the TARDIS is knocked off course, an event so minor it merely knocks Mel unconscious. (Baker is also very obviously not present – it's McCoy wearing a wig.) The Rani impersonating Mel is the worst kind of camp old nonsense, as is most of the action. However, Kate O'Mara is better at playing Mel than Bonnie Langford is, which is a shocking indictment of how bad Langford is here. The Lakyertyans' day-glo costumes are *very* mid-1980s.

Availability: Issued on VHS in 1995 as BBCV 5617 (UK), WHV E1301 (US).

Verdict: 'The more I know me, the less I like me.' New Doctor, same old rubbish. In spite of being McCoy's debut, 'Time and the Rani' still feels like the watered-down dregs of Colin Baker's era.

All the Colin staples are here – garish design, histrionic performances and scripts packed with hyperbolic gibberish. It's a shame
that, after having McCoy's Doctor jump up in full effect after his
regeneration, Pip and Jane Baker elect to introduce an amnesia
plotline that stops the character from settling down. In spite of a
script which has the Doctor not really knowing who he is,
McCoy's performance nonetheless makes the character different
from his predecessor – there's a melancholic aspect to his Doctor,
and a refreshing absence of the arrogance and bluster that made
Colin Baker's Doctor so irritating. Unfortunately McCoy is stuck
in bog-standard kid's television acting mode. Although some of
the effects are actually quite impressive, 'Time and the Rani' is a
total mess.

146
Paradise Towers

Part One: 5 October 1987
Part Two: 12 October 1987
Part Three: 19 October 1987
Part Four: 26 October 1987

Written by Stephen Wyatt
Directed by Nicholas Mallett

Notable Cast: Richard Briers (Chief Caretaker) is best known for
his roles in the sitcoms *Marriage Lines* (1963–66), *The Good Life*
(1975–78) and *Ever Decreasing Circles* (1985–89). He's also an
accomplished dramatic actor, as evidenced by his brilliant performances in *Henry V* (Kenneth Branagh, 1989) and *Hamlet*
(Kenneth Branagh, 1996). Judy Cornwell (Maddie) was a regular
in *Keeping Up Appearances* (1990–6) and is a prolific novelist.
Elizabeth Spriggs (Tabby) starred in *Shine On Harvey Moon*
(1982–85, 1995). Clive Merrison (Deputy Chief Caretaker) is also
in **37**, 'The Tomb of the Cybermen'.

Writer: Andrew Cartmel invited Stephen Wyatt to work on *Doctor
Who* on the strength of his play *Claws*.

Doctor Who?: McCoy's Doctor is playful, fretting, occasionally
sinister and driven by curiosity. He has a tendency to think out
loud and would hate to live his life by 'a boring old rule book'.

History 101: Paradise Towers is a housing development designed by the self-styled 'great architect' Kroagnon. It won awards 'way back in the twenty-first century'. Only teenagers, old women and a few staff (caretakers) live there, having been moved there from their own homes when the majority of the male population went off to fight a war that none returned from. The various communities within the towers loathe one another and gangs of teenage girls roam the streets.

Villains: The Chief Caretaker, the officious senior executive of the Towers who really just wants to make sure everyone follows the rules while he feeds his ostensible charges to the pet monster he keeps in the basement. Said monster is actually the container for the bodiless brain of Kroagnon.

Science/Magic: Kroagnon transfers his consciousness into the Chief Caretaker's body by putting him into a large metal tube. The Doctor calls this 'corpolectroscopy'. (Mind you, he calls a phone an example of 'audio-architectural synchronicity'.)

Things Fall Apart: The cleaning robots are cumbersome and utterly unmenacing. Mel doesn't exactly seem threatened by the pool-cleaning robot either. Why didn't Kroagnon just possess the Chief Caretaker years ago? Indeed why did the previous generation imprison rather than kill the clearly barking architect?

Availability: Issued on VHS in 1995 as BBCV 5686 (UK), WHV E1379 (US).

Verdict: 'Yellow Kang the last believed unalive. Reason not known.' A story that starts off as a jokingly played parable about inner city decay and ends up as a comedy zombie thriller which everybody plays worryingly straight, 'Paradise Towers' is very peculiar in terms of style, tone and content but rather ordinary in terms of quality. There are a number of memorable scenes (the Doctor using the caretakers' own rule book to escape them, the Kangs' ceremonies, the cannibalistic old ladies, the Doctor and the Chief Caretaker's regulation 'final conversation') and Wyatt's scripts demonstrate a sheer pleasure in the use of language ('taken to the cleaners', 'all sound and safe', 'talkie phone', 'build high for happiness', 'mayhaps') rare amongst *Doctor Who* writers. Mallett's cameras are mobile, spiralling presences – with characters drifting in and out of shot – in a very effectively realised physical world, one with grubby technology and harsh green, red and blue lighting.

That said, some of the guest performances are rather too broad, the Doctor contributes little to the story's resolution and, while the Kangs look far too old, the caretakers and Pex (Howard Cooke) look far too young. Most importantly you just can't shake the feeling that the production should be fundamentally less literal in how it deals with its big ideas (which include social alienation and the inflexibility of government, while the Red, Blue and Yellow Kangs obviously represent the three major British political parties) and how it implements them on screen.

147
Delta and the Bannermen

Part One: 2 November 1987
Part Two: 9 November 1987
Part Three: 16 November 1987

Written by Malcolm Kohll
Directed by Chris Clough

Notable Cast: Legendary musical comedian Stubby Kaye (Weismuller) appeared in *Cat Ballou* (Elliot Silverstein, 1965) and *Guys and Dolls* (Joseph L Mankiewicz, 1955). Don Henderson (Gavrok) starred on TV as George Kitchener Bullman in *The XYY Man* (1976–77), *Strangers* (1978–82) and *Bullman* (1985–87) and appeared in *Star Wars* (George Lucas, 1977) and on TV in *The Paradise Club* (1989). Brian Hibbert (Bounty Hunter) was in a capella pop group 'The Flying Pickets'. Ken Dodd (Tollmaster) is the Squire of Knotty Ash, although the position was not, as far as we are aware, legally conferred upon him. Hugh Lloyd (Goronwy) was a TV comedy star of the 1950s and 1960s.

Writer: This was Malcolm Kohll's first television credit. He has since moved into film, producing *The 51st State* (Stel Pavlou, 2001) and writing and producing *Barry* (Marleen Gorris, 2004).

Villains: The Bannermen, merciless warlike humanoids led by Gavrok. Their look was inspired by Japanese soldiers as seen in films like Akira Kurosawa's *Seven Samurai* (1954).

Other Worlds: The Chimeron home planet is briefly seen at the beginning (it's another quarry).

The Plan: The Bannermen are attacking the Chimeron, but it's not entirely clear why. Some sort of territorial dispute? Chimeron Queen Delta (Belinda Mayes) later speaks of taking the case to a higher interplanetary authority. Delta flees the planet with the egg from which her child will soon hatch. (Do the Chimeron women lay those things themselves? Ouch!) The Bannermen pursue.

History 101: After landing at an intergalactic toll booth, the Doctor and Mel win a holiday with Nostalgia Tours, a company run by the friendly Navarinos offering trips back in time. Delta also arrives at the toll booth and joins the holidaymakers in the hope of evading the Bannermen. They are heading for Disneyland 1959, but end up in Wales ('The real 50s,' comments the Doctor). Amusingly the alien Navarinos dress in a garish parody of 1950s fashions, and therefore look exactly like tourists (compare them with the genuine Happy Hearts Holiday Club who turn up at the end).

Elements such as the toll booth, the bounty hunter and the Navarino holidaymakers bear resemblance to the Marvel Comics *Doctor Who* strips of the 1980s: this attempt at stylisation is welcome after recent faux-'grittiness' and it's balanced out by well-drawn 'ordinary' characters like Burton (Richard Davies), who runs the camp.

Doctor Who?: The Doctor is recognised by a bounty hunter and there is evidently profit in killing him, suggesting that at least one person has put a price on the Doctor's head.

Science/Magic: The Chimeron baby food turns Billy into a Chimeron, which seems dumb – would human baby food turn a Chimeron into a human? And will Billy eventually turn into one of those horrid green Chimeron males we saw at the start?

Things Fall Apart: The Chimeron males look like their faces are made of papier-mâché. Weismuller's baseball cap and jacket are far too 1980s. The slimy puppet version of Delta's child looks a lot better than the green baby in a space romper suit. The bus explosion and Gavrok's death both look like bad stage-magic tricks.

Availability: Released on VHS in 2001 as BBCV 7131 (UK), WHV E1649 (US).

Verdict: 'You are not the Happy Hearts Holiday Club from Bolton, but instead are spacemen in fear of an attack from some other spacemen?' A lurch in the right direction for *Doctor Who*, 'Delta and the Bannermen' was the first script to be written after McCoy's casting and he gratefully stamps some authority on the role. The Doctor's tirade against Gavrok plays to the actor's strengths: emotional outbursts make him look silly, but he's good at simmering anger. This serial also marks more extensive use of location shooting in *Doctor Who*, resulting in fewer visual weaknesses.

Yet there's some weak lighting on indoor sequences, and genuine 1950s music would be preferable to covers and 'homages'. Also, while the peripheral stuff is solid, the central plotline of Delta's flight from the Bannermen and romance with Billy (David Kinder) is incredibly vague. This being *Doctor Who* the romance has to appear chaste, but surely a few sparks in their conversation wouldn't destroy the innocence of younger viewers. There is no sense of any bond between them, partly because both give a weak performance. Overall the story is not bad, but would very soon be trumped.

148
Dragonfire

Part One: 23 November 1987
Part Two: 30 November 1987
Part Three: 7 December 1987

Written by Ian Briggs
Directed by Chris Clough

Notable Cast: This is the last story for Bonnie Langford as a regular: replacing her is Sophie Aldred (Ace), best known for children's TV shows *Corners* (1989) and *Melvin and Maureen's Music-a-grams* (1991). Tony Selby returns as Sabalom Glitz (see **144**, 'Trial of a Time Lord'). Edward Peel (Kane) played DCI Mark Perrin in *Juliet Bravo* (1983–5), Anthony Cairns in *Emmerdale* (1997–98) and the Chief Superintendent in *Cracker* (1993–95). Patricia Quinn (Belazs) appeared in *The Rocky Horror Picture Show* (Jim Sharman, 1975), *Monty Python's The Meaning of Life* (Terry Jones, 1980), and on television in *I, Claudius* (1976) and *The Box of Delights* (1984), the latter opposite her husband, the late Sir Robert Stephens. Stuart Organ played Mr Robson in *Grange Hill* (1988–2003) and had a recurring role in *Brookside* (1984–89). Tony

Osoba (Kracauer) previously appeared in **104**, 'Destiny of the Daleks'. Daphne Oxenford (The Archivist) was an original cast member of *Coronation Street* playing Esther Hayes (1960–68) and play Mrs Pumphreys in *All Creatures Great and Small* (1978–90).

Writer: Ian Briggs has written for *Casualty* and *The Bill*.

Other Worlds: The Doctor follows a tracking signal to Iceworld, a 'space trading colony on the dark side of the planet Svartos', where local boss Kane is building up an army of mercenaries and cryogenically freezing them for later use. Iceworld is part supermarket and part ice-walled labyrinth where a dragon guards a lost treasure.

Villains: Kane, a native of the planet Proamon whose body temperature is far below that of humans – he has an ideal body temperature of minus 193 degrees Celsius, and can kill a man with his frozen touch. When he recruits a new servant, he offers them a golden sovereign, which is at such a low temperature that it brands the print of the coin on to their skin. He has a sculptor working on an ugly ice statue of his late lover, the criminal genius Xana.

Scary Monsters: The dragon is a tall 'biomechanoid' with lasers for eyes.

The Plan: Kane is manipulating treasure hunters to try and get them to kill the dragon. He has been in exile for three thousand years, with the dragon as his jailer. Only with the power of the dragonfire can he return to Proamon to destroy his enemies.

Doctor Who?: The Doctor is fascinated by stories of the dragon and considers himself to be on a scientific expedition to discover it. He's terribly disappointed when he thinks he won't get to meet it. The Doctor distracts a guard by engaging him in a debate on philosophy and theology, but is left lost for words when the guard asks him a question about 'semiotic thickness'. He stops Glitz from shooting the dragon, saying they have 'no right to kill'. When Mel decides to leave, the Doctor is melancholy but affectionate; his speech about her leaving before she's even arrived referring to the paradox of her joining the TARDIS in **144**, 'Trial of a Time Lord'. His mood is lightened by welcoming explosive-obsessed waitress Ace into the TARDIS.

Science/Magic: Cryosleep 'freezes the neural pathways', wiping the memory, although strong feelings of hatred can survive. Nitro-9 is nitro-glycerine 'with a bit more wallop'. The 'singing trees' are crystals that make noise as they vibrate, and are actually a system of 'opto-electric' circuits. The 'ice garden' is a stellar map.

Things Fall Apart: Sylvester McCoy theatrically slides around when the Doctor is walking on an icy surface – but none of the rest of the cast bother. It's hard to see what the Doctor is trying to achieve by hanging off a rail at the end of Part One.

Availability: Issued on VHS in 1994 as BBCV 5181 (UK) and WHV E1352 (US).

Verdict: 'Time for a quick adventure, then back for tea.' Evoking both the films of James Whale and 1960s *Doctor Who*, 'Dragonfire' feels like it should be in black and white, which is no bad thing. Ian Briggs's clever, witty script combines an adventure narrative with threats co-opted from Universal horror films – the vampiric Kane (superbly played by Edward Peel) is the best new villain the series has seen in years, while the monster in the basement is strangely sympathetic in the best tradition of Karloff. It even has that horror staple, zombies, in the form of Kane's frozen army.

By splitting the plot between two double acts – Doctor/Glitz and Mel/Ace – Briggs keeps the smart banter flowing, and the script is full of references to philosophy and the numerous film theory in-jokes. There's tension, jokes, some great effects work, a Doctor who is a scientist and explorer . . . Although the production is far from perfect (the 'ANT hunt', which attempts to ape the *Aliens* (James Cameron, 1986) bug hunt on a feebly smaller scale, just doesn't work), 'Dragonfire' is nonetheless the kind of highly entertaining and imaginative serial that hadn't been seen in the series for quite some time.

149
Remembrance of the Daleks

Part One: 5 October 1988
Part Two: 12 October 1988
Part Three: 19 October 1988
Part Four: 26 October 1988

Written by Ben Aaronovitch
Directed by Andrew Morgan

Notable Cast: Michael Sheard (Headmaster) previously appeared in **23**, 'The Ark', **56**, 'The Mind of Evil', **82**, 'Pyramids of Mars', **93**, 'The Invisible Enemy' and **116**, 'Castrovalva'. George Sewell (Ratcliffe) was a regular in *Z Cars* (1967–68), *Paul Temple* (1969–71) and *The Detectives* (1993–97). Joseph Marcell (John) played Geoffrey, the butler in *The Fresh Prince of Bel-Air* (1990–96). Pamela Salem (Rachel) previously appeared in **89**, 'The Face of Evil' and **90**, 'The Robots of Death'. Simon Williams (Gilmore) played James Bellamy in *Upstairs, Downstairs* (1971–75) and was in *Don't Wait Up* (1983–90), and has been seen more recently in *Holby City*. Harry Fowler (Harry) was a comic British film and radio star immediately after World War Two. John Leeson, who plays the Dalek Battle Computer, was the voice of K9.

Writer: This was Ben Aaronovitch's first television credit: he later worked on *Casualty* and *Jupiter Moon*, as well as writing three original *Doctor Who* novels during the 1990s.

History 101: The TARDIS lands in London 1963, implicitly not long after the Doctor left in **1**, 'An Unearthly Child'. The story takes place around the two locations of the first-ever episode, Coal Hill School and the junkyard at 76 Totters Lane.

Scary Monsters: The Daleks, this time divided into two factions – the white Imperials and the grey Renegades. The former regard the latter as genetically impure and wish to destroy them.

The 'remembrance' of the title ostensibly refers to the funereal theme of the story, but more accurately describes the way that it plays on the audience's memory of the Daleks. The attention to detail is remarkable (the inside of the Dalek mothership even makes the same noises as the control room in **2**, 'The Daleks'), but elsewhere expectations are subverted. What looks like Davros turns out to be something entirely different, whilst the end of Part One, as the Dalek climbs the stairs, is one of the most satisfying moments in all of *Doctor Who*. Their exterminating blasts pack a real punch for the first time and there's great joy in watching the two factions clash in London's streets.

That said, they do still waste time chanting 'Exterminate!' when they should be getting on with the business of actually extermina-ting, and they still spin around when they encounter something illogical.

The Plan: Both Dalek factions are trying to locate the Hand of Omega, a powerful Gallifreyan device which the Doctor has left behind on Earth. The Hand can transform a star into the kind of power source which the Gallifreyans used to develop mastery over time. However, the Doctor has a plan of his own, which involves letting the Daleks take the Hand.

Villains: The Daleks have often been used to represent Nazism: Aaronovitch develops this by involving them in an internecine race war and allying the Renegade Daleks with a genuine British Nazi in the form of Ratcliffe, who believes that Britain fought on the wrong side in World War Two.

Doctor Who?: There's an implication that the Doctor may have been present when Omega (see **65**, 'The Three Doctors') and Rassilon (see **88**, 'The Deadly Assassin') developed time travel. Prior to this story Omega and Rassilon had each been cited as solely responsible for this discovery. 'Remembrance' adopts the solution put forward by comics legend Alan Moore (whom Cartmel greatly admired) when writing for *Doctor Who Weekly*: the two men were contemporaries and colleagues. This Doctor also appears to feel more responsibility than his predecessors: in the wonderful café scene in Part Two he worries about the effect his decisions have (although any portentousness is neatly deflated by John: 'Life's like that. Best thing is just to get on with it'). The Doctor has a calling card which he plucks out of the air. (See **53**, 'The Ambassadors of Death'.)

Science/Magic: The Doctor constructs a device to interfere with the Daleks' systems and temporarily disable them: 'I rigged something like it on Spiridon.' (See **68**, 'Planet of the Daleks'.) Despite his confidence, he seems surprised and elated when it actually works.

Things Fall Apart: Occasionally you can spot a modern car or vehicle in the background. There are some very 1980s-looking buildings behind the churchyard. Mike's slip about the Hand of Omega is rather an 'Ooh, what a giveaway!' moment.

Availability: Released on DVD in 2001 BBCDVD 1040 (Region 2), WHV E1183 (Region 1) and on VHS as part of a boxed set with **16**, 'The Chase' in 1993 as BBCV 5007 (UK), WHV E1145 (US).

Verdict: 'You will be on the right side in *this* war.' One often encounters a popular perception that *Doctor Who* steadily declined in quality during the 1980s and that by the end it was basically unwatchable. Nonsense, we say. The show's last couple of years produced some of its best serials, including what is arguably the best Dalek story. By setting the action in 1963, 'Remembrance of the Daleks' demonstrates that *Doctor Who* had run for so long that it could revisit itself with a sense of historical perspective. Aaronovitch plunders the series' past for iconography: the army parallels UNIT, as the Doctor blithely calls Gilmore 'Brigadier', Professor Jensen is described as the group's 'chief scientific adviser' with her own Liz Shaw in the form of Miss Williams, and the traitor in the ranks is called Mike. Other programmes are also referenced, such as *Quatermass* ('I wish Bernard was here') and *Grange Hill* (a generation of children finds confirmation that Mr Bronson is indeed a Dalek agent).

Ultimately, though, 'Remembrance' succeeds because it's aware that if it is to match up to the audience's rose-tinted memory of what *Doctor Who* used to be like, it must in fact be bolder and better. It resembles the mid-1980s revamps of comic-book super-heroes in which the character's past is acknowledged and commented on within the context of an adventure which feels like the ones the reader remembers. On the surface 'Remembrance' functions perfectly as straightforward Doctor Who-versus-the-Daleks action, with cool imagery and satisfying battle sequences: underneath, there's much more going on.

150
The Happiness Patrol

Part One: 2 November 1988
Part Two: 9 November 1988
Part Three: 16 November 1988

Written by Graeme Curry
Directed by Chris Clough

Notable Cast: One of the UK's most admired actresses, Sheila Hancock (Helen A) played Carol in *The Rag Trade* (1961–62), Senna Pod in *Carry on Cleo* (Gerald Thomas, 1964), Martha Thompson in *Take A Girl Like You* (Jonathan Miller, 1970), Mrs Stitch in *Scoop* (1972) and Gwendolen in *Fortysomething* (2003). Harold Innocent (Gilbert M) appeared in *Brazil* (Terry Gilliam, 1985), *Porterhouse Blue* (1987), *Little Dorritt* (Christine Edzard, 1988), *Henry V* (Kenneth Branagh, 1989), and *Robin Hood: Prince of Thieves* (Kevin Reynolds, 1991). A stalwart of British film from the 1960s to his death in 1997, Ronald Fraser (Joseph C) was latterly best known as the 'Lord of Love' on *TFI Friday*. Rachel Bell was best known as Louise in *Dear John* opposite Ralph Bates. Georgina Hale is in several Ken Russell films including *The Boyfriend* and *The Devils*. John Normington (Trevor Sigma) previously appeared in **135**, 'The Caves of Androzani'. Lesley Dunlop (Susan Q) previously appeared in **132**, 'Frontios'.

Writer: Graeme Curry has written for *EastEnders* and *The Bill*.

Other Worlds: Terra Alpha, an Earth colony where happiness is enforced, public grief is illegal and 'killjoys' are executed by the Happiness Patrol. Lift music is piped in the streets, everything is brightly coloured and everyone wears jolly make-up. Galactic Centre has sent a census conductor to Terra Alpha, so clearly the planet is under some kind of central control. Citizens are ranked by alphabetical surnames – so Helen A is the leader, Joseph C her husband, and so forth. Offworlders are classified with the surname 'Sigma' and must stay within the 'tourist zones'. The 'drones' are workers from the flatlands, who aren't allowed within the city. Sugar appears to be the planet's main product.

Doctor Who?: The Doctor continues to be a crusader, instigating his battles – he goes to Terra Alpha because of disturbing rumours about the colony, with the intent of seeking out the evil and dealing with it one night. The Doctor has an uncanny ability to confuse and distract people: he spins census-taker Trevor Sigma around to the point where Sigma starts treating him as an authority figure; and he talks a sniper out of shooting protestors, demanding that he look him in the eye and shoot him ('pull the trigger, end my life'). He likes the blues, and sings 'As Time Goes By' in a French accent. The Doctor acts hysterically happy to stop the Happiness Patrol from firing on them. He believes happiness is only meaningful when it exists alongside sadness. The Doctor met a Stigorax in Birmingham in the 25th century, and recalls the Brigadier meeting a triceratops in **71**, 'Invasion of the Dinosaurs'.

Villains: Helen A, dictator of Terra Alpha. A vicious matriarch, her only affection is for her pet, Fifi.

Scary Monsters: The Kandyman, a tall robot made from sweets who designs elaborate executions for Helen A. These include the 'fondant surprise', where victims are drowned in strawberry fondant. The Kandyman has a distinctly marital relationship with his creator, the portly Gilbert M – when Gilbert is late returning, the Kandyman asks, 'What time do you call this?'

The ratlike natives of Terra Alpha have been driven underground, and live in the pipes under the city. Fifi is a Stigorax, a spiny doglike creature that her mistress uses to hunt.

The Plan: Helen A tried to abolish unhappiness. When she failed, she started to enforce it through the 'routine disappearances', which reduced the population by 17 per cent.

Science/Magic: Lemonade has an 'adhesive effect' on the Kandyman's sweetie feet. If the Kandyman stops moving, he starts to coagulate into 'a slab of toffee'. The 'sympathetic vibration' of a note in A flat causes a blockage of hardened sugar in the pipes beneath the city to shatter and collapse.

Things Fall Apart: The studio sets never convince as supposedly exterior streets. The go-kart the Doctor and Ace escape on in Part One moves slower than walking pace – perhaps the Happiness Patrol are worried about running in those heels.

Availability: Issued on VHS in 1997 as BBCV 5803 (UK), WHV E1081 (US).

Verdict: 'I can feel one of my moods coming on.' Political in a very scattershot, non-specific way, 'The Happiness Patrol' is not so much an allegory about any real political situation as a portrayal of a generic oppressive society and a critique of the falsity of governments that pretend everything is perfect. Helen A is an obvious Thatcher figure, but Sheila Hancock's excellent performance goes well beyond mere impersonation, and the society of Terra Alpha has aspects of Maoism, Stalinism, Nazism and probably a few other -isms along the way.

Politics aside, the serial is a mixed bag of superb elements (the Doctor talking to the sniper, the squabbling of the Kandyman and Gilbert M) and lacklustre production values. The direction is uninspired, and the budget is pitifully low – notably, this is the last time to date a *Doctor Who* story has attempted to recreate an alien world in the studio. The Patrol of the title aren't much of a convincing threat and McCoy seems barely present in some scenes. Ultimately, 'The Happiness Patrol' is smart in places – but not smart enough to be a total success.

151
Silver Nemesis

Part One: 23 November 1988
Part Two: 30 November 1988
Part Three: 7 December 1988

Written by Kevin Clarke
Directed by Chris Clough

Notable Cast: Anton Diffring (De Flores) made a career playing Nazis in films such as *The Colditz Story* (Guy Hamilton, 1955) and *The Black Tent* (Brian Desmond Hunt, 1956). Leslie French (Mathematician) was on the shortlist to play Doctor Who in 1, 'An Unearthly Child' and is the physical model for the statue of Ariel outside BBC Broadcasting House. Fiona Walker's (Lady Peinforte) first television acting job was as Kala, *Doctor Who's* first ever villainess in 5, 'The Keys of Marinus'. She played Aggripina in *I, Claudius* (1976). Dolores Gray was a Broadway superstar and the lead in musicals like *It's Always Fair Weather* (Gene Kelly, Stanely Donen, 1955).

Writer: Playwright Kevin Clarke came to *Doctor Who* after Andrew Cartmel was impressed by his episode of French Resistance drama *Wish Me Luck* (1987). He later wrote *Casualty* (for Cartmel) and episodes of *The Bill*.

Doctor Who?: 'Doctor who? Have you never wondered where he came from? Who he is?' asks Lady Peinforte at the story's climax. Peinforte claims the Doctor has a 'secret' which is connected to 'Gallifrey, the Old Time, the Time of Chaos' but doesn't reveal it. The implication seems to be that the Doctor is much older than he claims (explaining his inconsistent ageing?) and was in fact a contemporary of the founders of Gallifreyan society Rassilon and Omega (not impossible given how long Time Lords live). This would explain his familiarity with the asteroid Nemesis, the Hand of Omega (see **149**, 'Remembrance of the Daleks') and how both Omega and Rassilon (**65**, 'The Three Doctors', **129**, 'The Five Doctors') knew him at their first (on-screen) meetings. Hiding such a secret would also explain his inconsistent background. This idea runs contrary to much of the spirit, and the letter, of 1970s (if not 1960s) *Doctor Who* though. (See, in particular, **88**, 'The Deadly

Assassin', **103**, 'The Armageddon Factor'.) The Doctor loves 'straight blowing' jazz.

Villains: Lady Peinforte, a seventeenth-century sorceress. She and the Doctor have previously fought over the Nemesis, from which she learned secrets about his past. De Flores is a Nazi hiding in South America who knows of the Nemesis's existence. He travels to England with some paramilitary fascists he calls his 'Fourth Reich'.

Scary Monsters: The Cybermen also want the Nemesis and intend to use it, and a fleet of invisible warships, to invade the Earth and turn it into their 'base planet, the New Mondas' (destroyed two years previously: see **29**, 'The Tenth Planet'). They recognise the Doctor and his TARDIS and are aware of regeneration.

The Plan: Various factions battle over the comet Nemesis (also called an asteroid in this serial), launched into space by the Doctor at some point not long before 1638. It has crashed in Windsor in 1988. It contains a statue made out of a sentient metal, which can act as a terrible destructive weapon. The Doctor, who has anticipated all this, allows his enemies to wipe each other out and then uses the Nemesis to destroy the Cybermen's invasion fleet.

Science/Magic: For the first time in the history of *Doctor Who* something which is unequivocally magical (Lady Peinforte's time travel) works and the Doctor acknowledges it as such (see **59**, 'The Dæmons', **153**, 'Battlefield').

Things Fall Apart: There are ludicrous scenes with a pair of skinheads who mug Lady Peinforte and a dreary American woman who gives her a lift. There's a ridiculous sequence with HM The Queen. The battle between the Cybermen and the Nazis is the least exciting gunfight ever shot. The Nazis use (Israeli-made) Uzi machine guns and are such stock hoods they might as well be anyone.

Availability: Issued in an extended form on VHS in 1993 as BBCV 4888 (UK), WHV E1269 (US). The original broadcast version has never been available commercially.

Verdict: 'The secrets of the Time Lords mean nothing to us.' A decent first episode gives way to an insipid runaround with lots of padding. This is followed by a climactic final scene which raises the spectre of defeat only to collapse into utter inconsequentiality. The period scenes are nice, Fiona Walker is terrific and it's all, at least, quite entertaining, but you expect more from the official '25th Anniversary Story'. The fact that the whole plot is a rerun of (the far superior) **149**, 'Remembrance of the Daleks' from mere weeks before doesn't exactly add lustre to the serial, either.

152
The Greatest Show in the Galaxy

Part One: 14 December 1988
Part Two: 21 December 1988
Part Three: 28 December 1988
Part Four: 4 January 1989

Written by Stephen Wyatt
Directed by Alan Wareing

Notable Cast: TP McKenna (The Captain) was in *Straw Dogs* (Sam Peckinpah, 1971) and appeared on television in *Blake's 7* (1978), *All Creatures Great and Small* (1980) and *Callan* (1974). Ian Reddington (Chief Clown) played 'Tricky Dicky' in *East-Enders* (1992–94) and has appeared in *Cadfael* (1994), *Being April* (2002) and *Holby City* (2004) and starred in the Madness musical *Our House* (2003). Gian Sammarco (Whizzkid) was Adrian Mole (1985–87). Chris Jury (Deadbeat) was Eric in *Lovejoy* (1986–94) and later became a TV director. Peggy Mount (Stallholder) was memorably in *Oliver!* (Carol Reed, 1968) and the TV series *John Browne's Body* (1969), *You're Only Young Twice* (1978–81) and *George and the Dragon* (1968). Daniel Peacock (Nord) was in *Robin Hood: Prince of Thieves* (Kevin Reynolds, 1991) and *Quadrophenia* (Franc Roddam, 1981) and was a regular writer and performer for *The Comic Strip Presents . . .* (penning the legendary 'The Yob' episode). He is now the writer/director of the BBC's excellent *Cavegirl* children's series. Fans should check out his hilarious turn in *Robin of Sherwood*: 'Herne's Son' (1986). Jessica Martin (Mags) was a well-known impressionist.

Director: Alan Wareing worked his way up through the ranks at the BBC, working as an assistant and production manager on series like *Lovejoy* and *Tenko* before taking the BBC director's course and then going freelance. He has directed *EastEnders*,

Emmerdale, *London's Burning*, *Casualty* and *Wycliffe* amongst many others and continues to work in British TV.

Doctor Who?: The Doctor claims that he has fought the Gods of Ragnarok 'all throughout time', but it's unclear exactly what he means by this. He can do a variety of magic tricks and juggle. He makes a sword appear in his hand with the power of words. He can 'sense' evil (see **27**, 'The War Machines'). He believes that anybody remotely interesting is mad by some definition or another.

History 101: Having successfully toured the galaxy the communal Psychic Circus settled on the planet Segonax at the insistence of Kingpin, a member of the circus. Having been tempted there by the promises of the Gods of Ragnarok Kingpin rebelled against his masters who broke his mind, turned his comrades against him and used his circus as a trap.

Villains: The Gods' enforcer, the Chief Clown is a self-centred sadist carrying out his masters' every whim. The famous intergalactic explorer Captain Cook has travelled to Segonax in order to do a deal with the power behind the Psychic Circus even though he doesn't know who they are yet.

Scary Monsters: Mags is a werewolf. Cool.

The Plan: The Doctor attempts to destroy the parasitic Gods of Ragnarok, who live on human misery.

Science/Magic: The clowns have kites built by Flowerchild (Dee Sadler), which they can use to track escapees from the circus. Bellboy (Christopher Guard) builds robot clowns, a robotic bus conductor and huge guardian robot which Ace finds half buried. The Gods can be in two places at the same time. The circus's bus/spaceship appears to be the same type (a modified Hellstrom II) as the one in **147**, 'Delta and the Bannermen'. The Gods put Kingpin's mind in an amulet and then hide it in the bus, knowing that any of their servants who rebel against them will attempt to seize it.

Things Fall Apart: McCoy gurns when breaking through to the Gods' domain.

Availability: Issued on VHS in 2000 as BBCV 6798 (UK), WHV E1494 (US).

Verdict: 'Did you really believe in all that talk of peace . . . and love?' That this is reminiscent of the wildly creative side of 1960s *Who* (**24**, 'The Celestial Toymaker', **45**, 'The Mind Robber') is entirely appropriate, given that the story is essentially about the corruption of 1960s idealism ('It's gone . . . the freedom of being what you want to be . . . all of it. Don't you understand?') and the unselfconscious selfishness at the core of hippy culture. There's a feeling of real pain and misery emanating from both the plight of the enslaved circus troupe and the horrific fates of their victims. The bitterness with which Bellboy mutters, 'They took everything that was bright and good about what we had and buried it where it will never be found again' is very affecting and his subsequent suicide is one of *Doctor Who*'s most chilling moments.

The cast are uniformly excellent, with Ian Reddington's fanatical Chief Clown and Chris Jury's twin performance as both the deranged Deadbeat and the self-assured Kingpin worthy of especial note. It's also the perfect showcase for McCoy's manipulative, righteous, melancholy clown and probably his best performance as Doctor Who. Unlike Wyatt's earlier **146**, 'Paradise Towers', the big ideas don't seem at all out of place in what is a very assured production. The Doctor's calm walk away from the exploding circus is one of the series' perfect moments. 'The Greatest Show in the Galaxy' combines vivid images with a queasy atmosphere that deftly mixes the wacky and the poignant to create a wonderful *Doctor Who* story.

153
Battlefield

Part One: 6 September 1989
Part Two: 13 September 1989
Part Three: 20 September 1989
Part Four: 27 September 1989

Written by Ben Aaronovitch
Directed by Michael Kerrigan

Notable Cast: Jean Marsh (Morgaine) previously appeared in **14**, 'The Crusade' and **21**, 'The Daleks' Master Plan'. James Ellis (Peter Warmsly) played Bert Lynch throughout *Z Cars* (1962–65, 1967–78) and Sarge in *Nightingales* (1990–92). Angela Bruce (Brigadier Winifred Bambera) was a regular in *Angels* (1976–79),

Chrissie Stuart in *Press Gang* (1989–93) and the female Lister in *Red Dwarf*: 'Parallel Universe' (1988). Marcus Gilbert (Ancelyn) appeared in *Riders* (1993) and *Army of Darkness* (Sam Raimi, 1993) and played Lucifer in *Robin of Sherwood* 'The Swords of Wayland' (1985).

Director: Michael Kerrigan's TV credits include *Mister Majeika* and *The Knights of God*.

History 101: Ancelyn, a knight from a parallel Britain, arrives in Carbury, England, in the near future, to locate the dormant King Arthur and bring him home. (The implication is that the Arthurian legends filtered through from this parallel world and mingled with tales of our historically real Arthur.)

Doctor Who?: Ancelyn hails the Doctor as 'Merlin': it becomes clear that a future incarnation of the Doctor adopts the name and place in legend. Ancelyn does not recognise his face, 'but your manner . . . betrays you. Do you not ride the ship of time, does it not deceive the senses being greater within than without?' The future Doctor/Merlin buried Arthur on 'our' Earth after his final battle, claiming that the King was not dead, but in suspended animation and would one day return. The Doctor is entirely unaware of this at the outset of the story, but seeing him bluff his way through the role is a joy.

Villains: Morgaine, a warrior queen and sorceress, and her son Mordred (Christopher Bowen). They respect their enemies, leading to a wonderful scene in which they hold a remembrance ceremony for Britain's war dead. Morgaine believes that she defeated 'Merlin' by sealing him in an ice cave.

The Plan: Morgaine seeks to engage Arthur in battle when he awakes, but upon finding the Doctor also decides to wreak revenge upon him.

Scary Monsters: The Destroyer (Marek Anton), a demon called up by Morgaine to devour this Earth. The costume is one of *Doctor Who*'s best, approaching the standard of more recent TV series such as *Angel*.

Science/Magic: Magic clearly works in the dimension from which Morgaine, Mordred and Ancelyn originate, and Morgaine carries her abilities over into our universe. A chalk circle is effective protection against her. At one point the Doctor touches Mordred on the forehead and disarms him with a small 'zap' noise, which seems to give him a minor yet irritatingly convenient 'superpower' (although in truth it's little different to the Pertwee Doctor's Venusian Karate). He does it again in **156**, 'Survival'.

Things Fall Apart: The BBC's lack of interest in making *Doctor Who* by this stage was demonstrated when they accidentally threw away the TARDIS console room set between seasons: the one seen here is a hasty and cheap replacement. The shot of Ancelyn flying over the wall is dodgy. The bit with the flaming tyre marks is the silliest *Bessie* moment since **64**, 'The Time Monster'. Mordred's maniacal laughter in Part Two goes on too long. The scene in which Ace and Shou Yuing bitch at each other inside the chalk circle is very stilted ('I bet nobody likes you!' – ooh, what a pithy retort).

Availability: Issued on VHS in 1998 as BBCV 6330 (UK), WHV E1078 (US). This release includes around three minutes of untransmitted material.

Verdict: 'Tell them I've retired. Tell them I've decided to fade away.' Sword-and-sorcery is tricky to pull off, especially when placed in a modern context: it's easy to look overblown and ridiculous. 'Battlefield' sometimes succumbs to this, but much of it works and it was about time *Doctor Who* offered its spin on Arthurian legends. It's clear that the series was still building for the future: the story not only opens up the enjoyable idea of the Doctor's future self leaving jobs for him to do, but UNIT return in a manner that does not seem intended as a one-off. The organisation is re-established and remodelled (the variety of nationalities makes it seem like a UN organisation for the first time) with a new commander, and Nicholas Courtney is on great form for the symbolic handover. Although not all the plot points are adequately explained, 'Battlefield' remains a decent story that, had the series continued, would probably have proved highly significant.

154
Ghost Light

Part One: 4 October 1989
Part Two: 11 October 1989

Part Three: 18 October 1989

Written by Marc Platt
Directed by Alan Wareing

Notable Cast: Ian Hogg (Josiah) played the lead in *Rockcliffe's Babies* (1987) and *Rockcliffe's Folly* (1988), and numerous Shakespearean roles on both stage and screen. John Hallam (Light) appeared in *The Mallens* (1978), *EastEnders* (1988–90) and *The Pallisers* (1974) and the films *The Wicker Man* (Robin Hardy, 1973), *Flash Gordon* (Mike Hodges, 1980), *Dragonslayer* (Matthew Robins, 1981) and *Robin Hood: Prince of Thieves* (Kevin Reynolds, 1991). Sylvia Sims (Mrs Pritchard) played Sister Diane Murdoch in *Ice Cold In Alex* (J Lee Thompson, 1958), Laura in *Victim* (Basil Dearden, 1961), and Rebecca in *A Chorus of Disapproval* (Michael Winner, 1988). Sharon Duce (Control) starred in *Stay Lucky* with Ray Brooks. John Nettleton (Rev Matthews) was Francis Bacon in *Elizabeth R* (1970) and was a frequent civil servant in *Yes, Minister* and *Yes, Prime Minister*. Michael Cochrane (Redvers Fenn-Cooper) previously appeared in **120**, 'Black Orchid' and Frank Windsor (Inspector Mackenzie) was in **128**, 'The King's Demons'.

Writer: Marc Platt is a *Doctor Who* fan who had been pitching ideas to script editors for many years before 'Ghost Light' was commissioned.

History 101: Gabriel Chase, a house full of stuffed animals and other bric-a-brac near Perivale village in 1883. The Doctor has brought Ace there as part of an 'initiative test'.

Villains: The decrepit, photo-phobic Josiah Samuel Smith, an alien being masquerading as a Victorian gentleman. Josiah is the 'Survey' part of an alien expedition, the other members of the team being Control and Light. Their ship has been buried under the site of Gabriel Chase for millennia. Josiah has 'evolved' into a Victorian gentleman and set himself up as master of Gabriel Chase.

The Plan: Josiah has taken control of the house from Sir George Pritchard, hypnotising family, staff and guests to maintain his cover. He imprisoned Control and left Light to sleep. Once he has completed his evolution into a gentleman, Josiah intends to take over the British Empire, using the explorer Redvers Fenn-Cooper to assassinate Queen Victoria (the 'crowned Saxe-Coburg'). Josiah tries to hire the Doctor as an assassin to kill Control.

Doctor Who?: The Doctor acts as manipulative mentor to Ace, subjecting her to an initiative test which takes her back to a hated place from childhood, forcing her to face her fear. He doesn't like burned toast or bus stations, and hates 'unrequited love, and tyranny, and cruelty'. The Doctor is intensely secretive, refusing to explain things to Ace. The Doctor carries a portable Geiger counter and the 'fang of a cave bear' with him. He's a member of the Royal Geographical Society. He claims that Ace's immodest dress is due to her being 'from a less civilised clime'. He awakens the Light creature out of curiosity, then realises he may have unleashed a threat greater than Josiah. He uses his enemies' lack of imagination against them. He can wake people from trances.

Scary Monsters: Two 'husks' reside in the basement of Gabriel Chase, a withered reptile and insect, both wearing evening dress, animated by Control to effect her escape from the basement. Light and his crew's ability to personally evolve extends to reversing evolution in others – reducing one man to an ape and another to primeval soup.

Science/Magic: The story revolves around the principle of evolution. Light 'travels at the speed of thought'. The energy of Light's ship causes the stuffed and mounted creatures in the house to come to life.

Things Fall Apart: The music is too high in the sound mix, rendering parts of the dialogue difficult to hear. McCoy has a full-on gurnfest in Part Three, pulling a series of ridiculous faces as the Doctor stands up to Light.

Availability: Issued on VHS in 1994 as BBCV 5344 (UK), WHV E1318 (US). A Region 2 DVD was released in 2004 as BBCDVD 1352.

Verdict: 'You must hunt the dark continent, seek out what you desire. But be warned – you may find it.' The last *Doctor Who* story made by the BBC in the original 1963-89 run (although not in transmission order), 'Ghost Light' is an emphatic repudiation of any suggestion that the series had run out of steam. It's a story that couldn't be told in any other series, combining science, history, philosophy and fantasy in a way that only *Who* can – and yet it breaks new ground, the finished product unlike anything the series had attempted before. The script is clever, densely packed with gags and references, and is brought to life by an astonishing cast. Confined to one house, this is the most all-round successful production of the McCoy era, with excellent sets and costumes. At the centre of a story about change versus stasis, there's the developing relationship between the Doctor and Ace. McCoy and Aldred are never better than here, rarely slipping into the weaker regions of their respective acting abilities, and with a constructive tension between them as the Doctor challenges Ace's fears and encourages her to grow up. Smart, funny, subtle and exciting.

155
The Curse of Fenric

Part One: 25 October 1989
Part Two: 1 November 1989
Part Three: 8 November 1989
Part Four: 15 November 1989

Written by Ian Briggs
Directed by Nicholas Mallett

Notable Cast: Nicholas Parsons (Rev. Wainwright) is best known for hosting *Sale of the Century* (1971–84) and *Just a Minute* (1967–present), but his acting credits include the superlative *Comic Strip Presents* film *Mr Jolly Lives Next Door* (1988). Dinsdale Landen (Dr Judson) appeared in *Digby, the Biggest Dog in the World* (Joseph McGrath, 1973) and *Freud* (1984). Anne Reid (Nurse Crane) was Ken Barlow's first wife in *Coronation Street* (1960–71) and starred in *The Mother* (Roger Michel, 2003). Janet Henfrey featured in *The Singing Detective* (1986) and *Tipping The Velvet* (2003).

History 101: The TARDIS lands at a naval base near Whitby, Yorkshire in 1943. Overseen by Commander Millington (Alfred Lynch), the base houses computer expert Dr Judson and his Ultima machine, the most sophisticated code-breaking computer in the world. A troop of Russian commandos led by Sorin (Tomek Bork) arrive on the coast with the intention of stealing the Ultima machine. Millington plans to let them (there are disquieting parallels here with the Doctor's methods in **149**, 'Remembrance of the Daleks').

Science/Magic: Millington is developing chemical weapons using the natural toxins that exist under the church near the base . . .

Scary Monsters: . . . these same toxins, however, have seeped into the sea and caused the many who have drowned off the coast to mutate into Haemovores, degenerate vampire creatures.

Doctor Who?: The Doctor forges credentials for himself and Ace, writing a letter which claims that they have been sent by the War Office (holding a pen in each hand, he adds the 'signatures' of the Prime Minister and the Head of the Secret Service at the bottom). Later, Kathleen (Cory Pullman) asks the Doctor if he has any family: he quietly replies that he doesn't know (see **37**, 'The Tomb of the Cybermen'). When threatened by the Haemovores, lip-reading reveals that the incantation by which he summons up faith comprises the names of his fellow travellers in the TARDIS.

Villains: Fenric is a force of pure evil that has existed since the dawn of time but which takes corporeal form to do its work. In third-century Constantinople it wore its body out trying to solve a chess problem the Doctor set for it: it was banished to a shadow dimension whilst its earthly form was confined to a flask.

The Plan: Fenric has been able to remotely manipulate those who have touched the flask, and their descendants. The flask was stolen by Vikings and brought to Yorkshire: they carved inscriptions on runes which, unbeknownst to them, form a computer program – a sort of highly complex incantation – which can free Fenric from the flask. Only now, with the development of the Ultima machine, is it possible to run this program.

Things Fall Apart: Aldred's 'mysterious and sultry' acting is about as sexy as dandruff, and the 'evil' acting of Joann Kenny (Jean) and Joanne Bell (Phyllis) falls short. The rack of 'bombs' in the chemical weapons store is clearly a single piece of moulded plastic.

Availability: Issued on DVD in 2003 as BBCDVD 1154 (Region 2), WHV E1099 (Region 1). This release includes both the broadcast version and a 104-minute 'director's cut' TV movie version including 12 minutes of extra material. The pacing and clarity of the narrative are much improved in the latter and it comes highly recommended. An earlier VHS (BBCV 4453, WHV E1099) is also extended, but only by six minutes.

Verdict: 'Don't interrupt me when I'm eulogising.' 'The Curse of Fenric' sees a revival of the Gothic horror stylings of the early Tom Baker years integrated superbly with the confident new direction established under Andrew Cartmel. The scene in which Sorin wards off the Haemovores by his faith in a revolution which, by 1989, was failing is wonderful, as is its counterpoint when Wainwright (a powerful performance from Nicholas Parsons, of all people) finds that his angst over British war atrocities has destroyed his faith in God. This sordid view of war (the chemical weapons are a grisly touch) forms an ideal backdrop for the plottings of a simple but effective villain.

Again, it's the Doctor's game but Ace is a highly significant player, and his underestimation of her almost costs him dear when he assumes that she won't realise the true nature of the Viking runes. The Doctor has stepped up his activities and is now playing for high stakes, but may be biting off more than he can chew: the result is great heroic drama.

156
Survival

Part One: 22 November 1989
Part Two: 29 November 1989
Part Three: 6 December 1989

Written by Rona Munro
Directed by Alan Wareing

Notable Cast: Gareth Hale and Norman Pace (Harvey and Len) were a then-successful comedy double act with their own show on ITV. Adele Silva (Squeak) grew up to become tabloid gossip and pin-up fodder via a role in *Emmerdale*. Julian Holloway (Sergeant Patterson) is the son of Stanley Holloway and appeared in *A Hard Day's Night* (Richard Lester, 1964), *Porridge* (Dick Clement, 1979) and a lot of *Carry On* films, including *Carry On Henry* (Gerald Thomas, 1971).

Writer: Rona Munro met Andrew Cartmel on a BBC training course. She went on to work for him on *Casualty* (1990) and then scripted *Butterfly, Butterfly* (1994) for Ken Loach. Now a multiple award-winning playwright for both television and the stage, mostly working within social drama, her later works include *Aimee* *and Jaguar* (1999) about a lesbian romance in Nazi Germany, and *Rehab* (Antonia Bird, 2003).

Doctor Who?: He's heard of the cheetah people, the Kitlings and their nasty habits but there's no planning or foreknowledge from the Doctor here. He knocks Patterson nearly senseless by placing a finger on his forehead (see **153**, 'Battlefield'). That he finds his way back to Earth when possessed by the cheetahs' influence might imply he now considers Earth his home. (That said, he materialises mere feet from the TARDIS, as does Ace, and she describes the TARDIS as 'the only home I've got'.)

Scary Monsters: The cheetah people, catlike humanoids who have the power to teleport themselves through space in order to go hunting and return home with their prey. They seem barely sentient, living to hunt, eat and kill. They were once human and were transformed into bestial creatures by the power of the planet (see **Other Worlds**). While they were still human they bred the Kitlings, feline vultures which look like domestic black cats, to seek out their prey for them by sending them to other worlds as scouts.

Other Worlds: The unnamed planet of the unnamed cheetah people. A rocky, volcanic desert planet, it has a symbiotic relationship with its inhabitants: their violence and destruction influence how long it exists; its inherent savagery influences their behaviour. When they fight each other they trigger explosions and hasten the planet's demise.

Villains: The Master, trapped on the planet of the cheetah people, TARDIS-less and infected by the planet's malignancy. He's desperate to escape.

Science/Magic: The Master uses the term 'bewitches' to describe the effect the planet has on people who spend any time there. Those possessed by the power of the cheetah planet can see through the eyes of the Kitlings when they choose to.

Things Fall Apart: The Kitlings look quite poor in close-up. The cheetah people are only fair-to-middling costumes, but their effectiveness is preserved by being well shot, choreographed and performed. In the scripts Patterson is a police sergeant, BBC pressure changed this to a Territorial Army sergeant. This somewhat dilutes the concept of the character (and his relation to story's themes) although Julian Holloway's performance is superb.

Availability: Issued on VHS in 1995 as BBCV 5687 (UK), WHV E1335 (US).

Verdict: 'Not a very efficient way to hunt is it? All that noise and pantomime just to slaughter one little animal.' 'Survival' is surprisingly confident in the maturity of its scripts, and the music, direction and the performances of its cast are great. It's a complex, clever story, difficult to do justice to in brief because so much of its appeal lies in the concepts and the visuals rather than the plot.

'Survival' is, in part, *Doctor Who*'s attempt to comment on the perceived ethos of then-contemporary Britain. It's a story about the futility of competition and the terrible allure of savagery, with the cheetah planet and its effects a metaphor for both the impulses that drive humanity and the individual's need to subjugate their baser desires to the needs of the common good. It links this into an environmentalist viewpoint, with the destruction of the cheetah planet being due to the irresponsible behaviour of its inhabitants. The story also pities, rather than merely hates, those caught the trap of 'survival of the fittest' and questions societal applications of that 'glib generalisation'. In the context of a story *about* selfishness and cruelty, the use of the deranged, pitiless and entirely self-centred Master makes perfect sense and Anthony Ainley's performance is his best in the role. 'Survival' is proof positive that, despite all the odds, *Doctor Who* could be worthwhile, beautiful, powerful and strange right up to the very end.

157
The Paradise of Death
BBC RADIO 5, 30-minute episodes

Episode One: 27 August 1993
Episode Two: 3 September 1993
Episode Three: 10 September 1993
Episode Four: 17 September 1993
Episode Five: 24 September 1993

Written by Barry Letts
Directed by Phil Clarke

Notable Cast: Jon Pertwee returns as the Doctor, along with Nicholas Courtney and Elisabeth Sladen. Richard Pearce (Jeremy Fitzoliver) is a voice actor whose credits include *Shakespeare: The*

Animated Tales (1992). Actors with previous *Who* credits include Harold Innocent (**150**) as Freeth, Maurice Denham (**136**) as the President and Peter Miles (**52, 71, 78**) as Tragan. Other cast members who play multiple roles are the writer's son Dominic Letts, Trevor Martin (from **50**, 'The War Games'), and Julian Rhind-Tutt, who appeared in *The Saint* (Philip Noyce, 1997), *Notting Hill* (Roger Michell, 1999), *Lara Croft: Tomb Raider* (Simon West, 2001) and sitcom *Hippies* (2000) and *Green Wing* (2004–present).

Director: Phil Clarke has produced and directed numerous BBC radio programmes, including several projects with educational funnyman Mark Steel and many adaptations, including Ellis Peters' *Cadfael*.

History 101: London, the near future, where Parakon Corporation's new theme park 'Space World' is about to open on Hampstead Heath. The theme park has an Apollo rocket that dominates the North London skyline. UNIT has been brought in to investigate a murder on the Space World site. The Parakon Corporation has the full support of the United Nations, tying the Brigadier's hands, having negotiated with the authorities on Earth for some time.

Doctor Who?: The Doctor quotes Venusian proverbs, and explains the events of **64**, 'The Time Monster' to Sarah. The Doctor survives a fall of 200 feet through 'bone relaxation', allowing his tissue to soften and regenerate. His vision is so good that he can see a hair less than a millimetre long under a man's fingernail. He used to fly skimmers when he was a boy on Gallifrey. The Doctor says that when he lost his mentor, he felt like it was his father who had died. The Doctor tries to hypnotise a gargon with a Venusian lullaby (see **61**, 'The Curse of Peladon'), but it doesn't work. He's willing to admit when he's wrong. (See **66**, 'Carnival of Monsters'.) The Doctor refers to President Richard Nixon and Watergate.

Villains: Freeth, piggy Chairman of the Parakon Corporation and son of the President of Parakon. The sadistic Tragan (Peter Miles), a Naglon, is Vice Chairman of the Corporation's Entertainments Division.

Scary Monsters: Tragan has bestial, doglike alien pets from Blestinu that he sets on intruders. Exhibits at Space World include the 'Crab Clawed Kamelius' from Aldeberon II, an 'Osteroid', a

'Flesh Eating Griffin' and a 'Stinkler' – real creatures, but not their real names. The savage creatures used in executions on Parakon include 'the great butcher toad', a 'cranjal ape', the insectoid 'soldier chice', and the lethal gargon (which never stops following its prey's scent). The Comminion Bats can be ridden by people.

Science/Magic: 'Experienced Reality' is a form of virtual reality that puts the user into the perspective of someone within the action: it can be as addictive as heroin, and controls the user's mind through the ER transmission needles. A more advanced version creates hallucinations in the human mind using 'a radiated matrix of modulated psychomagnetic beams'. The Doctor repairs the 'psychotelemetric circuit' so that the TARDIS can locate a planet using matter from that world. The Blinovitch Limitation Effect only applies when going into your own past. The rapine plant can be used to synthesise almost anything, but reduces the land it grows on to desert.

Other Worlds: Parakon, on the other side of the galaxy from Earth, where the aged President rules a society of unemployed 'shareholders' entranced by ER broadcasts of public executions and alcoholic 'blip juice'. Blestinu is a battlefield of a planet.

The Plan: Freeth and Tragan are plotting against the President, shielding him from the truth. Hospital patients on Parakon are being implanted with ER technology, allowing the plotters to control them. The Parakon Corporation relentlessly expands, sowing rapine on each new planet.

Things Fall Apart: The character of Jeremy Fitzoliver is fingers-down-blackboard irritating. The 'cockneys' in Episode One are pretty bad, while Elisabeth Sladen isn't very good at acting Sarah's grief in Episode Five. The story is clearly meant to happen after **70**, 'The Time Warrior' but **71**, 'Invasion of the Dinosaurs' follows on directly from it.

Availability: Issued on CD as ISBN 0563553235.

Verdict: 'One backflip and a double somersault will be quite sufficient.' A straightforward, nostalgic adventure on the series' 30th anniversary, 'The Paradise of Death' is a lot of fun. It doesn't pretend to have been made in 1974, instead offering an entertaining runaround which is reminiscent of all sorts of *Who*, not just Pertwee's era. The cast give it 110 per cent and there's some fantastic sound design (the end of Episode Two sounds like something from the *Terminator* films). Not great, but certainly very good.

158
Dimensions In Time

Part One: 26 November 1993 (8 minutes)
Part Two: 27 November 1993 (5 minutes)

Written by John Nathan-Turner and David Roden
Directed by Stuart McDonald (uncredited)

Notable Cast: Kate O'Mara returns as the Rani (see **139**, **145**). Sam West (Cyrian) is an accomplished theatre actor who narrated *The Nazis: A Warning From History* (1998) and played Doctor Frankenstein in *Van Helsing* (Steven Sommers, 2004). The story is a comical crossover with BBC soap *EastEnders*, and has many members of the then-regular cast of that programme in cameo roles including Mike Reid (Frank Butcher) who was an extra in **37**, 'The War Machines'. Returning *Who* actors (Doctors aside) are: Sophie Aldred, Bonnie Langford, Carole Ann Ford, Elisabeth Sladen, Sarah Sutton, Nicola Bryant, Caroline John, Richard Franklin, Nicholas Courtney, Lalla Ward, Deborah Watling, Louise Jameson and the voice of John Leeson.

Writer: David Roden is a pseudonym for David Mansell.

Director: Stuart McDonald is a light entertainment director who has worked on *Robot Wars* and *Trisha*.

History 101: The East End of London in a twenty-year time-loop between 1973, 1993 and 2013, including the Cutty Sark, the Greenwich Meridian and Albert Square. In 2013 prices on market stalls are in barcodes, a monorail runs through East London and people are legally obliged to wear sunblock out of doors.

Villains: The Rani, from **139**, 'Mark of the Rani', whose TARDIS now more closely resembles the Doctor's, albeit with a black console, purple walls and a cheap carpet. Its exterior resembles a satellite, then the Queen Victoria pub (from *EastEnders*) and Richard's tombstone (from **151**, 'Silver Nemesis').

Doctor Who?: The Tom Baker Doctor, trapped somewhere odd, discovers the Rani's plan to trap the Doctors and sends a message to his other selves. The Hartnell and Troughton Doctors have already been captured, their severed heads floating in space. The Rani diverts the McCoy Doctor and Ace to 1973, and a time distortion turns him into the Colin Baker Doctor, then the Pertwee Doctor, and the Davison Doctor. (Ace then changes into other companions, as the Doctor's personal timestream disrupts, or something.) The Davison Doctor uses his telepathic powers to contact his other selves (see **65**, 'The Three Doctors'), and apparently summon the power of the Pertwee Doctor. The McCoy Doctor does the same to free his other selves.

The Plan: The Rani is assembling a menagerie from all over the universe, and needs an earthling to complete the set. When the Doctor(s) get closer to understanding the time distortion, she unleashes her monsters to kill them. A computer with genetic codes and brain prints of every species in the galaxy will, along with a time tunnel transferred to the Greenwich meridian, allow the Rani to control all evolution.

Scary Monsters: Unleashed from the Rani's menagerie are a Cyberman, an Ogron, a Vanir, a Tractator, a Tetrap, a prop from a *Doctor Who* stage play (don't ask), Fifi, a Time Lord, something dressed as Mawdryn, the Dragon from 'Dragonfire', a Vervoid, a Voc Robot, a Mogarian, an Argolin, a Plasmaton, a very tall Thoros Betan and a Sea Devil.

Science/Magic: The in-rush of timezones will apparently trap all the Doctors and companions in the East End together. Greenwich is centre of 'the Earth time meridian'. Two time brains in the Rani's computer will cause it to overload.

Things Fall Apart: The production uses a form of 3D which requires specific types of motion to maintain the effect – hence the random floating objects and bits in the foreground. The technology can cause a splitting headache. The *Who* actors may be bad in this, but some of the *EastEnders* cast are even worse.

Availability: As a *Children in Need* charity production for which all concerned gave their time for free, 'Dimensions in Time' was made on the contractual basis that it could never be repeated or released commercially. As such, it is the only *Who* production in this book which is unavailable in any legitimate form.

Verdict: 'I can hear the hearts-beat of a killer.' Thirteen minutes of psychotic nonsense, 'Dimensions in Time' is a blissfully short burst of gibberish for a good cause. As part of the BBC's annual *Children in Need* event it received a relative blaze of publicity, and was widely seen on broadcast. While it was nice at the time to see so many old faces, it's hardly the series' finest hour, and not much of a celebration – only Peter Davison gives a decent performance in the entire mess, cementing his status as the most capable actor of all the leads alive at the time. Davison aside, 'Dimensions of Time' has little to offer. It's done its job for charity, and can now be safely forgotten . . .

159
Doctor Who and the Ghosts of N-Space
BBC RADIO 2, 30-minute episodes

Episode One: 20 January 1996
Episode Two: 27 January 1996
Episode Three: 3 February 1996
Episode Four: 10 February 1996
Episode Five: 17 February 1996
Episode Six: 24 February 1996

Written by Barry Letts
Directed by Phil Clarke

Note: Produced as a follow-on to **157**, 'The Paradise of Death' in late 1994 (Jon Pertwee, Nicholas Courtney, Elisabeth Sladen and Richard Pearce all return) but transmission was delayed for over a year. The novelisation states that the story 'occurs' between **72**, 'Death To The Daleks' and **73**, 'The Monster of Peladon' from the Doctor and Sarah's point of view.

Notable Cast: Sandra Dickinson (Maggie) is best known for playing Trillian in the television *The Hitch-Hiker's Guide to the Galaxy* (1981). Jim Sweeney (Guido) is widely rated as Britain's top improvisational comedian. Stephen Thorne (Max) was in **65**, 'The Three Doctors', **67**, 'Frontier in Space' and **87**, 'The Hand of Fear'.

Science/Magic: Every world in the universe has a counterpart in 'Null Space' (which is 'Nowhere, literally') and every sentient being on Earth has a counterpart 'N-Body' which is 'co-terminus with the normal body'. N-Space can normally only be crossed by the dying, whose N-Bodies (seemingly a secular concept of the soul) pass through N-Space on their way 'elsewhere'. Some get trapped in N-Space (usually due to an unhappy death) and manifest themselves as ghosts and poltergeists. It is 'their own ignorance of the truth of the situation' and their inability to 'move on into the light leaving all the fear, hate and despair behind' that condemns them to walk the Earth. The trapped N-Bodies also 'generate negativity' while in N-Space (see **The Plan**). This N-Space is not the same as N (for Normal) Space referred to in **111**, 'Full Circle' et al.

Scary Monsters: 'Diabolo, the fiends from the Pit': physical manifestations of all the 'hatred, despair and rage' in N-Space.

Doctor Who?: The Doctor says he knew 'Bertie' (HG) Wells and helped him with 'invisibility experiments' (which contradicts **141**, 'Timelash'). He goes on a lot about 'synchronicity' and 'serendipity' (usually to 'explain' plot contrivances) and mentions that the latter term was coined by his old friend novelist Horace Walpole. Leonardo Da Vinci is another old friend (**86**, 'The Masque of Mandragora', **105**, 'City of Death'). The Doctor builds both a 'multi-vectored, null-dimensional temporal and spatial probe' (to recreate Sarah's encounter with a ghost) and a 'dimensional transducer' (to traverse N-Space) from scratch; the latter involves both the skull of a rat and a hard-boiled egg in its workings. He believes in a form of afterlife.

Villains: Max Vilimio (Stephen Thorne), a one-armed mafia billionaire and entrepreneur who is actually the immortal fifteenth-century sorcerer Maximilian. His sidekicks are Brother Nico (David Holt), the spirit of a fifteenth-century monk, and Maggie Pulaski, a self-confessed 'dumb broad from Brooklyn' who might have killed her abusive father.

The Plan: The story's main 'threat' is that the barrier between N-Space and Earth will collapse due to the pressure on the hole in it created by Max in the process of gaining immortality. Then all the evil in N-Space will burst through and swamp the Earth.

Things Fall Apart: The script commits the radio-technique sin of having characters talk out loud to themselves so that the audience can know what's going on. The occasional minor profanities ('cow-shit') seem out of place in *Doctor Who*. The extent of research for the Mafia subplot seems to be a viewing of *The Godfather* (Francis Ford Coppola, 1972) as there are characters called Clemenza and Bruno and the terms 'Godfather' and 'Consigliore' are bandied about.

Availability: Available on CD as ISBN 0563477016.

Verdict: 'Impossible? Evidently not, since it happened!' This is an epic, taking in heaven, hell and everything in between. Unfortunately, that 'in between' includes cod-Italian accents, clichéd Mafiosi, Elvis impersonators and an old man who talks in 'comedy' malapropisms. That said, this is hugely enjoyable: atmospheric, funny, darkly bizarre and occasionally genuinely horrific. Whilst the Doctor is traditionally characterised, the plot itself is very unlike any other *Doctor Who*, despite containing old staples like time-travel and slavering monsters (Letts must surely be given points for trying to stretch both himself and the series). It's also very well-produced radio with terrific music (by Peter Howell of the Radiophonic Workshop) and sound effects.

The scripts' spiritual relativism and the attempt to create pseudo SF/fantasy rationales for 'Big Questions' without explicitly taking from any specific faith seem much less odd in our post-*Buffy The Vampire Slayer* era than they did on transmission. While Pertwee's voice has noticeably aged there's enormous authority, warmth and a daredevil charm to his final performance as Doctor Who. It's also worth noting that while 'Gothic' is a term overused when discussing *Doctor Who* this, with its sorcerer walled up in a medieval castle, Rococo setting, casual sadism, ghost monks, despairing suicides and 'fiends from the pit', is arguably the real deal. Compare with **160**, 'The Movie' and seriously ask which demonstrates the more ambitious, wide-ranging and entertaining conception of *Doctor Who*.

160
Doctor Who/'The Movie'
(85 minutes)

27 May 1996
(US: 14 May 1996)

Written by Mathew Jacobs
Directed by Geoffrey Sax

Notable Cast: Sylvester McCoy returns as 'the Old Doctor' before regenerating into Paul McGann (born 1959). One of four acting

McGann brothers, Paul is best known as the 'I' in *Withnail and I* (Bruce Robinson, 1987), and for being almost entirely cut out of *Alien³* (David Fincher, 1992). He has more recently played Bush in *Hornblower* (2001–03). Eric Roberts (the Master), brother of Julia, played Paul Snider in *Star 80* (Bob Fosse, 1983), Paulie in *The Pope of Greenwich Village* (Stuart Rosenberg, 1984) and was Oscar-nominated for the Akira Kurosawa-scripted *Runaway Train* (Andrei Konchalovsky, 1985). Daphne Ashbrook played Dawn Atwood in early episodes of *The O.C.* (2003). Any other familiar faces are actors who've worked in more successful Canada-lensed productions like *The X-Files* or *Smallville*.

Writer: Matthew Jacobs wrote *Paperhouse* (Bernard Rose, 1988), and contributed to *The Young Indiana Jones Chronicles*. He scripted Activision's *Star Wars: Starfighter* videogame and his father played Doc Holliday in **25**, 'The Gunfighters'.

Director: Geoffrey Sax has directed episodes of *Lovejoy*, *The New Statesman*, Andrew Davies' update of *Othello* (2002, starring Christopher Eccleston) and adaptation of Sarah Waters' lesbian period drama *Tipping the Velvet* (2002).

Producer: Executive Producer Philip David Segal, the main creative impetus behind this project, worked on *Earth 2* (1994–95) and Gene Rodenberry's *Andromeda* (2003).

History 101: The Doctor is taking the Master's ashes to Gallifrey when the Master sabotages the TARDIS and the Doctor has to land in San Francisco on 30 December 1999.

Other Worlds: We see the planets Skaro and Gallifrey, but the former for a few seconds and the latter only from space. Gallifrey is '250 million light years' from Earth.

Doctor Who?: The McCoy Doctor is explicitly described as being at the end of his seventh life. He walks out of the TARDIS into a hail of bullets, two going into his leg and one through his shoulder. He doesn't die from his wounds, but is taken to hospital where he's sent for heart surgery due to his frantic double-pulse. Cardiologist Dr Grace Holloway then kills him by jabbing a fibre-optic camera into one of his hearts. The Doctor is dead for some time, regenerating later in the morgue (he later says this was due to the anaesthetic, which 'almost destroyed the regenerative process'). His regeneration involves muscle convulsions and gurning, and he is shown to start breathing again.

The regenerated Doctor has the strength to punch his way out of a morgue freezer, knocking the door off its hinges. The McGann Doctor suffers from amnesia, and wears a 'Wild Bill Hickock' costume he finds in a hospital locker, with a green velvet frock coat, waistcoat, grey trousers and cravat. He's not pleased to find the camera wire still jammed in one of his hearts. He remembers meeting Da Vinci, Puccini, Freud and Marie Curie. This new Doctor comes out with random insights about the people he meets, and talks in a dreamy, spaced-out way. He has random excitable outbursts, sometimes related to shoes. He remembers watching a meteor storm with his father on Gallifrey. He has a romance with Dr Grace Holloway (the woman who killed him, lest we forget), kissing her passionately a number of times. He regains his memory when the Eye of Harmony opens (see **The Plan**). The Doctor is half human, as shown by his human retinas. He says that he's half human on his mother's side, but it may be a joke. He doesn't recognise the Master until he sees his eyes. He agrees with Grace when she describes him as British. After his last life, he will be able to turn into another creature (the Doctor says that 'in the fight for survival there are no rules' – or any other kind of logic or sense, by the looks of it). He can only interfere because he's a Time Lord. He keeps a spare key to the TARDIS in a hole above the door, and likes its exterior shape. He doesn't consider himself to have seen death, and doesn't believe in ghosts. He seems to regret leaving Grace behind but the goes into the TARDIS and puts a record on.

Villains: The Master, who has been executed by the Daleks. Having survived disintegration, he exists as a gooey, snakelike liquid monster (he has reptilian eyes even before he dies). His liquid form leaps down the throat of a man called Bruce, taking possession of his body. This stolen body begins to decay almost immediately, and clearly isn't a permanent solution. He dresses as the Terminator (leather coat, shades) or in Gallifreyan robes for special occasions. He gets himself a young assistant, juvenile gangster Chang Lee (Yee Jee Tso), who he treats in a mock-paternal way. The Master is specific about grammar, and can vomit acidic goo as well as a mind-controlling acid. He can drain the goo from an infected human with a kiss.

The Plan: The Master wants to steal the Doctor's body. He opens the Eye of Harmony in the Doctor's TARDIS. Looking into the Eye will destroy the Doctor's soul, allowing the Master to steal his body. The Eye being left open will destroy the Earth, coincidentally at midnight on New Year's Eve 1999.

Science/Magic: The TARDIS has a vast wood-panelled control room and a handbrake that the Doctor applies during a 'critical timing malfunction'. The cloister room is a cathedral-like space with the stone Eye of Harmony in the middle. The Eye only opens when a human eye looks into the beam of light underneath the 'reflector staffs'. It's the power source of the TARDIS and opening it causes the 'molecular structure of the planet' to break down, allowing the Doctor to bend plate glass and walk straight through it. The Doctor needs a beryllium atomic clock to fix the TARDIS and close the Eye again. The TARDIS has the power to bring people back to life with magic fairy dust.

Things Fall Apart: The cut from the Police Box exterior floating in space to the TARDIS interior doesn't indicate that one is inside the other, which must have been baffling for new viewers. McCoy's dying scream on the operating table sounds more like a bark of annoyance. Daphne Ashbrook seems to think she's in a screwball comedy, trying far, far too hard to be quirky. The denouement is confused, pointless and twee.

Availability: Issued on VHS under the generic title *Doctor Who* in 1996 as BBCV 5882 (UK), and on DVD as *The Movie*, BBCDVD 1043 (Region 2). Rights issues have prevented any North American release, either on VHS or DVD.

Verdict: 'Only children believe that crap.' A well-directed but otherwise average Canadian-filmed TV movie of the kind that clutters up American network television and British cable channels every day of the week, 'The Movie' fails to give even the slightest indication of the possibilities of *Doctor Who* as a series. The threat to the world seems tacked on, and the Doctor is portrayed as a wandering eccentric rather than an adventurer, scientist, explorer or even hero. All we're left with is a fight-to-the-death between two aliens who don't seem to be able to die, which is exactly as pointless as it sounds. The TARDIS sets are fantastic, and there's a buzz to seeing the police box and other bits of *Who* iconography appear, but otherwise this is uninspiring stuff. Paul McGann never really convinces or appeals as the Doctor, so kudos to Eric Roberts (an actor who talked of fond memories of watching the show in the 1970s) for injecting a highly entertaining note of gleeful malice to the part of the Master. You know there's something wrong when the Master is more charming, funny and engaging than the Doctor – perhaps the most glaring symptom of the problems with this glossy misfire.

161
The Curse of Fatal Death
5-minute episodes

Part 1: 12 February 1999
Part 2: 12 February 1999
Part 3: 12 February 1999
Part 4: 12 February 1999

Written by Steven Moffat
Directed by John Henderson

Notable Cast: Writer, comedian and actor Rowan Atkinson (The Doctor) is best known as the various incarnations of Edmund Blackadder (1983–89, 2000), for playing *Mr Bean* and appearing in *Not The Nine O'Clock News* (1980–84). Richard E Grant (The Doctor) will for ever be Withnail of *Withnail and I* (Bruce Robinson, 1986). Jim Broadbent (The Doctor) won an Oscar for *Iris* (Richard Eyre, 2001) and appeared in *Moulin Rouge!* (Baz Luhrmann, 2001), *Gangs of New York* (Martin Scorsese, 2003) and much light British TV comedy. Hugh Grant (The Doctor) is arguably the biggest living British film star. You know who he is. Joanna Lumley (The Doctor) was Purdey in *The New Avengers* (1976–77) Sapphire of *Sapphire and Steel* (1979–82) and Patsy in *Absolutely Fabulous* (1992–present) among many other things. Julia Sawalha (Emma) starred in *Press Gang* (1989–93), *Absolutely Fabulous* (1992–present) and *Jonathan Creek* (2002–present) and is utterly adored by the authors of this book. Jonathan Pryce can be seen in *Brazil* (Terry Gilliam, 1983), *Tomorrow Never Dies* (Roger Spottiswode, 1997) and *Evita* (Alan Parker, 1986) and is amazing as the Master.

Writer: Steven Moffat created and wrote all of the consistently brilliant BAFTA-winning *Press Gang* (1989–93) and the sitcoms *Joking Apart* (1991–5), *Chalk* (1996–7) and *Coupling* (2000–present) the last of which won him a Silver Rose of Montreux, European TV's highest award for a situation comedy.

Director: An experienced TV comedy director, John Henderson also has several feature film credits including *Loch Ness* (1996) and *Two Men Went to War* (2002).

Producer: Sue Vertue, the writer's wife, is the producer of numerous British comedy series including *Coupling* (2000–present), *Gimme, Gimme, Gimme* (1999–2001) and *The Vicar of Dibley* (1998–2001). Moffat claims that her allowing him to cast five Doctor Whos was the best wedding present ever.

Other Worlds: Terserus (see **88**, 'The Deadly Assassin'), a planet whose population communicated by 'precisely modulated gastric emissions' and were all killed when they discovered fire.

Villains: The Master, who fails to anticipate his betrayal by his enemies and is identified by the Doctor as 'the camp one'. So he's basically characterised how he's always been.

Scary Monsters: The Daleks. Moffat deserves some kind of medal for including no stair-climbing jokes.

The Plan: The Master plots to lure the Doctor to his doom, whilst helping the Daleks to take over the universe with a Zectronic Energy Beam.

Doctor Who?: The Atkinson Doctor is identified (by the Master) as the 'ninth body'. He's self-assured, a little smug and planning to retire and marry his assistant Emma. He then regenerates four times: first into the arrogant, narcissistic Richard E Grant Doctor; then the shy, bumbling Broadbent Doctor; the foppish, charming Hugh Grant Doctor and finally into the Lumley Doctor, who is forthright, spirited and female. Because the series had previously claimed (see **88**, 'The Deadly Assassin' et al) that Time Lords have thirteen lives, this 'using up' of the Doctor's incarnations was seen by some as a BBC sop to 'finish off' the show, but this is inaccurate and unfair: the script is overwhelmingly positive, suggesting that the Doctor will *never* die. Besides, *Doctor Who*'s various producers have always thrown out established ideas if they were inconvenient. If the BBC wants to keep making the show, it won't let an old bit of continuity get in the way.

Things Fall Apart: For once, the ropy bits are intentional – and some of the effects are better than anything the programme had seen up to that point.

Availability: Released on VHS in 1999 as BBCV 6889 (UK), presented in the production team's favoured two-part format (and with a different title sequence on the first part) along with a 'making of' documentary and a collection of *Doctor Who* spoofs and sketches.

Verdict: 'You fools! This Zectronic Beam Controller will not only explode, it will *im*plode!' Everything you wouldn't normally be able to do in *Doctor Who* covered in the space of twenty minutes dispersed across 1999's *Comic Relief* telethon. Even when the series has been played for laughs in the past, it observed certain rules without which it would've fallen to bits: having the Doctor nip back and set things up for himself wouldn't be viable on a weekly basis, as the stories would all be over inside five minutes. The fact that everybody's thought of it at some point, though, is what makes it funny when you see it happen.

For those who know *Doctor Who* very well there are details like recycling of obscure dialogue and music, whilst people who vaguely remember the series will have seen tabloid speculation about the Doctor romancing his assistants (see **160**, 'The Movie') or the casting of a female Doctor (which, unfailingly, would suggest Joanna Lumley) and recognise that rules are being broken for comic effect. For those in-between this feels like an archetypal *Doctor Who* story with jokes and famous people (all of whom give excellent performances – Hugh Grant looks remarkably at ease in the role). 'The Curse of Fatal Death' therefore works for a general audience fuelled by the alcohol and hearty goodwill generally involved in watching *Comic Relief*, whilst for the fans it's a far better celebration than the last charity runaround (**158**, 'Dimensions in Time') and a signal that public attitude towards *Doctor Who* was growing fonder in its absence.

162
Death Comes to Time
BBCi

At the Temple of the Fourth: 16 July 2001*
Planet of Blood Part 1: 14 February 2002**
Planet of Blood Part 2: 22 February 2002
Planet of Blood Part 3: 1 March 2002
The Child Part 1: 8 March 2002
The Child Part 2: 15 March 2002

The Child Part 3: 22 March 2002
No Child of Earth Part 1: 29 March 2002
No Child of Earth Part 2: 5 April 2002
No Child of Earth Part 3: 12 April 2002
Death Comes to Time Part 1: 19 April 2002
Death Comes to Time Part 2: 26 April 2002
Death Comes to Time Part 3: 3 May 2002
*30-minute pilot episode.
**30-minute episodes, divided into three 10-minute instalments.

Written by Colin Meek
Directed by Dan Freedman

Notable Cast: Sylvester McCoy and Sophie Aldred return as the Doctor and Ace. Kevin Eldon (Antimony) is a comic writer and actor whose credits include *Brass Eye* (1997), *Fist of Fun* (1996) and *Nighty Night* (2004). Leonard Fenton (Casmus) played Dr Legg in *EastEnders*, and as such is referred to, but doesn't appear, in **158**, 'Dimensions in Time'. Novelist, writer, actor and director Stephen Fry (Minister of Chance) is best known for the lead role in *Wilde* (Brian Gilbert, 1997), playing Melchett in *Black-Adder II* (1985) and *Blackadder Goes Forth* (1989) and his comic collaborations with Hugh Laurie. Actor and performer John Sessions (Tannis) appeared in *Gangs of New York* (Martin Scorsese, 2002) and Kenneth Branagh's *Henry V* (1989) and *In The Bleak Midwinter* (1995), but is best known in the UK for *Whose Line Is It Anyway?* and *Stella Street*. He auditioned for the role of *Doctor Who* in **160**, 'The Movie'. Anthony Stewart Head (St Valentine) played Giles in *Buffy the Vampire Slayer* (1997–2003). Julienne Davis (Computer) appeared in *Eyes Wide Shut* (Stanley Kubrick, 1999). David Soul *is* Hutch in *Starsky and Hutch* (1975–79).

Writer: Colin Meek is a pseudonym for several people who contributed to the script, principally . . .

Director: Dan Freedman writes, directs, produces, performs and lectures on comedy for radio.

Script Editor: Nev Fountain writes comedy for radio and television including for impressions show *Dead Ringers*.

Doctor Who?: The Doctor is a powerful, melancholy figure, capable of bending time to his will with the power of words and tormented at being 'bound by a code' that prevents him from interfering. The Doctor gets possibly his best entrance in the entire series – an unstoppable invasion force sweeps on to a planet, crushing all resistance. One of the invaders makes a speech about how all hope is lost for the oppressed people ... and *then* the TARDIS arrives, the Doctor walks out and the theme music begins. The Doctor has a new friend, the purple-skinned Antimony, an innocent young man whom the Doctor gets to hit people. He says he doesn't mind dying. He's very persuasive. He thinks he was once eaten by an Allosaurus. He describes himself as being alien 'to everywhere'. He was never a baby.

Villains: General Tannis, Supreme Commander of the military forces of the Canisian Empire. He is expanding his power base across the universe, and destroys the lives of millions for fun.

The Plan: Tannis has sent the vampire Nessican to kill two Time Lords, Antinor and Valentine, to cover up a distortion they discovered in space and time. He has reduced the Canisian leader to a puppet, so that Tannis can continue his conquests uninterrupted.

Other Worlds: Alpha Canis One, homeworld of the Canisian Suns. Santini, a democratic planet invaded by the Canisians. Myson Island is a planet in the Crab Nebula, where the Time Lords built the Temple of the Fourth to mark the decision not to use their powers, a decision they made after their powers destroyed the people they tried to help. Anima Persis is a dead planet inhabited by 'mutant monstrosities and the vengeful spirits of the dead'. On a peaceful planet, Mount Plutarch is home to the Kingmaker, who appoints Time Lords and gives them their TARDISes.

Scary Monsters: Nessican, a vampire sent to Earth to kill the Saints, Antinor and Valentine. Vampires are naturally drawn to darkness and cold, and have hypnotic powers over their prey. They can be killed by garlic, or severing of the spine.

Science/Magic: There are black holes expanding, tearing a hole in the fabric of space–time. The Doctor considers this to be the result of someone changing time. The TARDIS is not so much a vehicle as 'the essence of transport'.

Things Fall Apart: The scenes set in the US are just not funny.

Availability: Released on CD in 2002 as ISBN 0563528230, remastered with some revised or extended scenes, and a number of extras. An MP3 CD was released in 2004 as ISBN 0563523670, including both the remastered audio and the original RealPlayer version with animated illustrations by Lee Sullivan.

Verdict: 'Twilight falls, and the strange dream ends.' Poetic, mythic and epic, 'Death Comes To Time' reinvents *Doctor Who*, providing a coda to the 1963–89 television series. The story picks up the characters of the Doctor and Ace ten years on from **156**, 'Survival' (the project was pitched to BBC Radio in 1999, almost exactly a decade on from the end of the TV series), and as such fits in that odd sub-genre of stories where ageing heroes come back for a great, final battle, and muse on their life and experiences.

A sweeping narrative concerning death, war, power and responsibility requires a script that reaches beyond conventional 'kitchen sink' drama or SF pulp hackwork, and Colin Meek's writing rises to the occasion, with some gorgeous dialogue and imagery. It's not all philosophising – there's a contemporary murder plot, spectacular space battles, witty jokes and a truly evil villain. Production is first rate, with excellent effects and genuine classical music preferred over an original score. While Lee Sullivan's cosmic illustrations, full of starfields and alien landscapes, are an appropriate accompaniment to such a lyrical story, this is primarily an audio drama, and as such rests heavily on its voice cast. Thankfully McCoy and Aldred are at their very best, with material that plays to their strengths, and the guest cast is high powered with Stephen Fry and Leonard Fenton simply wonderful as the two troubled Time Lords, the Minister and Casmus. John Sessions is deliciously, fruitily evil as Tannis, and there are starry cameos from Anthony Stewart Head and David Soul.

'Death Comes To Time' takes the omnipotent aspect of the McCoy Doctor to its natural conclusion, from being a manipulative character playing god with the universe, dropping hints of being part of a mythic history of the Time Lords (as in **149** and **151**), to his role here as an ageing, melancholy individual sinking under his sense of responsibility, one of a diminishing number of Time Lords. Although the portrayal of the Time Lords' godlike abilities is more mystical than seen before, it's thematically consistent with their status in the series' mythology and, frankly, there have been bigger leaps and inconsistencies in previous *Who* continuity. These kinds of changes are justified by the quality of the story, which boldly attempts to provide a suitably epic 'final *Doctor Who* story'. The astonishing thing about 'Death Comes To Time' is that, had it been the end for the series, it would have been an appropriately dramatic finale. The best of the BBCi webcasts, and way ahead of any other post-1989 *Who* production to date.

163
Real Time
BBCi, 15-minute episodes

Episode One: 2 August 2002
Episode Two: 9 August 2002
Episode Three: 16 August 2002
Episode Four: 23 August 2002
Episode Five: 30 August 2002
Episode Six: 6 September 2002

Written, Directed and Produced by Gary Russell

Notable Cast: Colin Baker returns to the role of the Doctor. Stewart Lee (Carey) and Richard Herring (Renchard) are a comedy duo responsible for *Fist of Fun* (1995–96) and *This Morning with Richard not Judy* (1998–99). Yee Jee Tso previously appeared in **160**, 'The Movie'.

Writer/Director: Gary Russell is a former child actor most notable as Dick in *The Famous Five* (1978). Having not made the transition to acting in adulthood, he has since worked in a variety of areas, including editing *Doctor Who Magazine*. A producer for Big Finish Productions, a company that sells *Doctor Who* CDs to fans via mail order and specialist shops, Russell wrote and directed the company's first (of two) webcasts for the BBC.

Doctor Who?: The Doctor's costume has exactly the same silhouette as before, but entirely in shades of blue. He's been called in to investigate the situation on Chronos by 'Central'. The Doctor is willing to sacrifice his friends if the Cybermen threaten them as leverage – he's aware that giving the Cybermen the TARDIS will sacrifice 'eternity'. He is presently travelling with Evelyn Smythe (Maggie Stables) a middle-aged History lecturer.

Other Worlds: 3286, a planet with an eighteen-hour day and a mysterious temple. Two human expeditions have gone missing around the temple, with reports of temporal waves and Cybermen.

Scary Monsters: The Cybermen, drawn in a slightly sleeker redesign by Lee Sullivan. Otherwise, they're the generic bad guys they've always been. Their aims are 'power, dominance, perfection'. There are a number of semi-completed Cybermen in the story. There's a potted history of the Cybermen in Episode One, which hastily reconciles various bits of continuity.

The Plan: The Cybermen are on the other side of a time portal within the temple, but can't correctly use it. They are based in the far future, when most of the Cybermen have been wiped out. They want the Doctor to help them, so that they can go back further into the planet's past to discover the secrets of the portal. The Cybercontroller wants to convert either the Doctor or Evelyn to become a Cybercontroller, piloting the TARDIS.

Science/Magic: The members of the expedition have subcutaneous transponders beneath the skin, which transmit a signal – they can be used to listen in to their conversations.

Things Fall Apart: One scene sees the Cybermen defeated in their schemes by a failure to get the TARDIS through a tight doorway. During the Doctor's monologues, the animation focuses on random bits of the Doctor's costume. Episodes Four to Six had to have a content warning due to the jarringly sadistic content.

Availability: Available online at http://www.bbc.co.uk/cult/doctor who/realtime.

Verdict: 'I've never known Cybermen to look so badly made before.' Following on from the sweeping excesses of **162**, 'Death Comes to Time', BBCi's second webcast is clearly attempting to be a more traditional, comprehensible and palatable *Who* story. So whose bright idea was it to include a baffling time paradox plot and violence that makes the second half unsuitable for young children? As the audio is accompanied by largely static illustrations, courtesy of Lee Sullivan, shouldn't the story be written to these strengths, rather than being a mindless action movie that requires something more than endless close-ups of the Doctor's lapel badge (or, in one baffling moment, the elderly Evelyn's torso)? Derivative and unimaginative, the script fails to arrange its clichés in a credible order, and the final 'twists' in the plot are risible. Colin Baker puts considerable effort into trying to lift the acting side of things, but most of the cast are poor, and the acting cannot save proceedings from the weak scripting.

164
Shada
BBCi

Episode One: 2 May 2003

Episode Two: 9 May 2003
Episode Three: 16 May 2003
Episode Four: 17 May 2003
Episode Five: 30 May 2003
Episode Six: 6 Jun 2003

Written by Douglas Adams
Adapted for Audio by Gary Russell
Additional Material by Nicholas Pegg
Directed by Nicholas Pegg

Note: The transmitted 'Shada' is a remake of a serial planned to run after **108**, 'The Horns of Nimon'. Its production (directed by Pennant Roberts) was interrupted by industrial action. It was never completed or transmitted, although excerpts were used in **129**, 'The Five Doctors'. Douglas Adams incorporated elements of his screenplay into his novel *Dirk Gently's Holistic Detective Agency* (1988). In 2003, BBCi commissioned a full-cast audio recording of the script. This was broadcast on the Internet with (rather good) semi-animated cartoon pictures accompanying it. Paul McGann (see **160**, 'The Movie') rather than Tom Baker plays the lead.

Notable Cast: James Fox (Professor Chronotis) gave his best-known performance in *Performance* (Nicholas Roeg, 1970). Andrew Sachs (Skagra) played Manuel in *Fawlty Towers* (1975, 1979), but he's also a prolific voiceover and radio artiste. Susannah Harker (Clare) was Mattie Storin in *House of Cards* (1990) and Jo in *Chancer* (1989–90). Melvyn Hayes (Wilkin) played 'Gloria' in *It Ain't Half Hot, Mum!* (1974–80). In the 1979 production Denis Carey (see **114**, 'The Keeper of Traken') played Chronotis. Christopher Neame, previously one of the stars of the BBC's *Colditz* (1973–74), took the part of Skagra. Wilkin was played by Gerald Campion – the BBC's Billy Bunter (1952–62). Lalla Ward plays Romana in both versions.

Director: Nicholas Pegg has worked extensively as a theatrical director. He is also the author of the dizzyingly well-researched *The Complete David Bowie*.

Doctor Who?: The Doctor's boyhood hero was the Time Lord criminal Salyavin – who was imprisoned before he was born. He knows the work of Saul Bellow well. He received an honorary degree from St Cedd's College, Cambridge in 1960.

Other Worlds: Shada – the Time Lords' prison planet. It can only be accessed by turning the pages of the book *The Worshipful and Ancient Law of Gallifrey* while inside a TARDIS: a typically Adams concept in that it blends a literary conceit (book = knowledge) with the trappings of science.

Villains: Skagra, an alien humanoid scientist who is, according to the Doctor, 'too clever by seven-eighths'. He is cold, officious and lacks the ability to laugh at himself.

Scary Monsters: Krargs – shaggy crystalline beasts, grown by Skagra in tanks.

The Plan: Skagra wants to free the imprisoned Salyavin and learn from him how to project his own mind into that of every other being. Skagra doesn't want to conquer the universe. He wants to *become* the universe – a nifty representation of the egomania common to *Doctor Who* villains.

Science/Magic: The Doctor ascertains that Cambridge graduate Chris Parsons understands the works of Isaac Newton, Max Planck as well as Quantum Theory and opines that he's 'got a lot to unlearn'. Skagra has a sphere that can drain the memories of individuals and flies a talking, invisible spaceship with a mellifluous feminine voice (Hannah Gordon).

Things Fall Apart: The 2003 'Shada' begins with a prologue which attempts to explain how and why the events of the story may (or may not) happen twice (once to Tom Baker's Doctor and once to McGann's). It's pointless, contrived and *horribly* written and played. A lot of 'stage direction' dialogue is added to Adams's script, ostensibly to make it suitable for audio, but the extra lines are often simply unnecessary.

Availability: In 1992 the 1979 'Shada' was released on VHS – BBCV 4814 (UK), WHV E1180 (US) – with linking narration by Tom Baker to explain what happened in the unrecorded scenes. The video was packaged with a script for greater clarity. The remake can be watched online at www.bbc.co.uk/cult/doctorwho/shada.html.

Verdict: 'His attempts to resist have caused severe cerebral trauma.' The first episode is dreadful. The rest are merely very bad. The references to Adams's other work ('Ford Prefect'), added to a scene where Skagra steals a car, are vilely grating as is the production's atmosphere of forced, joyless bonhomie. Paul McGann's performance falls very flat, he sounds either confused by, or totally uninterested in, what's going on. He can't make the jokes funny and lacks the steel to make his final confrontation with Skagra work. Without a dynamic lead at the centre the whole serial simply fails to cohere. The 1979 'Shada' is, even in its VHS release form, a dysfunctional epic enlivened by flashes of wit and held together by Tom Baker's charisma. The 2003 'Shada' is an out-of-tune pub karaoke rendition of a song that, you suddenly realise, didn't really have much going for it in the first place.

165
Scream of the Shalka
BBCi, 15-minute episodes

Episode One: 13 November 2003
Episode Two: 20 November 2003
Episode Three: 27 November 2003
Episode Four: 4 December 2003
Episode Five: 11 December 2003
Episode Six: 18 December 2003

Written by Paul Cornell
Directed by Wilson Milam

Note: *Doctor Who*'s first fully-animated adventure was visualised by Cosgrove Hall, famous for *Danger Mouse* and *The Wind in the Willows*.

Notable Cast: Richard E Grant (born 1957) plays the Doctor for a second time, although this Doctor is rather different to the one seen in **161**, 'The Curse of Fatal Death'. Sophie Okenodo (Alison) appeared in *Dirty Pretty Things* (Stephen Frears, 2002) and *Hotel Rwanda* (Terry George, 2004). Craig Kelly (Joe) played *Who* fan Vince in *Queer As Folk* (1999–2000). Jim Norton is instantly recognisable, even in cartoon form, as Bishop Brennan from *Father Ted* (1994). Sir Derek Jacobi (The Master) played Claudius in *I, Claudius* (1976): he was also the BBC's *Hamlet* (1980), played a very different Claudius in a very different *Hamlet* (Kenneth Branagh, 1997) and Francis Bacon in *Love is the Devil* (John Maybury, 1998) among many other great stage and screen credits. Diana Quick (Prime) starred in *Brideshead Revisited* (1982).

Writer: Paul Cornell received his television break with the play *Kingdom Come* (1990). He went on to write for *Coronation Street*, *Springhill* and *Casualty*, and create the children's series *Wavelength* (1997). He has also written comic strips for *2000AD*, published two mainstream sci-fi novels and eight *Doctor Who* novels.

Director: Wilson Milam has largely worked as a theatre director, with credits including *Defender of the Faith* and *On Such As We*.

History 101: The TARDIS lands in contemporary Lannet, Lancashire. The village is ominously quiet and the inhabitants are cowed, unable to leave and afraid of reprisals from . . .

Scary Monsters: . . . the Shalka. 'Never heard of you,' says the Doctor. 'So, if you'll forgive me, you can't be *all that*.' However, the Shalka are a clandestine presence on 'eighty per cent of the worlds in the universe. Worlds *you* think of as dead.' They prey upon ecologically damaged planets, destroy the population and move in underground.

The Plan: The Shalka cannot breathe our oxygen-rich atmosphere, so they are gradually modifying the inhabitants of Lannet (and other communities around the world) to emit their 'scream'. The 'scream' will agitate the air molecules and transform the atmosphere.

Doctor Who?: The Doctor twice implies (although never states) that this is his ninth incarnation. He is spiky and withdrawn, following some traumatic experience (this seems to be the death of a woman). He is being directed on missions – 'They keep putting me in places where terrible things are going to happen' – but is going through the motions. At one point he is about to die and opines that he was finished anyway. However, he subsequently notes that 'I appear to have found some form' and is more effective thereafter. His new friend Alison says Lannet is the dullest place in the universe, to which he responds that she should see *his* home planet. He acknowledges the contradictions in his own character and methods: 'I say I do not kill, but then I exterminate thousands.'

Villains: The Master – although he is no longer a villain and now travels with the Doctor: 'I was of aid to the Doctor . . . during the events that so damaged him. In return, he offered me a last chance for salvation.' It seems his body has been destroyed, as his intelligence is now housed in a robotic construct. He is restricted from leaving the TARDIS.

Things Fall Apart: The Doctor's use of his mobile phone to escape from the black hole is a neat trick, but it does give him an easy way out of any life-or-death situation.

Availability: Available online at www.bbc.co.uk/cult/doctorwho/shalka.

Verdict: 'I only come to this planet for the wine and the total eclipses. And I do love a nice old-fashioned invasion.' Produced as a bold first step into a new medium, 'Scream of the Shalka' is now likely to remain a curio – but one well worth investigating. It seems very much intended as a pilot, offering an archetypal adventure whilst hinting at an intriguing backstory. The threat is original and, although the plotting is archetypal base-under-siege stuff (with an informal UNIT-style military presence), this traditional *Who* feel allows writer Cornell space to develop a very different Doctor from any we've seen before. Had there been more animated adventures then excursions outside the regular format would have been necessary, but it seems churlish to criticise an opening story for being straightforward.

The design is great, and although the animation itself drew negative comparisons with *South Park* this is mainly because it's quite a new form for narrative animation and there is little to compare it to. The sound mixing is a little off – it's been recorded with the in-the-room intimacy of a radio drama, which sits oddly when you're watching pictures on a screen at the same time. But these are minor complaints. 'Shalka' stands up as a successful experiment nixed only by the return of *Doctor Who* to television.

Doctor Who – The New Series

Thirteen 45-minute episodes
Spring 2005

Notable Cast: Doctor Who is played by Christopher Eccleston (born 1964), which is a remarkable coup as he is widely considered to be one of the best actors working in Britain today. His film credits include *Shallow Grave* (Danny Boyle, 1994), *Elizabeth* (Shekhar Kapur, 1998) and *The Others* (Alejandro Amenabar, 2001), whilst on TV he has appeared in *Cracker* (1993–94), *Our Friends in the North* (1996) and *The Second Coming* (2003). Billie Piper (Rose Tyler) trained as an actress at the Sylvia Young Theatre School, but was diverted into a pop career during her teenage years and hit the number one spot with her 1998 debut single 'Because We Want To' (still her best-known song, although the follow-up 'Honey to the B' is superior). After two albums she returned to acting, appearing on TV in *The Canterbury Tales* and *Bella and the Boys* during 2003.

Noel Clarke (Mickey) was awarded the 2003 Laurence Olivier Theatre Award for Most Promising Newcomer: he appeared on TV in *Metrosexuality* (1999) and the revival of *Auf Wiedersehen, Pet* (2002–present). Penelope Wilton appeared in *Ever Decreasing Circles* (1985–89), *Calendar Girls* (Nigel Cole, 2003) and *Shaun of the Dead* (Edgar Wright, 2004). Camille Coduri (Jackie) had roles in *Nuns on the Run* (Jonathan Lynn, 1990) and *King Ralph* (David S Ward, 1991).

Simon Callow (Charles Dickens) is best known for *Four Weddings and a Funeral* (Mike Newell, 1994), but his career also includes *Postcards from the Edge* (Mike Nichols, 1990), *Shakespeare in Love* (John Madden, 1998) and *Bright Young Things* (Stephen Fry, 2003). He has portrayed Dickens on stage and screen numerous times and has written books on acting and a biography of Orson Welles. John Barrowman (Captain Jack), Glasgow-born but raised in the USA, presented by BBC1's Saturday morning show *Live & Kicking* (1993–4) and was a regular in the soap *Titans* (2000). Navin Chowdhry was in *Gulliver's Travels* (1996) and *NY-LON* (2004), but is best known as Kurt McKenna in *Teachers* (2001–03).

Executive Producers: Russell T Davies originally worked in children's television as a producer, then moved into writing with the children's serials *Dark Season* (1991) and *Century Falls* (1993). He won a BAFTA for a 1996 episode of *Children's Ward*: the same year saw him scripting *The Grand* (1996–97) for ITV. However, it was *Queer As Folk* (1999–2000) – a Channel 4 series set on Manchester's gay scene – which confirmed his position among Britain's foremost television writers. Subsequently Davies seemed set upon producing work for ITV, writing *Bob and Rose* (2002) and *The Second Coming* (2003), until the offer of *Doctor Who* came along.

Whilst Davies is the main creative force in this new series, he is joined by two other executive producers in the form of Julie Gardner and Mal Young. Gardner is Head of Drama at BBC Wales: she was previously script editor and producer of *Sunburn* (1999) and script editor of *The Mrs Bradley Mysteries* (1999). Young is Controller of BBC Continuing Series: he has also acted as executive producer on *Dalziel and Pascoe* (1996–present) and *Holby City* (1999–present), and was producer of *Brookside* (1992–96).

Producer: Phil Collinson has also produced *Linda Green*, *Born and Bred* and *Sea of Souls* (2004–present).

Writers: Eight of the thirteen episodes are written by Davies himself. Other episodes are by Paul Cornell (see **165**, 'Scream of the Shalka'), Steven Moffat (see **161**, 'The Curse of Fatal Death'), Mark Gatiss and Robert Shearman. Gatiss writes and performs with the League of Gentlemen, best known for their eponymous television series (1999–2002): he also worked on the Reeves and Mortimer revival of *Randall and Hopkirk (Deceased)* (2001) and has written four *Doctor Who* novels. Shearman is an award-winning playwright whose works for the stage include *Breaking Bread Together* (1994) and *Binary Dreamers* (1996): he has also written episodes of the TV series *Born and Bred*.

Directors: Keith Boak directs episodes one, four and five: his other TV credits include episodes of *The Knock* (2000), *Mersey Beat* (2001), *Holby City* (2004) and *NY-LON* (2004). Euros Lyn directs episodes two and three; his other credits include *Casualty*, *Belonging III* (2002), *Cutting It* (2004) and Welsh-language series such as *Pam Fi Duw?* (1997). Joe Ahearne directs six and eight. He previously worked as a writer/director on *This Life* (1997). He was sole writer/director of the excellent vampire series *Ultraviolet* (1998) and the drama-documentary *Space Odyssey: Voyage to the Planets* (2004). He also directed episodes of *Strange* (2002–03).

* * *

On 25 September 2003, BBC1 controller Lorraine Heggessey announced that she had commissioned the first new series of television *Doctor Who* since 1989.

The programme had never actually been cancelled: no announcement had been made that the 1989 season would be the last. The BBC had merely decided to seek a co-production deal in the US and quietly put *Doctor Who* on hold until such a deal could be struck. This plan eventually came to fruition with **160**, 'The Movie', but Universal Television did not exercise its option to make a full series. BBC Worldwide then reserved the property whilst it sought to secure a co-production deal on a feature film, but this came to nothing and the rights were eventually conceded back to BBC Television, which had started to consider that the time might be right to produce *Doctor Who* as an in-house TV series once more.

There was another key motivating factor in the return of *Doctor Who*: Russell T Davies. Generally acknowledged to be among the best writers currently working in British television, Davies' interest in *Doctor Who* was well known: indeed, in 1996 he published a *Who* novel called *Damaged Goods*. In 1999 he commented on whether he would write for the series if and when it returned to television. 'Oh, I'd love to do it, absolutely,' he told *Doctor Who Magazine*. 'Although it would depend what they were doing. If the producer was a fool, and I thought the way they were doing it was wrong, then no, I'd rather die. Trouble is, I'm reaching a point in my career where I'm insisting on a lot of control over what I do.' He added, 'God help anyone in charge of bringing it back – what a responsibility!'

Come 2003, the BBC was interested in getting Davies to write something for BBC1 and there was only one thing it could offer him which the independent sector could not: *Doctor Who*. The extent to which he is in demand is demonstrated by the fact that the BBC was not only willing to bring *Doctor Who* back as a means of 'poaching' him, it was willing to make Davies executive producer and place the production under the wing of BBC Wales to give him a degree of independence from the central BBC hierarchy. The return of *Doctor Who* would always have attracted huge interest, but its dual identity as 'the latest project from Russell T Davies' adds an unexpected level of prestige.

By the same token, it's a testament to *Doctor Who*'s influence that one of the most acclaimed writers in television unashamedly counts himself a fan of the show. When *BBC Wales Today* asked

Davies to account for the enduring popularity of the series he replied, 'Because it's the best idea ever invented in the history of the world! I really think so. I love it.' (He's not alone: Stephen Poliakoff – writer/director of *Shooting the Past* (1999) and one of Britain's most notable living playwrights – rates the early Hartnell serials as his favourite television of all time.)

Doctor Who in 2005 is the same show as it was back in 1963, but it's also very different. The lead character is the same man we met back in 'An Unearthly Child': the story is continuing on, not starting again. He'll remain as flexible and changeable as he ever was, but essentially normal service is being resumed: we hope that it will not be disrupted again for quite some time, but that depends on how the public responds to the return of *Doctor Who*.

The main differences can be attributed to the ways in which television has moved on in the last fifteen years. Serials comprised of 25-minute episodes can no longer find a place in the schedule (even in the 1980s the format was starting to look like a relic) and *Doctor Who* is now produced in 45-minute instalments, with 13 episodes to a season. This bears a resemblance to the show's aberrant 1985 season, but crucially differs in that most of its episodes will be standalone stories with a few two-parters mixed in. It is shot on film and mostly on location, avoiding where possible the artifice of the television studio.

Perhaps most importantly, it won't be cheap. It has often been said that the cheapness of old *Doctor Who* is a key component of its appeal, that this aspect is somehow endearing and reassuringly 'British'. Quite apart from what this says about the British psyche, if it is true then the series is nothing more than a kitsch nostalgia trip and bringing it back is a waste of time. We don't believe that. It has also been claimed that because *Doctor Who* couldn't rely on production gloss, the scriptwriters and actors had to work that much harder and that's what made the series great. If you follow this argument through to its logical conclusion, *Doctor Who* would ideally be made on a bare stage by Lars Von Trier, which would be an interesting experiment but hardly a formula for mass-market family entertainment. Television is a visual medium (hence the name), yet the visuals in this series have often detracted from the action where they should augment it.

We love *Doctor Who* – but like so many of the people who worked on it, we would like it to have been afforded the time and money that its nature demanded. Apparently the BBC now agrees, as this programme that was once legendary for its shoestring production values is currently being made for an estimated cost of £1 million per episode. It's the most expensive drama the Corporation has ever made, and this demonstrates its ambition to create a series that it can sell around the world and take pride in.

At the time of going to press plot details are being kept firmly under wraps, 'for the fun of the viewers, really', as Davies told *BBC Wales Today* during filming. 'I hate watching stuff where I know what's going to happen. I think we all know that a fair bit's going to leak on to the Internet but really most people, and I hope millions of people, will be sitting down watching a brand new series of *Doctor Who*, the first proper series in fifteen years, so: it's a surprise!' We do know, however, that the Daleks are set to return after negotiations with the estate of their creator, Terry Nation, grabbed newspaper headlines twice in 2004: first to announce that terms had not been agreed and the Daleks could not be used, then again to announce that everything had been resolved. In addition, set reports reveal that the Autons (see **51**, 'Spearhead from Space') are set to appear in an early episode.

Davies has said that he initially thought that sticking with Earthbound adventures might be a wise choice, to keep costs down, but quickly abandoned this in favour of a variety of settings: episodes will take place both on and off Earth, in the past, present and future. This seems a wise move, regardless of financial concerns: the go-anywhere nature of the series is what keeps even the most mundane serial afloat. *Doctor Who* is a pretext for the extraordinary to happen on a weekly basis, and it's good to hear that it will continue to be so.

Since 1989, science fiction and fantasy have been near-dead genres on British television: most of what has been produced has either been poor (1996's *Invasion Earth*, 2003's *Strange*) or very firmly rooted in a realistic contemporary setting (2004's *Sea of Souls*, 1997's *Ultraviolet*). Monsters, other worlds and spaceships have largely been the preserve of American series, so it's inevitable that *Doctor Who* will be influenced by the likes of *The X-Files* (1993–2002) and *Babylon 5* (1993–98): in addition, Davies has cited *Buffy the Vampire Slayer* (1997–2003) as his favourite television series of all time (a sentiment with which the present authors have some sympathy). Davies has given his writers basic ideas to work from, so it seems likely that the season will tell some kind of overall story – a mode that *Buffy* developed very successfully. However, *Doctor Who*'s ever-changing backdrop demands an individually crafted approach and so it's likely to be different from any series we've seen before.

Davies believes that the series is consistent with his own body of work, whilst also remaining immediately recognisable as *Doctor Who*. *BBC Wales Today* asked how he was dealing with the pressure of wildly varying audience expectations: 'To be honest, I just sort of ignore them,' he replied. 'I make the *Doctor Who* that I wanted to make, which is going to be new and exciting: it's also going to be very, very traditional. People are going to have the same old thrill that they always had watching it, it's just going to look more year 2005, more of a sort of upbeat kick to it, and it's very much the same old show.'

Index

Aaronovitch, Ben 348, 358

'Abominable Snowmen, The' 97–9

Adams, Douglas 231, 232, 244, 246, 330, 386

Agnew, David 226, 227, 244

Ainley, Anthony 264, 297, 311, 367

Aldred, Sophie 346, 381, 383

Alexander, Terence 320, 322

Allen, Ronald 111, 130

'Ambassadors of Death, The' 130–2

'An Unearthly Child' 9–13

'Android Invasion, The' 196–8

'Androids of Tara, The' 235–7

'Arc of Infinity' 285–7

Archard, Bernard 194

'Ark in Space, The' 181–3

'Ark, The' 63–6

'Armageddon Factor, The' 239–41

Arnatt, John 227, 228

Ashbrook, Daphne 375, 377

Atkinson, Rowan 378, 379

'Attack of the Cybermen' 316–18

'Awakening, The' 303–5

'Aztecs, The' 23–5

Bailey, Christopher 274, 275–6, 287

Bailie, David 212, 213

Baker, Bob 139, 140–1, 153, 157, 183, 205, 218, 220, 224, 239, 249

Baker, Colin 62, 285, 314, 316, 321, 323, 324, 330, 332, 339, 341–2, 370, 371, 384, 385

Baker, Jane 320, 321, 335, 339

Baker, Pip 320, 321, 335, 339

Baker, Tom 102, 179, 180, 187, 190, 191, 200–1, 202, 228, 230, 233, 235, 237–8, 240, 241, 245, 249, 250, 253, 256, 257, 268, 271, 298, 300, 318, 365, 386, 387, 388

Barkworth, Peter 100, 101

Baron, Lynda 294, 295

Barron, Keith 294, 295

Barry, Christopher 13, 14, 16, 36, 37, 39, 70, 79, 144, 153, 179, 198, 246

Barry, Morris 85, 86, 95, 111

'Battlefield' 358–60

Beckley, Tony 201, 202

Benjamin, Christopher 133, 214

Bennett, John 171, 214

Bennett, Rodney 181, 183, 203

Benson, Peter 292, 294

Bernard, Paul 146, 147, 148, 155, 162

Bidmead, Christopher H 253, 260, 266, 268, 305

'Black Orchid' 278–80

Black, Ian Stuart 70, 72, 88, 89

Black, John 263, 264, 271

Boucher, Chris 209, 210, 211, 213, 221, 222

'Brain of Morbius, The' 198–201

Brayshaw, Edward 29, 123, 126

Briant, Michael E 142, 151, 166, 188
Briggs, Ian 346, 347, 348, 363
Bromly, Alan 168, 169
Bryant, Peter 92, 95, 105, 264
Bulloch, Jeremy 44, 169
Butterworth, Peter 48, 50, 57
Byrne, Johnny 263, 301

Camfield, Douglas 31, 42, 43, 48, 50, 57, 104, 115, 117, 133, 190, 201
Cant, Brian 57, 111
Carey, Dennis 263–4, 325, 386
'Carnival of Monsters' 160–2
Cartmel, Andrew 340, 342, 354, 365
'Castrovalva' 268–71
Caunter, Tony 42, 294
'Caves of Androzani, The' 311–14
'Celestial Toymaker, The' 66–8
Chadbon, Tom 244, 246, 331–2
Challis, John 201, 203
'Chase, The' 46–8
'City of Death' 244–6
Clarke, Phil 367, 368, 372
'Claws of Axos, The' 139–41
Clough, Chris 335, 344, 346, 351, 354
Clunes, Martin 287, 289
Coburn, Anthony 9, 10
Cochrane, Michael 278, 361
Colbourne, Maurice 307, 316, 318
Cole, Tristan De Vere 108, 109
Collings, David 188, 190, 212, 290
'Colony in Space' 142–4
Combe, Timothy 128, 130, 137
Cooklin, Shirley 95, 97
Cornell, Paul 388, 389

Cotton, Donald 54, 55, 56, 68
Courtney, Nicholas 57, 104, 115, 134, 298, 360, 367, 372
Cox, Frank 16, 17, 26
Craze, Michael 72, 76
'Creature from the Pit, The' 246–8
Crockett, John 18, 19, 23
'Crusade, The' 41–3
Cullen, Ian 23–4, 25
Cumming, Fiona 268, 269, 287, 289, 294, 309
Curry, Graeme 351, 352
'Curse of Fatal Death, The' 378–80
'Curse of Fenric, The' 363–5
'Curse of Peladon, The' 148–51
Cushing, Peter 15–16, 35
Cutherbertson, Iain 229, 30

'Daemons, The' 144–6
Daker, David 169, 249
'Dalek Invasion of Earth, The' 33–6
'Daleks, The' 13–16
'Daleks' Master Plan, The' 56–61
Danielle, Suzanne 242
Darrow, Paul 128, 325, 326
David, Hugh 82, 85, 106
Davies, Russell T 391–2, 393, 395, 396
Davis, Gerry 61, 66, 74, 76, 77, 82, 87, 92, 95, 188
Davison, Peter 268, 269, 271, 273, 275, 277, 278, 284, 285, 287, 292, 302–3, 306, 308, 311, 313–14, 316, 331, 372
'Day of the Daleks' 146–8
'Deadly Assassin, The' 207–9
'Death Comes to Time' 380–4

'Death to the Daleks' 173–4

Delgado, Roger 135, 140, 156, 163, 267

'Delta and the Bannermen' 344–6

Denham, Maurice 314, 316

'Destiny of the Daleks' 241–4

Dicks, Terence 3, 115, 123, 131, 179, 199, 217, 259, 260, 297, 300, 301

'Dimensions In Time' 370–2

'Doctor Who and the Ghosts of N-Space' 372–4

'Doctor Who and the Silurians' 128–30

'Doctor Who/'The Movie' 374–8

'Dominators, The' 110–12

'Dragonfire' 346–8

Dudley, Terence 255, 271, 278, 296

Dunlop, Lesley 305, 352

'Earthshock' 280–2

'Edge of Destruction, The' 16–18

Ellis, David 89, 90

Emms, William 50, 51

'Enemy of the World, The' 102–4

'Enlightenment' 294–5

'Evil of the Daleks, The' 92–5

'Face of Evil, The' 209–11

'Faceless Ones, The' 89–91

Fenton, Leonard 381, 383

Ferguson, Michael 72, 119, 120–1, 130, 139, 141

Fielding, Janet 266, 289, 307

Fisher, David 233, 235, 244, 246, 253

'Five Doctors, The' 297–301

Ford, Carole Ann 9–10, 18, 30, 34–5, 298

'Four To Doomsday' 271–3

Francis, Derek 37, 38, 39

Franklin, Richard 135, 298

'Frontier in Space' 162–4

'Frontios' 305–6

Fry, Stephen 381, 383

'Full Circle' 257–9

'Fury from the Deep' 106–8

'Galaxy 4' 50–2

'Genesis of the Daleks' 185–8

'Ghost Light' 360–3

Glover, Julian 42, 244, 296, 318

Gooderson, David 244

Goodwin, Derrick 218, 219

Gorrie, John 21, 29

Gostelow, Gordon 121, 122

Gough, Michael 66, 285

Grainger, Gawn 320, 322

Grant, Hugh 378, 379, 380

Grant, Richard E. 378, 379, 388

'Greatest Show in the Galaxy, The' 356–8

'Green Death, The' 166–8

Grimwade, Peter 257, 259, 266, 274, 280, 283, 284, 289, 309, 311

'Gunfighters, The' 68–9

Haisman, Mervyn 97, 104, 111

Halliday, Peter 115, 160, 245

Hancock, Prentis 164, 193

Hancock, Sheila 351, 353

'Hand of Fear, The' 205–7

'Happiness Patrol, The' 351–3

Harper, Graeme 311, 312, 327

Hartnell, William 4, 9, 11, 13, 14, 18, 22, 24, 25, 28, 30, 37,

38, 39, 41, 48, 50, 54, 55, 63,
65, 67, 69, 77, 78, 83, 125,
136, 157, 159, 187, 200, 204,
278, 298, 300, 371, 394
Hayes, Michael 235, 239, 244
Hayles, Brian 66, 74, 100, 101,
119, 149, 175
Hayman, Damaris 144, 145–6
Head, Anthony Stewart 381,
383
Hellings, Sarah 321, 322
Henderson, John 378, 379
'Highlanders, The' 82–3
Hill, Jacqueline 9, 25, 43, 47,
56, 255, 256
Hinchcliffe, Philip 174, 181
Hines, Frazer 82, 83, 112,
159–60, 298, 323, 324
Hinsliff, Geoffrey 221, 249
Holloway, Julian 365, 366
Holmes, Robert 117, 121, 126,
135, 160, 168, 181, 187–8,
194, 198, 199, 207, 223, 229,
231, 237, 311, 313, 323, 331,
336
'Horns of Nimon, The' 250–2
'Horror of Fang Rock' 216–18
Horsfall, Bernard 113, 123,
164, 208, 209
Houghton, Don 133, 137
Hughes, Geoffrey 337, 339
Hughes, Nerys 274, 275
Hulke, Malcolm 89, 123, 128,
130, 131, 142, 151, 152,
162–3, 172
Hunter, Russell 212, 213
Hurndall, Richard 298, 299
Hussein, Waris 9, 10, 18

'Ice Warriors, The' 99–101
'Image of the Fendahl' 220–2
'Inferno' 132–5

Innocent, Harold 351, 368
'Invasion of the Dinosaurs'
171–3
'Invasion of Time, The' 226–8
'Invasion, The' 114–17
'Invisible Enemy, The' 218–20

Jacobs, Mathew 374, 375
Jaeger, Frederick 70, 192, 219
Jameson, Louise 209, 211, 218,
227
Jarvis, Martin 39, 171, 318, 320
Jayston, Michael 331
Jeffrey, Peter 88, 235
John, Caroline 126, 134, 298
Johns, Stafford 271, 273
Jones, Emrys 82, 114
Jones, Glyn 44, 183
Jones, Ron 278, 283, 305, 333
Joyce, Paul 261–2

Kay, Bernard 33, 90, 142
'Keeper of Traken, The' 263–6
Kerrigan, Michael 358, 359
'Keys of Marinus, The' 21–3
'King's Demons, The' 296–7
'Kinda' 273–6
'Krotons, The' 117–19
Kwouk, Burt 271

Lambert, Verity 10–11, 26, 28,
68
Lane, Jackie 61, 65, 74
Langford, Bonnie 335, 338,
341, 346
Leeson, John 219, 240, 253,
255, 261, 298, 349
Leigh-Hunt, Ronald 119, 188,
190
'Leisure Hive, The' 253–4
Letts, Barry 102, 135, 144, 160,
177, 192, 196, 198, 367, 372

Lill, Dennis 221, 303, 304
Lincoln, Henry 97, 104, 111
Lindsay, Kevin 169, 177, 184
Lloyd, Innes 66, 67, 74, 76, 77, 78, 92
Lockwood, Preston 287
'Logopolis' 266-8
Lucarotti, John 18, 21, 23, 25, 61
Lumley, Joanna 378, 379

Mackay, Angus 209, 289
Madoc, Philip 117, 123, 126, 199, 237
Mallett, Nicholas 331, 332, 342, 363
Maloney, David 112, 113, 117, 123, 164, 185, 187, 192
Manning, Katy 135, 150, 166
'Marca Terror, The' 88-9
Marcell, Joseph 349
'Marco Polo' 18-21
'Mark of the Rani, The' 320-2
Marks, Louis 31, 146, 192, 203
Marsh, Jean 42, 57, 358
Marter, Ian 160, 179, 181, 183, 190
Martin, Dave 139, 140-1, 153, 157, 183, 218, 220, 224, 239
Martin, Philip 319, 333
Martin, Richard 13, 14, 16, 35, 39, 46
Martinus, Derek 50, 51, 52, 76, 79, 92, 100, 126
'Masque of Mandragora, The' 203-5
'Massacre, The' 61-3
'Mawdryn Undead' 289-91
Mayne, Lennie 149, 157, 175, 205
McBain, Kenny 250, 251, 252

McCoy, Sylvester 340, 346, 348, 362, 363, 371, 374, 377, 381, 383
McGann, Paul 374-5, 377, 387, 388
McNally, Kevin 314, 316
Meek, Colin 381, 383
'Meglos' 255-7
Merrison, Clive 95, 342
Milam, Wilson 388, 389
Miles, Peter 128, 171, 185, 186, 368
'Mind of Evil, The' 137-9
'Mind Robber, The' 112-14
'Mission to the Unknown' 52-4
Moffatt, Peter 259, 276, 284, 289, 297, 314, 323, 378, 379, 392
Molloy, Terry 307, 318
'Monster of Peladon, The' 175-6
'Moonbase, The' 85-7
Morgan, Andrew 339, 340, 348
Morris, Michael Owen 303, 304
'Mutants, The' 153-4
'Myth Makers, The' 54-6

Nathan-Turner, John 253, 297, 340, 370
Nation, Terry 13, 14-15, 21, 33, 34, 46, 52, 57, 164, 185, 196, 198, 242, 243, 395
Newman, Sydney 10, 12, 26
'Nightmare of Eden' 248-50
Normington, John 311-12, 352

O'Brien, Maureen 36, 56
O'Mara, Kate 321, 341, 370
Osaba, Tony 242, 346-7

Palmer, Geoffrey 128, 153
'Paradise of Death, The'
    367–70
'Paradise Towers' 342–4
Parsons, Nicholas 363, 365
Pastell, George 95, 97
Patrick, Kay 38, 70
Pearce, Richard 367–8, 372
Pedler, Kit 76, 77, 78, 85, 86,
    95
Pemberton, Victor 106, 107
Pertwee, Jon 126, 131, 134–5,
    144, 145, 150, 151, 155, 158,
    159, 160, 168, 173, 176, 178,
    180, 181, 190, 192, 200, 203,
    208, 298, 360, 367, 371,
    372
Pickering, Donald 90, 340
Piggott-Smith, Tim 139, 203
Pinfield, Mervyn 26, 44
'Pirate Planet, The' 231–3
Pitt, Ingrid 155, 156, 301
'Planet of Evil' 192–4
'Planet of Fire' 309–11
'Planet of Giants' 31–3
'Planet of the Daleks' 164–6
'Planet of the Spiders' 177–9
'Power of Kroll, The' 237–9
'Power of the Daleks, The'
    79–81
Purves, Peter 46, 48, 50, 56, 67,
    69, 74
'Pyramids of Mars' 194–6

Read, Anthony 225, 227, 233,
    241, 250
'Real Time' 384–5
Reddington, Ian 356, 358
'Reign of Terror, The' 29
'Remembrance of the Daleks'
    348–51
'Rescue, The' 36–7

'Resurrection of the Daleks'
    307–9
'Revelation of the Daleks'
    327–9
'Revenge of the Cybermen'
    188–90
'Ribos Operation, The'
    228–31
Richfield, Edwin 151, 314
Ringham, John 24, 74, 142
Robbins, Michael 276, 277
Roberts, Eric 375, 377
Roberts, Pennant 209, 210,
    223, 231, 301, 325
Robinson, Matthew 307, 316
'Robot' 179–81
'Robots of Death, The' 211–13
'Romans, The' 37–9
Rouse, Simon 274, 275
Rowe, Alan 169, 217, 257
Ruskin, Sheila 264, 265
Russell, Gary 384, 386
Russell, Paddy 61, 62, 194
Russell, William 9, 18, 25, 41,
    290
Ryan, Christopher 33, 339

Salem, Pamela 212, 349
Sallis, Peter 100, 101
'Savages, The' 70–2
Saward, Eric 269, 271–2, 276,
    279, 280, 307, 309, 316, 317,
    327, 329, 330
Sax, Geoffrey 374, 375
Schofield, Leslie 123–4, 209
'Scream of the Shalka'
    388–90
'Sea Devils, The' 151–2
'Seeds of Death, The' 119–21
'Seeds of Doom, The' 201–3
'Sensorites, The' 25–8
Sessions, John 381, 383

Shaban, Nabil 318, 320, 333, 339
'Shada' 385–8
Shaps, Cyril 95, 177, 235
Sheard, Michael 5, 64, 137, 194, 219, 269, 349
Sherwin, Derrick 92, 104–5, 112, 115
'Silver Nemesis' 354–6
Silvera, Carmen 66, 171
Sims, Joan 331, 361
Sladen, Elizabeth 168, 203, 205, 207, 255, 287, 367, 369, 372
'Slipback' 329–31
Sloman, Robert 155, 166, 177
Smith, Julia 74, 84
'Smugglers, The' 74–6
'Snakedance' 287–9
'Sontaran Experiment, The' 183–4
'Space Museum, The' 43–5
'Space Pirates, The' 121–3
'Spearhead from Space' 126–8
Spencer, Paul 329–30
Spenton-Foster, George 221, 229
Spooner, Dennis 29, 37, 38, 39, 48, 56, 57
'State of Decay' 259–61
Stewart, Norman 225, 237
Stewart, Robert Banks 190, 201
Stoney, Kevin 57, 115, 188
'Stones of Blood, The' 233–5
Strickson, Mark 289, 291, 294, 295, 310
Strutton, Bill 39, 40
Sullivan, Lee 383, 384, 385
'Sun Makers, The' 223–4
'Survival' 365–7
Sutton, Sarah 264, 270

Tamm, Mary 229, 230, 237, 240, 243
'Terminus' 291–4
'Terror of the Autons' 135–7
'Terror of the Zygons' 190–2
'Talons of Weng-Chiang, The' 213–16
'Tenth Planet, The' 76–9
'Three Doctors, The' 157–60
Thorne, Stephen 144, 157, 159, 372, 373
Tierney, Malcolm 335, 339
'Time and the Rani' 339–42
'Time-Flight' 282–5
'Timelash' 325–7
'Time Meddler, The' 48–50
'Time Monster, The' 155–7
'Time Warrior, The' 168–70
Todd, Richard 274, 275
'Tomb of the Cybermen, The' 95–7
Tosh, Donald 61, 66
'Trial of a Time Lord, The' 331–9
Troughton, David 149
Troughton, Patrick 11, 62, 77, 79, 81, 83, 86, 87, 94, 102, 104, 110, 112, 114, 116, 122, 126, 130, 143, 149, 157, 159, 160, 200, 203, 298, 299, 323, 340, 371
Tucker, Rex 10, 68
'Twin Dilemma, The' 314–16
'Two Doctors, The' 323–4

'Underwater Menace, The' 84–5
'Underworld' 224–6

'Vengeance on Varos' 318–20
'Visitation, The' 276–7

Walker, Fiona 354, 356
Ward, Lalla 239–40, 246, 256, 261
Wareing, Alan 356, 361, 365
'War Games, The' 123–6
'War Machines, The' 72–4
'Warriors of the Deep' 301–3
'Warriors' Gate' 261–3
Warwick, David 231, 233
Waterhouse, Matthew 257, 270, 280
Watling, Deborah 92, 97, 106–7
Watling, Jack 97, 104
'Web of Fear, The' 104–6
'Web Planet' 39–41
'The Wheel in Space' 108–10

Whitaker, David 14, 16, 17, 18, 36, 42, 43, 78, 79, 92, 94, 102, 104, 108, 110, 130, 131, 172
Whitsun-Jones, Paul 74, 153
Williams, Graham 181, 217, 222, 227, 244, 246
Wills, Anneke 72, 76, 83
Wisher, Michael 161, 188, 193
Woodnutt, John 126, 162
Woodvine, John 239, 264
Woolf, Gabriel 196, 223
Wyatt, Stephen 342, 343, 356, 358
Wyngrade, Peter 309, 311

Yardley, Stephen 185, 318